D1606040

USB

Hardware and Software

John Garney Ed Solari Shelagh Callahan

Kosar Jaff Brad Hosler

Annabooks

San Diego

USB
Hardware and Software
by
John Garney Ed Solari Shelagh Callahan
Kosar Jaff Brad Hosler

PUBLISHED BY

Annabooks
11838 Bernardo Plaza Court
San Diego, CA 92128-2414
USA

619-673-0870
800-462-1042
619-673-1432 FAX
info@annabooks.com
http://www.annabooks.com

Printed in the United States of America

ISBN 0-929392-37-X

First Printing October 1998

Information provided in this publication is derived from various sources, standards, and analyses. Any errors or omissions shall not imply any liability for direct or indirect consequences arising from the use of this information. The publisher, authors, and reviewers make no warranty for the correctness or for the use of this information, and assume no liability for direct or indirect damages of any kind arising from technical interpretation or technical explanations in this book, for typographical or printing errors, or for any subsequent changes.

The publisher and authors reserve the right to make changes in this publication without notice and without incurring any liability.

All trademarks mentioned in this book are the property of their respective owners. Annabooks has attempted to properly capitalize and punctuate trademarks, but cannot guarantee that it has done so properly in every case.

Dedications

I always wanted to find out what it was like to write a "real" book, and now I know. It is a lot of work that always takes longer than you expect. Time will tell whether we have produced the useful reference we all wanted.

A completely inadequate "thank you" goes to my family (Pauline, Ben, and James) for putting up with me occupying space, but not "being there" while trying to put thoughts to paper and get it all finished.

To my co-authors: I couldn't ask for a better set of people to take on something like this project. I just wish we had fewer other things competing for our time so we could have focused on doing more.

John Garney

I would like to thank all of the co-authors for moving forward with this book. Due to the shortcomings of the official bus specification, it required extra effort by everyone to get the job done. I would also like to thank my wife Deborah for allowing me to "go off and write yet another book."

Ed Solari

I would like to acknowledge my colleagues at Intel Architecture Labs who helped develop USB from concept to reality: Bala Cadambi, Shelagh Callahan, John Garney, Brad Hosler, John Howard, Jeff Morriss, and Jim Pappas. I would also like to thank the following people at Microsoft for their efforts to support USB: Brad Carpenter, John Dunn, Mike Glass, Tom Green, and Glen Slick (among many others). Finally, I would like to thank Michelle for her patience and encouragement. I wish to dedicate this work to my Kurdish compatriots, my family, friends, and to my dog Bailey.

Kosar Jaff

Acknowledgments

The authors and publisher would like to thank the USB Implementers Forum for their permission to quote portions of the specification. For information on USB IF, please visit http://www. usb.org.

Contents

List of Figures

List of Tables

Foreword

The birth of the Universal Serial Bus (USB) represented a huge step forward in the computer's evolution. The dream of peripheral plug-and-play without rebooting the PC, and nearly limitless expansion became a reality. Now dip switches, jumper cables, IRQs, DMAs, and I/O addresses are replaced by dynamic insertion and removal, automatic configuration, and virtually unlimited peripheral connectivity.

Originally developed in 1994 by Compaq, Digital, IBM, Intel, Microsoft, NEC, and Northern Telecom, the Universal Serial Bus has grown into an industry-wide specification backed by a collection of over 450 technology companies. USB represents one of the best examples of industry-wide cooperation.

In the design of USB we implemented two bandwidth options, thus allowing devices like keyboards, mice, and game controllers to communicate at 1.5 Mbps at extremely low cost points, while providing a 12 Mbps rate for applications like audio, telephony, and digital imaging. Up to 127 devices can now be attached to a single PC, allowing virtually limitless expansion. By the year 2000, serial, parallel, and analog game ports will no longer be necessary, and the plug-in card will virtually disappear. PC's will come equipped with USB, and IEEE 1394 allowing the attachment of almost any class of external device.

To further simplify the ease of use of the PC, USB can automatically recognize the power needed by any given device, up to 500 milliamps, and can then provide that power through the cable. Many new peripherals can now be attached to the PC without the requirement for power adapter bricks, providing better power management abilities for both the system and its peripherals.

Developers no longer need to design drivers from scratch. The base USB driver, with some device class specifics, can be built upon to provide maximum support with a minimum of effort.

USB Hardware and Software is your magic ticket to accessing USB design and development. The authors have been key members in the development of USB and its specification. Whether you are just starting your design or are well into the development cycle, this is the reference you shouldn't be without. Its detailed examination of every aspect of USB makes it the best source of information available. USB's time has come, so "Hop on the Bus".

Jim Pappas
Director of Technology Initiatives
Intel Corporation

Preface

The authors of this book have been involved in most aspects of the PC industry for many years (collectively about 75 person-years!) before having the opportunity to participate in USB. For most of us, many of those years were involved in new technology development and/or one PC related standard or another.

One author started in the early days of the IEEE AT bus standard and evolved into developing PCI chip sets. Two of us participated as architects in the development of the PCI standard. Another two were primary architects of PC Card (PCMCIA) and CardBus standards. Then, over an almost two year period, four of us phased into working on the definition of the USB standard.

With that extensive exposure to technology standards, we have all come to appreciate the impact successful new technologies can have on the PC and embedded industry. We also have first-hand experience with the length of time it can take for a technology to become commonplace.

The adoption of a new technology is strongly influenced by how clearly it can be explained so that developers know how to apply it and achieve compatibility with other developers' designs. We know how difficult it is to fully explain a new technology in the framework of a technical specification. It is hard enough to clearly define what must be done, let alone describe why something is defined the way it is and how it is intended to be used.

When we were presented with the chance to write a book on USB, we jumped at it. We all wanted to try our hands at writing something less formal than a PC standard specification. We hope this book will enhance understanding of how to use USB beyond the definitions in the USB specifications.

It has taken us longer to write the book than we expected. It turns out to be harder to explain things than to define them. And we did all this on our own time whereas our previous specification work was done for a company paying our salaries.

Ed provided excellent guidance through the mazes of general book writing, given his involvement with several other PC technical books. He also had the challenge to start at the bottom of USB and explain the arcane aspects of USB, including electrical, mechanical, and signaling.

John took the middle ground and followed up writing the USB specification architecture description in the system architecture chapter, along with packets (with Ed), frames, and data transfer chapters.

Shelagh used her extensive telephony experience to describe USB's view of isochrony, and reprised her involvement with the USB specification descriptor, request, and class definitions to write the framework and class chapters.

Brad brought his experience with PCI and USB compliance to write the compliance, enumeration, and host controller (with John) chapters.

Kosar reapplied his efforts in writing code for USB to produce the software chapter. Kosar and Ed also wrote the extensive chapter on hubs.

We expect there may be future revisions of this book that will include more information, but as with any "product" we needed to "finish it" and "ship it".

Last, but not least, thanks to the staff at PC2 Consulting LLC and Annabooks for supporting the logistics of getting this book completed. Also, the authors would like to express special thanks to John Choisser for his long-term commitment to the book. The development of the book took longer than anticipated and John kept the faith that it would be worth the effort.

The Authors

Oregon, USA

1. Introduction

This book was written in the interest of expanding on the information provided in the Universal Serial Bus Specification version 1.0. The USB specification describes the basics of what is required according to the standard, but it sometimes leaves out important background or explanatory information. Since most of us have been intimately involved in the creation of the original specification, we wanted to take the opportunity to provide the "rest of the story" to help the USB development community at large. It turned out to take a lot longer to write than any of us expected, but hopefully it will fill the need intended.

1.1 Background

Universal Serial Bus was created out of a desire to provide solutions for many problems associated with low to medium data rate, cable connected, external peripherals for the Personal Computer (PC) market. The back panel of a PC has been cluttered with too many different I/O port connectors for a variety of specific devices. There's usually an RS232 port for a modem, printer, or mouse, a Centronics-style parallel port for printers, plotters, and scanners, and a SCSI port for disk, tape, and scanners. The list of peripherals and connectors has continued to grow.

1

Peripheral vendors wanting to create a new peripheral have been faced with several problems. If they used a standard I/O port connector, it was likely that the end user already had something attached to that connector. If they used their own I/O port connector, they had to develop an add-in card in the "hostile" internal electrical environment of the PC. In addition, the development of an add-on card usually requires a significantly different set of skills than those required for the peripheral itself. Another consideration, even if a vendor wanted to use a standard connector, was that the data rate available might not be sufficient for the peripheral. Many of the PC connectors had been unchanged for almost the lifetime of the PC industry, and the data rates of modern peripherals are generally increasing.

Also, each I/O port connector has required its own special cable. The poor end user was constantly confused about what to connect and where. Some I/O port connectors looked almost the same, but weren't. Further, some I/O port connectors could be changed with the PC running and some couldn't. In general, end users were not always successful in connecting a peripheral without a lot of effort.

The bottom line was that the ability to attach new and innovative PC peripherals was fraught with problems; consequently few interesting or exciting PC peripherals were being developed. Something had to be done.

1.2 Universal Serial Bus Approach

A group of companies started discussions with each other to determine whether a better I/O port connector could be designed that would be easier for the developer to create and also easier for the end user to understand. This better I/O port connector should allow a large number of peripherals to be attached at any time. Also, there was a desire to try to create one bus that would do everything for everyone for any particular peripheral. Therefore, the scope of devices that USB would deal with was intentionally limited to provide a greater chance of "getting it right" and to focus the engineering team.

It was recognized at the time that there was a significant amount of energy in the PC industry working to connect the PC and the telephone in various ways. Also, there was a lot of interest in enabling the PC to do a better job of enabling human interactive devices: joysticks, tablets, pens, steering wheels, pedals, etc. Most of these devices require modest bandwidth and latency compared to devices like hard disks and video monitors. Therefore, it was arbitrarily decided to focus the USB solution on the former types of devices, in the 10 Mbit/second and below bandwidth range. In addition, USB bus would focus on desktop area connectivity as opposed to wide area or local area networks of devices and interconnects.

With attention directed at these areas, the selection of technologies was simplified.

1.3 Solution

There were a number of alternatives in progress at the time, such as access.bus, Geoport, and Apple Desktop Bus. Each had different advantages and disadvantages. None of the other buses had the combined focus of relatively high data rates, large number of possible simultaneous devices, and interactive/telephony type devices.

The USB bus originally was targeted at a 5 Mbps data rate, but it was soon determined that for the same cost, a 12 Mbps bus could be developed. The companies developing the USB bus consciously chose to make the bus definition asymmetric, *i.e.*, the cost/complexity of the host controller would be greater than that of a device. This was done so devices would be easier to create. Even though the host controller was slightly more complicated and expensive, it was expected that it could easily be incorporated in the standard silicon included on every PC.

These factors made the deployment of the USB bus easy compared to many other technology developments. People were not asking why they should be interested. The key question was "Why isn't it available yet"? Everyone involved knew it was simply a matter of time before the "bus" was on its way. End users liked the simplicity of attaching new Plug and Play devices. Peripheral developers liked the range of peripherals they could create and sell. It sounded like a winner all around.

1.4 Overview of this Book

This book describes the hardware, software, device, bus, and host controller details of the Universal Serial Bus version 1.0. Our desire has been to expand on the technical information presented in the official specification. We expect that you have a copy of the official specification, which should be considered the final word on correct and required bus, device, and host controller behavior. We believe this book is an accurate interpretation, but this book is not the official specification unless and until it becomes adopted as such by the USB Implementers Forum (USB-IF).

The focus of this book is to address the needs of developers creating USB device hardware/firmware and device driver software. We feel that there would be many more USB devices created in the coming years, while relatively few host controller implementations and probably few operating system bus driver software implementations will be developed. Therefore, we want to provide more information to make the job of developing devices easier.

The book is organized to present Universal Serial Bus from a number of complementary perspectives. Early chapters provide critical information in understanding later chapters. However, not all of you will need to read all chapters to gain a full understanding of USB. The material is sequenced through the book in roughly a bottom-up fashion. This book is related in style and approach to classes that we have collectively taught on the subject for several years. Hopefully, it is easier to understand than just wading through the official specification.

This chapter presents some of the background motivation for the creation of the Universal Serial Bus.

Chapter 3 presents the basic overview of the whole Universal Serial Bus environment. It is required reading to help understand the terminology of USB and to gain forward references for various specific areas of the rest of the book.

Chapters 4 and 5 describe the lowest level foundations of the bus. Many developers that use building block components provided by other developers won't need to read these chapters.

Chapter 4 describes the electrical and mechanical basics of the bus.

Chapter 5 describes the details of the bus signaling mechanisms.

Chapters 6, 7, and 8 present common aspects of the bus that will be of interest to all developers. These chapters should be read by all developers; especially if you are using a bus analyzer to determine exactly how a device is interacting with the USB bus's activities.

Chapter 6 describes how the primitive data is moved over the USB bus via packets and transactions.

Chapter 7 describes how USB provides a common time base useful for some data transfer types.

Chapter 8 describes how USB has optimized different stylized forms of data communication.

Chapters 9 and 10 are more specialized chapters that may not be of general interest.

Chapter 9 describes some unique features that USB provides for easing the handling of certain data types such as audio and video.

Chapter 10 presents some of the minimum behavioral features that a USB Host Controller must provide to correctly support USB devices.

Chapters 11, 12, 13, and 14 describe details of USB that are at the heart of implementing USB devices.

Chapter 11 describes how devices describe themselves to ensure that they all work properly on the shared USB bus.

Chapter 12 presents information on the most important USB device class. Without this class definition, Universal Serial Bus would not be able to support the number of different devices that it does. This chapter is of most interest to developers of hub devices or compound packages. However, it may be useful to developers interested in how their device fits into the bus as a whole.

Chapter 13 describes some of the emerging types of USB devices and how they are being standardized. If a designer is developing a device that fits into one of these categories, it is very useful information.

Chapter 14 pulls together many of the previous chapter details and describes in detail how a USB device is recognized and "connected" to its respective device driver software.

Chapter 15 briefly touches on some aspects of Windows Driver Model (WDM) programming with respect to USB device drivers.

Chapter 16 presents the types of tests that devices will be expected to pass in order to ensure they share usage of the bus correctly.

Device software developers can get the most use of the book by reading Chapters: 3, 6, 7, 8, 11, 14, and 15.

Device hardware developers can get most use of the book by reading Chapters: 2, 4, 5, 6, 7, 8, 11, and possibly 14.

2. Glossary

2.1 USB Terminology

Most readers are aware that glossaries are normally found at the end of the book. However, reading this book already places you at the forefront of leading-edge development, so you must be open to new ideas and new definitions. You will be less confused and more likely to get the most out of the rest of this book if you read through this chapter before proceeding.

USB terminology has been carefully crafted so that developers will have a common set of terms to use when communicating with each other. Of course, there are other words and phrases that have similar or identical meaning. Therefore it is highly recommended that you use the following standard terminology:

active:
- See link states

adaptive endpoint: (An endpoint synchronization type)
- An isochronous endpoint which is not synchronized to the USB clock. Within the tolerance of its local clock, it can adapt to one of the following:
- The timing of the data streams it consumes
- The timing of the data stream it produces

Advanced Power Management (APM):
- A set of interfaces to power information and control for a USB system

asynchronous endpoint: (An endpoint synchronization type)
- An isochronous endpoint which is not synchronized with the USB clock and whose local clock cannot adapt to the timing requirements of the producer or consumer of its data stream
- Data rate is determined by the device

attachment:
- Act of attaching a device (including a hub) to a hub's downstream port.

awake:
- See hub's functional state

babble:
- Upstream transmission of data and handshake packets that do not include an EOP by the end of the Frame period.

bit stuffing:
- Act of inserting an additional 0 in the <u>bit stream</u> whenever there are six consecutive 1's.
- Bit stuffing limits the maximum time between signal transitions to allow clock recovery with NRZI data encoding.

Bps: (bytes per second)
- Transmission rate in terms of 8 bit bytes.

bps:(bits per second)
- Transmission rate in terms of packet bits. Instantaneous rate is 12 Megabits per second for full speed links and 1.5 Megabits per second for low speed links.

bit period:
- The time between two information bits in a packet. For full speed the bit period is 83.33 nanoseconds. For low speed the bit period is 666.67 nanoseconds.

byte time:
- The amount of bus time required to transmit one byte (8 bits) of information.

buffer:
- A portion of the host controller's memory that contains data transferred from a device endpoint or to be transferred to a device endpoint.
- Portion of a device's memory, associated with its endpoint, that contains data to be transferred to the host controller, or data that has been transferred from the host controller.

bulk transfer:
- See transfer types.

cable:
- The mechanical entity that includes two signal wires (D+ and D- signal lines), connectors, and two power wires (Vbus and ground). The functional USB bus name is "link".

class:
- A USB class describes an interface or device that is organized in a particular way to deliver a capability like audio. Each USB class specification describes one or more USB classes.

class specifications:
- audio
- communications
- hub
- human interface device (HID)
- imaging (video & still)
- monitor
- physical interface device (PID)
- power
- printer
- storage

client:
- A software module (can be an application, device driver, or library) that initiates USB bus activities via the USBD (USB Driver) interface.

client pipe:
- A pipe under the control of a client device driver.

client software:
- Host software that interacts with USB devices to manage communications with a device. Each interface on a device is owned by exactly one client.

communication class:
- USB class describing a framework in which a variety of class interfaces are used to support remote activities such as phone calls. The same specification also describes the data class, which is an undifferentiated data stream.

composite device: (a device type)
- A type of device that does not contain a hub, but does contain one or more embedded functions in a single mechanical package.

compound package: (a device type)
- A type of hub with an upstream port and downstream port(s), and one or more embedded functions in a single mechanical package.

configuration:
- The act of administrating a device to communicate what resources it is using and what features have been enabled. Each device has one or more mutually exclusive configurations.

consumer:
- The recipient of the data in a transfer.

control transfer:
- See transfer types.

data packet:
- See packet types.

data toggle:
- Some transfers have transactions with data packets of alternating DATA0 and DATA1 PIDs (Packet Identifications).

default address:
- All devices respond to a unique address after configuration. Prior to configuration, all devices respond to the default address of "0".

default pipe:
- The message pipe associated with Endpoint 0. It is always owned by the USBD (USB Driver) and is available for use by any client interfacing with the device. It is used primarily for configuration and other control activities.

descriptor:
- A data structure that reports the attributes of a device. Standard, class-specific and vendor-specific descriptors are defined and may be applied to the entire device or to a single configuration, interface, or endpoint.

descriptor type:
- Each descriptor type has a predefined format. Current standard descriptors include device configuration, interface, endpoint, and string.

device(s): (a device type)
- The term "device" is a generic term for all hubs, compound packages, composite devices, embedded functions, and function-only entities (commonly called a device) connected to a hub port. In order to assist in explanations, some chapters will provide a greater distinction in the exact definition of device.

device address:
- Each device is assigned a unique address. The address "0" is reserved as the default address and the root hub also requires an address, thus a total of 126 addresses are available for assignment.

device driver:
- Host software that controls one or more interfaces of one or more devices.

device power classes:
- Defined relative to power requirements of the device as viewed by the downstream port of the upstream hub or compound package. Regardless of power class, each device listed below is required to draw one unit load (100 milliamps) or less until it is configured.

- **Self-powered hub:** Always appears as one unit load (100 ma) or less on the upstream link connected to the upstream port of the hub. All power for the hub controller and hub repeater comes from the upstream link. Devices connected to the hub's downstream ports and embedded functions are powered by non-bus sources.
    - When the hub is suspended, the load on the upstream link is 500 microamps.
- **Bus-powered hub:** Initially requires one unit load or less on the upstream link connected to the upstream port of the hub. All power for the hub controller, hub repeater, embedded functions, and devices connected to the hub's downstream ports comes from the upstream link.
    - Long term power supplied by the upstream link connected to the upstream port of the hub is 1 to 5 unit loads.
    - When the hub is suspended, the load on the upstream link connected to the upstream port of the hub is 500 microamps per downstream port (a maximum of 2.5 ma).
- **Low load & self-powered device:** A device that draws one unit load or less of power from the bus, and has other sources of power to provide device functionality.

- **High load & bus-powered device:** A device that draws more than one unit load of power from the bus and has no other source of power to provide device functionality.
- **Low load & bus-powered device:** A device that draws one unit load or less of power from the bus and has no other source of power to provide device functionality.

device states:
- **connected:** Device has been physically attached to a downstream port of a hub but is not powered.
- **powered-on:** Bus power is applied to the device.
- **default:** The device has observed a reset and will now respond to the default address.
- **addressed:** The device has been assigned a unique, non-default address.
- **configured:** A specific configuration has been chosen for the device. This configuration is specified by a non-zero configuration value.
- **suspended:** The device has seen no bus activity for a period of time and will thus consume a reduced level of power.

device types: (Please see individual listings for the following terms)
- **root hub**
- **hub**
- **device**
- **compound package**
- **composite device**
- **embedded function**

disabled:
- See hub port states

disconnected:
- See hub port states

downstream connection:
- See hub's functional state

downstream port:
- See port types.

embedded function: (a device type)
- A portion of a hub, compound package, or composite device that performs as a "stand alone" device

enabled:
- See hub port states

End-of-Frame (EOF):
- End of bus frame period. Two types are defined:EOF1 and EOF2. Each is a count value of the hub frame timer to identify the end of a frame period and to detect a babble condition.

End-of-Packet (EOP):
- Identifies the end of packet with two bit periods of SE0 followed by one bit period of a (idle) J state of the link.

endpoints:
- A unique source or sink of transactions used for transfers between the host controller and devices. All devices are required to implement a bi-directional endpoint 0 for configuration. Full speed devices can implement up to 15 additional endpoints (1 to 15). Low speed devices can implement up to two additional endpoints (1 to 2).
- Endpoint 0 is a required endpoint of a device.

endpoint synchronization types: (Please see individual listings for the following terms)
- **adaptive**
- **asynchronous**
- **synchronous**

enumeration: (different from configuration)
- Ongoing process of identifying, configuring, and binding to a device driver each connected device.

frame:
- A reference time base that bounds the execution of transactions. A frame is the time between two consecutive SOFs.

frame period
- The time reference of nominally 12,000 full speed bit periods.

full speed link or full speed devices:
- Transmits and receives bits at the rate of 12 Megabits per second.

handshake packet:
- See packet types.

host:
- The entire standard PC

host controller:
- The hardware and software interface between the PC and a USB bus. There may be more than one host controller per PC, but only one host controller per USB bus. The host controller communicates with the USB bus via the root hub.

Host Controller Driver (HCD):
- Host software unique to the particular host controller and root hub implementation. It is only accessed by the USBD (USB Driver).

hot plug:
- Action of attaching or removing a link when the system is already powered-on.

hub: (a device type)
- A device with downstream ports to expand the USB bus to other downstream devices, and an upstream port to connect to the USB bus.
- There are there types of hubs:
- The typical "hub" simply supports upstream and downstream ports
- The "root hub" is the most upstream hub on a USB bus and interfaces between the host controller and the entire downstream USB bus.
- A "compound package" contains upstream and downstream ports, plus embedded function(s).

hub controller:
- The hub controller contains the configuration registers; and controls the hub repeater, hub port states, and the hub's functional states.
- The hub controller also contains the hub frame timer for the EOF protocol.

hub functional states:
- The hub's functional states represent hub operations reflecting packet transmission, clock operation, and power. The hub's functional states are:
  - **awake**: Hub is actively transmitting packets upstream and downstream.
  - **transient suspend**: Hub is not transmitting packets between its upstream and downstream ports.
  - **time suspend**: Hub is not transmitting packets between its upstream and downstream ports. Internal clock has equal or less

accuracy than during awake, transient, suspend, or send resume hub functional states.
- **low power suspend**: Similar to time suspend except internal clocks are disabled.
- **send resume**: Hub is transmitting resume signaling.
- **downstream connection**: Hub is transmitting downstream binary patterns.

hub port states:
- Defined for only the hub's downstream ports. The hub port states are:
    - **powered-off**: No power is provided to the downstream link and thus no packets are moving upstream or downstream.
    - **disconnected**: No downstream device is connected to the port
    - **disabled**: A downstream device is connected and power is supplied to the link, but the port has been deactivated and no packets are moving upstream or downstream .
    - **enabled**: A downstream device is connected, power is provided, and packets are moving upstream or downstream .
    - **suspended**: A downstream device is connected, the port is activated, and power is provided; but no packets are moving upstream or downstream.
    - **not configured**: The hub has not been configured and will not yet support normal USB bus operation.

hub frame timer (HFT):
- The HFT counts the number of full speed bit periods from the most recent SOF or EOF event. 12,000 bit periods nominally define a frame period.

hub repeater:
- The portion of the hub that repeats all downstream packets from the upstream port to all of the downstream ports in the enabled hub port state. The repeater also repeats the upstream packets from a downstream port to the upstream port.

hub repeater states:
- The hub repeater states define the packet flow protocol to establish appropriate transmit and receive modes of the transceiver's upstream and downstream ports. The primary states for hub repeaters are waiting for SOP and EOP.

hub power classes:
- See device power classes.

idle:
- See link states.

IN packet:
- See packet types.

information:
- The generic term for the binary pattern of the packet that contains PID, data, synchronization pattern, CRC, etc.

interrupt transfer:
- See transfer types.

isochronous transfer:
- See transfer types.

Lack of Activity (LOA)
- Upstream transmission of data and handshake packets that begin with an SOP, no EOP has been transmitted, and becomes stuck in a constant link state.

link:
- Represents both the physical and logical connection between hubs and devices. A physical implementation is typically a cable consisting of D+ and D+ signal lines, Vbus, and ground. A composite device or compound package has an implied link between the hub repeater and the embedded functions.

link states: The different states are defined by the binary pattern on the D+ and D- signal lines.
- **reset**: The binary pattern of SE0 for more than 2.5 microseconds. Re-establishes a device in powered or suspended state to a known initialized state
- **idle**: A constant J state.
- **suspended**: An idle state for more than 3 milliseconds.
- **resuming**: 20 milliseconds of the K state after a suspended idle state.

low power suspend:
- See hub's functional state and global suspend

low speed link or low speed device:
- Transmits and receives bits at the rate of 1.5 Megabits per second.

message pipe:
- A pipe that uses a USB-defined structure. Currently, the only defined structure is the one defined for control transfers.

monitor class:
- Describes the control mechanisms for a PC monitor. The video monitor data for the monitor is assumed not to be conveyed over USB; only the control information is conveyed. This class is an example of a class that reuses another class definition; in this case the HID class.

ms:
- millisecond

not configured: See hub port states.

OUT packet:
- See packet types.

PID: (class)
- See Physical Interface Device

PID: Packet identifier (protocol)
- The PID is a field within each packet that identifies the type packet.

packets:
- A series of logical transitions of the D+ and D- signal lines to encode a synchronization pattern, PID, inverted PID, CRC, and address endpoint, data, or frame number.

packet types:
- **token packet:** First or second packet transferred in a transaction always sent by host controller. Contains transaction type: direction of data transfer, device address, and endpoint number. The token packet types are:
  - **SOF** (Start of Frame): A token packet PID that indicates the start of a USB frame. Occurs every 1 millisecond (1 kHz).
  - **SETUP:** A token packet PID that indicates the first phase of a transaction used for a control transfer.
  - **OUT:** A token packet PID that indicates the beginning a transaction that includes a data packet transmitted by the host controller.
  - **IN:** A token packet PID that indicates the beginning a transaction that includes a data packet transmitted by a downstream device, compound package, and composite device.

- **data packet:** Contains data of a transaction. Data packet types are identified by either DATA0 (even) or DATA1 (odd) PIDs, depending on the appropriate data toggle value.
- **handshake packet:** Used to complete transactions for bulk, control, and interrupt transfers. The handshake packet types are:
  - **ACK:** Acknowledges the reception of an error free data packet
  - **NAK:** A downstream device's endpoint cannot transmit or receive a data packet at this time, but will be able to later.
  - **STALL:** A downstream device's endpoint is not able to continue with transmitting or receiving packets.
- **special packet**
  - **PRE (Preamble):** A special token packet to indicate that a low speed packet will be transmitted next on the link by the host controller.
- **reserved packet:** PID encoding not used for one of the other packet types

participants: (of a USB transaction)
- Host controller and the specific endpoint addressed

phases:
- A transaction has one to three phases. Each phase contains one or two packets.

pipes:
- A pipe is a data transport connection between an endpoint of a device and a buffer associated with a client on the host.

port types:
- **upstream**: The port of the hub or compound package connected to another upstream hub or compound package. For a device or composite device, it is the single USB compatible port connected to an upstream hub or compound package. The name "upstream port" is another name for "root port".
- **downstream**: The port of a hub or compound package connected to the upstream port of another hub or compound package, or the upstream port of a device or composite device.

powered-off:
- No power is available from a downstream port over the link to the upstream port of a hub, composite device, compound package, or device. Also, defines one of the hub port states.

powered-on:
- Power is available from a downstream port over the link to the upstream port of a hub, composite device, compound package, or device. Also, defines one of the device states.

PRE (preamble packet):
- See packet types.

producer:
- The provider of the data in a transfer.

receiver:
- The recipient of packets.

removal:
- Act of removing a device (including a hub) from a hub's downstream port.

reset:
- See link states.

resuming:
- See link states.

root hub: (a device type)
- Hub uniquely associated with the host controller.

root port:
- See port types.

selective resume:
- An action that causes one of the hub's downstream ports to transition out of the suspended hub port state.

selective suspend:
- An action that causes one of the hub's downstream ports to transition into the suspended hub port state.

SE0: (Single ended zero)
- The binary pattern when the D+ and D- signal lines are both logically and electrically low. The SE0 is used as part of the EOP and reset protocol.

SOP: (Start of Packet)
- The binary pattern of the D+ and D- signal lines on the link that changes from idle (J state) to the beginning of the synchronization pattern.

SETUP:
- See packet types.

sink:
- Endpoint of the device that is the recipient of a transaction.

SOF (Start of Frame)
- See packet types.

software: (Please see individual listings for the following terms)
- **Client software**
- **USB Driver (USBD)**
- **Host Controller Driver (HCD)**

source:
- Endpoint of device that is the provider of a transaction.

special packet:
- See packet types.

subtree:
- By definition, one of the following:
  - A device connected to a single downstream port by a single link.
  - Collection of hub(s), compound packages, composite devices, or device(s) connected to a single downstream port by a single link.

suspended:
- See link and hub port states.

synchronous endpoint: (An endpoint synchronization type)
- An isochronous endpoint synchronized to the USB bus clock.
- Clock synchronization established to SOFs.
- Data rate is fixed or previously programmed
- Can be a source or sink of isochronous data.

system:
- PC, host controller including all hubs, compound packages, composite devices, and devices connected by links.

time suspend:
- See hub's functional state.

token packet:
- See packet types.

transfer:
- The mechanism to move data between host controller memory and the endpoint of a downstream device, hub, composite device, compound package, or embedded function.

transfer types:
- **bulk:** A transfer type that does not provide guaranteed USB bus bandwidth or delivery latency. It does guarantee correct data delivery via limited retry. This type of transfer is only available to full speed devices.
- **interrupt:** A transfer type that provides limited guaranteed USB bus bandwidth and delivery latency. It also guarantees correct data delivery via limited retry. It is used to transmit interrupt requests from downstream devices to the host controller.
- **isochronous:** A transfer type that provides guaranteed USB bus bandwidth and delivery latency. There is no guarantee of correct data delivery. This type of transfer is only available to full speed devices.
- **control:** A transfer type that provides limited guaranteed USB bus bandwidth and delivery latency. It also guarantees correct data delivery via limited retry. It consists of three stages: setup, data, and status. It is used to control and configure devices and interfaces.

transaction:
- Each transfer consists of a series of transactions. Each transaction consists of phases, and each phase contains one or two packets.

transient suspend:
- See hub's functional state and global suspend.

transmission:
- Actual sequence of bits of a packet.

transmitter:
- The provider of packets.

upstream port:
- See port types.

us:
- microsecond (μs)

USB bus:
- All devices, compound packages, composite devices, hubs, and links connected directly or indirectly to a root hub.

USB Driver (USBD):
- Host software which is the single point of access for other host software wanting to communicate with devices, compound packages, composite devices, and hubs. It is also responsible for providing standard USB configuration and control mechanisms to its clients and pipe access to USB devices.
- It also manages one or more host controllers via their individual HCDs.

3. System Architecture

3.1 Introduction

Traditional personal computer system interconnects have been based on buses with multiple parallel signal wires. The physical and logical concepts of these buses are familiar to most PC developers. These buses have typically been physically constructed with combinations of address, data, and control signal wires. Such interconnects have directly provided common types of logical system resources such as memory addresses, I/O addresses, DMA channels, and IRQs.

Universal Serial Bus (USB) is a much different interconnect. It has some attributes that are more familiar to communication systems than bus interconnects. In order to fully understand a USB system, it is important to know what its physical and logical components are and how they interrelate. This chapter provides an overview of the major USB physical and logical components with references to other chapters that provide more details about each area of the bus. All developers should read this chapter first to gain a basic understanding of the overall USB Architecture.

Three viewpoints are followed at various points in the book: the end user viewpoint, the host side of the USB bus viewpoint, and the device side of the USB bus viewpoint. Each viewpoint focuses on different aspects of USB. The end user viewpoint points out aspects of USB with which the end user will interact, *e.g.*, connectors, cables, peripherals, etc. The host side of the USB bus viewpoint describes how devices appear from the host perspective, *e.g.*, aspects of USB of interest to developers writing device drivers. The device side of the USB bus viewpoint describes how the host appears to a device, e.g., aspects of USB of interest to developers of USB peripherals with the firmware or hardware composing those devices.

Most of the book focuses on explaining the details of interest to device and driver developers. Core attributes of the bus are explained so those developers will understand how the bus operates and how to build superior devices. The book does not go into detail on how to build host controllers or bus drivers as it is expected that most of the USB industry activity will be in creating USB peripherals. Few host controllers and USB bus drivers will be designed as those pieces of USB will be difficult to add real value and are expected to rapidly become commodities that are present on every mass market computer system.

The physical architecture describes the physical USB components that can be seen and touched in some form by an end user. The logical architecture describes the key technical features of USB that are of interest to developers. These features typically span different aspects of the USB environment and need to be understood globally before diving into specific details of certain aspects of the bus.

3.1.1 End User Perspective

An end user sees a USB system as connector sockets located on a personal computer and cables with plugs on peripherals. For example, Figure 3.1 shows a USB system with a telephone and headset that the end user has just purchased and wants to attach and use. In general, the end user believes that a USB device's cable simply connects to a USB socket and upon attachment, the device "just works." For implementers of USB components, it is important to understand the more detailed internal view of how the end user perspective is supported. There is, in fact, more that must be done to deliver the desired end user results.

Figure 3.1: Universal Serial Bus End User View

3.2 Physical Architecture

The physical architecture of USB focuses on the pieces of plastic and metal that an end user must deal with to construct a USB environment. Every USB physical environment is composed of five types of components: host, host controller, link, hub, and device. The components of the USB physical environment are presented starting from the host proceeding through the architecture toward a device.

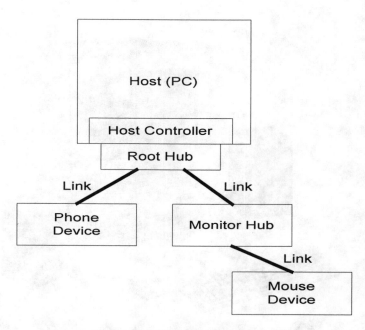

Figure 3.2: Simple Physical Architecture

Figure 3.2 shows an overview diagram of the main components of a simple USB environment. The host, host controller, and root hub are typically contained within a Personal Computer (PC). The example architecture shows the root hub connected via links to Phone Device and Monitor Hub. The Monitor Hub in turn connects via a link to the Mouse Device.

The remainder of this section describes the key features of each component of the USB physical architecture. Each description concludes with references to other chapters for further detailed information about a component.

3.2.1 Host

The host is the complete computer system including software and hardware that anchors USB. The USB Core Specification has a single chapter that describes the host and the host controller. This book spends more time presenting information about both the overall host and the host controller.

The software on the host includes the device drivers used to control the end user desired features of the USB devices. A host has the processing ability to manage the configuration changes that can occur on the bus during runtime. The host manages system and bus resources such as system memory usage, bus bandwidth allocation, and bus power. The host also assists the end user by automatically configuring USB devices that are attached, reacting to devices that are removed, and adhering to any policies the user may have adjusted for his custom system. Generic requirements on the actions that a host is responsible for are described later in the book. Specific details of exactly what the host does and how it is done are very computer system- and operating system-dependent and are outside the scope of this book. For example, exactly how to write a particular operating system driver for a host controller is not discussed. However, the sequence of actions that a host is required to take to identify a newly attached device is described.

A host can support one or more USB buses. The host manages each bus independently of any others. Bus-specific resources such as allocated bandwidth are unique to each bus. Each bus is connected to the host via a host controller.

See Chapter 10 for more detailed information about the host.

3.2.2 Host Controller

The host controller is made up of the hardware and software that allows USB devices to be connected to a host. The host controller is the initiating agent on the bus that starts every bus transfer. The host controller is the master of a USB bus. Other buses, such as PCI, allow multiple masters to be present on a bus where each master arbitrates for its bus access. There is exactly one and only one host controller for each USB bus. Therefore there is no arbitration for bus access.

A USB host controller operates as a form of bus bridge, *i.e.*, it connects a USB bus to some other system bus such as PCI. Data transfers from a device on USB result in data transfers on the other system bus. Since device data transfers can occur based on data or space availability of a USB device, most host controllers are implemented as PCI bus master devices. This allows the host controller to initiate a data transfer on the system bus as it needs to, without requiring host CPU involvement for each data transfer. The host controller behaves as a multiple channel programmable PCI bus master to support the data transfer needs of the multiple devices connected to the USB bus.

> USB was designed to be very asymmetric in cost/complexity of the host controller versus a USB device. The host controller side bus interface is significantly more costly/complex than the device side bus interface. Typical host controllers can be implemented in about 10,000 gates. A device side bus interface is very inexpensive/simple, *e.g.*, it can be implemented in an ASIC or with a microcontroller. Typical device size bus interfaces require on the order of 1500 gates to implement.

When there are multiple USB buses in a personal computer, there is a dedicated host controller for each bus. A required feature of every host controller is a root hub to provide the initial attachment points for USB devices.

See Chapter 10 for more detailed information about the host controller.

3.2.3 Hub

A hub is a standardized type of USB device. A hub is the only USB device that provides connection points for additional USB devices. The root hub is the hub that is an embedded part of every host controller. From an end user perspective, a hub provides the sockets that are used to plug in other USB devices. There are no limitations on the number of sockets that a hub can provide beyond the addressing limits of USB and the amount of power that the hub can supply to its sockets. Hubs can attach to other hubs to provide connections for up to a total of 126 devices. The number of devices connected includes all hubs, since hubs also are devices.

Figure 3.3 shows an example of how hubs can be used to support the range of devices shown in Figure 3.1. In this example, the root hub has two connections: one to the phone device and one to a hub device contained as part of the monitor.

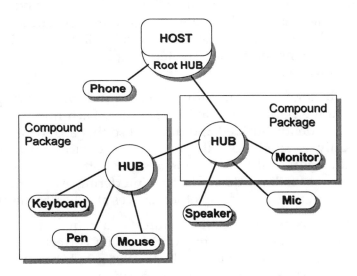

Figure 3.3: Hub Fan-out Example

The monitor hub has four connections: another hub, the monitor control device, a microphone device, and a speaker device. The last hub is contained as part of the keyboard. It has three connections: the keyboard device, a pen device, and the mouse device.

> USB is not a single point-to-point interconnect like a serial RS232 communications port or a Centronics style parallel port. Multiple devices can be simultaneously attached to USB. A hub is the USB device that provides additional attachments.

A hub provides hardware support for detecting dynamic attachment and removal of USB devices. The hub is directly responsible for providing hot plug support for USB. Hot Plug is a common PC industry term identifying the ability to attach and remove some electronic device without powering off the PC or rebooting the operating system.

A hub is connected to the bus via ports. A hub has a single upstream port, i.e., the cable/connectors leading in the direction of the host controller. A hub has one or more downstream ports, *i.e.*, the sockets/cables that allow connection of other USB devices. Downstream ports are uniquely identifiable and have explicitly controllable features. Upstream ports are transparent and provide no controllable features. The term "port" will normally be used to refer to a downstream port. The term "upstream port" will be fully qualified when used as such.

Host bus software can turn power on and off to each port and therefore the port's connected USB device. Each hub port can also be independently enabled and disabled so that a USB device can be electrically isolated from the rest of the devices on a bus. This individual port control allows the host bus software to prevent an ill behaved or failing device from interfering with the normal operation of the bus and any other devices attached to the bus.

A hub has many specific features and required behaviors to support a normally operating USB bus. Its correct functioning is critical to having a useful USB bus. After a hub has been used to detect, report, and enable communication to a newly attached device, it becomes essentially transparent for normal communication involving the devices attached to it.

Communication with devices attached to USB is done over a link.

See Chapter 12 for more detailed information about the hub.

3.2.4 Link

A link is the connection between a USB hub and some other device. A USB bus consists of a set of USB devices and their links. The link is physically composed of a four-wire cable. Two wires are used to provide power and ground so that some USB devices can be designed without their own local power supply. The remaining two wires provide a differential signal pair that is electrically robust.

This differential signal operates half duplex and carries all signaling defined for the bus. The link is conceptually a single logical wire that carries data across the USB bus.

Some form of a conceptual link connects the host controller to the root hub. However, that particular link will seldom be a physical cable. Some form of a link always connects each USB device to the bus. There are also other links which are not required to be implemented via physical cables. For example, in some highly integrated devices, links can be implemented as metal layers on a single silicon die. The key requirement is that all links obey the behavioral rules of USB.

Signaling across a link is generated by a transmitter and accepted by a receiver. There is never more than one transmitter on a link at any given time. There can be multiple receivers. All transmissions on the bus must obey strict signaling protocol to preserve the robustness of the USB bus. These rules will be described later.

See Chapter 5 for more information about signaling and Chapter 6 for more information about USB protocol.

Data is transmitted across a USB link at one of two signaling speeds: full speed or low speed. Each device can only operate on the bus at one speed. Electrical voltage levels on the signal wires at attachment time identify to the host the speed of a newly connected device. These voltage levels determine the speed used for the link: full or low speed.

3.2.5 Full Speed

Full speed data transmissions operate at 12 Mbps. A full speed device and link can make use of all bus transfer types. Shielding cable and twisted signal line wires in the cables are required on full speed devices.

3.2.6 Low Speed

Low speed data transmissions operate at 1.5 Mbps. A low speed device and link is limited to a subset of the bus transfer types. Low speed cables don't require a shield or twisted signal line wires in the cable, and can consequently be lower cost. The main reason for defining the low speed mode was to allow a lower cost for some devices.

> Several bus definitions were consciously made to make low speed devices less attractive to implement. Low Speed was defined to allow building very cost competitive, limited feature devices such as mice. For these devices, the cost of the shield copper is a significant portion of the device cost. However, if all devices are implemented as low speed devices, the bus becomes a 1.5 Mbps bus that was designed (with associated costs) for a 12 Mbps bus. In some regards, "low speed" could have been named "reduced feature" to better indicate the impact of its attributes.

See Chapter 4 for more detailed signaling information dealing with transmission speeds.

3.2.7 Link Data Organization

Information on the link is organized to support multiple devices being present on the bus at the same time. This organization is called Enhanced Time Division Multiplexed (ETDM). Time on the bus is organized into units called frames.

Each frame is a 1 ms time period. The frame period is precisely controlled by the host controller, in order to provide better support for devices requiring isochronous information transfer. Each device present on the bus is given some time during one or more frames for its data transmission.

An expanded overview of how data is transmitted over the bus is presented below in the *Logical Architecture* section. Additional details regarding the rules of organizing data on the bus is described in the communication model for USB.

See Chapter 8 for more detailed information about the impact of the communication model on transmission speeds.

3.2.8 Device

A device is a collection of functionality that performs some useful purpose. For example, a device could be a mouse, keyboard, joystick, telephone, audio speaker, or video camera. A device is uniquely addressable on the bus. Multiple devices can be present on the bus at the same time. Each device carries information that can be used to identify its features and characteristics.

Host bus software is able to determine the type of device that is attached by making use of a hub's individual port addressing and control and the device-carried information. Once a device has been recognized and identified, the host bus software can cause the appropriate device drivers to be given control of the newly attached device.

Each device is dynamically assigned an address when it attaches to a bus. The address is unique within the scope of the currently connected bus and is only used while the device is connected. After a device is disconnected, the address it had been assigned may be reused for the device connected next.

A device only participates in bus transactions when the host controller identifies it as a participant of a bus transaction. A device is always a slave to the host controller in that it only participates in bus transactions when requested to do so by the host controller.

Many implementations of devices provide similar functionality. Such devices can be built to adhere to a specific device class. USB defines several device classes for many common types of devices such as Display Monitor control, Audio, Human Interface, etc. See Chapter 13 for more information about these specific USB device classes.

There is a great deal of flexibility possible in the construction of a USB device. A single USB device may provide a single type of functionality such as a simple microphone or speaker. Alternatively, a device can be composed of multiple different types of functionalities, such as a speaker and an LCD panel. This latter type of device is called a multiple function or composite device. Chapter 11 *USB Device Framework* describes more details about the possible organization of devices.

A compound package is another way of constructing a product with multiple functions. A compound package is the term used when a hub along with multiple USB devices is grouped into one package. An end user probably sees a single unit on the end of a USB cable, but internally there is a hub and one or more additional devices. A compound package has a unique bus address for each device contained within it. In contrast, a composite device has only one bus address.

> A compound package is called a compound device in the USB specification. The specification term is somewhat misnamed. It is only interesting from an end user or packaging perspective. The name compound device is confusing because it appears to be a different type of USB device, while in fact it is not. The individual devices comprising a compound package are the actual USB devices and the compound package has no controllable attributes or characteristics. A compound package is transparent when looked at from within the bus.

Figure 3.3 shows two example compound packages. One is the monitor that contains the monitor device along with a hub providing some additional external connections for other USB devices. The example monitor compound package could typically allow a large number of additional connectors for attachment of other USB devices. This type of compound package can provide sufficient power to each connector since a power supply with appropriate capacity can be included in the monitor without the addition of a power cord.

The other compound package is composed of a keyboard, mouse, and pen device along with a hub. In this case, the diagram suggests that the hub has no other externally accessible USB connectors. This could allow the keyboard compound package along with its mouse and pen to be implemented in a low power fashion that would not need an external power supply or power cord.

> Throughout this book, whenever a device is referenced, it can typically mean either a hub or compound package, since a compound package always contains a hub and a hub is also a USB device.

3.3 Logical Architecture

This section takes the physical architecture presented in the last section and describes how the physical USB components are viewed from a logical perspective. This viewpoint presents layers of abstractions that are relevant to different designers and implementers. The logical architecture describes how to bind a piece of USB device hardware to a device driver on the host so that some end user desired behavior can be provided. After the general logical architecture is introduced, three detailed sections are presented:

- The communications view describes the abstraction layers of the link presented in the physical architecture.
- The device view describes the abstraction layers within a USB device.
- The host view describes the abstraction layers within the USB host.

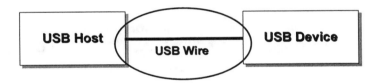

Figure 3.4: General Logical Connection

The general logical architecture is simple, as shown in Figure 3.4. The host provides a connection to a device. This connection is via a single USB link. Most other buses like PCI, ISA, etc. provide multiple connections to a device. Device drivers manipulate their device via some combination of these connections, i.e. via I/O and memory addresses, interrupts, and DMA channels.

USB physically has only a single wire bus that is shared by all devices on the bus. However, the logical view presented is that each device has its own point to point connection with the host. The abstraction layers contain the mechanisms that deliver the simple logical view over the physical architecture. The developers of USB wanted to make the details of the shared bus as transparent as possible to minimize the new learning implementers would need to build USB devices.

3.4 Logical Communications View

The logical architecture is described from the lowest abstraction layer building up to higher level abstraction layers. Figure 3.5 shows the abstraction layers present in a USB environment.

The communication view of the logical architecture as shown in Figure 3.5 focuses on the logical view of the wire that connects a host to a device. The view of the wire shifts to match each abstraction layer being discussed.

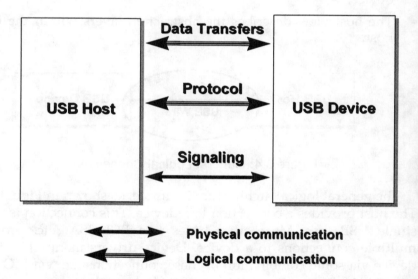

Figure 3.5: Logical Communication Abstraction Layers

The signaling layer uses electrical conditions to move bits of information between the host and a device via bus interfaces. The protocol layer organizes these bit streams of information carried by the signaling layer into packetized byte streams moving between USB system software on the host and a corresponding logical device connected to the USB bus. The data transfer layer allows the transfer of meaningful information between a device driver or some other client software on the host and its corresponding device specific interface of the USB device.

The following sections describe each layer of the logical communication abstraction from the bottom signaling layer up through the top data transfer layer. Even though the three abstraction layers are described in the remainder of this chapter, the actual data flow between some entity on the host and its corresponding entity on the device is always carried via the signaling layer.

3.4.1 Signal Layer: Packets

Information is moved over the bus in one or more packets. A packet is the smallest unit of coherent data moved over the bus. Packets are carried by the physical signaling over the link. Figure 3.6 shows that the physical signaling defines the start and end of a packet and carries the bits/bytes contained within the packet.

There are different types of packets defined to carry different types of information. token packets identify the device that communication will involve and the direction of data movement. data packets carry information specific to a communication. handshake packets can be used to indicate the success of a data delivery, return an indication of error to the host, or can be used for flow control to indicate that there is no data to deliver at this time.

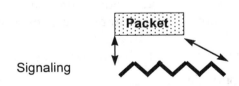

Signaling

Figure 3.6: Signaling to Packet

Every packet includes some form of error detection so that errors in or corruption of a packet are detectable. Different mechanisms are used for packet delivery retry when errors are detected.

Data packets are variable sized while token and handshake packets are fixed length.

Packets are organized into bus transactions.

See Chapters 4 and 5 for more information about signaling. See Chapter 6 for more detailed information about packets and bus protocol.

3.4.2 Protocol Layer: Transaction

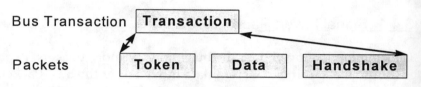

Figure 3.7: Packets to Transaction

A transaction consists of one or more packets involving the host and zero or more devices. Some transactions are broadcast and aren't targeted for a particular device. Most transactions involve data movement between a specific USB device and the host in a specified direction: i.e. outward from the host to a device or inward from a device to the host.

Figure 3.7 shows that a transaction is composed of one to three phases: token phase, optional data phase, and optional handshake phase. A phase is composed of one or two packets. Two packets are required for certain phases of transactions of low speed links. The additional packet is a preamble packet indicating that the next packet will be transmitted with low speed signaling.

The host controller defines the source and sink for every bus transaction. The host controller is always either the source or the sink. The identified USB device is the corresponding sink or source involved in the data movement. The source generates a data packet during the data phase and the sink accepts the data packet. There are no peer to peer bus transactions for USB. The host controller is always involved in every bus transaction.

Strict protocol is defined to ensure that normally there will never be more than one source operating on the bus at a time. Even in error cases, possibly due to failing devices, the bus has features that ensure correct operation after error recovery actions have been taken. For example, there are specific limits to the maximum times allowed between packets. This limit allows quick detection and recovery of conditions that could otherwise lead to a hung bus.

The token phase identifies the direction of bus transaction and the address of the device (if there is one) involved with the host in data movement for this transaction. This information establishes the source and sink for a following data phase in a transaction that includes a data phase.

There are three general types of bus transactions identified by the token phase: setup, data, and start of frame (SOF). Setup and data transactions identify the source and sink involved in a bus transaction. SOF transactions are broadcast transactions and don't identify a source or sink. These are described in more detail in Chapter 6.

The optional data phase immediately follows the token phase of the bus transaction. The data phase is used to deliver data from the source to the sink. If no data needs to be delivered, there is no data phase. The data packet contains within it a data field that carries the source data from source to sink.

The optional handshake phase immediately follows either the token or data phase. A handshake phase follows the token phase in the case that a device has no data to provide to the host for an inward data movement. This handshake is used as flow control and is not an error condition. A handshake phase can follow the token or data phases so that a device can indicate a successful data phase or an error condition. A handshake phase follows the data phase to indicate back to the source the success of the data movement during the data phase.

Multiple bus transactions may be required to transfer a meaningful unit of data between a host device driver and the device hardware.

See Chapter 6 for more detailed information about packets and protocol.

3.4.3 Data Transfer Layer: Transfer

Figure 3.8 shows that a transfer is composed of one or more transactions. A transfer delivers a meaningful collection of data between a host device driver and a USB device.

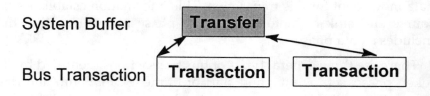

Figure 3.8: Transactions to Transfer

There are four transfer types to allow a range of optimizations of bus utilization and good bus sharing. The four transfer types are control, interrupt, bulk, and isochronous. Each transfer type places limits on:

- the size of the data field of a data packet during a bus transaction's data phase
- the frequency of bus transactions, and
- the composition of a bus transaction

In particular, the data size limits of a particular transfer type may require that a desired data transfer be split up into multiple bus transactions to be moved over the bus.

The host controller determines when bus transactions move over the bus, subject to the definitions of each transfer type. In general, host device drivers will present a data transfer to the host controller's driver and can be unaware of the fact that the transfer may be split up into multiple bus transactions. However, a device implementer must understand the transfer type rules to correctly design a USB device. Device driver writers may also need to understand the rules to correctly recover from transfer errors.

A transfer is to or from an endpoint of a device.

See Chapter 8 *Data Transfer* for more detailed information about the communication model and the details of each transfer type. See Chapter 10 *Host Controller* for more information about how the host controller manages transfers.

3.5 Logical Device View

The logical view of a device has abstraction layers corresponding to the communication view. Figure 3.9 shows USB bus interface, endpoint, and interface device layers.

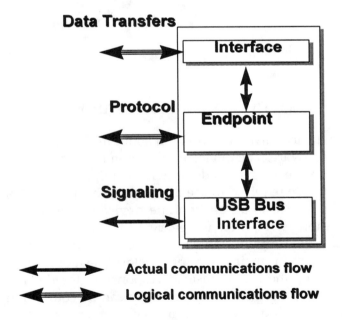

Figure 3.9: Logical Device Architecture

Each implementation of a device consists of one or more endpoints and interfaces. The logical communication architecture allows point to point connections between each logical device side entity with its corresponding host side entity. The definition of the USB transfer mechanisms allows this point to point connection to be done in an implementation generic fashion. The bus provides generic multiplexing and de-multiplexing of the data moving over the shared bus as shown in Figure 3.10 for the device side. Device AddressA contains two endpoints (EP0 and EP2). Device AddressB contains a single Endpoint (EP0). All data for each endpoint is moved over the shared link, but each endpoint can view its usage of the bus as transparent with any other endpoint.

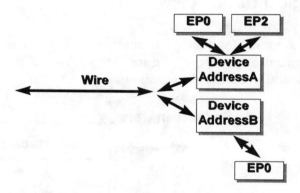

Figure 3.10: Device Side Data (De-)Multiplexing

Each device carries information about itself that can be probed by system software. The device information is used to determine what type of device is connected and what configurations, interfaces, and endpoints are required to use the device. This information is used to bind the device to an appropriate device driver (or drivers). This information is required for every USB device due to the shared nature of the USB bus. Drivers are not allowed to probe the devices on the bus in their own proprietary fashion. The controlling software for the bus is instead responsible for determining what devices are present and whether they can be configured and used. Devices can be attached and removed from the bus at any time. For these reasons the device enumeration process is standardized for all devices.

See Chapter 11 *USB Device Framework* for more information about how devices describe themselves. See Chapter 14 *Enumeration* for details about USB device enumeration.

3.5.1 Signaling Layer: Bus Interface

The device's bus interface contains the logic that recognizes a unique device address for all endpoints of the device. This device address is assigned to the device as part of the enumeration process. The device address is a seven-bit number from 0 to 127. Whenever a packet is sent on the bus, each device's bus interface unit receives the packet and determines whether the device address contained within the packet is for this device or not. If the packet is not for this device, it is ignored. Otherwise, the packet is kept and it is routed internally by the device logic to the correct device endpoint.

See Chapters 4, 5, and 6 for more information about the Bus Interface Unit.

3.5.2 Protocol Layer: Endpoint

An endpoint is a uniquely addressable part of a device that is the source or sink of a transaction. Endpoints are similar in some respects to memory or I/O addresses in other bus environments. That is, just as an I/O or memory location accepts or generates data, so an endpoint accepts or generates data. Each endpoint has a direction associated with it; i.e., IN or OUT. IN endpoints generate data to the host. OUT endpoints accept data from the host.

All devices are required to have an endpoint zero (0). This endpoint is used for device enumeration and configuration purposes. It can also be used for other device-specific purposes. A full speed device can have no more than fifteen (15) IN and fifteen (15) OUT endpoints. A low speed device can have no more than two (2) endpoints besides endpoint zero.

A host device driver transfers data to/from a device endpoint to manipulate the behavior of the device, which is logically connected via its endpoints. This is similar to how a device driver manipulates an ISA or PCI device via memory or I/O reads and writes. An endpoint is the end of a data connection between the host and a device. An endpoint typically has a device FIFO associated with it.

Endpoints have associated information describing the capabilities and requirements of their data connection. The design of the endpoint allows the data communication requirements of the device to be matched to the data communication resources of the bus and host. An endpoint on a device is matched with a memory buffer area on the host.

Endpoints are organized into interfaces.

See Chapter 8 *Data Transfer* for more detailed information about the communication model and Chapter 11 *Device Framework* for more information about the endpoint descriptors.

3.5.3 Data Transfer Layer: Interface

An interface is a collection of zero or more endpoints that provide a means of manipulating a USB function. A device can provide several interfaces simultaneously, *e.g.*, multiple functions. Each interface carries associated information on the device that allows the correct device driver to be identified and bound to the interface. At any point in time, each interface is manipulated by a single device driver.

A device can provide different interfaces that can be alternatively selected via configuration actions. These alternate interfaces allow a device to match its capabilities to the requirements of the host device driver(s) present in the system. Interfaces can also be selected during operation of the device after the device has been configured.

See Chapter 11 *Device Framework* for more detailed information about interfaces.

3.6 Logical Host View

The logical view of the host as shown in Figure 3.11 contains the abstraction layers corresponding to the layers of the logical communication and device views. The host also contains a USB Bus interface as part of the host controller. The USB system software manages access to device endpoints. Client software manipulates device interfaces.

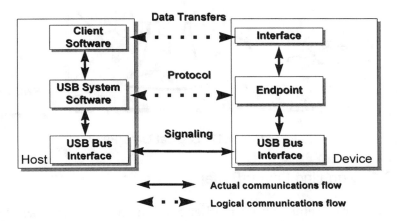

Figure 3.11: Complete Logical Architecture

Figure 3.12 shows an overview of the logical host-device data flow. There are three endpoints in this example composing a single interface of a device. One of the endpoints supports data flow from host to device. The second endpoint supports data flow from device to host and the third endpoint pair allows bi-directional data flow. Each data flow is associated with a host buffer via a pipe. Each of these features will be discussed in turn.

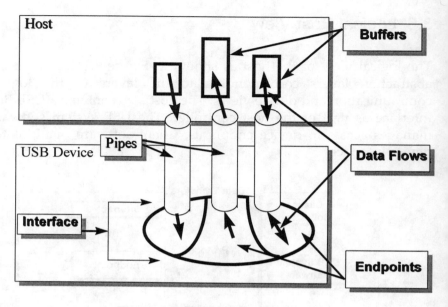

Figure 3.12: Logical Data Flow

3.6.1 Signaling Layer: Buffer

A host side memory buffer either contains the data that will be sent through a pipe to a device endpoint or contains the space into which data will be written when sent through a pipe from a device endpoint. Buffers are typically allocated from system memory with the involvement of a device driver.

The details of buffer management are usually operating system specific. Consult your operating system device driver writer's documentation for more information.

Just as the device side of USB is involved in data multiplexing and de-multiplexing, so also is the host side. Figure 3.13 shows how the host controller is the agent that internally routes data to and from buffers on to and off of the bus. Device drivers put data into or take data from a buffer and notify the system software that the buffer needs to be handled. System software is responsible for directing the host controller to transmit data on or receive data from the bus as appropriate.

See Chapter 10 *Host Controller* for more information about Host Controllers.

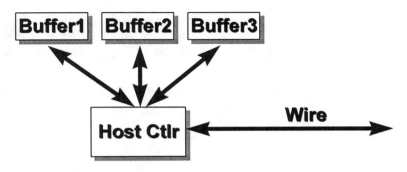

Figure 3.13: Host Side Data (De-)Multiplexing

3.6.2 Protocol Layer: Pipe

A pipe is the conceptual connection of an endpoint of a device and a host memory buffer area. Data flows through the pipe between the host memory buffer and the device endpoint. There are two types of pipes defined for USB: stream and message.

A stream pipe is unidirectional and has no USB imposed format on the data that flows through the pipe. Bulk, interrupt, and isochronous transfer types use stream pipes. The unidirectional pipes and endpoints of Figure 3.12 are used for bulk, interrupt, or isochronous transfers.

A message pipe is bi-directional and USB requires a specific format for how data moves through the pipe. Control transfers use message pipes. The bi-directional pipe and endpoint of Figure 3.12 are used for control transfers.

See Chapter 8 *Data Transfer* for more detailed information about the transfer type details.

3.6.3 Data Transfer Layer: Device Driver

The device driver is the agent on the host that is responsible for manipulating a USB function via interface endpoints. A device driver can use multiple interfaces to manipulate a function. Multiple device drivers can be simultaneously using a single USB device. Typically a single device driver is responsible for each USB interface.

See Chapters 10, 11, and 15 for more detailed information about device drivers and how they interact with interfaces.

4. Electrical and Mechanical

4.1 Introduction

This chapter describes the electrical and mechanical aspects of USB. As discussed in Chapter 3, the USB architecture does not include a bus on a fiberglass backplane compared to other typical system buses. Rather, a USB Bus is composed of cables and devices where the wiring topology is organized in a tree structure (See Figure 4.1).

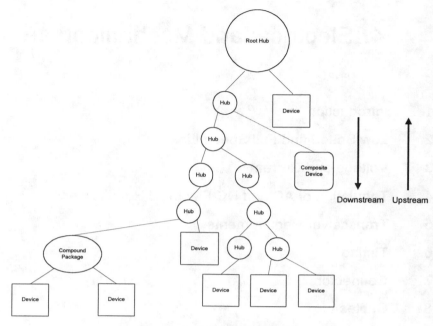

Figure 4.1: USB Architecture

In the USB architecture, the number of device connection points is expanded by the addition of hubs or compound packages. Each hub or compound package provides additional downstream ports that can be used to attach more USB devices. The interconnects between hubs, compound packages, composite devices, and devices are called links. The links contain wires for power, and the D+ and D-. signal lines.

> In this chapter, the term "hub" refers to both hubs and compound packages. The term "device" refers to both non-hub devices and composite devices.

4.2 Low Speed and Full Speed Links

USB bus protocol defines two speed rates for the links and associated devices: low and full. Low speed links are connected between hubs and low speed devices. Full speed links are connected between hubs and full speed devices, and between hubs. Full speed links support an instantaneous transmission rate of 12 Megabits per sec (Mbps). However, to support full speed, the links have EMI requirements of twisted pair signal lines and a shielded cable for the link. The low speed link supports an instantaneous transmission rate of 1.5 Mbps and does not require twisted pair signal lines or shielded cable. Consequently, the low speed cable is lower in cost and performance, but may be sufficient for specific cost sensitive applications.

Throughout this chapter, information will be provided for both low and full speed links. The requirements of the two link types differ in terms of bit speed, impedance, mechanical requirements, cable length, voltage, current, and the I/O buffers of the transmitters and receivers at the ports. Also, the voltage polarity of the D+ and D- signal lines are different for the two types of link speed.

Another consideration is that both low and full speed devices must be supported throughout the USB system. Consequently, all links between hubs are required to be full speed to insure that the downstream port of a hub can support both low and full speed devices. The low speed link cannot support full speed transmission rates, but a full speed link can support both low and full speed transmission rates.

See Chapter 5 *Signaling Characteristics* for more information about USB link protocol.

4.3 Voltage and Current

Each link consists of two signal wires and two power wires. The two signal wires are electrically differentially driven and labeled as D+ SIGNAL LINE and D- SIGNAL LINE. The electrical values of the D+ and D- signal lines are defined individually as differential states of DIFFERENTIAL 1 and DIFFERENTIAL 0, and as QUIESCENT STATES "1" AND "0". Also, together the D+ and D- signal lines define the electrical value of a single ended zero (SE0). Finally, to provide a convenient naming convention between full and low speed links, both differential and quiescent states of the D+ and D- signal line pair are defined in terms of J states and K states.

The power wires are labeled **VBUS** and **GND** (ground). The important considerations of the power lines are the current load of a downstream hub or device, the associated voltage drop in the link, and the voltage drop in a hub.

4.3.1 Signal Line Definitions

For both full and low speed links, a Differential 1 is identified whenever the D+ signal line voltage is 200 mv more than the D- signal line voltage. Similarly, a Differential 0 is identified whenever the D+ signal line voltage is 200 mV less than the D- signal line voltage. The quiescent states of "1" and "0" are defined when the Differential 1 and Differential 0 are driven onto the signal lines during the idle periods between packet transmissions. In Figures 4.2 and 4.3, the quiescent state is identified as "1" and "0" in the Binary row of the drawing. The quiescent state of "1" and "0" reflect a constant Differential 1 and 0, respectively.

When the transmission of a packet begins, the D+ and D- signal lines will change polarity during the synchronization and data portions of the packet transmission. The differential value of the D+ and D- signal lines alternate dependent on the information transmitted and the non-return to zero inverted protocol (NRZI), as will be discussed in Section 5.5.3. In Figures 4.2 and 4.3, the information transmitted in both full and low speed links is the same. The synchronization portion of the information is 0000001 and the data portion of the information is 110101000100, as defined in the binary row of the figures. The link transmission of the synchronization and data uses a differential pattern on the D+ and D- signal lines. Figures 4.2 and 4.3 show that the polarity of the D+ and D- signal lines during the packet transmission is opposite between full and low speed links.

For protocol convenience that is independent of the link speed, the USB specification has adopted the convention of using "J" and "K" states. The value of the J and K states for the full speed link is opposite of the values for the low speed link. Consequently, as shown in Figures 4.2 and 4.3, the sequence of J and K states are identical for the two link speeds across the idle periods and the packet transmission.

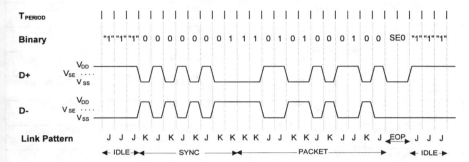

Figure 4.2: Full Speed Link

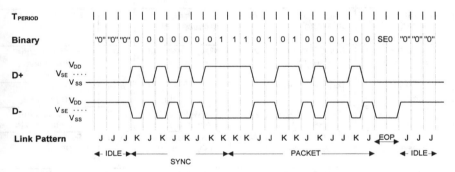

Figure 4.3: Low Speed Link

A unique definition of the D+ and D- signal lines is SE0, and is defined when both D+ and D- signal lines are less than Vse. As will be discussed in Chapter 5 *Signaling Characteristics*, the SE0 is part of the end of packet (EOP) protocol and also defines the reset of the link. The D+ and D- signal lines are also used to determine whether a device is connected to a link and the speed of that link. Table 4.1 summarizes the D+ and D- signal line definitions.

Item	D+ (1)		D- (1)		Absolute Value of (D+)- (D-)
Quiescent "0" for D+	<Vse (min)		N/A		N/A
Quiescent "0" for D-	N/A		<Vse (min)		N/A
Quiescent "1" for D+	>Vse (max)		N/A		N/A
Quiescent "1" for D-	N/A		>Vse (max)		N/A
Differential 0 Full Speed Link	<Vse(min)	And	>Vse (max)	And	>200millivolts
Differential 1 Full Speed Link	>Vse (max)	And	<Vse(min)	And	>200millivolts
Differential 0 Low Speed Link	<Vse(min)	And	>Vse (max)	And	>200millivolts
Differential 1 Low Speed Link	>Vse (max)	And	<Vse(min)	And	>200millivolts
J State Full Speed Link	Per quiescent >Vse (max)	And	Per quiescent <Vse (min)		Per quiescent N/A
J State Low Speed Link	Per quiescent <Vse (min)	And	Per quiescent >Vse (max)		Per quiescent N/A
J State Full Speed Link	Per differential >Vse (max)	And	Per differential <Vse (min)	And	Per differential >200millivolt
J State Low Speed Link	Per differential <Vse (min)	And	Per differential >Vse (max)	And	Per differential >200millivolts
K State Full Speed Link	Per differential <Vse (min)	And	Per differential >Vse (max)	And	Per differential >200millivolts
K State Low Speed Link	Per differential >Vse (max)	And	Per differential <Vse (min)	And	Per differential >200millivolt
Single Ended Zero (SE0)	<Vse (min)	And	<Vse (min)		N/A
Disconnected	<Vse (max) for >=2.5 usec	And	<Vse (max) for >=2.5 usec		N/A
Connected Full Speed Link	>Vse (max) for >=2.5 usec	And	<Vse (min) for >=2.5 usec		N/A
Connected Low Speed Link	<Vse (min) for >=2.5 usec	And	>Vse (max) for >=2.5 usec		N/A

Table 4.1: Summary of D+ and D- Signal Line Definitions

Note: (1) Vse is the single-ended receiver threshold. Vse = 0.8 volts min. and 2.0 volts max.

4.3.2 Voltage Drop, Voltage Droop, and Cable Requirements

USB defines two minimum voltages, as shown in Figure 4.4. The first is 4.75 volts as the minimum voltage at any downstream port of any root hub or self-powered hub. The second is 4.40 volts as the minimum voltage at any downstream port of a bus-powered hub. Both of these voltages are steady state voltages that USB devices can rely upon. Transient conditions, such as device insertions or port power enabling, may cause voltages to droop for short periods of time.

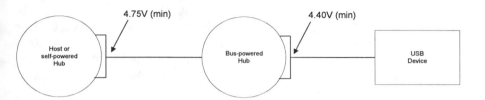

Figure 4.4: Minimum DC Voltages

There are two elements of voltage definition in the USB bus: voltage drop and voltage droop. The voltage drop is due to the physical attributes of the cable, FET voltage switch, connector, and voltage regulator requirements in the host root hub and other downstream hubs. The voltage droop is primarily due to the in-rush current when a USB hub or device is attached to a hub. Voltage droop is also affected by the physical elements listed above for voltage drop.

Voltage Drop

As will be discussed in Chapter 12 *Hub Devices*, a hub or a device is either bus-powered or self-powered. When a hub is bus-powered or a device is high power bus-powered, the maximum current that must be supplied by an upstream hub port is 500 milliamps. When the hub or the device is self-powered or the device is low power bus-powered, the maximum current that must be supplied by an upstream hub port is 100 milliamps. A bus-powered hub is required to have an FET switch (or equivalent) for the power control of the downstream ports. This FET affects the voltage drop/droop requirements.

The power systems of hubs (root, self-powered, and bus-powered), and the cable characteristics of both permanently attached and detachable cables, must all play together to meet the USB defined minimum voltages when maximum current is supplied to downstream devices. As components in these power calculations, USB defines connector resistance as 30 milliohms and FET voltage drop (which includes voltage drop for board traces) as 100 millivolts. Calculations for voltage drop must assume (worst case) that the USB GND is isolated from any environmental ground so that any current flowing through the Vbus wire will also be flowing in the ground wire. For some components in the calculation (like connectors and cables), the resistance must be used twice since current is flowing in both directions. For example, for USB connectors there will be a voltage drop on both the Vbus connection and the GND connection.

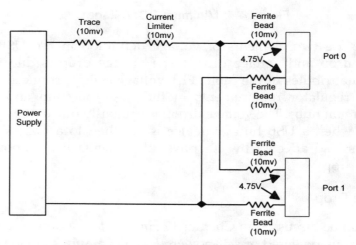

Figure 4.5: Voltage Drops in Power Providers

The design factors for root hubs and self-powered hubs to meet the 4.75 volt requirement are shown in figure 4.5. These factors include the tolerance of the power supply, required current limiting devices, and trace and ferrite bead impedances. When all ports are providing maximum current (500 ma), there will be a voltage drop from the power supply output to the USB connectors because of the DC impedance of some of these devices. Voltage drop across the current limiting device can vary, but can be as much as 70 mV for 1 amp of current. Trace resistance and DC impedance of the ferrite beads is small, but non-zero. If a total voltage drop of 100 mV is assumed across all components, then the minimum output of the power supply has to be 4.85 volts. An appropriate power supply for this design would be 5.0 V nominal with a tolerance of +5% (yielding 5.25 V) and -3% (yielding 4.85 V). Careful selection of components can yield different designs that meet the 4.75 V requirement, but in no case can a 5 volt supply with a -5% tolerance meet the requirement.

The design factors for bus-powered hubs and cables to meet the 4.40 volt requirement are shown in Figure 4.6. The total voltage drop budget for this configuration is 4.750V - 4.400V, or 350 mV. The figure shows four different connector-related drops at 15 mV each for a total of 60 mV. A bus-powered hub is required to provide power control for its downstream ports, and USB defines the voltage drop across this control as 100 mV. So connector drop and power control drop total 160 mV. Subtracting this from the voltage budget (350 mV) leaves 190 mV, which is the allowed voltage drop across BOTH wires in the cable. This translates to a maximum voltage drop across one wire of 95 mV (1/2 of 190 mV).

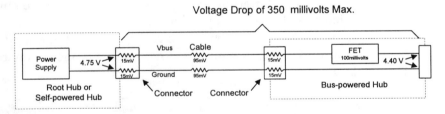

Figure 4.6: Voltage Drop Summary

Cable Requirements

Applying Ohms Law (V=IR) to the values above (V=.095V and I=.5A) for cables yields a maximum cable resistance of .190 ohms. This maximum resistance can be translated to maximum cable length based on the resistance per meter of various gauge wires, as shown in Table 4.2.

Vbus and Ground Gauges @ 20 degrees centigrade	DC resistance per meter (1)	Maximum Length in Meters
28 gauge	0.232 ohms max	.81
26 gauge	0.145 ohms max	1.31
24 gauge	0.091 ohms max	2.08
22 gauge	0.057 ohms max	3.33
20 gauge	0.036 ohms max	5.00

Table 4.2: Cable Requirements for 500 Millivolt Current Load

Note: (1) The resistance listed is measured along Vbus wire plus gnd wire, Thus the resistance for each wire is ½ the value listed

All detachable cables must meet the maximum length requirements shown in Table 4.2. These cables must also be full speed links, meaning the D+ and D- signal lines are a twisted wire pair with a twist every 6 to 8 centimeters.

Bus-powered hubs with permanently attached cables may be able to have cable lengths that are longer than those shown in Table 4.2 because there is no upstream connector resistance, and the actual current consumption of the hub and its downstream devices may be less than 500ma.

Table 4.2 establishes the longest cable length to support 500 milliamps for various DC resistances for Vbus and GND wires. The actual cable length can be longer if the cable is permanently attached to a hub or device that requires less current. The actual cable length may be shorter than what is allowed for current and voltage reasons. The shorter length may be required due to skew, attenuation per meter, and cable propagation requirements for D+ and D- signal lines as outlined in Table 4.3. The maximum cable length must comply with all of these specifications.

Figure 4.7 outlines the voltage drops throughout a USB system for various typical configurations using detachable cables. The values used in this figure are:

- 500 ma maximum current for a bus-powered hub or a high power device.

- 100 ma maximum current for a self-powered device or a low power device.

- .190 ohms maximum resistance per cable power wire.

- 30 milliohms maximum resistance per connector.

Items (1) to (7) discussed below are referenced in Figure 4.7. Similar calculations can be applied to devices with attached cables where appropriate adjustments are made for known currents (less than maximum), cable resistance (different because of shorter lengths), and connector resistance (because one connector is not used).

Item (1): The minimum voltage at a downstream port of a root hub or self-powered hub is 4.75 volts.

Item (2): The minimum voltage at a downstream port of a bus-powered hub is 4.40 volts.

Item (3): The voltage drop across the cable and two connectors when 500 ma is being supplied is 250 mV. This is the sum of the cable drop (.190 ohms times .5 amps times 2 wires (Vbus and ground) = 190 mV) plus the connector drops (30 milliohms times .5 amps times 2 connections (Vbus and GND) times 2 connectors = 60 mV).

Item (4): The voltage drop across the cable and the two connectors when 100 ma is being supplied is 50 mV. This is the sum of the cable drop (.190 ohms times .1 amps times 2 wires (Vbus and ground) = 38 mV) plus the connector drops (30 milliohms times .1 amps times 2 connections (Vbus and GND) times two connectors = 12 mV).

Item (5): The voltage to a device drawing 500 ma from its upstream port is 4.500 volts. This is calculated from the required supply of 4.750 volts (Item 1) minus the voltage drop across the cable and connector of 250 mV (Item 3).

Item (6): The voltage to a device drawing 100 ma from its upstream port if the upstream port is on a root hub or self-powered hub is 4.70 volts. This is calculated from the required supply of

4.750 volts (Item 1) minus the voltage drop across the cable and connectors of 50 mV (Item 4).

Item (7): The voltage to a device drawing 100 ma from its upstream port if the upstream port is on a bus-powered hub is 4.350 volts. This is calculated from the required supply of 4.400 volts (Item 2) minus the voltage drop across the cable and connectors of 50 mV (Item 4).

Note that there are certain configurations that are not shown in Figure 4.7 because they are disallowed. For instance, a bus-powered hub plugged into a bus-powered hub is not an allowed configuration, because the voltage provided at the second bus-powered hub would be too low. Similarly, a high power bus-powered device plugged into a bus-powered hub is not allowed because bus-powered hub ports cannot normally provide more than 100 ma of current. End users who try a disallowed configuration will find that their device does not operate as expected, (and with some OS's will be given a warning), but will not endanger the operation of the rest of the USB.

> All hubs and devices are required to support configuration operation with a minimum Vbus voltage relative to ground of 4.400 volts (see Item (1) above) at the upstream end of its cable (whether permanently attached or detachable). Hubs and devices with detachable cables must be able to support configuration operation with a minimum voltage (measured at the device) of 4.35 volts (see Item (7) above). The configuration operation voltage must be independent of the voltage required for normal operation.

4.3.3 Voltage Droop

Voltage droop is a momentary voltage reduction due to the in-rush current when a hub or device is attached. The in-rush current is a result of charge sharing between the bulk capacitance of the added device, and the bulk capacitance of the upstream port (either host or hub). Voltage droop is defined and measured at hub ports other than the one where the new connection is taking place. For example, on a three port hub, two of the ports would have devices connected that are drawing the maximum current allowed (500 ma for self-powered hubs or root hubs, and 100 ma for bus-powered hubs). The voltage at these ports is then monitored when a device is attached to the remaining port. The momentary reduction in voltage at these ports is the voltage droop.

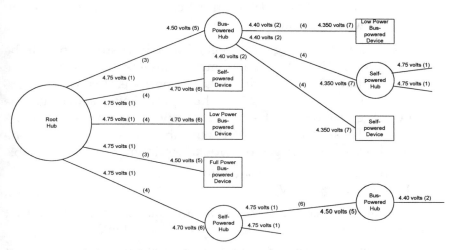

Figure 4.7: Voltage Drop Distribution

The specified maximum voltage droop at any downstream port of a hub is 330 millivolts. Electrical factors on both the upstream hub and the attaching device contribute to how much voltage droop will actually occur.

Devices must present a maximum load of 10 microfarads in parallel with 44 ohms. The 44 ohm resistor represents 1 unit load (100 ma) assuming that Vbus is 4.40 volts. All devices are limited to 100 ma (steady state) when first attached. The 10 microfarads consists of any bulk capacitance plus any inherant capacitance visible through the device's voltage regulator (if there is one). Some devices may need more than 10 µF of bulk capacitance to meet their application needs, and if so they must provide some sort of surge current limiter such that the device behavior matches the 10 µF - 44 ohm characteristics above.

Note that bus-powered hubs must meet the same characteristics (10 µF – 44 ohms) as any other device when they are connected to the USB. Bus-powered hubs also have to limit the amount of surge current drawn when the its downstream ports are powered. This is typically done using a switch that has slow turn-on characteristics (*i.e.*, the switch resistance gradually goes from infinite to a very small value). The resulting behavior of the bus-powered hub when its downstream ports are enabled must conform to the standard 10 μF – 44 ohm load behavior.

USB specifies the voltage droop at a hubs downstream port to be a maximum of 330 mV. Actual measurements of systems have determined that the voltage droop at the peripheral is at least 15% less than the voltage droop at the hub port. This means that the actual voltage droop seen at a device is approximately 280 mV (85% of 330 mV). These values, coupled with the minimum steady state voltages shown in Figure 4.7, provide the following rules of thumb:

- Minimum voltage at a root hub or self-powered hub port is 4.42V (4.75V – 330 mV).

- Minimum voltage at a device drawing 500 ma attached to a root hub or self- powered hub is 4.22V (4.50V – 280 mV).

- Minimum voltage at a device drawing 100 ma attached to a root hub or self- powered hub is 4.42V (4.70V – 280 mV).

- Minimum voltage at a bus-powered hub port is 4.07V (4.40V – 330 mV).

- Minimum voltage at a device drawing 100 ma attached to a bus-powered hub is 4.07V (4.35V – 280 mV).

Power providers (root hubs and self-powered hubs) can manage the voltage droop seen at their downstream ports by careful design of their power connections. The specification indicates that the port power lines should be bypassed by a bulk capacitor (specifically a 120μF tantalum capacitor). Careful placement of this capacitance with respect to current limiting devices and ferrite beads can lead to power connections that meet minimum DC voltage requirements and meet the maximum droop requirement of 330 mV. The figures below illustrate some designs for USB power providers. Each figure shows two downstream ports, but the concepts described can be applied to hub designs with more downstream ports.

Figure 4.8 shows an optimal design for a USB power provider. The separate current limiting device for each port minimizes the voltage drop because of the lower current flowing through it. The individual bulk capacitors (C1 and C2) for each port provide ample charge to keep the voltage from drooping, and this current only goes through the small resistance of the ferrite beads. The ferrite beads on both the Vbus and GND lines act as small inductors and help limit the magnitude of the current surge thus reducing droop.

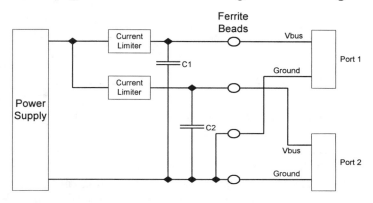

Figure 4.8: Optimal Power Provider Design

Figure 4.9 is another acceptable design for USB power provider and is slightly lower cost than the previous case. The primary difference in this design is that there is a single current limiting device and a single bulk capacitor (C1). The current limiting device needs to be chosen such that it has a relatively high trip point since this will result in a smaller voltage drop for the larger current needed to supply power to both ports. The single bulk capacitor has to provide current to both ports in the case of a hot plug resulting in more severe voltage droop than the previous design. The ferrite beads on all lines are still required to help minimize the surge current which help limit voltage droop.

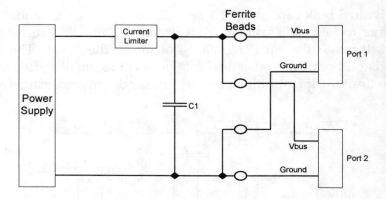

Figure 4.9: Acceptable Power Provider Design

Figures 4.10 and 4.11 illustrate power designs that do not have acceptable voltage drop and voltage droop characteristics. In Figure 4.10 the bulk capacitance is placed behind the current limiter so any current supplied by the capacitor during the hot plug incurs a voltage drop across the current limiter resulting in poor voltage droop behavior.

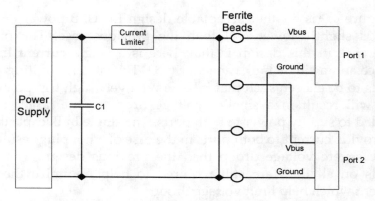

Figure 4.10: Unacceptable Power Provider Design

Figure 4.11 has the bulk capacitance in the correct location but the shared ferrite beads means that the voltage droop seen on the port where the hot plug occurred (which has no maximum droop requirements) is also directly seen by the other port.

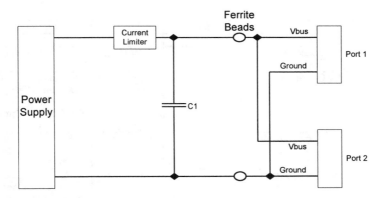

Figure 4.11: Unacceptable Power Provider Design

From the examples above (both good and bad), several general rules of thumb for USB power providers can be derived:

- Per-port bulk capacitance is best.

- Bulk capacitance always has to be between the current limiting device and the USB ports. Failure to do this results in too large a voltage drop across the current limiting device when a hot plug occurs.

- Ferrite beads are needed on each port on both the Vbus and ground lines.

4.4 Tabulation of AC and DC Electrical Requirements

Table 4.3 tabulates the AC voltage and current electrical requirements for the USB bus of the different elements of the USB bus.

Item	Min.	Max.	Comments
Connector			
Connector Voltage rating		30 VAC rms	For 0 to 40 degrees C
Connector Current rating		1A max. per contact	Not to exceed 30 degree C Temp. rise For 0 to 40 degrees C
Shield coupling capacitor impedance to chassis (2), (3)		250K ohms	Required to be equal to or less than at 60Hz
Shield coupling capacitor impedance to chassis (2), (3)		15 ohms	Required to be equal to or less than at 3 MHz to 30 MHz
Cable ground signal line coupling capacitor impedance to chassis (2), (3)		250K ohms	Required to be equal to or less than at 60Hz
Shield coupling capacitor impedance to chassis (2), (3)		15 ohms	Required to be equal to or less than at 3 MHz to 30 MHz
D+ and D- Signal Line Characteristics (One way directions)			
Skew between two signal line pairs		Less that 65.6 ps/m max.	At 10kHz (1)
Signal line attenuation @ 0.064 MHz		4.80 db max	Db/305 meters (1)
Signal line attenuation @ 0.256 MHz		6.70 db max	Db/305 meters (1)
Signal line attenuation @ 0.512 MHz		8.20 db max	Db/305 meters (1)
Signal line attenuation @ 0.772 MHz		9.40 db max	Db/305 meters (1)
Signal line attenuation @ 1.000 MHz		12.0 db max	Db/305 meters (1)
Signal line attenuation @ 4.000 MHz		24.0 db max	Db/305 meters (1)
Signal line attenuation @ 8.000 MHz		35.0 db max	Db/305 meters (1)
Signal line attenuation @ 10.000 MHz		38.0 db max	Db/305 meters (1)
Signal line attenuation @ 16.000 MHz		48.0 db max	Db/305 meters (1)

Table 4.3: AC Electrical Characteristics

Item	Min.	Max.	Comments
D+ and D- Signal Line Characteristics (One way directions)			
Characteristic Impedance	76.5 ohms	103.5 ohms	Measured 1 to 16 MHz
Signal Line Length for Propagation Delay of 9.0 nsec/m		3.3 m	
Signal Line Length for Propagation Delay of 8.0 nsec/m		3.7 m	
Signal Line Length for Propagation Delay of 7.0 nsec/m		4.3 m	
Signal Line Length for Propagation Delay of 6.5 nsec/m		4.6 m	
Propagation delay		30 nsec.	Measured 1 to 16 MHz
Full Speed D+ and D- Signal Charateristic Impedance Zo	76.5 ohms	103.5 ohms	Measured 1 to 16 MHz
D+ or D- Pull-up resistor at upstream port of device or hubs	1.43 K ohms	1.58 K ohms	Connected to a voltage level of 3.0 to 3.6 volts
D+ or D- Pull-down resistor at down stream port of root hub and hubs	14.25 K ohms	15.75 K ohms	Connected to cable ground
Transmitter Characteristics			
Rise and Fall times Full Speed Transmission	4 nanosec. min.	20 nanosec. max.	Measured at 10% and 90% of 2.8 volts at CL = 50 pF See Figure 4.12
Rise and Fall times Low Speed Transmission	75 nanosec. min.	300 nanosec. max.	Measured at 10% and 90% of 2.8 volts at CL = 350 pF See Figure 4.12
Output impedance of transmitter	30 ohms (4)	42 ohms (5)	Optional resistors may have to be added to insure the impedance meets this range See Figure 4.13

Table 4.3: AC Electrical Characteristics (continued)

Notes:

(1) The skew and attenuation requirements will establish the longest cable length for AC operation. The actual cable length may be shorter to meet the voltage drop requirements for specific current requirements. See Table 4.2 and Voltage Drop and Droop Requirements section for more information.

(2) The cable shield is terminated to the ground signal line of the plug for all connectors. Only at the root hub are the shield, DC power source ground, and chassis ground all connected together. Consequently, the entire USB bus is reference to ground only at the root hub. The chassis of downstream devices and hubs are not connected to the cable shield or cable ground signal lines.

(3) Shield EMI coupling of a capacitor from shield and chassis to ground is permitted. Dielectric voltage rating of capacitor is 250 Vac (rms) min.

(4) Minimum output impedance for a full speed transmitter. An optional series resister may have to be added to achieve the minimum impedance and still meet the maximum impedance. No requirement for low speed transmitter.

(5) Maximum output impedance for a full speed transmitter. An optional series resister may have to be added to achieve the minimum impedance and still meet the maximum impedance. No requirement for low speed transmitter.

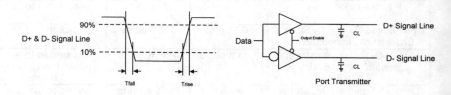

Figure 4.12: Rise and Fall of Signal Lines

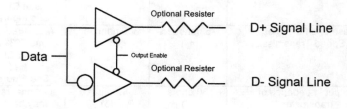

Port Transmitter

Figure 4.13 CMOS Transmitter

Note: Figs 4.13 and 4.14 are referenced in Table 4.3.

Figure 4.14 defines the input characteristics for a receiver. The minimum requirement is 200 millivolts differential sensitivity for the D+ and D- signal lines in the voltage range of 0.8 to 2.5 volts of common mode input voltage. If the common mode input voltage is beyond the 0.8 to 2.5 volts range, the minimum input sensitivity is shown in Figure 4.14.

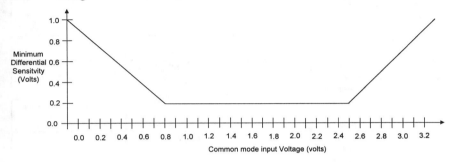

Figure 4.14: Differential Input Sensitivity

Table 4.4 tabulates the DC voltage and current electrical requirements for the USB bus of the different elements of the USB bus.

Item	Min	Max.	Comment
Vbus for Power Relative to Ground			
Vbus on downstream port of self-powered hub or root hub	4.65 volts	5.25 volts	Original specification defined the minimum voltage as 4.75 volts
Vbus on downstream port of bus-powered hub	4.40 volts	5.25 volts	
Vbus on upstream port of self-powered hub	4.150 volts	5.25 volts	
Vbus on upstream port of low power bus-powered device	4.150 volts	5.25 volts	
Vbus on upstream port of self-powered device	4.150 volts	5.25 volts	
Vbus on upstream port of full power bus-powered device	4.40 volts	5.25 volts	

Table 4.4: DC Electrical Characteristics

Item	Min	Max.	Comment
Downstream Port Supply Currents from:			
Root hub	500 ma		
Self-powered hub or Self-powered compound device	500 ma		
Bus-powered hub or Bus-powered compound device	100ma		
Upstream Port Load Currents to:			
Self-powered hub or Self-powered compound device or Self-powered device Or Self-powered composite device		100 milliamps	
Bus-powered hub or Bus-powered compound device or Bus-powered high powered device or Bus-powered high powered composite device		500 milliamps	
Bus-powered low powered composite device or Bus-powered low powered device		100 milliamps	
Suspended device		500 microamps	
Receiver or Transmitter for D+ or D- Signal Line			
Hi-Z Leakage Current	-10 microamps	+10 microamps	
Receiver for D+ or D- Signal Line			
Differential Input Sensitivity See Figure 6.4-3			Absolute difference between D+ and D-
Differential Common Mode range	0.8 volts	2.5 volts	
Single ended receiver threshold Vse	0.8 volts	2.0 volts	
Input voltage tolerance	-0.5 volts	3.8 volts	
Transmitter for D+ or D- Signal Line			

Table 4.4: DC Electrical Characteristics (continued)

Item	Min	Max.	Comment
Static Output Low Vol (1)		0.3	Load resistance of 1.5 K ohms pull-up to 3.6 volts
Static Output High Voh (1)	2.8	3.6	Load resistance of 15 K ohms pull-down to ground
Voltage that is required to be tolerated on the output pins when transmitter is actively driving the D+ or D- signal line.	-0.5 volts	3.8 volts	Transmitter is required to tolerate these voltages for a minimum of 10 microsec.
Termination			
D+ or D- Pull-up resistor at upstream port of device or hubs	1.43 K ohms	1.58 K ohms	Connected to a voltage level of 3.0 to 3.6 volts
D+ or D- Pull-down resistor at down stream port of root hub and hubs	14.25 K ohms	15.75 K ohms	Connected to cable ground
Capacitance			
Transceiver Input Capacitance		20 picofarads	Measured from input to ground
At the upstream port of a device	1.0 microfarads	10.0 microfarads	See note Attached between Vbus to ground
At the downstream port of a hub or composite device	120 microfarads		Tantalum

Note: The low to high output swing versus the high to low output swing of the transmitter is required to be balanced to insure a minimum signal slew. The transmitter is required to support the three state operation for bi-directional half duplex operation and powered-on attachment of removal of downstream links.

Table 4.4: DC Electrical Characteristics (continued)

4.5 Transceiver Requirements

As previously discussed, the quiescent voltage level of the D+ and D- signal lines establish the speed of the link which reflects the speed of a downstream device or hub attached to the link. Either a low or full speed link can be connected to the downstream port of a hub; consequently, the downstream transmitter is required to meet both low and full speed electrical requirements. Table 4.5 lists the transceiver requirements for hubs, low speed devices, and full speed devices. The transceiver of a low speed device only supports low speed electrical characteristics and timing.

Location of Transceiver	Transceiver Required to Support	Associated Link
Downstream port of a hub or compound package	Full/Low speed (1)	Link speed dependent on speed of the downstream device
Upstream port of a ful-speed device (other than hub or compound package)	Full speed	Full speed
Upstream port of a low speed device	Low speed	Low speed
Upstream port of a hub or compound package	Full and low speed (2)	Full and low speed

Notes:

(1) Buffer required to meet both low and full speed electrical

(2) Buffer required to meet full speed electrical

Table 4.5: Full/Low Speed Buffer Requirements

4.6 Timing

All packet transmissions on the USB bus begin at either the host controller through the root hub to a downstream device, or from a downstream device to the root hub. As used in this section, the word "device" includes devices, hubs, compound packages, and composite devices. Also, the word "hub" includes hubs and compound packages.

There are three elements of packet transmission timing between the root hub and the device: transmitter, link, and hub. The transmitter element is required to consider the transmitter's reliance on an internal clock to define bit periods for the D+ and D- signal lines transition points, the performance of the transmitter varies for rising versus falling transitions, and the enabling of the transmitter per SOP. The transition points are the low to high and high to low voltage swings of the D+ and D- signal lines. The link element is required to consider the transmission line effects due to capacitance and reflective waves of the electrical cable. The hub element is required to consider that packet transmission passes through one or more hubs. Each hub operates as a repeater, which does not exactly replicate the input signal and does not instantaneously repeat the waveform.

The receiver at the device or the root hub is required to accommodate the three elements identified above. These three elements contribute to the timing of the signal line transmission waveform and are defined by waveform jitter and delay.

The "simplest" packet transmission path is between the root hub and device via a single link (see Figure 4.15). This packet transmission path includes only a link (shortest path A to B), the root hub, and the device. There are several possible paths with multiple links and hubs. Configuration software will only allow a maximum of five hubs between the root hub and any downstream device (longest path A to D). The hubs between the transmitters and receivers of the root hub and device simply repeat the signal line waveform. When a hub is the device participant, the same receiver and transmitter considerations as those of the root hub or a downstream device apply.

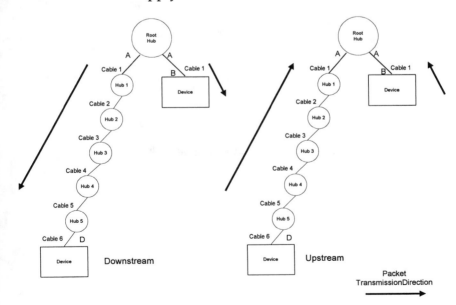

Figure 4.15: A Long and Short Path Topology

4.6.1 Basic Waveform

Figure 4.16 and Tables 4.6 and 4.7 define the basic timing references of the signal line waveforms between any transmitter and receiver. The tolerance of the timing and the delays are defined in terms of jitter. Jitter will be precisely defined in the next section. For clarity, the waveforms in this figure exemplify either D+ or D- signal lines, and do not have D+ and D- explicitly labeled. The Vcr reference line in this figure is the crossover voltage of the D+ and D- signal lines as defined in the previous section. The timing values in Tables 4.6 and 4.7 represent the nominal values. These values will subsequently be used as the base for additional attributes of waveform jitter and delay discussed later.

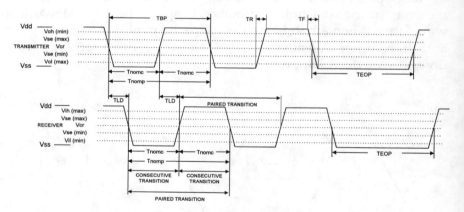

Figure 4.16: Full and Low Speed Waveform

Item	Timing Reference	Nominal Value	Tolerance
Frame period (as generated by host controller) (1) (3)	N/A	1.00 millisec.	+/- 0.05% (initial frame
Bit Rate	N/A	12 Mb/sec	+/- 0.25%
Bit Period	TBP	8.33 nsec.	+/- .021 nsec
Signal Line Rise Time (2) (3)	TR	12 nanosec.	+/- 8 nanosec. With CL = 50pf
Signal line Fall Time (2) (3)	TF	12 nanosec.	+/- 8 nanosec. with CL = 50pf
Rise and Fall Matching (3)	N/A	100%	+/- 10%
Output Signal Crossover Voltage (3)	VCR	1.65 volts	+/-0.35 volts
SE0 period for EOP indication at transmitter	TEOP	167.5 nsec.	+/- 7.5 nsec.with CL = 50 pf
Nominal period between Consecutive Transitions	Tnomc	83.33 nsec.	N/A
Nominal period between Paired Transitions	Tnomp	16.66 nsec	N/A
Removal detection period	Trem	2.5 microsec.	Min.
Attachment detection period	Tatt	2.5 microsec.	Min.
Reset	N/A	20 millisec.	Min. time of SE0 binary pattern

Notes:

(1) The frame period is 1.000 millisec. long with a tolerance of +/- 0.05%.

(2) Measured at 10 and 90% of data signal swing at transmitter. The data signal full swing is Vdd max - Vss (at 0 volts). The transitions are required to be monotonic changes.

(3) Measured at the transmitter.

Table 4.6: Full Speed Signal Timing

Item	Timing Reference	Nominal Value	Tolerance
Frame period (as generated by host controller) (1) (3)	N/A	1.00 millisec.	+/- 0.05% (initial frame
Bit Rate	N/A	1.5 Mb/sec	+/- 1.5%
Bit Period	TBP	666.66 nsec.	+/-10.0 nsec.
Signal Line Rise Time (2) (3)	TR	75 nanosec.	Min. with CL = 70pf
Signal Line Rise Time (2) (3)	TR	300 nanosec.	Max. with CL = 350pf
Signal Line Fall Time (2) (3)	TF	75 nanosec.	Min. with CL = 70pf
Signal Line Fall Time (2) (3)	TF	300 nanosec.	Max. with CL = 350pf
Rise and Fall Matching (3)	N/A	100%	+/- 20%
Output Signal Crossover Voltage (3)	VCR	1.65 volts	+/-0.35 volts
SE0 period for EOP indication at transmitter	TEOP	137.5 microsec.	+/- 12.5 microsec. with CL = 70 to 350 pf
Nominal period between Consecutive Transitions	Tnomc	666.67 nsec.	N/A
Nominal period between Paired Transitions	Tnomp	1333.33 nsec.	N/A
Removal detection period	Trem	2.5 microsec.	Min.
Attachment detection period	Tatt	2.5 microsec.	Min.
Reset	N/A	20 millisec.	Min. time of SE0 binary pattern

Notes:

(1) The frame period is 1.000 millisec. long with a tolerance of +/- 0.05%.

(2) Measured at 10 and 90% of data signal swing at transmitter. The data signal full swing is Vdd max - Vss (at 0 volts) The transitions are required to be monotonic changes.

(3) Measured at the transmitter.

Table 4.7: Low Speed Signal Timing

Figure 4.17 defines the timing for attachment and removal of the cable. The timing references are contained in Tables 4.6 and 4.7. See Chapter 5 *Signaling Characteristics* for more information.

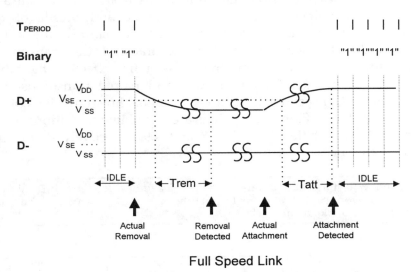

Full Speed Link

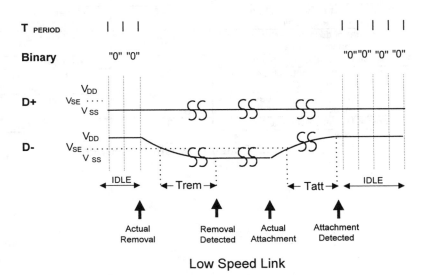

Low Speed Link

Figure 4.17: Attachment and Removal Signaling Sequence

4.6.2 Waveform Jitter

The synchronization pattern and data portions of the packet transmission waveforms contain transitions from low to high and high to low voltage levels. The exact time and profile of the transitions are defined by waveform jitter (or simply jitter). The jitter is due to elements of clock accuracy of the transmitter, transmitter characteristics, and transmission line effects of the cable. The jitter is defined for consecutive and paired transitions (See Figure 4.18). Consecutive transitions are signal line transitions of the opposite polarity. Paired transitions are signal line transitions of the same polarity. Tables 4.6, 4.7, 4.8 and 4.9 collectively define the timing references in Figure 4.18.

> The figures in this section show a sample waveform for D+ and D- signal lines. Waveforms of the opposite polarity of those shown also apply to both D+ and D- signal lines.

Item Path in Figure 4.15	Contributes to Timing Reference	Tolerance
Transmitter Jitter at Root Hub and 1st downstream cable	TJC	+/- 2 nanosec. with CL = 50pf
Transmitter Jitter of downstream device and connected cable	TJC	+/- 2 nanosec.
Repeater at Hub and connected cable	TJC	+/- 3 nanosec.
Transmitter Jitter at Root Hub and 1st downstream cable	TJP	+/- 1 nanosec. with CL = 50pf
Transmitter Jitter of downstream device and connected cable	TJP	+/- 1 nanosec.
Repeater at Hub and connected cable	TJP	+/- 1 nanosec.

Table 4.8: Full Speed Downstream Device

Item Path in Figure 4.15	Contributes to Timing Reference	Tolerance
Transmitter Jitter of Root Hub and 1st downstream cable non short path	TJC	+/- 2 nanosec.
Transmitter Jitter of Root Hub and 1st downstream cable short path	TJC	+/- 45 nanosec.
Transmitter Jitter of downstream device and connected cable	TJC	+/- 25 nanosec.
Repeater at Hub and connected cable	TJC	+/- 3 nanosec.
Transmitter Jitter at Root Hub and 1st downstream cable non short path	TJP	+/- 1 nanosec. with CL = 50pf
Transmitter Jitter of Root Hub and 1st downstream cable short path	TJP	+/- 15 nanosec.
Transmitter Jitter of downstream device and connected cable	TJP	+/- 10nanosec.
Repeater at Hub and connected cable	TJP	+/- 1 nanosec.

Table 4.9: Low Speed Downstream Device

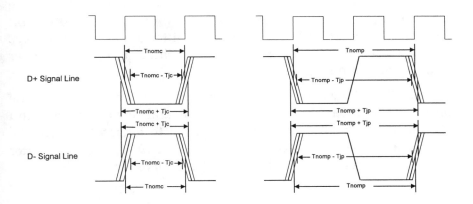

Figure 4.18: Minimum Jitter Definition

The above discussion is referenced to one bit clock period for consecutive transitions and two bit clock periods for paired transitions. The transition protocol for the USB bus also consists of consecutive and paired transitions with greater than one and two bit periods, respectively. The consecutive transition has two other conditions: extended jitter and EOP. The paired transition has only one other condition: extended jitter.

The requirements of extended jitter for consecutive and paired transitions are due to the NRZI protocol. As will be explained in Chapter 5 *Signaling Characteristics*, the NRZI coding protocol creates transitions on the signal lines as multiples of bit periods. The individual bit periods are referenced in the transmitter to an internal clock and encoded with the NRZI. The first eight bit periods of the transmission packet comprise the synchronization pattern which allows the phase lock loop in the receiver to lock onto the transmitter's clock and establish a reference clock integral to the receiver. For an upstream packet the receiver is contained within the root hub and transmitter is contained within the downstream device. For a downstream packet the receiver is contained within the downstream device and the transmitter is contained within the root hub.

The NRZI encoding allows for no consecutive transitions for seven bit periods and no paired transitions for 14 bit periods (see Figure 4.19). For extended jitter of consecutive transitions, the receiver is required to accept the jitter accumulated over seven bit periods as defined by Tjxc. For extended jitter of paired transitions, the receiver is required to accept the jitter accumulated over fourteen bit periods as defined by Tjxp.

Thus, the total waveform jitter at the receiver is dependent on the bit sequence, internal clocks in root hubs and devices, cables, and repeaters in hubs. The receiver is required to tolerate jitter for the extended bit periods as defined in Figure 4.19 for the other jitter elements involved with the long path (A to D) of Figure 4.15.

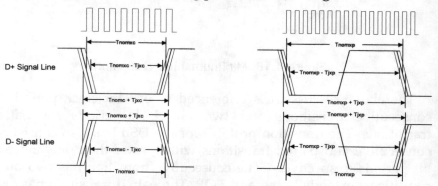

Figure 4.19: Extended Jitter Definition

The following tables and associated explanations define the jitter and delays that must be considered in the design of USB hubs and devices.

Tables 4.10 and 4.11 are for paths defined according to Figure 4.15. The columns in these two tables are defined as follows:

For Table 4.10: *Synchronization Packet and Data Portion of Downstream Packets*, the columns are:

1. This column identifies the path in Figure 4.15 under consideration and the speed of the device.

2. This column tabulates the jitter from the transmitter of the root hub and the 1st downstream cable.

3. This column tabulates the jitter from the repeater in each hub and the connected downstream cable.

4. This column tabulates the jitter from the internal clock of the root hub.

5. This column tabulates the jitter from the internal clock of the device.

6. This column tabulates the total jitter at the receiver in the device. It is a summation of columns 1 to 5.

7. This column tabulates the total jitter at the receiver in the device. It is a summation of columns 1 to 5.

Timing

1	2		3		4
Item	Transmitter Jitter (including 1st Cable) Downstream from Root Hub nsec.		5 Hubs + 5 Cables Between Root Hub and Device Jitter nsec.		Transmitter Freq. Jitter (3) Full Spd = +/- .21 per bit Low Speed = +/- 1.7 per bit nsec.
	Tjc	Tjp	Tjc	Tjp	
Shortest path A - B Figure 4.15 Full Speed Device	+/-2.0	+/-1.0	N/A	N/A	1b = .21 2b = .42 7 b = 1.47 14 b = 2.94
Longest path A - D Figure 4.15 Full Speed Device	+/-2.0	+/-1.0	5 x +/- 3.0 = +/- 15 (4)	5 x +/- 1.0 = +/- 5.0 (5)	1b = .21 2b = .42 7 b = 1.47 14 b = 2.94
Shortest path A - B Figure 4.15 Low Speed Device	+/-45	+/-15	N/A	N/A	1b = 1.7 2b = 3.4 7b = 11.9 14b = 23.8
Longest path A - D Figure 4.15 Low Speed Device	+/-2.0	+/-1.0	4 x +/- 3.0 + +/-45 = +/- 57 (4)	4 x +/- 1.0 + +/-15 = +/- 19 (5)	1b = 1.7 2b = 3.4 7b = 11.9 14b = 23.8

1	5	6		7	
Item	Receiver Freq. Jitter (3) Full Speed = +/- .21 per bit Low Speed = +/- 10 per bit nsec.	Total Minimum Jitter per Figure 4.18 nsec		Total Extended Jitter per Fig. 4.19 nsec.	
		1 bit Tjc	2 bit Tjp	7 bits Tjxc	14 bits Tjxp
Shortest path A - B Figure 4.15 Full Speed Device	1b = .21 2b = .42 7 b = 1.47 14 b = 2.94	+/-2.21 (1) +/-2.42 (2)	+/-1.21 (1) +/-1.42 (2)	+/-3.47 (1) +/-4.94 (2)	+/-3.94 (1) +/-6.88 (2)
Longest path A - D Figure 4.15 Full Speed Device	1b = .21 2b = .42 7 b = 1.47 14 b = 2.94	+/-17.21 (1) +/-17.42 (2)	+/-6.21 (1) +/-6.42 (2)	+/-18.47 (1) +/-19.94 (2)	+/-8.94 (1) +/-11.88 (2)
Shortest path A - B Figure 4.15 Low Speed Device	1b = 10 2b = 20 7b = 70 14b = 140	+/-46.7 (1) +/-56.7 (2)	+/- 16.7 (1) +/- 26.7 (2)	+/- 55.9 (1) +/-125.9 (2)	+/- 38.8 (1) +/- 178.8 (2)
Longest path A - D Figure 4.15 Low Speed Device	1b = 10 2b = 20 7b = 70 14b = 140	+/- 60.7 (1) +/-70.7 (2)	+/-21.7 (1) +/-31.7 (2)	+/- 70.9 (1) +/-140.9 (2)	+/- 43.8 (1) +/- 183.8 (2)

Table 4.10: Synchronization Pattern and Data Jitter for Downstream Transmission

Notes:
(1) This number is jitter presented to the upstream port of the downstream device.

82

(2) This number is the incremental jitter tolerance of the receiver required over the tolerance of the received transmission due to the tolerance of the receiving device's integral clock. For a full speed device this is .21 nsec per bit. For a low speed device this is 10 nsec per bit.

(3) 12 Mbps x +/- .25% results in +/-.21 nsec per bit for a full speed root hub or device … 1.5 Mbps x +/- .25% results in +/- 1.7 nsec per bit for a full speed root hub … 1.5 Mbps x +/- .25% results in +/- 10 nsec per bit for a low speed device.

(4) This number reflects that the propagation delay though the hub and cable of a J to K state transition is the same as K to J state transition within +/- 3.0 nsec. data transmission.

(5) This number reflects that the propagation delay though the hub and cable of a J to K state transition is the same as another J to K state transition within +/- 1.0 nsec. data transmission.

The columns for Table 4.11: *Synchronization Pattern and Data Portions of Upstream Packets* are defined as follows:

1. This column identifies the path in Figure 4.15 under consideration and the speed of the device.

2. This column tabulates the jitter from the transmitter of the device upstream cable attached to the device.

3. This column tabulates the jitter from the repeater in each hub and the connected upstream cable.

4. This column tabulates the jitter from the internal clock of the device hub

5. This column tabulates the jitter from the internal clock of the root hub.

6. This column tabulates the total jitter at the receiver in the root hub. It is a summation of columns 1 to 5.

7. This column tabulates the total jitter at the receiver in the root hub. It is a summation of columns 1 to 5.

1	2		3		4
Item	Transmitter Jitter (including 1st cable for short and 6th cable for long) Upstream from Device nsec		5 Hubs + 5 Cables between Root Hub and Device Jitter nsec		Transmitte Freq. Jitter Full Speed +/- .21 per b Low Speed +/- 10 per b nsec.
	Tjc	Tjp	Tjc	Tjp	
Shortest path A - B Figure 4.15 Full Speed Device	+/-2.0	+/-1.0	N/A	N/A	1b = .21 2b = .42 7 b = 1.47 14 b = 2.94
Longest path A - D Figure 4.15 Full Speed Device	+/-2.0	+/-1.0	5 x +/- 3.0 = +/- 15 (4)	5 x +/- 1.0 = +/- 5.0 (5)	1b = .21 2b = .42 7 b = 1.47 14 b = 2.94
Shortest path A - B Figure 4.15 Low Speed Device	+/-25	+/-10	N/A	N/A	1b = 10 2b = 20 7 b = 70 14 b = 140
Longest path A - D Figure 4.15 Low Speed Device	+/-25	+/-10	4 x +/- 3.0 + +/-45 = +/-57 (4)	4 x +/- 1.0 + +/-45 = +/- 49 (5)	1b = 10 2b = 20 7 b = 70 14 b = 140

1	5	6		7	
Item	Receiver Freq. Jitter (3) Full Speed = +/- .21 per bit Low Speed = +/- 1.7 per bit nsec.	Total Minimum Jitter per Figure 4.18 nsec		Total Extende Jitter per Figure nsec	
		1 bit Tjc	2 bit Tjp	7 bits Tjxc	14 Tj
Shortest path A - B Figure 4.15 Full Speed Device	1b = .21 2b = .42 7 b = 1.47 14 b = 2.94	+/-2.21 (1) +/-2.42 (2)	+/-1.21 (1) +/-1.42 (2)	+/-3.47 (1) +/-4.94 (2)	+/-
Longest path A - D Figure 4.15 Full Speed Device	1b = .21 2b = .42 7 b = 1.47 14 b = 2.94	+/-17.21 (1) +/-17.42 (2)	+/-6.21 (1) +/-6.42 (2)	+/-18.47 (1) +/-19.94 (2)	+/-
Shortest path A - B Figure 4.15 Low Speed Device	1b = 1.7 2b = 3.4 7 b = 11.9 14 b = 23.8	+/-35 (1) +/-36.7 (2)	+/-20 (1) +/-21.7 (2)	+/-95 (1) +/-106.9 (2)	+/-1
Longest path A - D Figure 4.15 Low Speed Device	1b = 1.7 2b = 3.4 7 b = 11.9 14 b = 23.8	+/- 92(1) +/-93.7 (2)	+/-69 (1) +/-70.7 (2)	+/- 152 (1) +/-163.9 (2)	+/-1 +/-2

Table 4.11: Synchronization Pattern and Data Jitter for Upstream Transmission

Notes:

(1) This number is jitter presented to the upstream port of the upstream root hub.

(2) This number is the incremental jitter tolerance of the receiver required over the tolerance of the received transmission due to the tolerance of the receiving device's integral clock. For a full speed device this is .21 nsec per bit. For a low speed device this is 10 nsec per bit.

(3) 12 Mbps x +/- .25% results in +/-.21 nsec per bit for full speed root hub or device ... 1.5 Mbps x +/- .25% results in +/- 1.7 nsec per bit for full speed root hub ... 1.5 Mbps x +/- .25% results in +/- 10 nsec per bit for low speed device.

(4) This number reflects that the propagation delay though the hub and cable of a J to K state transition is the same as a K to J state transition within +/- 3.0 nsec. data transmission.

(5) This number reflects that the propagation delay though the hub and cable of a J to K state transition is the same another J to K state transition within +/- 1.0 nsec. data transmission .

(6) EOP and SOP are two special waveform patterns within a transmission packet. The EOP is two bit periods in length of the SE0 at the transmitter and indicates the end of the packet. As part of a conservative worst case condition, the receiver will assume an EOP with one bit period of SE0. EOP occurs with SE0 waveform followed by a transition to the J state.

Tables 4.12 and 4.13 refer to paths defined in Figure 4.15. The columns in these two tables are defined as follows:

For Table 4.12: *EOP Jitter of Downstream Packets:*

1. This column identifies the path in Figure 4.15 under consideration and the speed of the device.

2. This column tabulates the jitter from the transmitter of the root hub and the 1ST downstream cable.

3. This column tabulates the jitter from the repeater in each hub and the connected downstream cable.

4. This column tabulates the jitter from the internal clock of the root hub.

5. This column tabulates the jitter from the internal clock of the device.

6. This column tabulates the total jitter at the receiver in the device for a minimum 1 bit and defined 2 bit periods.

7. This column tabulates the minimum and maximum width of the SE0 for 1 bit period at the device.

8. This column tabulates the minimum and maximum width of the SE0 for 2 bit periods at the device.

1	2	3	4	5
Item	Transmitter Jitter (including 1st cable) Downstream From Root Hub nsec. Tjc	5 Hubs + 5 Cables between Root Hub and Device Jitter nsec. Tjc	Transmitter Freq. Jitter (3) Full Speed = +/- .21 per bit Low Speed = +/- 1.7 per bit nsec.	Receiver Freq Jitter (3) Full Speed = +/- .21 per bit Low Speed = +/- 10 per bit nsec.
Shortest path A - B Figure 4.15 Full Speed Device	+/-2.0	N/A	1b = .21 2b = .42	1b = .21 2b = .42
Longest path A - D Figure 4.15 Full Speed Device	+/-2.0	5 x +/- 3.0 = +/- 15 (5)	1b = .21 2b = .42	1b = .21 2b = .42
Shortest path A - B Figure 4.15 Low Speed Device	+/-45	N/A	1b = 1.7 2b = 3.4	1b = 10 2b = 20
Longest path A - D Figure 4.15 Low Speed Device	+/-2.0	4 x +/- 3.0 + +/-45 = +/- 57 (5)	1b = 1.7 2b = 3.4	1b = 10 2b = 20

1	6		7		8	
Item	Total EOP Jitter per Figure 4.20 nsec		Total SE0 Extended Jitter per Figure 4.20 Full Speed = 83.33 Low Speed = 666.67 (4)(6) 1 bit period nsec.		Total SE0 Width Jitter per Figure Full Speed = 166 Low Speed = 133 (4)(6) 2 bit periods nsec.	
	1 bit period	2 bit period	Min.	Max.	Min.	Ma
Shortest path A - B Figure 4.15 Full Speed Device	+/-2.21 (1) +/-2.42 (2)	+/-2.42 (1) +/-2.84 (2)	80.91 (2)	85.75 (2)	163.82 (2)	169
Longest path A - D Figure 4.15 Full Speed Device	+/-17.21 (1) +/-17.42 (2)	+/-17.42 (1) +/-17.84 (2)	65.91 (2)	100.75 (2)	148.82 (2)	184
Shortest path A - B Figure 4.15 Low Speed Device	+/-46.7 (1) +/-56.7 (2)	+/-48.4 (1) +/-68.4 (2)	609.97 (2)	723.37 (2)	1264.93 (2)	1401
Longest path A - D Figure 4.15 Low Speed Device	+/-60.7 (1) +/-70.7 (2)	+/- 62.4 (1) +/-82.4 (2)	595.97 (2)	749.07 (2)	1250.93 (2)	1415

Table 4.12: EOP Jitter for Downstream Transmission

Notes:

(1) This number is jitter presented to the upstream port of the downstream device.

(2) This number is the incremental jitter tolerance of the receiver required over the tolerance of the received transmission due to the tolerance of the receiving device's integral clock. For a full speed device this is .21 nsec per bit. For a low speed device this is 10 nsec per bit.

(3) 12 Mbps x +/- .25% results in +/-.21 nsec per bit for full speed root hub or device ... 1.5 Mbps x +/- .25% results in +/- 1.7 nsec per bit for full speed root hub ... 1.5 Mbps x +/- .25% results in +/- 10 nsec per bit for low speed device.

(4) Add data from page 126 and 127 of spec.

(5) This number reflects that the propagation delay though the hub and cable of a J to K state transition is the same as for a K to J state transition within +/- 3.0 nsec. data transmission.

(6) A full speed receiver is required to accept bus activity as a valid EOP provided the minimum value for the SE0 in the table is followed by a J state of one bit period. If the period of the SE0 is less than 40 nanosec. and/or the SE0 is not followed by a J state for one bit period, the receiver is required to not accept the bus activity as an EOP. If the SE0 is between 40 and 82 nanosec. and is followed by a J state for one bit period, the receiver may accept the bus activity as an EOP. A low speed receiver is required to accept bus activity as a valid EOP provided the minimum value for the SE0 in the table is followed by a J state of one bit period. If the period of the SE0 is less than 330 nanosec. and/or the SE0 is not followed by a J state for one bit period, the receiver is required to not accept the bus activity as an EOP. If the SE0 is between 330 to 670 nanosec. and is followed by a J state for one bit period, the receiver may accept the bus activity as an EOP.

For Table 4.13: *EOP Jitter of Upstream Packets,* the columns are defined as follows:

1.   This column identifies the path in Figure 4.15 under consideration and the speed of the device.

2.   This column tabulates the jitter from the transmitter of the device upstream cable attached to the device.

3.   This column tabulates the jitter from the repeater in each hub and the connected upstream cable.

4.   This column tabulates the jitter from internal clock of the device hub.

5.   This column tabulates the jitter from internal clock of the root hub.

6.   This column tabulates the total jitter at the receiver in the root hub for a minimum 1 bit and defined 2 bit periods.

7.   This column tabulates the minimum and maximum width of the SE0 for 1 bit period at the root hub.

8.   This column tabulates the minimum and maximum width of the SE0 for 2 bit periods at the root hub.

1	2	3	4	5
Item	Transmitter Jitter (including 1st Cable for short and 6th Cable for long) Upstream from Device nsec Tjc	5 Hubs + 5 Cables between Root Hub and Device Jitter nsec Tjc	Transmitter Freq. Jitter (3) Full Speed = +/- .21 per bit Low Speed = +/- 10 per bit nsec.	Receiver Freq. Jitter (: Full Speed = +/- .21 per bi Low Speed +/- 1.7 per bi nsec.
Shortest path A - B Figure 4.15 Full Speed Device	+/-2.0	N/A	1b = .21 2b = .42	1b = .21 2b = .42
Longest path A - D Figure 4.15 Full Speed Device	+/-2.0	5 x +/- 3.0 = +/- 15 (5)	1b = .21 2b = .42	1b = .21 2b = .42
Shortest path A - B Figure 4.15 Low Speed Device	+/-25	N/A	1b = 10 2b = 20	1b = 1.7 2b = 3.4
Longest path A - D Figure 4.15 Low Speed Device	+/-25	4 x +/- 3.0 + +/-45 = +/-57 (5)	1b = 10 2b = 20	1b = 1.7 2b = 3.4

1	6		7		8	
Item	Total EOP Jitter per Figure 4.20 nsec 1 bit period	2 bit period	Total SE0 Extended Jitter per Figure 4.20 Full Speed = 83.33 Low Speed = 666.67 (4)(6) 1 bit period nsec. Min.	Max.	Total SE0 Exten Jitter per Figure Full Speed = 16 Low Speed = 13: (4)(6) 2 bit periods nsec. Min.	M:
Shortest path A - B Figure 4.15 Full Speed Device	+/-2.21 (1) +/-2.42 (2)	+/-2.42 (1) +/-2.84 (2)	80.91 (2)	85.75 (2)	163.82 (2)	169.
Longest path A - D Figure 4.15 Full Speed Device	+/-17.21 (1) +/-17.42 (2)	+/-17.42 (1) +/-17.84 (2)	65.91 (2)	100.75 (2)	148.82 (2)	184.
Shortest path A - B Figure 4.15 Low Speed Device	+/-35 (1) +/-36.7 (2)	+/-45 (1) +/-48.4 (2)	629.97 (2)	703.37 (2)	1284.93 (2)	138 (
Longest path A - D Figure 4.15 Low Speed Device	+/- 92 (1) +/-93.7 (2)	+/- 102(1) +/-105.4 (2)	572.97 (2)	760.376 (2)	1227.93 (2)	143 (

Table 4.13: EOP Jitter for Upstream Transmission

Notes:

(1) This number is jitter presented to the upstream port of the upstream root hub.

(2) This number is the incremental jitter tolerance of the receiver required over the tolerance of the received transmission due to the tolerance of the receiving device's integral clock. For a full speed device this is .21 nsec per bit. For a low speed device this is 10 nsec per bit.

(3) 12 Mbps x +/- .25% results in +/-.21 nsec per bit for full speed root hub or device ... 1.5 Mbps x +/- .25% results in +/- 1.7 nsec per bit for full speed root hub ... 1.5 Mbps x +/- .25% results in +/- 10 nsec per bit for low speed device.

(4) Add data from page 126 & 127 of the specification.

(5) This number reflects that the propagation delay though the hub and cable of a J to K state transition is the same as a K to J state transition within +/- 3.0 nsec. data transmission.

(6) A full speed receiver is required to accept bus activity as a valid EOP provided the minimum value for the SE0 in the table is followed by a J state of one bit period. If the period of the SE0 is less than 40 nanosec. and/or the SE0 is not followed by a J state for one bit period, the receiver is required to not accept the bus activity as an EOP. If the SE0 is between 40 and 82 nanosec. and is followed by a J state for one bit period, the receiver may accept the bus activity as an EOP. A low speed receiver is required to accept bus activity as a valid EOP provided the minimum value for the SE0 in the table is followed by a J state of one bit period. If the period of the SE0 is less than 330 nanosec. and/or the SE0 is not followed by a J state for one bit period, the receiver is required to not accept the bus activity as an EOP. If the SE0 is between 330 to 670 nanosec. and is followed by a J state for one bit period, the receiver or may accept the bus activity as an EOP.

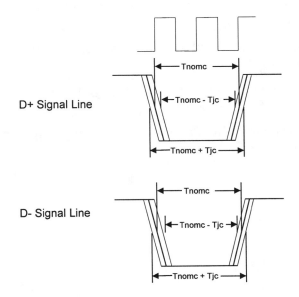

Figure 4.20: EOP Jitter

Note: Figure 4.20 is referenced in Table 4.13.

SOP is the portion of the transmission packet that indicates the beginning of a transmission packet. The SOP is the transition from the idle to the K state. The K state is for one bit period in length. The SOP is slightly different in that the transmitter requires additional time to be enabled, which adds to the jitter value of the transmitter. See Chapter 5 for more information.

Tables 4.14 and 4.15 are for paths defined in Figure 4.15. The columns in these two tables are defined as follows:

For Table 4.14: *SOP Jitter of Downstream Packets*:

1. This column identifies the path in Figure 4.15 under consideration and the speed of the device.

2. This column tabulates the jitter from the transmitter of the root hub and the 1ST downstream cable.

3. This column tabulates the jitter from the repeater in each hub and the connected downstream cable.

4. This column tabulates the jitter from the internal clock of the root hub.

5. This column tabulates the jitter from the internal clock of the device.

6. This column tabulates the total jitter at the receiver in the device for 1 bit period.

7. This column tabulates the minimum and maximum width of the K state at the device.

1	2	3	4
Item	Transmitter Jitter (including 1st Cable) Downstream From Root Hub nsec. Tjc	5 Hubs + 5 Cables between Root Hub and Device Jitter nsec. Tjc	Transmitter Freq. Jitter (3) Full Speed = +/- .21 per bit Low Speed = +/- 1.7 per bit nsec.
Shortest path A – B Figure 4.15 Full Speed Device	+/-2.0	N/A	1b = .21
Longest path A – D Figure 4.15 Full Speed Device	+/-2.0	5 x (+5.0 or -3) = +25 or -15 (5)	1b = .21
Shortest path A – B Figure 4.15 Low Speed Device	+/-45	N/A	1b = 1.7
Longest path A – D Figure 4.15 Low Speed Device	+/-2.0	4 x (+5.0 or -3) + +/-45 = +65 or -57 (5)	1b = 1.7

1	5	6	7	
Item	Receiver Freq. Jitter (3) Full Speed = +/- .21 per bit Low Speed = +/- 10 per bit nsec.	Total for K State Jitter per Figure 4.21 nsec 1 bit period	Total for K State per Figure 4.21 Full Speed = 83.33 Low Speed = 666.67 (4) 1 bit period nsec.	
			Min.	Max.
Shortest path A – B Figure 4.15 Full Speed Device	1b = .21	+/-2.21 (1) +/-2.42 (2)	80.91 (2)	85.75 (2)
Longest path A – D Figure 4.15 Full Speed Device	1b = .21	+ 27.21 (1) +27.42 (2) - 17.21 (1) - 17.42 (2)	65.91 (2)	110.75 (2)
Shortest path A – B Figure 4.15 Low Speed Device	1b = 10	+/-46.7 (1) +/-56.7 (2)	609.97 (2)	723.37 (2)
Longest path A – D Figure 4.15 Low Speed Device	1b = 10	+ 68.7 (1) + 78.7 (2) - 60.7 (1) - 70.7 (2)	595.97 (2)	745.37 (2)

Table 4.14: SOP Jitter for Downstream Transmission

Notes:

(1) This number is jitter presented to the upstream port of the downstream device.

(2) This number is the incremental jitter tolerance of the receiver required over the tolerance of the received transmission due the tolerance of the receiving device's integral clock. For a full speed device this is .21 nsec per bit. For a low speed device this is 10 nsec per bit.

(3) 12 Mbps x +/- .25% results in +/-.21 nsec per bit for full speed root hub or device ... 1.5 Mbps x +/- .25% results in +/- 1.7 nsec per bit for full speed root hub ... 1.5 Mbps x +/- .25% results in +/- 10 nsec per bit for low speed device.

(4) The extra delay to enable the transmitter creates a different jitter timing than the subsequent transitions of the synchronization patterns. Consequently, the first bit of the synchronization pattern should be used for the internal phase lock loop of the receiver. This number reflects that the propagation delay though the hub and cable of an idle to K state and includes the transmitter enable time.

For Table 4.15: *SOP Jitter of Upstream Packets*:

1. This column identifies the path in Figure 4.15 under consideration and the speed of the device.

2. This column tabulates the jitter from the transmitter of the device upstream cable attached to the device.

3. This column tabulates the jitter from the repeater in each hub and the connected upstream cable.

4. This column tabulates the jitter from the internal clock of the device hub.

5. This column tabulates the jitter from the internal clock of the root hub.

6. This column tabulates the total jitter at the receiver in the root hub for a 1 bit period.

7. This column tabulates the minimum and maximum width of the K state at the root hub.

1	2	3	4
Item	Transmitter Jitter (including 1st Cable for short and 6th Cable for long) Upstream from Device nsec Tjc	5 Hubs + 5 Cables between Root Hub and Device Jitter nsec Tjc	Transmitter Freq. Jitter (3) Full Speed = +/- .21 per bit Low Speed = +/- 10 per bit nsec.
Shortest path A – B Figure 4.15 Full Speed Device	+/-2.0	N/A	1b = .21
Longest path A – D Figure 4.15 Full Speed Device	+/-2.0	5 x (+5.0 or -3) = +25 or -15 (5)	1b = .21
Shortest path A – B Figure 4.15 Low Speed Device	+/-25	N/A	1b = 10
Longest path A – D Figure 4.15 Low Speed Device	+/-25	4 x (+5.0 or -3) + +/-45 = +65 or -57 (5)	1b = 10

1	5	6	7	
Item	Receiver Freq. Jitter (3) Full Speed = +/- .21 per bit Low Speed = +/- 1.7 per bit nsec.	Total EOP Jitter per Figure 4.21 nsec 1 bit period	Total SE0 Extended Jitter per Figure 4.21 Full Speed = 83.33 Low Speed = 666.67 (4) 1 bit period nsec. Min.	Max.
Shortest path A – B Figure 4.15 Full Speed Device	1b = .21	+/-2.21 (1) +/-2.42 (2)	80.91 (2)	85.75 (2)
Longest path A – D Figure 4.15 Full Speed Device	1b = .21	+ 27.21 (1) +27.42 (2) - 17.21 (1) - 17.42 (2)	65.91 (2)	110.75 (2)
Shortest path A – B Figure 4.15 Low Speed Device	1b = 1.7	+/-35 (1) +/-36.7 (2)	629.97 (2)	703.37 (2)
Longest path A – D Figure 4.15 Low Speed Device	1b = 1.7	+100 (1) +101.7 (2) - 92 (1) -93.7 (2)	572.97 (2)	768.37 (2)

Table 4.15: SOP Jitter for Upstream Transmission

Notes:

(1) This number is the jitter presented to the upstream port of the upstream root hub.

(2) This number is the incremental jitter tolerance the receiver requires over the tolerance of the received transmission due to the tolerance of the receiving device's integral clock. For a full speed device this is .21 nsec per bit. For a low speed device this is 10 nsec per bit.

(3) 12 Mbps x +/- .25% results in +/-.21 nsec per bit for a full speed root hub or device ... 1.5 Mbps x +/- .25% results in +/- 1.7 nsec per bit for a full speed root hub ... 1.5 Mbps x +/- .25% results in +/- 10 nsec per bit for a low speed device.

(4) The extra delay to enable the transmitter creates a different jitter timing than the subsequent transitions of the synchronization patterns. Consequently, the first bit of the synchronization pattern should be used for the internal phase lock loop of the receiver. This number reflects that the propagation delay though the hub and cable of an idle to K state and includes the transmitter enable time.

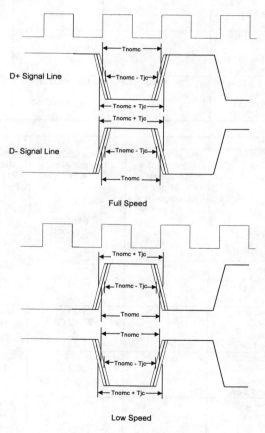

Figure 4.21: SOP Jitter

Note: Figure 4.21 is referenced in Tables 4.14 and 4.15.

4.6.3 Waveform Delay

As previously discussed, a portion of the packet transmission waveform is delay. One element of delay occurs when the transmitter is enabled for an SOP. This specific element of delay is included in the waveform jitter numbers defined above. The other elements of delay are outlined below.

The other elements of delay are due to the cable and the hub. These delays are outlined as an example for a downstream flow of data bits or EOP in Figure 4.22. The same concepts apply for the synchronization pattern, data bits, or EOP flowing in the upstream direction. The cable and hub delays are defined in Table 4.16 for the synchronization pattern and data, and Table 4.17 for the EOP. These are referenced to the long path (A to D) defined in Figure 4.15, but individual cable and hub delays apply to shorter paths, such as in Figure 4.22.

In these tables, the cable delay is defined as 30 nanoseconds given the maximum of 5.0 and 3.0 meters for full and low speed cables, respectively. The delay will vary depending on the actual cable characteristics, which affect the maximum cable length:

- 9.0 nsec/m .... Max length of 3.3 meters
- 8.0 nsec/m .... Max length of 3.7 meters
- 7.0 nsec/m .... Max length of 4.3 meters
- 6.5 nsec/m .... Max length of 4.6 meters

Item	Each cable delay for 1st to 5th cable nsec. Max. Tcab	Each hub delay for 1st to 4th hub (1) nsec. Max. Thub	6th cable delay nsec. Max. Tcab	5th hub delay (1) nsec. Max. Thub
Longest path A – D Figure 4.15 Full Speed Device	30	40	30	40
Longest path A – D Figure 4.15 Low Speed Device	30	300	30	300

Note: (1) Measured with no cable and a 50 pF load.

Table 4.16: Downstream & Upstream Synchronization Pattern and Data Delay

Item	Each cable delay for 1st to 5th cable nsec. Max. Tcab	Each hub delay for 1st to 4th hub (1) nsec. Max. Thub	6th cable delay nsec. Max. Tcab	5th hub delay (1) nsec. Max. Thub
Longest path A - D Figure 4.15 Full Speed Device	30	15	30	15
Longest path A - D Figure 4.15 Low Speed Device	30	200	30	200

Note: (1) Measured with no cable and a 50 pF load.

Table 4.17: Downstream and Upstream EOP Delay

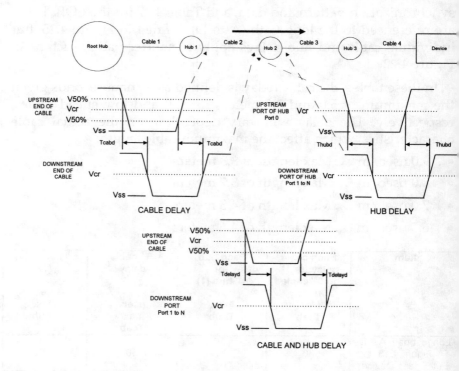

Figure 4.22: Summary of Delays

From Tables 4.16 and 4.17 the total delay over the longest possible path can be computed. As will be discussed in Chapter 6, some of the token packets transmitted require a responding data (read) or handshake packet. Similarly, some data packets transmitted require a responding handshake packet. The number of cables and hubs between the root hub and the device determines the delay for a packet transmission in one direction and a response packet in the opposite direction. An additional USB requirement is that the device or root hub providing a response packet is required to wait two J states after the EOP before transmitting the response packet. All of these considerations determine the time a root hub or device is required to wait prior to assuming that no response will be received.

The amount of time for a root hub to wait for a response can be computed from the Table 4.18. The definitions of the columns in Table 4.18 are as follows:

1. This column identifies the path in Figure 4.15 under consideration and the speed of the device.

2. This column tabulates the delay due to cables between hubs, root hubs, and devices.

3. This column tabulates the delay of each hub.

4. This column tabulates the delay for the shortest path.

5. This column tabulates the delay for the longest path.

6. This column tabulates the delay for each packet transmission in one direction.

7. This column tabulates the maximum bit time a device or root hub can wait between the SE0 of EOP and the SOP of a response.

8. This column tabulates number of bit times a root hub waits for a response.

9. This column tabulates number of bit times a root hub waits for a response.

1	2	3	4	5
Item	Cable Delays (1)(2) nsec	Hub Delay (1) Full Speed = 40 Low Speed = 300 For EOP and additional delay of Full Spd = 15 Low Spd = 200 nsec	0 Hub + 1st Cable Figure 4.15 nsec	5 Hubs + 5 Cables Figure 4.15 nsec
Shortest path A – B Figure 4.15 Full Speed Device	30	N/A	30	N/A
Longest path A – D Figure 4.15 Full Speed Device	30	40 for EOP total is 55	N/A	5 x 70 = 350 for EOP 5 x 85 =425
Shortest path A – B Figure 4.15 Low Speed Device	30	N/A	30	N/A
Longest path A – D Figure 4.15 Low Speed Device	30	300 for EOP total is 500	N/A	5 x 330 = 1650 for EOP 5 x 500 = 2500

1	6		7	8	9
Item	Total Full Spd = 83.33 Low Spd = 666.67 Bit Times nsec. EOP Response Trip Trip		Required to Respond Device = 6.5 Root hub = 7.5 Device/Root hub Max. Bits Times	Total Bits Times Root hub required to wait for response (3)(4) Bit Times	Total Bits Times Downstream device required to waits for response (4) Bit Times
Shortest path A – B Figure 4.15 Full Speed Device	.36	.36	6.5/7.5	7.22	8.22
Longest path A – D Figure 4.15 Full Speed Device	5.46	4.56	6.5/7.5	16.52	17.52
Shortest path A – B Figure 4.15 Low Speed Device	0.05	0.05	6.5/7.5	6.6	7.6
Longest path A – D Figure 4.15 Low Speed Device	3.80	2.53	6.5/7.5	12.83	13.83

Table 4.18: EOP and SOP Upstream and Downstream Transmission Delays

Notes:

(1) Measured with a 50pF load

(2) Full Speed = 5 meters Max. Low Speed = 3 meters Max.

(3) USB spec. requires that the host controller does not begin the next transmission until 18 bits time has elapsed.

(4) This number includes 2 bit clocks for two J states after the SE0 of the EOP. These 2 bit clocks are included in the 6.5 and 7.5 bits times of column 7.

4.7 Connectors

To connect a device to a downstream port of a hub or a compound package requires a link, which consists of a connector pair (plug and receptacle) and cable. The plug is connected to the cable and the receptacle is connected to the hub or device. There are two types of connector pairs: series A and series B. These are defined as follows:

- Series A connector pair
  - Used when the cable is permanently connected to the upstream port of the device. The device including the permanent cable and series A plug is attached or removed from the downstream port of a hub as a single unit.
  - The downstream port of a hub always contains a permanently connected series A receptacle.
- Series B connector pair
  - Used when the cable is not permanently connected to the device. The cable is connected to a series B plug that mates with the series B receptacle on the upstream port of the device. When the downstream end of the cable has a series B plug it is required to have a series A plug on the opposite upstream end of the cable.
  - A cable with a series B plug must be a full speed cable, *i.e.*, it must have twisted signal lines and a shield. This is because even if it was provided as part of a low speed device product, it can be used with a full speed device that has a series B receptacle.

The electrical requirement for power, signal line electrical requirements, EMI characteristics, speed of the link, and the length of the cable are all independent of the series of the connector used. However, the series A connector components (plug and receptacle) are not mechanically compatible with the series B connector components. The reason for the non-compatible mechanical aspects of the two series of connectors is to control the electrical integrity of the USB bus. That is, cables cannot be attached in series to create long links with non-compliant electrical characteristics.

The USB specification requires that the series A receptacles are connected to the downstream ports of hubs, thus:

- When a cable is permanently connected to a device, the series A plug is connected to one end of the cable to allow attachment to a hub's downstream port.
- When the cable is not permanently connected to the device, the series A plug is connected to one end of the cable and the series B plug is connected to the other end of the cable.
  - The end of the cable with the series A plug can only be attached to a hub's downstream port which has a series A receptacle.
  - The end of the cable with the series B plug can only be attached to the upstream port of a device that has a series B receptacle.

The use of the above convention insures the proper connection of hubs or the root hub and devices:

- A cable permanently connected to a device can only be connected to a downstream port of a hub, and cannot be connected to the upstream port of another device.
- A removable cable can only attach one end to the upstream port of a device and the other end to a downstream port of a hub. The cable cannot be used to connect two downstream ports of a hub together, or two upstream ports of two devices together.

4.8 Cables

As previously outlined, there are two speeds for a link: full and low. The speed of the link depends on the construction of the cable. For the full speed link, the cable is shielded, twisted pair wire. For the low speed link, the cable is unshielded, non-twisted pair wire. The choice of the cable reflects cost and the compliance to industrial standards for EMI and the required capabilities of the device being attached.

Either cable type (shielded twisted pair or unshielded non-twisted pair) contains four individual wires defined as follows:

- Shielded twisted pair for full speed link:
  - Two 20 to 28 AWG wires assembled as a non-twisted pair for power distribution
    - V_{cc} has red color insulation
    - Gnd has black insulation
  - Two 28 AWG wires assembled as a twisted pair for signal lines D+ and D-. The twist shall be one complete twist every 6-8 cm.
    - D+ has green insulation
    - D- has white insulation
- Unshielded non-twisted pair low speed link:
  - Two 20 to 28 AWG wires assembled as a non-twisted pair for power distribution
    - V_{cc} has red color insulation
    - Gnd has black insulation
  - Two 28 AWG wires assembled as non-twisted pair for signal lines D+ and D-.
    - D+ has green insulation
    - D- has white insulation

4.9 Environmental

The operating environment for USB is 0C to 70C ambient.

USB must meet the following regulatory requirements:

EMI:

FCC part 14 class B

EN55022:1994 (Based on CISPR-22:1993)

EN5082-1:1992 (Generic Immunity standard)

VCCI (Japan version of CISPR-22)

Safety:

UL, CSA

4.10 Mechanical

This section reproduces the mechanical portions of the USB v1.0 specification for convenient reference. Mechanical designers should rely on current drawings available from http://www.usb.org. The authors and publisher gratefully acknowledge the permission of the USB Implementer's Forum to include this material.

4.10.1 Connector (Series A)

Figures 4.23 through 4.29 describe the Series A connector. The original figure number from the specification is shown in parentheses for each drawing. Notes within some drawings refer to other drawings, which will refer to those drawing numbers in parentheses.

Plug (Series A)

The USB (Series A) plug is a four-position plug with a shielded housing compatible with the cabling as described in Section 4.8 (Specification Section 6.3). The following guidelines ensure intermateability. The recommended color is frost white for the overmold. Internal plastic features can be frost white or equivalent.

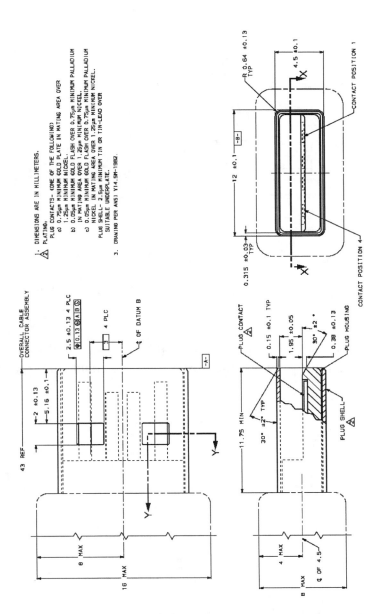

Figure 4.23 (Spec. Fig. 6-1): Plug Connector (Series A)

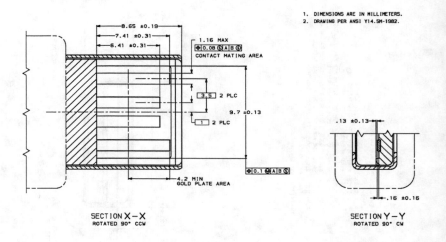

Figure 4.24 (Spec. Fig. 6-2): Plug Contact Detail (Series A)

The termination of the conductors to the plug contacts may be done as deemed appropriate by the connector's manufacturing process.

Receptacle (Series A)

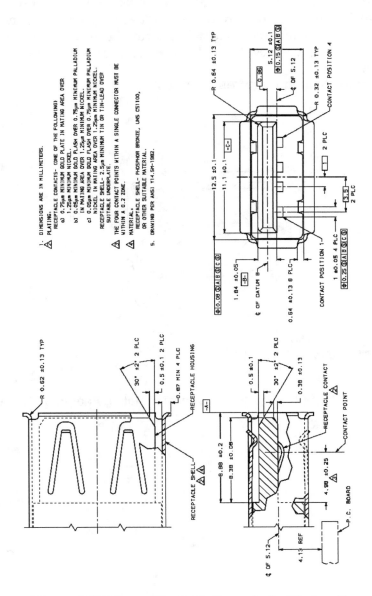

Figure 4.25 (Spec. Fig. 6-3): Receptacle (Series A)

There are four variants of the receptacle available for general use. They are vertical, right angled, panel mount, and stacked right angled with SMT as well as through-hole variants. However, as long as the interface requirements of the specification are met, it is up to the implementer as to what form the receptacle will take. Internal plastic features should be frost white or equivalent.

Connector Mating Features (Series A)

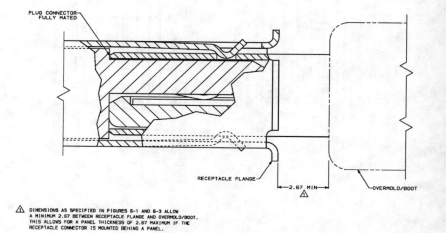

△ DIMENSIONS AS SPECIFIED IN FIGURES 6-1 AND 6-3 ALLOW
A MINIMUM 2.67 BETWEEN RECEPTACLE FLANGE AND OVERMOLD/BOOT.
THIS ALLOWS FOR A PANEL THICKNESS OF 2.67 MAXIMUM IF THE
RECEPTACLE CONNECTOR IS MOUNTED BEHIND A PANEL.

Figure 4.26 (Spec. Fig. 6-4): Connector Mating Features (Series A)

Receptacle PWB Foot Print (Series A)

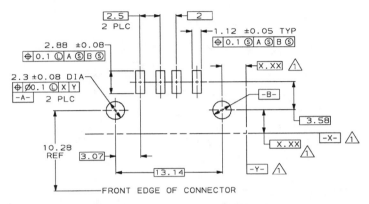

1. DATUM AND BASIC DIMENSIONS ESTABLISHED BY CUSTOMER.
2. RECOMMENDED PC BOARD THICKNESS OF 1.57
3. DRAWING PER ANSI Y14.5M-1982.

Figure 4.27 (Spec. Fig. 6-5): PWB Footprint for Receptacle, SMT (Series A)

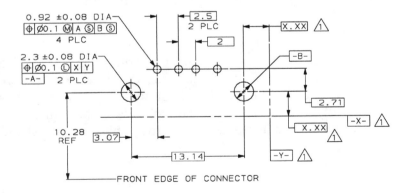

1. DATUM AND BASIC DIMENSIONS ESTABLISHED BY CUSTOMER.
2. RECOMMENDED PC BOARD THICKNESS OF 1.57
3. DRAWING PER ANSI Y14.5M-1982.

Figure 4.28 (Spec. Fig. 6-6): PWB Footprint for Receptacle, Throughhole (Series A)

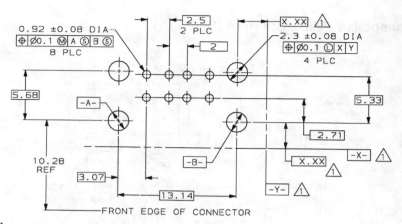

0.92 ±0.08 DIA
⊕ Ø0.1 Ⓜ A Ⓢ B Ⓢ
8 PLC

2.5
2 PLC

2

X.XX ⚠

2.3 ±0.08 DIA
⊕ Ø0.1 Ⓛ X Y
4 PLC

5.68

-A-

5.33

2.71

10.28 REF

-B-

X.XX ⚠

-X- ⚠

3.07

-Y- ⚠

13.14

FRONT EDGE OF CONNECTOR

⚠ DATUM AND BASIC DIMENSIONS ESTABLISHED BY CUSTOMER.
2. RECOMMENDED PC BOARD THICKNESS OF 1.57
3. DRAWING PER ANSI Y14.5M-1982.

**Figure 4.29 (Spec. Fig 6-7): PWB Footprint for Receptacle, Stacked
Right Angle (Series A)**

4.10.2 Connector (Series B)

Figures 4.30 through 4.34 describe the Series B connector.

Plug (Series B)

The USB (Series B) plug is a four position plug with shielded
housing compatible with the cabling as described in Section 4.8
(Specification Section 6.3). The following guidelines ensure
intermateability. The recommended color is frost white for the
overmold. The internal features can be frost white or equivalent.

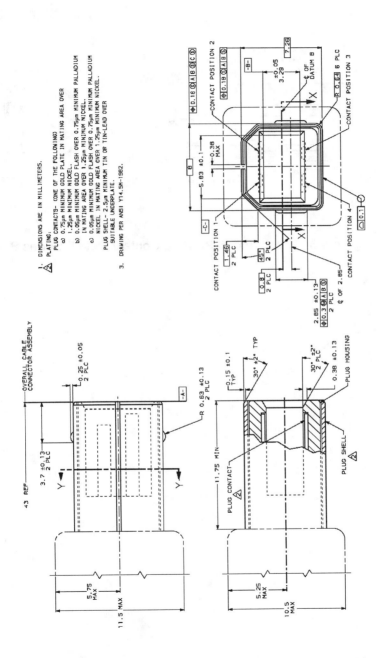

Figure 4.30 (Spec. Fig. 6-8): Plug Connector (Series B)

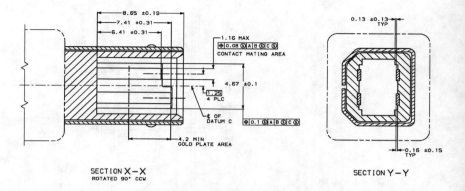

Figure 4.31 (Spec. Fig. 6-9): Plug Contact Detail (Series B)

Receptacle (Series B)

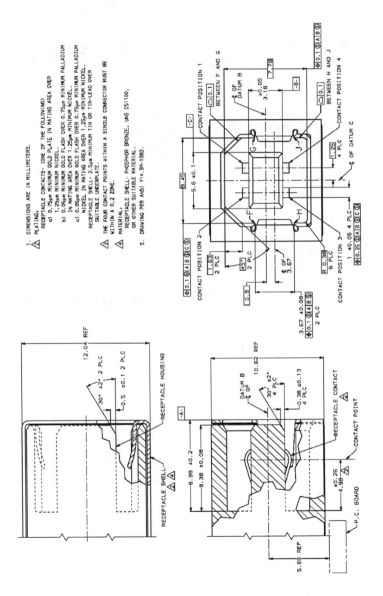

Figure 4.32 (Spec. Fig. 6-10): Receptacle (Series B)

Connector Mating Features (Series B)

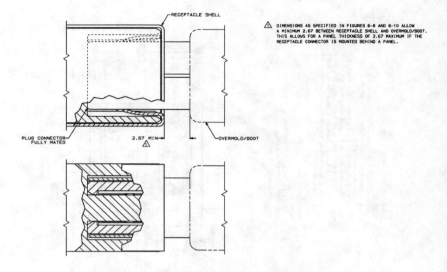

Figure 4.33 (Spec. Fig. 6-11): Connector Mating Features (Series B)

Receptacle PWB Foot Print (Series B)

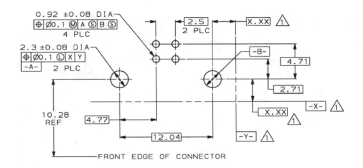

△ DATUM AND BASIC DIMENSIONS ESTABLISHED BY CUSTOMER.
2. RECOMMENDED PC BOARD THICKNESS OF 1.57
3. DRAWING PER ANSI Y14.5M-1982.

Figure 4.34 (Spec. Fig. 6-12): PWB Footprint for Receptacle, Throughhole (Series B)

4.10.3 Serial Bus Icon

The USB icon, shown in Figure 4.35 (Specification Figure 6-13), should be molded into the connector and also placed on the product for ease of identifying the USB port. It is recommended that the icon on the product and the one on the plug be adjacent to each other when the plug and receptacle are mated. This icon can be used for both series A and B connector schemes. On the plug, there should be a 0.635 mm rectangular recessed area around the icon such that there is a perceptible feel of the icon.

Figure 4.35 (Spec. Fig. 6-13): USB Icon Artwork

4.10.4 Plug/Receptacle Mechanical and Electrical Requirements

Contact Numbering (Series A and B)

Contact Number	Signal Name	Comment
1	V_{cc}	Cable power
2	- Data	
3	+ Data	
4	Ground	Cable ground

Table 4.19 (Spec. Table 6-6): Contact Numbering

Ratings

Voltage: 30 Vac (rms).

Current: 1 A maximum per contact not to exceed 30°C temperature rise.

Temperature: -40 °C to 60°C storage; 0 °C to 40 °C operating.

Performance and Test Description

Product is designed to meet electrical, mechanical, and environmental performance requirements specified in Table 4.20 (Specification Table 6-7). Unless otherwise specified, all tests shall be performed at ambient environmental conditions. Cable construction and/or part number used for testing must be included with test report.

Test Description	Requirement	Procedure
Examination of product	Meets requirements of Section 6.3	Visual, dimensional, and functional compliance
ELECTRICAL		
Termination resistance	30 mΩ maximum	EIA 364-23 Subject mated contacts assembled in housing to 20 mV maximum open circuit at 100 mA maximum. See Figure 6-14.
Insulation resistance	1000 MΩ minimum	EIA 364-21 Test between adjacent contacts of mated and unmated connector assemblies
Dielectric withstanding voltage	750 Vac at sea level	EIA 364-20 Test between adjacent contacts of mated and unmated connector assemblies
Capacitance	2 pF maximum	EIA 364-30 Test between adjacent circuits of unmated connectors at 1 kHz
MECHANICAL		
Vibration, random	No discontinuities of 1 μs or longer duration. See Note.	EIA 364-28 Condition V Test letter A. Subject mated connectors to 5.35 G's rms. Fifteen minutes in each of three mutually perpendicular planes. See Figure 6-15.
Physical shock	No discontinuities of 1 μs or longer duration. See Note.	EIA 364-27 Condition H. Subject mated connectors to 30 G's half-sine shock pulses of 11 ms duration. Three shocks in each direction applied along three mutually perpendicular planes, 18 total shocks. See Figure 6-15 for the test setup.
Durability	See Note.	EIA 364-09 Mate and unmate connector assemblies for 1500 cycles at maximum rate of 200 cycles per hour

Table 4.20 (Spec. Table 6-7): Test Requirements and Procedures Summary

Test Description	Requirement	Procedure
Mating force	35 Newtons maximum	EIA 364-13 Measure force necessary to mate connector assemblies at maximum rate of 12.5 mm per minute.
Unmating force	10 Newtons minimum	EIA 364-13 Measure force necessary to unmate connector assemblies at maximum rate of 12.5 mm per minute.
Cable Retention	Cable shall not dislodge from cable crimp.	Apply axial load of 25 Newtons to the cable.
ENVIRONMENTAL		
Thermal shock	See Note.	EIA 364-32 Test Condition I. Subject mated connectors to five cycles between -55 °C and 85 °C.
Humidity	See Note.	EIA-364-31 Method II Test Condition A. Subject mated connectors to 96 hours at 40 °C with 90 to 95% RH.
Temperature life	See Note.	EIA-364-17 Test Condition 3 Method A. Subject mated connectors to temperature life at 85 °C for 250 hours.

Table 4.20 (Spec. Table 6-7): Test Requirements and Procedures Summary (continued)

Note:

Shall meet visual requirements, show no physical damage, and shall meet requirements of additional tests as specified in the test sequence listed in Table 4.21 (Specification Table 6-8).

Test or Examination	Test Group (a)		
	1	2	3
	Test Sequence (b)		
Examination of product	1,10	1,5	1,9
Termination resistance	3,7	2,4	
Insulation resistance			3,7
Dielectric withstanding voltage			4,8
Capacitance			2
Vibration	5		
Physical shock	6		
Durability	4		
Mating force	2		
Unmating force	8		
Thermal shock			5
Humidity			6
Cable Retention	9		
Temperature life		3(c)	

Table 4.21 (Spec. Table 6-8): Product Qualification Test Sequence

Notes:
(a) Refer to Specification Section 6.3.5.4 (Book Section *Sample Selection*).
(b) Numbers indicate sequence in which tests are performed.
(c) Precondition samples with 10 cycles durability.

Sample Selection

Samples shall be prepared in accordance with applicable manufacturers' instructions and shall be selected at random from current production. Test groups 1, 2, and 3 shall consist of a minimum of eight connectors. A minimum of 30 contacts shall be selected and identified. Unless otherwise specified, these contacts shall be used for all measurements.

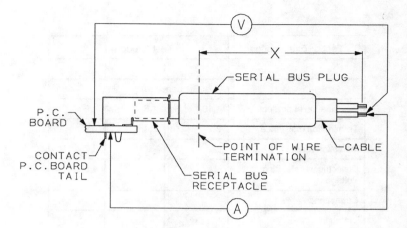

1. RESISTANCE DUE TO X INCHES OF WIRE
   IS TO BE REMOVED FROM ALL READINGS.

Figure 4.36 (Spec. Fig. 6-14): Termination Resistance Measurement Points

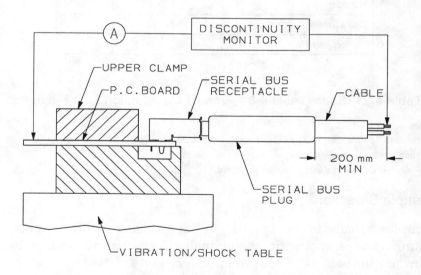

Figure 4.37 (Spec. Fig. 6-15): Vibration and Physical Shock Mounting Fixture

Additional Requirements

Flammability: Plastic material used in the construction of this item shall be rated 94V-0, per UL-STD-94.

Marking: USB icon per Figure 4.35 (Specification Figure 6-13) on plug. Recommended that OEM's add an icon near the receptacle on end product where possible or practical.

Qualification: All suppliers when requested must be able to supply appropriate documentation to show conformance to the requirements of this chapter.

5. Signaling Characteristics

5.1   Introduction

5.2   Signal Line Operation

5.3   Link States

5.4   Link Transmission Speeds

5.5   Packet Signaling Protocol

5.1 Introduction

The USB bus incorporates a pair of signal lines on the link: D+ and D-. These signal lines operate as a differentially driven pair with quiescent levels. The differential driving of the signal lines is used to transmit packets of the transaction. The quiescent levels defined are: reset, attachment, removal, link speed identification (also defined as idle), and end of packet.

There are two possible transmission speeds of the link: FULL for 12 Mbps and LOW for 1.5 Mbps. The speed difference allows the link to be constructed from either shielded cable with twisted wire for full speed links or unshielded cable with non-twisted wire for low speed links. The low speed link allows for low rise and fall times; consequently, the requirements for FCC class B EMI can be achieved more inexpensively.

5.2 Signal Line Operation

5.2.1 Overview

As previously outlined in Chapter 4 *Electrical and Mechanical*, the USB link consists of a cable of four wires. Two of these wires are used for power, and two (D+ and D-) are used for signaling. There are no other signal lines defined in the USB link; thus these signal lines provide two types of binary values: Quiescent and Differential. These two types of values are defined as follows:

- Quiescent levels of the D+ and D- signal lines define attachment/removal, link idle (speed), reset, suspend, and end of packet. When these signal lines are connected to a pull-up resistor to V_{DD} or pull-down resistor to V_{ss} ground, the quiescent levels of "1" and "0" are defined and reflect the independent voltage levels of the D+ and D- signal lines. The quiescent level is also defined when a transmitter of the device's port buffer drives the signal lines to a constant voltage. The quiescent levels are written as "1" and "0" in the text.

- Differential driving of the signal lines is used to transmit USB transactions in the form of packets. The differential information within the packet includes start of packet, the synchronization pattern, and transaction data. The differential driving occurs between the start and end of packet (SOP and EOP), respectively. When the voltage level of the D+ signal line is 200 millivolts greater than the D- signal line, the value of "differential 1" is defined. When the voltage level of the D- signal line is 200 millivolts greater than the D+ signal line, the value of "differential 0" is defined.

- Logical data 0 and 1

  - The traditional definition of binary data in a processor and traditional buses. That is, 1 has a value greater than 0 in a processor and 1 is a more positive voltage level than 0 on a bus. Written as 0 and 1 in the following text.

- J and K

- As previously outlined, at the time of device attachment the link speed is established. The J and K notation supports discussion of link activity without regard to link speed. J and K notation also refers to the quiescent state defined during the idle link state. Written as J and K in the following text.

See Chapter 4 *Electrical and Mechanical* for more information about the electrical characteristics of the D+ and D- signal lines.

In this chapter the term "hub" refers to both hub and compound package. The term "device" refers to both composite devices and devices that are not hubs.

By convention, the D+ and D- signal lines cannot be defined as differential 1 or 0 during quiescent levels even though the polarity of these signal lines define such a dynamic interpretation. The dynamic driving definition of these signal lines only exists from the start of a packet until the completion of EOP (SE0, then J state), or EOF2 event has occurred.

The USB bus uses pull-up and pull-down resistors on the D+ and D- signal lines to establish the quiescent levels and thus the connection of a device and the speed of the link. Figure 5.1 outlines the location of the pull-up and pull-down resistors that establish the quiescent level.

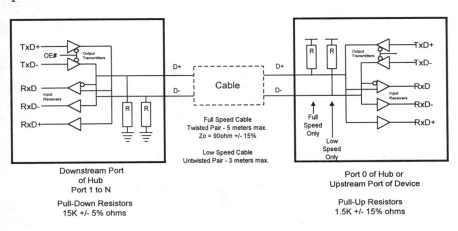

Figure 5.1: Location of Pull-Up and Pull-Down Resistors

> Notice in Figure 5.1 the location of the pull-up and pull-down resistors. All downstream ports of a hub are required to attach 15K ohm pull-down resistors between D+ and D- signal lines and ground. All upstream ports of a hub or device are required to attach a 1.5K ohm pull-up resistor between D+ or D- signal line and V$_{ss}$ to establish the speed of the link.

5.2.2 Quiescent Levels for Attachment/Removal and Link Idle (Speed)

> In this book the terms "attachment" and "removal" of a device refer to the real time dynamic event of plugging and unplugging the cable. The terms "connected" and "disconnected" refer to the condition that exists before and after "attachment" and "removal", respectively. "Disconnected" also refers to the condition when the cable has not been plugged in.

When power is supplied to the upstream port of a device or hub, the pull-resistors will encode the connection of the device or hub to the downstream port of a hub. The encoding defines the link idle state and the link speed. If no device is connected, the pull-down resistors of the downstream port of the hub would encode this information. The quiescent levels of the D+ and D- signal lines provide the connection and link speed information outlined in Table 5.1.

Connection and Speed	Quiescent level of D+	Quiescent level of D-
Full speed device or hub connected with full speed link ... idle state	"1"	"0"
Low Speed device connected with low speed link ... idle state	"0"	"1"
Device or hub not connected	"0"	"0"
Not possible	"1"	"1"

Table 5.1: Device Connection and Speed Protocol

5.2.3 Attachment and Removal

The connected and disconnected encoding on pull-up and pull-down resistors relies on the downstream port of the hub and the upstream port of the downstream device or hub to identify attachment and removal. This information is shown in Figures 5.2 and 5.3 for full and low speed links.

124

Bounce time is defined as the momentary indeterminate electrical state of the signal lines prior to making or breaking a clean electrical connection. This bounce time may be proportionally longer than the rise and fall times to establish the quiescent levels of the signal lines. In these figures no bounce time is shown. It is assumed that the receiver in the hub's downstream port will mask the bounce time from the rest of the hub port circuitry that is measuring the 2.5 microseconds in Figures 5.2 and 5.3.

Once the 2.5 microsecond removal or attachment period has occurred, there are further requirements placed on the hub relative to these hardware events as follows:

- When a hub or device is attached to a hub, the SE0 encoding on the downstream port is no longer sensed. The downstream port transitions from the Disconnected hub port state to the Disabled hub port state as follows:

  - If the hub is in the suspended hub functional state, the attachment will not be sensed until the hub is in the awake hub functional state.

  - If the hub is in awake hub functional state or when it transitions to the awake hub functional state, the attachment of a hub or device will cause the downstream port to sense a non-SE0 encoding. After 2.5 μsec. of non-SE0 encoding, the downstream port has 2.0 milliseconds to transition to the Disabled hub port state. The 2.0 milliseconds is measured from a stable non-SE0 encoding (*e.g.*, allowing for de-bounce time after attachment is completed).

- When a hub or device is removed from a hub, the SE0 encoding on the downstream port is sensed. The downstream port transitions from the Disabled, Enabled, or Suspended hub port state to the Disconnected hub port state as follows:

  - If the hub is in the suspended hub functional state and the remote wakeup feature is enabled, the removal of a hub or device will cause the downstream port to sense an SE0 encoding. After 2.5 μsec. of SE0 encoding, the downstream port has 12.0 milliseconds to transition to the Disconnected hub port state. The 12.0 milliseconds is measured from a stable SE0 encoding (*e.g.*, allowing for de-bounce time after removal is completed).

- If the hub is in the suspended hub functional state and the remote wakeup feature is disabled, the removal of a hub or device will not be sensed until the hub is in the awake functional state.

- If the hub is in the awake hub functional state the removal of a hub or device will cause the downstream port to sense an SE0 encoding. After 2.5 μsec. of SE0 encoding the downstream port has 2.0 milliseconds to transition to the Disconnected hub port state. The 2.0 milliseconds is measured from a stable SE0 encoding (*e.g.*, allowing de-bounce time after removal is completed).

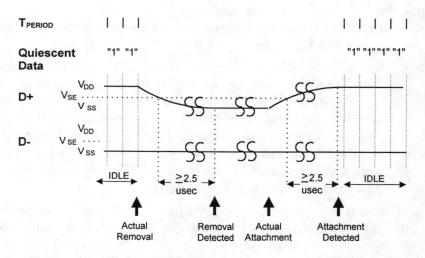

Figure 5.2: Signal Line Electrical Profile for Full Speed Attachment and Removal

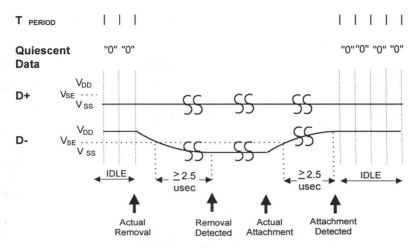

Figure 5.3: Signal Line Electrical Profile for Low Speed Attachment and Removal

Once the attachment of a device or hub has been established, the downstream port can identify the speed of the link and the device as outlined in Table 5.1. The speed of the device is defined at the time of design and manufacture. The type of cable used by the device is defined by the speed of the device. A full speed cable can be used on a low speed device, but would usually not make sense from an economic point of view. See Chapter 4 *Electrical and Mechanical* for more information.

> The speed of the device or hub and the link connected to its upstream port is defined at the time of design and manufacture. The physical attachment of the device or hub establishes this speed with the upstream hub's downstream port. If the device is already connected prior to the system being powered-up, the speed is established by the quiescent level of the D+ and D- signal lines.

If the detection of the hub or device speed is after a hardware reset event (SE0 encoding on the upstream port of the hub), the hub is required to determine the speed between 2.5 µsec. and 1.0 millisecond. The determination time is optional and is referenced to the transitioning of the SE0 to a stable non-SE0 encoding (*e.g.*, allowing de-bounce time after attachment is completed).

5.2.4 Quiescent Levels for Reset, Suspend, and End of Packet

As shown in Table 5.1, once the attachment of a device or hub has been established, the link immediately enters the idle link state, which also defines the speed of the link. There are three quiescent levels of the link state defined: reset, suspend, and end of packet. See more detailed information in Section 5.3

Reset

The reset link encoding is defined when both D+ and D- signal lines are driven to "0" by the downstream port transmitter of a hub for a minimum amount of time. By convention, when both D+ and D- signal lines are driven to "0", these signal lines encode a single ended zero (SE0). A hub is required to transmit a reset link encoding downstream for a SetPortFeature(Port_Reset) request. Under this condition the hub is required to transmit this reset link encoding between 10 milliseconds and 20 milliseconds. The upstream ports of all downstream devices (including hubs) are required to identify a reset link state when both D+ and D- signal lines are driven to "0" between 2.5 μsec. and 5.5 μsec.

Suspend

The suspend link encoding is defined when the idle link encoding has existed on the link for a minimum of three milliseconds. The suspended encoding remains until a packet transmission begins, the resume protocol is executed, or reset occurs. See Figures 5.4 and 5.5.

EOP

The end of packet (EOP) link encoding is a unique quiescent level in that it is integral to the successful completion of a packet. The previous portions of the packet were transmitted with differential levels of the D+ and D- signal lines. The end of packet (EOP) quiescent link encoding is similar to reset in that the SE0 encoding is used. It differs from reset as follows:

- The SE0 encoding is driven by the transmitter associated with the packet for only two bit periods maximum. In the subsequent bit time (third bit time) the transmitter drives the J encoding onto the D+ and D- signal lines.

- The receiver will assume an EOP after one bit time of SE0 if it is followed by the J binary pattern (see below).

- The EOP is driven by the transmitter of the downstream port of the hub or the upstream port of the hub or device.

> If the SE0 encoding is driven onto the D+ and D- signal lines for more than two bit times but less than 2.5 μsec, an EOP is assumed to have occurred.

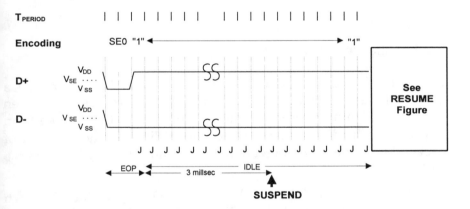

Figure 5.4: Suspend and EOP for Full Speed Link

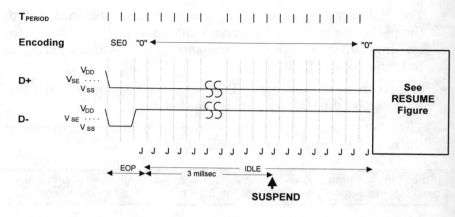

Figure 5.5: Suspend and EOP for Low Speed Link

5.2.5 Differentially Driven Signal Lines on the Link

When the D+ and D- signal lines on the link do not encode a quiescent level, then by definition they are being driven differentially and are used to transmit USB transactions in the form of packets. The differentially driven signal lines define the start of packet (SOP), the synchronization pattern, and data (see Figures 5.6 and 5.7).

The differential driving of the D+ and D- signal lines for each packet is terminated with the EOP encoding. It is possible that due to an operational problem on the USB bus that the D+ and D- signal lines are driven differentially until the end of frame. That is, no EOP encoding was generated. This activity of differentially driven D+ and D- signal lines is defined as babble. For more information, see Section 12.4.2.

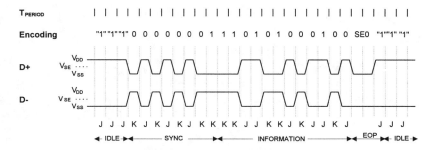

Figure 5.6: Full Speed Link Differential Levels (Sync Pattern and Information)

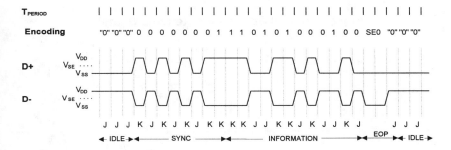

Figure 5.7: Low Speed Link Differential Levels (Sync Pattern and Information)

5.2.6 Resume Signaling Protocol

The conditions for a suspended link state were outlined in Figures 5.4 and 5.5. The link exits the suspended link state when a packet is transmitted or the resume protocol is executed. As outlined in Figures 5.8 and 5.9, the resume protocol begins when the encoding of idle for the suspend link state changes to the binary encoding for K. In order to propagate throughout the USB bus, the K pattern is maintained for a minimum of 20 milliseconds. After that time expires, an EOP is transmitted. For both the full and low speed links, the length of the SE0 and the subsequent J encoding that comprises an EOP is required to equal the elapsed period for a low speed version of EOP. Upon completion of the EOP, the link returns to the idle or active link state. The active link state is the beginning of a packet transmission. See more information in Section 5.3.

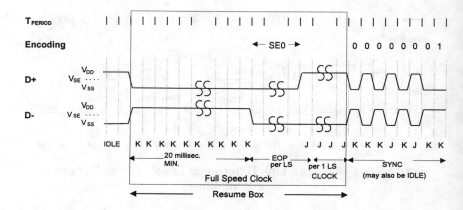

Figure 5.8: Full Speed Link Resume Signaling

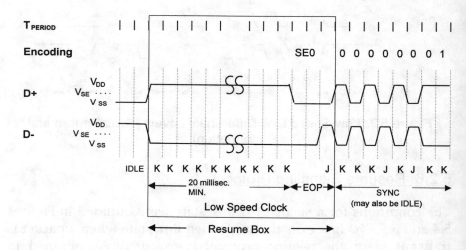

Figure 5.9: Low Speed Link Resume Signaling

5.3 Link States

5.3.1 Definition

Once the quiescent level link encoding has established that a device is connected to a downstream port of a hub and the port is not in the powered-off or disconnected hub port state, the link states can be defined. Obviously, it is meaningless to define link states for unconnected downstream devices and downstream ports of a hub that are in the powered-off or disconnected hub port states. The link states are summarized in Table 5.2. See more information associated with each link state in the previous Section 5.2.

It is important not to confuse link states with the hub port states. The link states specifically define the activity of the D+ and D- signal lines of the link between the downstream port of a hub and the upstream port of the connected device or hub. The hub port states define the operational condition of the transmitter and receiver in the hub's downstream port. See Chapter 12 *Hub Devices* for more information about hubs.

Link States	Quiescent level of D+	Quiescent level of D-	Differential level of D+ and D-	D+ and D- driven by
Reset.... Requirement for both D+ and D- must be met for a minimum of 2.5 usec. at receiver	"0"	"0"	N/A	Transmitters of the downstream port of the hub
Reset.... Requirement for both D+ and D- must be met for a minimum of 10 millisec. at transmitter	"0"	"0"	N/A	Transmitters of the downstream port of the hub
Idle full speed Requirements for both D+ and D- must be met	"1"	"0"	N/A	Pull-downs and pull-up resistors on downstream port of hub and upstream port of device
Idle low speed Requirement for both D+ and D- must be met	"0"	"1"	N/A	Pull-downs and pull-up resistors on downstream port of hub and upstream port of device
Suspended as defined for full speed link Occurs when both D+ and D- conditions are met for a continuous 3.0 millisec.	"1"	"0"	N/A	Pull-downs and pull-up resistors on downstream port of hub and upstream port of device
Suspended as defined for low speed link Occurs when both D+, D- conditions are met for a continuous 3.0 millisec.	"0"	"1"	N/A	Pull-downs and pull-up resistors on downstream port of hub and upstream port of device
Resume full speed Requirements for both D+ and D- must be met for suspend prior to resume	N/A	N/A	Start of Packet defined when D+ and D- driven to differential 0	Transmitter of either the upstream port of the device or downstream port of the hub depending on direction of resume signaling
Resume low speed Requirements for both D+ and D- must be met for suspend prior to resume	N/A	N/A	Start of Packet defined when D+ and D- driven to differential 1	Transmitter of either the upstream port of the device or downstream port of the hub depending on direction of resume signaling
Active	N/A	N/A	Differential 1 or Differential 0	Transmitter of either the downstream port of the hub or the upstream port of the device depending on direction of packet flow

Table 5.2: Link States

Further definitions of the links states in the above table follow.

Reset Link State

- The reset state of the link occurs when the D+ and D- signal lines both have a quiescent level of "0" (defined as SE0).
- The reset condition is only defined in the downstream direction and only occurs for the following conditions:
    - A device is connected to a hub's downstream port and the downstream port buffer transmits an SE0 for 20 milliseconds or more. The receivers of the downstream device will assume a reset of the link after 2.5 μsec of SE0.

> The downstream port of a hub contains pull-down resistors that will cause a quiescent SE0 when no downstream device is connected. By convention, the "link" is not in the reset state because it is meaningless when no device or hub is connected.

Idle Link State

- This link state indicates no bus activity. The signal lines are only driven by the pull-up and pull-down resistors of the downstream port of the hub and the upstream port of the downstream device. One exception is the EOP. After the transmitter drives an SE0 onto the link, it is required to drive the J encoding for one bit time.
- The idle link state also establishes the speed of the link at attachment time.

Suspend Link State

- This state begins when the idle link state exists on the link for more than 3.0 milliseconds. The signal lines are only driven by the pull-up and pull-down resistors of the downstream port of the hub and the upstream port of the device.
- Any bus activity within the aforementioned 3.0 milliseconds prevents the link from entering the suspend state. Bus activity is any change of state of the D+ and D- signal lines from the idle link state.
- Once the link is in the suspend link state it will exit this link state when any bus activity occurs. This bus activity includes

any change of state of the D+ and D- signal lines from the idle link state.

Resume Link State

- The resume state indicates that the suspended link state is ending and bus activity of packet transmission will start.

- The resume state is defined for the resume signaling protocol previously outlined in this chapter. It is also implied when packet transmission begins (including SOF), or reset encoding is transmitted.

Active Link State

- The active link state typically occurs when a data packet is being transmitted. A data packet is transmitted between an SOP and EOP.

- The active link state can also be defined as one of the following:

  - Between SOP and EOF when no EOP occurs after SOP and the D+ and D- signal lines are not in the idle link state. This is defined as babble and is not a typical link operation.

  - Between SOP and the time the downstream hub port transmitters drive SE0 onto the link.

  - Between the SOP and the idle link state when no EOP has been transmitted. This is defined as loss of activity (LOA) and is not a typical link operation.

5.3.2 Next State Tables

Listed below are the next state tables of the link that outline the correct sequence for the link to transition from state to state. There are three link activities that determine the link state sequence. These next state tables are summarized at the end of this section in Figure 5.10.

Activity 1: Link states following SE0 transmitted onto the link are:

- The hub's downstream port is transmitting an SE0 to a connected device. The connected device has received the SE0 for a minimum of 2.5 µsec. (Arc "A" in Figure 5.10.)

Present State	Reset	Suspended	Resume	Active	Idle
Next State	Reset				

> The downstream port of a hub contains pull-down resistors that will appear as SE0 when no downstream device is connected. By convention, the "link" is not in the reset state because it is meaningless when no device is connected.

- The hub's downstream port is transmitting SE0 as part of EOP protocol. (Arc "B" in Figure 5.10.)

Present State	Reset	Suspended	Resume	Active	Idle
Next State	N/A			Idle	Idle

Activity 2: Link states related to typical operation (without reset, lack of activity, attachment/removal, or babble):

- Typical operation (Arc "C" in Figure 5.10).

Present State	Reset	Suspended	Resume	Active	Idle
Next State	Idle	Resuming	Active	Idle	Idle or Suspend or Active

Activity 3: Link states related to atypical operation of lack of activity and babble:

- When LOA has occurred, *i.e.*, link activity between SOP and EOF without any EOP. (Arc "D" in Figure 5.10.)

Present State	Reset	Suspended	Resume	Active	Idle
Next State	N/A			Active	N/A

- When babble has occurred, *e.g.*, link activity between SOP and EOF without any EOP. Typical operation (Arc "D" in Figure 5.10)

Present State	Reset	Suspended	Resume	Active	Idle
Next State	N/A			Active	N/A

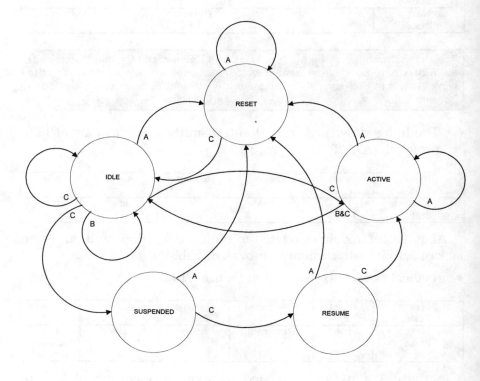

Figure 5.10: Summary of Link States

5.4 Link Transmission Speeds

5.4.1 Full and Low Speed

As previously discussed in Section 5.1, the two possible speeds of the link are "full" and "low" which provide a packet bit rate of 12 Mbps and 1.5 Mbps, respectively. The purpose of the different link speeds is to allow for two types of cables and transceivers. A full speed link requires a shielded cable with a twisted wire pair. The low speed link allows for less expensive cable and easier-to-design buffers. The electrical requirements for the full and low speed links are defined in Chapter 4 *Electrical and Mechanical*.

A low speed or full speed device requires a low speed or full speed cable, respectively. The flow of packets for either speed device will occur over the path of hubs and cables upstream to the device. The sequence of hubs between the root hub and a full speed device require the transceivers of the upstream and downstream ports of the hubs to operate at full speed. Similarly, the cables between these hubs are required to be full speed.

When a low speed device is connected to the downstream port of a hub, the cable between it and the downstream port is low speed. The transceiver on the device's upstream port is low speed. The downstream port of the hub has no control over the speed of the device connected to it. Consequently, the transceiver of the downstream port of the hub is required to support both full and low speed links. Similarly, the other upstream hubs and cables are required to support both full and low speed transmission (see Figure 5.11). Table 5.3 outlines the transceiver and cable requirements for full and low speed devices shown in Figure 5.11.

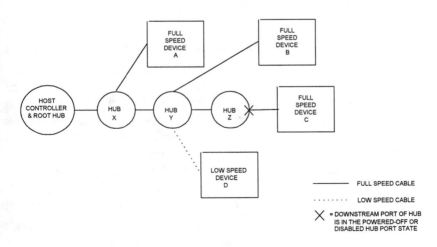

Figure 5.11: Full and Low Speed Packet Paths

Transceiver of Upstream Port of Hub	Transceivers of Downstream Ports of Hub	Transceiver of Upstream Port for Immediate Downstream Hub or Device	Link Speed	Cable Type for Link	Between Hub / Hub or Device in Figure 5.11
Full 1.5K ohm pull-up resistor on D+	Full & Low 15K ohm pull-down resistor on D+ and D-	Full 1.5K ohm pull-up resistor on D+	Full	Shielded - Twisted	Any Hub / Any Hub
Full 1.5K ohm pull-up resistor on D+	Full & Low 15K ohm pull-down resistor on D+ and D-	Full 1.5K ohm pull-up resistor on D+	Full	Shielded - Twisted	Hub "X" / Device "A" or Hub "Y" / Device "B" or Hub "Z" / Device "C"
Low 1.5K ohm pull-up resistor on D+	Full & Low 15K ohm pull-down resistor on D+ and D-	Low 1.5K ohm pull-up resistor on D-	Low	Unshielded - non-twisted	Hub "Y" / Device "D"

Table 5.3: Transceiver and Cable Requirements

It is important to remember that the 12 Mbps and 1.5 Mbps are instantaneous transmission rates of bits within a packet. It does not define the transmission rate of transferred data.

5.4.2 Establishment of Transmission Path

As discussed in Chapter 3 *System Architecture*, the host controller begins and controls all transactions. To establish the device participating in the transaction, the host controller sends a token packet downstream. The token packets are sent to all downstream full speed devices. The device or hub at the end of the path participating with the host controller transmits packets directly back to the host controller by a path that is moving the packet always in the upstream direction, never in the downstream direction. For example, in Figure 5.11, the host controller transmits full speed packets in the downstream direction to devices A and B via hubs X and Y. If the participant in the transaction is device B, then all upstream packets will flow from device B through hub Y, through hub X, and finally to the host controller. These upstream packets will not flow downstream to device A (not a participant), nor through hub C (not a participant), nor device D (not a participant).

As was discussed in Chapter 3 *System Architecture*, in order for the host controller to communicate to low speed device D, a full speed Preamble special packet (PRE) must be broadcast to all full speed hubs. The PRE enables signal repeating of all enabled downstream ports of downstream hubs connected to low speed devices. Downstream low speed packets are broadcast from the host controller to all devices connected via enabled downstream hub ports. Upstream packets are only transmitted from the device through intervening hubs to the host controller. For example, in Figure 5.11, the host controller transmits downstream the full speed PRE packet to hubs X, Y, and Z. Devices A, B, C, and D all receive the PRE and ignore it. If the downstream port of hub Y is in the enabled hub port state, the hub repeater and transceivers will be prepared for low speed packet transmission to device D. All upstream packets will flow from device D through hub Y, through to hub X, and finally to the root hub. These upstream packets will not flow downstream to device A (not a participant), through hub Z (not a participant), or to device B (not a participant). See Chapter 3 *System Architecture* for more information.

> The ability to transmit any packet through a hub is dependent on the hub's repeater state and the hub's downstream port hub port state. See Chapter 12 for more information about these hub-related states.

5.5 Packet Signaling

5.5.1 Bit and Byte Sequencing

For purposes of the following discussion, "data" (written as "data" in the following text) will collectively include bits of a packet after the synchronization pattern and before the EOP. Also, for this discussion, the conventions outlined in Section 5.2 will be used:

The sequence that bits of a byte are transmitted on the USB bus is the Least Significant bit (LSb) is the first bit transmitted, and the

Most Significant bit (MSb) is the last bit transmitted. Similarly, the Least Significant Byte (LSB) is the first byte transmitted and the Most Significant Byte (MSB) is the last byte transmitted. Figure 5.12 shows the conversion of 32 parallel bits into a series of bits on the USB bus. This example is to demonstrate order and thus does not show the SOP, synchronization pattern, and so forth.

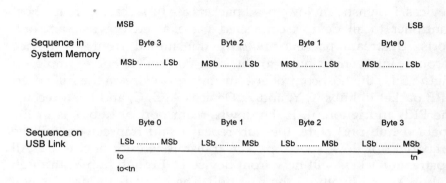

Figure 5.12: USB Packet Data Sequence

5.5.2 Signaling Link States

Table 5.4 outlines the encoding of the packet bits. Chapter 4 *Electrical and Mechanical* contains the electrical specifications for the data transmitted on the link.

The D+ and D- signal lines encode the quiescent link state of "1" and "0" for the idle link state depending on the link speed. The quiescent value is achieved by the pull-down and pull-up resistors on the downstream port of the hub and the upstream port of the device, respectively. There are two boundary conditions that occur when the value for the idle link state is not driven by the pull-down and pull-up resistors. The boundary conditions (see Figure 5.13) require careful consideration as to which USB device is driving the D+ and D- signal lines. The boundary conditions are as follows:

Representations	D+	D-
Idle Link State for Full Speed Link	"1" appears as J	"0" appears as J
Idle Link State for Low Speed Link	"0" appears as J	"1" appears as J
Start of Packet (SOP) (SOP is the first bit of the sync pattern below)	Switch from idle link state to K	Switch from idle link state to K
"Sync pattern" (SOP above is the first bit of the sync pattern)	Sequence of seven bits of 0 followed by a bit of 1 ... appears as a sequence of KJKJKJKK	Sequence of seven bits of 0 followed by a bit of 1 ... ... appears as a sequence of KJKJKJKK
End of Packet (EOP) at transmitter	"0" for 2 bit times followed by idle link state	"0" for 2 bit times followed by idle link state
End of Packet (EOP) at receiver	"0" for 1 bit times followed by J	"0" for 1 bit times followed by J
J per low speed link	Differential 0	Differential 0
J per full speed link	Differential 1	Differential 1
K per low speed link	Differential 1	Differential 1
K per full speed link	Differential 0	Differential 0
Single Ended Zero (SE0)	"0"	"0"

Table 5.4: Signaling Definitions

- After the current transmitter drives the SE0 for two bit times and then drives the idle state value one bit time as part of the EOP.

- For the idle link state after the EOP, the D+ and D- signal lines are driven by pull-up and pull-down resistors. When the next transmitter is ready to drive the idle link state or SOP encoding onto the D+ and D- signal lines, these signal lines are driven by the transmitter and not the resistors. It is required that a minimum of "one bit time" exists between the previous transmitter driving the D+ and D- signal lines for EOP and the next transmitter driving these signal lines with idle link state or SOP encoding.

- The aforementioned "one bit time" is required to insure that the previous USB transmitter and next USB transmitter do not cause transmitter buffer contention.

If the previous transmitter and next transmitter is the same, then the aforementioned "one bit time" when the D+ and D- single lines are driven by the pull-down and pull-up resistors can instead be driven by the that same USB transmitter. However, in order to maintain USB bus protocol, a minimum of "one bit time" is still required between the EOP and the SOP.

For the purposes of this book, the idle link state for the D+ and D- signal lines include (a) the one bit time associated with the EOP protocol, (b) any bit times driven by the pull-up and pull-down resistors, and (c) any bit times when the idle link state is driven by a transmitter.

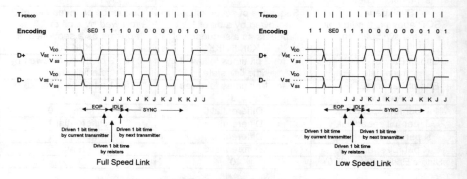

Figure 5.13: Boundary Conditions for Idle

5.5.3 Data Encoding, Decoding, and Synchronization

The USB bus implements a non-return to zero inverted (NRZI) transmission encoding of the bits between an SOP and an EOP. The idle link state prior to SOP is not encoded with NRZI encoding and is represented by quiescent levels of the D+ and D- signal lines. Also, as previously discussed, the EOP consists of SE0 (both D+ and D- signal lines are quiescent "0" level) and the idle link state. All of the synchronization and information bits between SOP and EOP are encoded with NRZI.

The NRZI encoding is applied to the synchronization pattern and the information transmitted prior to EOP. The encoding and decoding of the NRZI occurs at the transmitter and receiver, respectively. Consequently, the encoding done by the transmitter and the decoding done by the receiver is invisible to logic outside of the NRZI encoder/decoder, host software, and higher level device hardware/firmware.

144

The protocol of NRZI is as follows:

- A sequence of multiple 0's requires the signal lines to toggle for each bit time.

- A sequence of multiple 1's requires the signal lines NOT to toggle for each bit time.

- The sequence of a single 1 to 0 pair requires the signal lines to toggle.

- The sequence of a single 0 to 1 pair requires the signal lines NOT to toggle.

A key element of the USB bus protocol is the lack of clock signal lines in the cable that contains the D+ and D- signal lines. The information is transmitted between the transmitter and receiver in packets. The value of the D+ and D- signal lines are sampled by the receiver relative to bit times. The boundary points of the bit times must align between the transmitter and receiver. To achieve alignment, a synchronization pattern is transmitted as the first part of each packet. The synchronization pattern allows the phase lock loop of the receiver to synchronize with the phase lock loop of the transmitter. This synchronization, in addition to the NRZI protocol constantly changing the D+ and D- signal lines, establishes a timing relationship between the transmitter and receiver.

The following are examples of how the NRZI encoding protocol is applied to different encodings. For instructional purposes, a specific information sequence was chosen. The sequence was chosen to convey encoding examples and does not necessarily represent actual PID, packet information, etc.

The synchronization pattern plus the following data sequence examples are used in Figures 5.14 to 5.17:

1. 110101000100

2. 001010111011

3. 1010100010

4. 0101011101

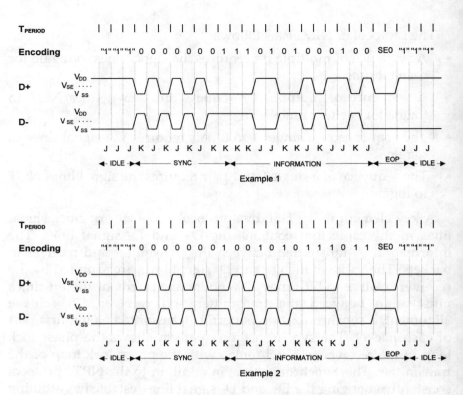

Figure 5.14: Full Speed Link without Bit Stuffing

146

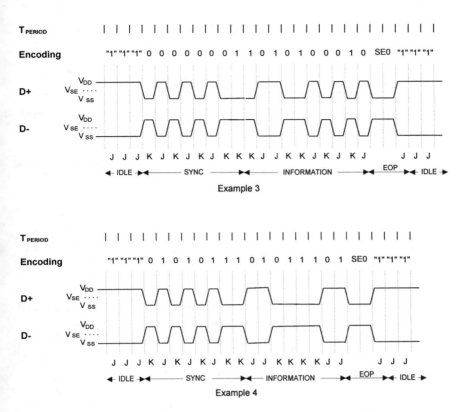

Figure 5.15: Full Speed Link without Bit Stuffing

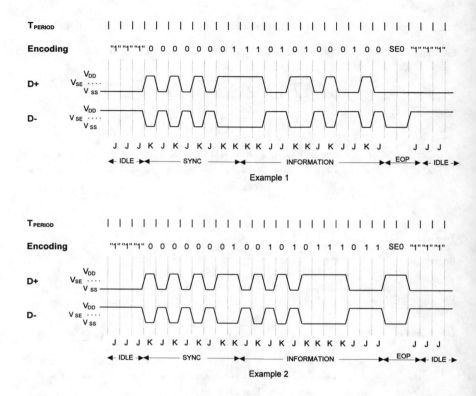

Figure 5.16: Low Speed Link without Bit Stuffing

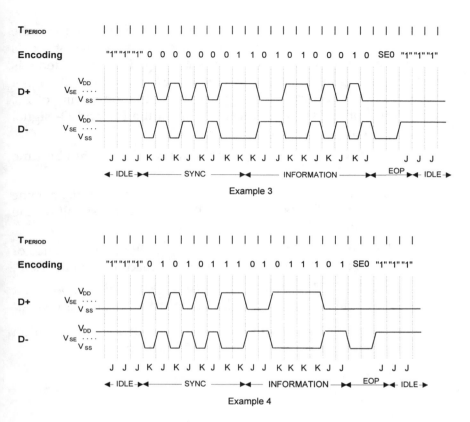

Figure 5.17: Low Speed Link without Bit Stuffing

5.5.4 Bit Stuffing

The NRZI encoding causes the toggling of D+ and D- signal lines for a sequence of 0's but not for a sequence of 1's. Consequently, the bit timing synchronization at the receiver for a sequence of 1's can become an issue when there are no changes in the D+ and D- signal lines over a period of time. As previously discussed, the bit timing relationship between the transmitter and receiver is initially established for each packet by the synchronization pattern. The timing relationship is maintained by the frequent toggling of the D+ and D- signal lines by the NRZI protocol. However, the NRZI protocol can result in sequences of no toggling of the D+ and D- signal lines for a sequence of 1's. To insure the bit timing relationship between the transmitter and receiver is maintained, the USB specification requires that every consecutive sequence of six 1's must have a 0 appended before NRZI encoding. This appended 0 is called bit stuffing and insures the toggling of the D+ and D- signal lines after NRZI encoding. The toggling prevents a long string of 1's, which would prevent frequent transitions on the D+ and D- signal lines. The specific rules are as follows:

- The sequence of 1's in six bit times requires the seventh bit time to transmit a 0 bit stuff

- The beginning of each packet is required to include a sync pattern (80H). All bits between SOP and EOP must follow the NZRI protocol.

- If the last bits of information prior to an EOP are a sequence of six 1's, then a bit stuff 0 is required to be added prior to the EOP.

- All of the NRZI encoding, decoding, bit stuffing, and bit unstuffing will be done in the device transmitters and receivers.

The synchronization pattern plus the following information sequence examples are used in Figures 5.18 to 5.21:

1. 111101

2. 1111101

3. 011111

4. 0111111

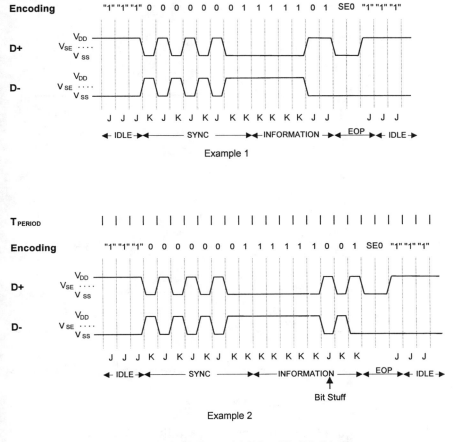

Figure 5.18: Full Speed Link with Bit Stuffing

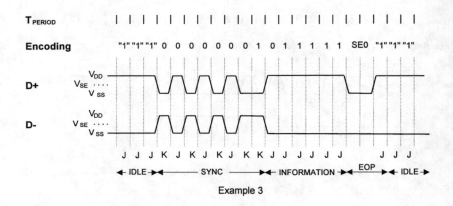

Example 3

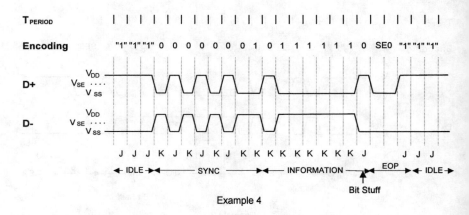

Example 4

Figure 5.19: Full Speed Link with Bit Stuffing

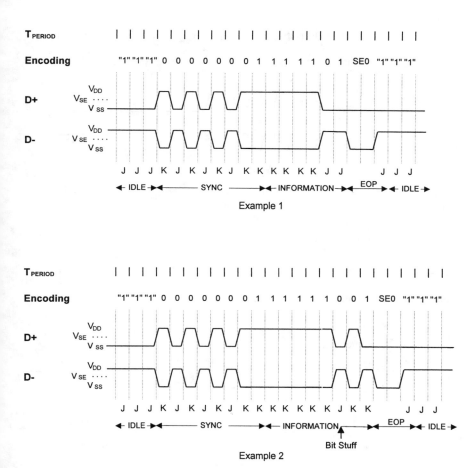

Figure 5.20: Low Speed Link with Bit Stuffing

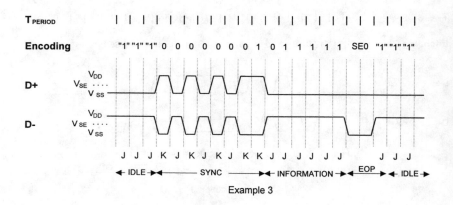

Example 3

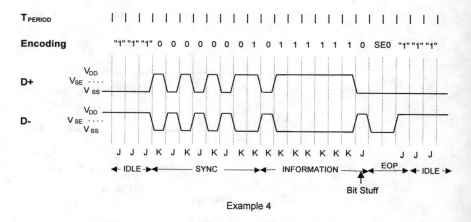

Example 4

Figure 5.21: Low Speed Link with Bit Stuffing

6. Packets and Transactions

6.1 Introduction

The transfer of information between system memory and the endpoint of a device is distributed across a series of transactions and over a series of frames. Each transaction within a frame consists of one or more packets. The information contained within each packet transmitted varies depending on the type of packet.

The transmission protocol of packets and transactions are discussed in this chapter. First, the various USB packets are described, including their internal organization and content. Then the rules for organizing packets into transactions are presented. Finally, additional information for supporting low speed transactions and bus retries is described. See Chapter 8 *Data Transfer* for more information on how transactions are organized to transfer data.

In this chapter the word "hub" will represent "hub(s)" (upstream port and N downstream hub ports with no embedded functions) and "compound package(s)" (upstream port and N downstream hub ports with embedded functions). Also in this chapter, the word "device" will represent "hub(s)" (upstream port and N downstream hub ports with no embedded functions), compound package(s) (upstream port and N downstream hub ports with embedded functions), composite device(s) (embedded functions with no downstream hub ports), and devices (upstream device port with no downstream USB ports).

6.2 Packets

As discussed in Chapter 4 *Electrical and Mechanical*, the levels on the D+ and D- signal lines define the start and end of a packet. Figure 6.1 shows examples of a full speed and a low speed packet. Between the start of packet (SOP) and end of packet (EOP), the signaling transitions carry the bits making up the body of the packet. Chapter 5 *Signaling* provides more details about specific signaling features of USB. This section discusses the format of the bits between the SOP and EOP for the USB-defined packet types.

6.2.1 General Packet Format

As shown in the example in Figure 6.1, each packet begins with an SOP, followed by an eight bit synchronization pattern ("SYNC") and potentially some number of additional bit periods ("INFORMATION") until the EOP. The SYNC pattern has been discussed in Chapter 4 *Electrical and Mechanical* and is used to allow the receiver of the packet to synchronize its internal bit clock to the transmitter's bit clock.

The information portion of the packet is after the sync pattern and consists of a PID, that PID inverted (IPID), and the packet body. The information portion of the packet is always a sequence of bytes. The USB bus signaling may encode those bytes, using NRZI and bit stuffing, into some number of bits that is not a multiple of eight. (See Figure 6.2.) The inverted PID (IPID) is a binary complement of each PID bit. Bit 0 of the IPID is the binary complement of bit 0 of PID, Bit 1 of the IPID is the binary complement of bit 1 of PID, etc.

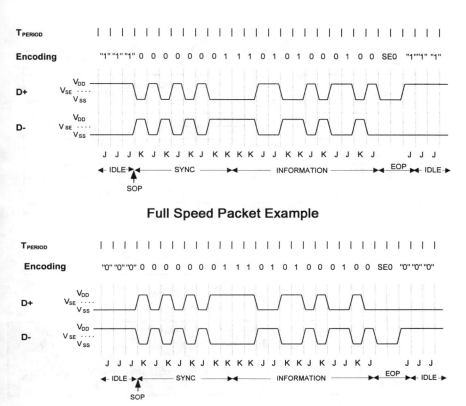

Full Speed Packet Example

Low Speed Packet Example

Figure 6.1: An Example of Full speed and Low Speed Packets

The PID defines the packet type within each packet category as shown in Table 6.1. There are four categories: token, data, handshake, and special. The remaining PID values are reserved. Each packet type has additional required fields besides arbitrary device specific data that may be allowed in the packet.

PACKET CATEGORY	PACKET TYPE	PID VALUE (MSb ... LSb)
TOKEN	OUT	0b0001
TOKEN	IN	0b1001
TOKEN	SOF	0b0101
TOKEN	SETUP	0b1101
DATA	DATA0	0b0011
DATA	DATA1	0b1011
HANDSHAKE	ACK	0b0010
HANDSHAKE	NAK	0b1010
HANDSHAKE	STALL	0b1110
SPECIAL	PRE	0b1100
RESERVED	RESERVED	0b0000, 0b0100, 0b0110, 0b0111, 0b1000, 0b1111

Table 6.1: Packet Types

Note: In the following sections the figures show the flow of packets from LSB (least significant byte) to MSB (more significant byte) from left to right. In relation to the transmission time line, the LSb (least significant bit) of each byte is transmitted first. See Chapter 4 *Electrical and Mechanical Characteristics* for more information.

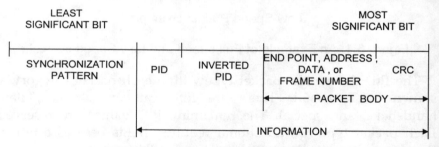

Figure 6.2: General Packet Format

The contents of the packet body are explained in detail in the following sections for each packet category.

6.2.2 Token Packets

There are four token packet types: OUT, IN, SETUP, and SOF. All token packets have additional fields for the remainder of the packet body. Table 6.2 summarizes the fields of the packet body for the four token packet types.

TOKEN PACKET PID	INFORMATION		
	PID FIELDS	PACKET BODY FIELDS LSb ... MSb	
OUT	8 bits PID/IPID	7 bits ADDR	4 bits ENDP	5bits CRC
IN	8 bits PID/IPID	7 bits ADDR	4 bits ENDP	5bits CRC
SETUP	8 bits PID/IPID	7 bits ADDR	4 bits ENDP	5bits CRC
SOF	8 bits PID/IPID	11 bits Frame Number		5bits CRC

Table 6.2: Token Packet Types

The last field in all token packets is a 5 bit cyclic redundancy check (CRC) of the packet body, *i.e.*, the CRC does not include the SYNC, PID, and IPID portions of the packet. See Section 6.7 for more information about the CRC formulas.

The OUT, IN, and SETUP token packets include two more fields in addition to the CRC field: ADDR and ENDP.

The ADDR field is a seven bit field that contains a device address. The ADDR field defines 128 (2^7) possible device addresses. Address 0000000b is used by each device temporarily until it is assigned its own unique device address as it is being configured. One other (arbitrary) address is used by the root hub. Consequently, two addresses are predefined, and an additional 126 devices can be connected to a USB bus.

The ENDP field is a four bit field that identifies an endpoint of the specified device. The PID itself also indicates the direction of data transfer.

See Chapter 3 *System Architecture* or Chapter 11 *USB Device Framework* for more information about devices and endpoints.

For the OUT, IN, and SETUP token packets, a CRC is computed over the ADDR and ENDP bits.

The SOF token packet includes only one field in addition to the CRC field: FRAME. The FRAME field is an 11 bit field that contains a monotonically increasing frame number. See Chapter 7 *Frames* for more information about USB frames. For the SOF token packet, the CRC is computed over the FRAME field.

Token Packet Meanings

Each token packet initiates a USB bus transaction. Token packets are transmitted only by the host controller and only propagate in a downstream direction.

The four token packets are:

- OUT: The OUT token packet preceeds "data out from the host controller to a device". The OUT token packet defines a data transaction from the host controller to an endpoint of a device. The ADDR field identifies the device and the ENDP field identifies the out endpoint of the device involved in this transaction. See Chapter 8 *Data Transfer* for information about the data transfer established by this token packet.

- IN: The IN token packet precedes "data into the host controller from a device". The IN token packet defines a data transaction from an endpoint of a device to the host controller. The ADDR field identifies the device and the ENDP field identifies the in endpoint of the device involved in this transaction. See Chapter 8 for more complete information about the data transfer established by this token packet.

- SETUP: The SETUP token packet is similar to an OUT token packet except that it always refers to a bi-directional endpoint of a device and also indicates a specific format for the subsequent data phase (see Chapter 11 *Device Framework*). The subsequent data phase is always from the host controller to an endpoint of a device. The ADDR field identifies the device and the ENDP field identifies the bi-directional endpoint within the device involved in the transaction. See Chapter 8 *Data Transfers* for information about the data transfer established by this token packet.

- SOF: The SOF token packet defines the "start of frame". The SOF token packet is different in several ways from the other token packets. First, it is only supported by hubs and full speed devices; low speed devices will never receive an SOF packet. Second, it is a single packet transaction that is not addressed to a particular endpoint. Third, there are no other packets as part of this transaction and no devices will respond during this transaction. See Chapter 7 *Frames* for more information.

6.2.3 Data Packets

Data packets are used to carry device-specific data between system memory and a device's endpoint as part of a bus transaction. There are two data packet types: DATA0 and DATA1. Data packets have two fields in the packet body: DATA and CRC. Table 6.3 summarizes the packet body fields of the two data packet types.

All data packets contain a 16 bit CRC field covering the data field, *i.e.*, the CRC does not include the SYNC, PID, and IPID portions of the packet. See Section 6.7 for more information about the CRC formulas.

The DATA field of the data packet carries the device-specific data of a USB bus transaction. The field can be varied in length according to device specifics or data transfer type definition constraints. See Chapter 8 *Data Transfer* for more information about limits on the DATA field length.

DATA PACKET PID	INFORMATION	
	PID FIELDS	PACKET BODY FIELDS LSb ... MSb
DATA0	8 bits PID/IPID	0-1023 bytes 16 bits DATA CRC
DATA1	8 bits PID/IPID	0-1023 bytes 16 bits DATA CRC

Table 6.3: Data Packet Types

Data Packet Meanings

There are two data packet types:

- DATA0: The DATA0 data packet (also known as the even data packet) is the first, third, fifth, seventh, etc. data packet to be transmitted for sequential transactions.

- DATA1: The DATA1 data packet (also known as the odd data packet) is the second, fourth, sixth, etc. data packet to be transmitted for sequential transactions.

See Section 6.6 for more information.

6.2.4 Handshake Packets

Handshake packets are used to return flow control information for a bus transaction. The receiver of a data packet can use a handshake packet sent to the transmitter to indicate its ability to send or receive data. There are three handshake packet types: ACK, NAK, and STALL. A handshake packet contains only the PID field and does not contain a packet body. Table 6.4 summarizes the PID fields of the three handshake packet types.

Since all handshake packets contain only the SYNC and PID/IPD fields; there is no CRC field in a handshake packet. The inverted PID provides error detection for the PID. The CRC was not included to save bandwidth on the bus.

HANDSHAKE PACKET PID	INFORMATION
	PID FIELDS LSb ... MSb
ACK	8 bits PID/IPID
NAK	8 bits PID/IPID
STALL	8 bits PID/IPID

Table 6.4: Handshake Packet Types

Handshake Packet Meanings

There are three handshake packet types:

- ACK: The ACK (acknowledged) handshake packet is transmitted when a data packet has been successfully received. The host controller transmits the ACK handshake packet to a downstream device when it has successfully received an upstream data packet. A device transmits the ACK handshake packet to the host controller when it has successfully received a downstream data packet. A successful reception of a data packet is defined as data packet received without errors in the PID/IPID, no bit stuffing protocol mistakes, and no CRC miss-compares. Some bus transfers do not allow ACK handshake packets as part of their bus transactions. Even though a data packet is transmitted and successfully received, no acknowledgment is provided. See Chapter 8 *Data Transfer* for more information.

- NAK: The NAK (not acknowledged) handshake packet is transmitted when the downstream device is not able to transmit or receive a data packet. By definition, the host controller can always receive or transmit a data packet; otherwise, the host controller would not have transmitted the token packet. Consequently, the NAK handshake packet can only be transmitted upstream by the downstream device and only received by the host controller.

  After the host controller transmits a data packet associated with an OUT token packet, the downstream device transmits a NAK handshake packet if the device cannot receive the data packet, *e.g.*, the device is not ready or the endpoint buffer is full. Also, after the host controller transmits an IN token packet, the device transmits a NAK handshake packet if the device is not ready to transmit the data packet. Some bus transactions do not allow NAK handshake packets as part of the bus transaction. See Chapter 8 *Data Transfer* for more information.

- STALL: The STALL handshake packet is transmitted upstream when the addressed endpoint is experiencing an error condition and requires intervention from the host to correct a problem before communication can be resumed. The STALL handshake packet can only be transmitted by a downstream device, and can be received only by the host controller. This is because the host can issue requests to handle the error conditions indicated by a STALL handshake. Devices are only polled by the host and have no ability to independently affect the status of the host.

The device transmits a STALL handshake packet after the host controller transmits a data packet associated with an OUT token packet if the device endpoint needs intervention by the host. In this case, the STALL handshake is transmitted even if the device receives a data packet with an error in the PID/IPID, a bit stuffing protocol mistake, or a CRC miss-compare. Also, the device transmits a STALL handshake packet after the host controller transmits an IN token packet if the endpoint needs intervention by the host. Some transfers do not allow STALL handshake packets as part of their bus transactions. See Chapter 8 *Data Transfer* for more information.

> The ACK handshake packet can only be transmitted by the host controller or device subsequent to receiving a successful data packet. A NAK or STALL handshake packet can only be transmitted by the device subsequent to receiving an IN token packet or a data packet associated with an OUT token packet.

6.2.5 Special Packet

The special packet has a very different usage than the other packet types. The only currently defined special packet is the PREAMBLE (PRE packet). The PRE packet contains only the PID/IPID field and does not contain a packet body, consequently, there is no CRC field. Table 6.5 summarizes the packet body fields of the only special packet type.

The inverted PID provides error detection for the PID. The CRC was not included to save bandwidth on the bus.

PRE Packet Meaning

When a low speed device is connected to a downstream port of a hub, that specific port is defined as a low speed port. The low speed port won't normally pass signaling downstream. This is to avoid full speed signaling moving across a low speed cable and causing uncontrolled EMI emissions.

The PRE packet is transmitted downstream from the host controller as a full speed packet to indicate to all downstream hubs that a low speed packet will be transmitted next. The hubs repeat the PRE packet through all full speed downstream ports in the enabled hub port state. The hub repeater will repeat the next packet to all enabled downstream hub ports (full and low speed).

The subsequent downstream packet will be a token, data, or handshake packet transmitted with low speed timing. The low speed downstream packet is transmitted through all enabled hub ports, both full speed and low speed ports. After the low speed packet is completed, the hub repeater will stop repeating signaling to enabled low speed ports until the next PRE packet. See Chapter 12 *Hub Devices* for more information.

SPECIAL PACKET PID	INFORMATION
	PACKET BODY FIELDS LSb ... MSb
PRE	8 bits PID/IPID

Table 6.5: Special Packet Types

6.3 TRANSACTIONS

A USB bus transaction is a sequence of packets that can accomplish the movement of one unit of data between system memory and a device. There are either one, two, or three phases in a transaction. The three possible phases are token, data, and handshake. Each phase of a transaction contains one or two packets. The data and handshake phases are optional based on the transfer type. Figure 6.3 outlines the phases for both full and low speed transactions. A full speed transaction consists of a single packet per phase. The protocol of a low speed transaction is slightly different. The low speed transaction begins with a PRE packet and a token packet as the first phase of the transaction. The second phase, if present, of the transaction is a PRE packet and a data packet if the direction is from host to device. If the direction is from device to host, the second phase is either a data or handshake packet. Finally, if a third phase is required by the transfer type, the third phase will be a PRE packet and a handshake if the host is performing the acknowledgement. If the device is performing the acknowledgement, the third phase consists of just a handshake packet. The PRE packets are only used for low speed transactions. The shaded packets of Figure 6.3 are the packets sent by the host. Unshaded packets are sent by a device.

Data is moved over the USB bus via a series of transactions distributed over a series of frames. It may take several bus transactions to move some volume of data between system memory and a device's endpoint. Consequently, the entire sequence of bus transactions to move a given volume of data will frequently take more than one frame period to complete.

As the host controller manages bus transactions on USB, it always keeps the packets of a bus transaction together in the same frame. A transaction is never split across a frame. The USB specification places strict limits on the maximum time allowed between the packets composing a bus transaction. That timeout limit does not allow a transaction to be split across a frame boundary.

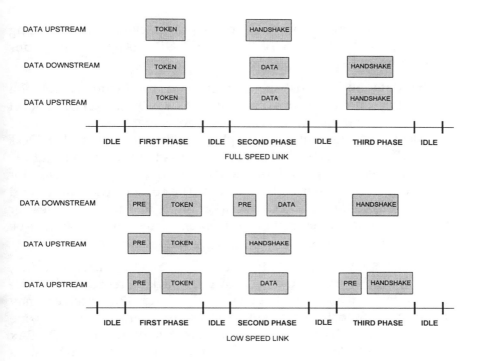

Figure 6.3: The Different Phases of a Transaction

The packets composing a bus transaction are also not allowed to be interspersed with packets for another bus transaction. All packets of a given transaction are sequential, *e.g.*, the token packet is followed by the data packet which is followed by the handshake packet.

> **All of the packets of a transaction are contiguous (no intervening packets not part of this transaction) and must be completed in a single frame.**

A transaction is always initiated by the host controller with an IN, OUT, or SETUP packet (preceded by a PRE packet if this is a low speed transaction) or an SOF packet. A device never transmits a token packet, *e.g.*, an IN, OUT, SETUP, PRE or SOF packet. The IN, OUT, or SETUP packet identifies the device and endpoint that will be involved in a bus transaction. Devices only transmit a packet at the appropriate phase for the bus transaction in which they are involved. A device never transmits a packet without being stimulated to do so via an IN, OUT or SETUP packet initiating a bus transaction.

The data and handshake phases of a transaction involve a transmitter and receiver. The initial IN, OUT or SETUP packet establishes the transmitter and receiver roles that the host controller and device will play in the data phase of the transaction. For OUT or SETUP transactions, the host controller is the transmitter and the device is a receiver. For IN transactions, the device is the transmitter and the host controller is the receiver. The roles of transmitter and receiver of the data packet are important in that they allow easier and more uniform description of USB error mechanisms as will be discussed later in this chapter.

As discussed previously, for an OUT or SETUP transaction (*i.e.*, one initiated with an OUT or SETUP packet, respectively), the transmitter transmits a DATAx packet and the receiver may transmit a handshake packet. For an IN transaction (*i.e.*, one initiated with an IN packet), the transmitter may transmit a DATAx packet or handshake packet while the receiver may transmit a handshake packet. The receiver never transmits a handshake without a DATAx packet having first been transmitted.

> A transmitter of the data packet for a bus transaction can both transmit and receive packets on the bus as part of the transaction. A receiver of the data packet for a transaction can both receive and transmit packets on the bus as part of the transaction. Don't confuse whether the host controller or device transmits the data packet in a transaction with their ability to also transmit and receive packets as part of the transaction.

See Chapter 8 *Data Transfers* for a more in-depth discussion of how transactions are used for different data transfers.

6.4 Changing Packet Transmission Speed

As described in the previous section, all of the packets are transmitted at full speed unless the Preamble (PRE) packet is used. The instantaneous signaling transmission rate of a full speed packet is 12 Megabits per second. The instantaneous signaling transmission rate of a low speed packet is 1.5 Megabits per second. All downstream full speed packets are repeated by a hub through all enabled full speed ports. A low speed packet can only be transmitted downstream after a PRE packet has been transmitted downstream. The downstream transmission of the PRE packet tells all hub repeaters to repeat the signaling for the subsequent packet to all enabled low speed downstream ports in addition to all enabled full speed downstream ports. An upstream low speed packet begins at a device and propagates upstream through the enabled low speed downstream port to which it is attached. The low speed packet continues upstream through enabled full speed downstream ports of the other hubs.

As outlined in the previous section, the PRE packet only allows one downstream low speed packet to be transmitted. Each additional low speed packet first requires the transmission of a PRE packet downstream. The protocol is as follows:

- The downstream transmission of the PRE packet only allows the subsequent transmission of a single downstream packet at low speed.

  - If the packet after that downstream packet is another low speed downstream packet (data or handshake), the PRE packet must be transmitted prior to that second downstream packet.

Hubs are required to switch between repeating full speed packets to repeating low speed packets as shown in Figure. 6.4:

- After completion of the last bit of a full speed PRE packet, each hub executes the following:

  - The hub switches to low speed timing on its enabled full speed downstream ports.

    - The hub must switch to low speed timing within four full speed bit periods and place the low speed J state idle binary pattern on the downstream port (Transition Full Speed to Low Speed in Figure 6.4).

  - After the completion of the last bit period of a low speed packet, the hub switches to full speed timing within four full

169

speed bit periods, and places the full speed J state idle binary pattern on the downstream port (Transition Low Speed to Full Speed in Figure 6.4).

- The hub repeater is required to begin and end repeating low speed signaling to the enabled low speed downstream ports within the transition periods stated above.

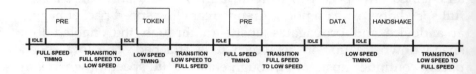

Figure 6.4: Hub Speed Switching Protocol

> Since there is no PRE packet that precedes an upstream packet, hubs must support both full and low speed timings for upstream packet transmission. The hub port identifies whether low speed timing is used.

All packets, except the SOF and PRE packets, can be transmitted at either low or full speed. SOF and PRE packets are only transmitted at full speed.

6.5 Low Speed Keep Alive

Low speed devices can't receive SOF packets. Since a low speed device may not be involved in bus transactions frequently, it may incorrectly enter a power management suspend state after 3 milliseconds have elapsed with no bus activity (*i.e.*, the suspended link state). Therefore, USB defines that each hub will toggle the D+ and D- signal lines for its enabled low speed ports every frame (*i.e.*, every 1 millisecond) to keep low speed devices alive. A hub only generates keep alives when it receives SOF's. Otherwise, low speed devices would stay awake after the host had suspended the bus. This ensures that there is bus activity every frame on low speed links. This prevents a low speed device from incorrectly entering a suspended state. See Chapter 12 *Hub Devices* for more information.

> Toggling of the D+ and D- signal lines (keep-alive toggling) is defined as two low speed bit periods of SE0 followed by at least 0.5 low speed bit period of a J binary pattern. Low speed toggling tracks the SOF token packet and EOF2.

Other attributes of the low speed keep alive are:

- The low speed keep alive must not start before the EOF2 event of the hub's frame timer. The SE0 portion of the keep alive toggling must be completed before the EOP of the subsequent SOF token packet (assuming the subsequent SOF is received 1 millisecond after the last SOF).

- No more than three low speed keep alives can be generated after the hub receives its last SOF token packet. Once the hub detects an SOF token packet reception, the keep alive toggling must begin within one frame period.

6.6 Data Toggle Synchronization

The ACK handshake packet is transmitted to acknowledge error-free reception of a data packet. If the ACK handshake packet is not received error-free or is not received at all (missing according to the timeout protocol), the transmitter of the associated data packet cannot be assured of the successful transmission and reception of the data packet. The data packet transmitter faces an ambiguous situation: Did the data packet arrive error-free and the subsequent data packet should consist of new data or was the data packet not received and the subsequent data packet should consist of a retry of the old data? USB defines a mechanism called data toggle to address this ambiguous situation.

> The data toggle protocol is not used for all transactions of all the different transfer types. The behavior of the USB system when data toggling does not apply will be discussed in a later section of this chapter.

When a data transfer starts, the transmitter and receiver each have a data toggle bit that is initialized to a starting value dependent on the transfer type. See Chapters 8 and 11 for information about how a data transfer is started.

The transmitter of the data packet uses a DATA0 data packet PID for a data phase when the data toggle bit is zero (0) and a DATA1 data packet PID for a data phase when the data toggle bit is one (1). Whenever the transmitter does not receive an error-free ACK handshake, the transmitter changes the logical value of the data toggle bit. If the transmitter does not receive an ACK handshake packet, the data toggle bit value is not changed and the transmitter re-transmits the data packet at its next opportunity. The re-transmission of the data packet is done by retrying the whole bus transaction.

The next opportunity to retry the bus transaction may or may not be immediately following the current bus transaction. Retries can occur several times in one frame or not for a number of frames. The timing of the retry depends on the particular transfer type and what other bus transactions are awaiting transmission. See Chapter 8 for more information on transfer types.

When the receiver of the data packet receives an error-free data packet, it compares the PID to the data toggle bit. If the data toggle bit is zero (0) and the PID is DATA0 or the data toggle bit is one (1) and the PID is DATA1, the receiver accepts the data in the packet, changes its data toggle bit value, and transmits an ACK handshake packet. If the data toggle bit and PID don't "match", the receiver

(1) discards the data in the packet,

(2) does not change the value of its data toggle bit, and

(3) transmits an ACK handshake packet.

The above protocol assumes that only one data-sequence-related error occurs at a time. Consequently, the data toggle bit allows the receiver to distinguish between a retried data packet versus a new data packet. When the ACK handshake packet is not correctly received but the associated data packet had been received error-free, the data packet transmitter re-transmits the data packet with the current unchanged value of the data toggle bit. The receiver recognizes a mismatch in the PID of the data packet and its data toggle bit. Consequently, the receiver identifies the new data packet as a re-transmission and discards the data. It transmits an ACK handshake to indicate successful reception. The receiver does not change its data toggle bit, which will now match the transmitter's data toggle bit when the transmitter successfully receives the ACK packet.

If a NAK or STALL handshake were being transmitted, it wouldn't matter that the handshake was not correctly received, since the transmitter that is awaiting the handshake packet will retransmit the data packet anyway.

6.7 CRC Protocol

The cyclic redundancy check (CRC) protocol is used to protect the non-PID portions of token and data packets. This protection addresses all single- and double-bit errors. There are two different generating polynomials used as follows:

- For token packets, the generating polynomial is $G(X) = X^5 + X^2 + 1$

  - This is represented by "01100" (generator polynomial). Error-free reception of information and CRC results in a 5 bit residue of "01100"

- For data packets, the generating polynomial is $G(X) = X^{16} + X^{15} + X^2 + 1$

  - This is represented by "1000000000000101" (generator polynomial). Error-free reception of information and CRC results in a 16 bit residue of "1000000000001101"

Shift registers can be implemented for the CRC generator and checkers. These are seeded with an all "1"s binary pattern. Each bit that is to be transmitted or received is XORed with the most significant bit of the shift register. The resulting pattern is "left shifted" (toward most significant bit) and a binary "0" is inserted into the least significant bit to provide a "remainder" to be used with the next bit to be transmitted or received. If the result of the

XOR operation was logical "1", the "remainder" is also XORed with the generator polynomial to create a new "remainder" to be used with the next bit to be transmitted or received.

After all of the bits to be sent have been processed through the CRC protocol outlined above, the remainder is inverted and transmitted (most significant bit first). The receiver applies the bits of the inverted remainder that was transmitted to the CRC shift registers as outlined above. The resulting remainder will equal the residue value listed above when it is received error-free.

> The CRC is calculated at the transmitter before bit stuffing is added according to the NRZI protocol. At the receiver, the bit stuffing is first removed and then the CRC is calculated. Also, bit stuffing is applied to the CRC bits but are not part of the CRC calculation.

> USB requires *all* transmitters to generate valid CRCs for the packets they transmit. Receivers, however, are not required to check the CRC.

6.8 Packet and Transaction Robustness

The USB bus protocol provides detection mechanisms to help ensure successful transfers. These detection mechanisms cover four categories:

- Signaling Errors
- Packet Errors
- Transaction Protocol Errors
- Transfer Errors:

Each error category and detection mechanism is discussed in the subsequent sections.

The effect of these errors is that any packet can be damaged or changed on the bus between the transmitter and receiver. The detection mechanisms attempt to identify the occurrence of one or more of these errors and respond in a way that avoids or minimizes the chance of treating erroneous packets as good packets. These responses may result in retries or in the host controller reporting errors to the host system software.

The basic error response concept varies according to the packet type. If a token packet is missing or received with an error, the token packet is ignored, and the following packets are ignored until the next token packet is correctly received, *i.e.*, the bus transaction never starts. If a data packet is missing or received with error, the data is discarded, and the data packet may or may not be re-transmitted. If a handshake packet is missing or received with error, the host controller may or may not retry the bus transaction. Each of these cases will be described in detail in the following sections.

> Retrying a data packet requires a retry of the complete transaction with token, data, and handshake (when applicable) phases.

6.8.1 Signaling Errors

Signaling errors are due to incorrect transition patterns of the D+ and D- signal lines. A receiver that detects a signaling error will ignore the packet. The occurrence of a signaling error results in the packet being defined as "received with error", and the packet is ignored. This is the most basic level at which an error can be detected in USB. A signaling error prevents the SIE from:

- Determining the correctness of the synchronization pattern, PID, and IPID.
- Decoding a packet PID to determine what packet was transmitted
- Interpreting the ADDR and ENDP or FRAME fields of a token packet body
- Continuing to accept data from the data payload portion of a packet body
- Checking the CRC residual for a CRC protected packet body field or fields

The detectable signaling errors are: NRZI Encoding and Bit Stuffing Violations and Babble.

NRZI Encoding and Bit Stuffing Violations

The transmitted encoding of the signal lines integrates timing information by implementing the non return to zero inverted (NRZI) protocol. This protocol allows the phase lock loop of the receiver to maintain correct bit period timing for decoding the binary pattern. The receiver is able to detect an NRZI encoding violation when the correct synchronization pattern is known, PID and inverted PID do not agree, or the CRC checking of the information reveals an error that cannot be recovered. Associated with the NRZI protocol is the requirement to implement bit stuffing. A bit stuffing error occurs when more than 6 consecutive "1" bits are received.

If the received packet has an NRZI encoding or bit stuffing violation, no reliable recovery of the current packet is possible and the error continues until an EOP is detected.

Babble

A packet cannot be considered fully or correctly received if the EOP is not received prior to the end of the frame period. This condition is called babble. See Chapter 12 *Hub Devices* for more information.

6.8.2 Packet Errors

A packet error occurs when the packet is not correctly received, but no signaling error was detected. A receiver that detects a packet error will ignore the packet.

> In some cases, a signaling error may appear as a packet error and vice versa. The result is the same; the packet is ignored.

There are three packet error types: Incorrect Packet Type, CRC Failure, and Packet Length Error.

Incorrect Packet Type

A PID/IPID mismatch error occurs either when the inverse of the PID on a bit by bit basis does not equal the IPID, or when an invalid PID is decoded.

CRC Failure

An address CRC (cyclic redundancy check) or data CRC error is identified by an incorrect residue from a CRC operation on the associated address and data.

Packet Length Error

Packet length errors occur when the packet length is below the allowed minimum length, or the maximum length of a packet is exceeded. If the maximum length of a packet is exceeded, any additional bits/bytes before the EOP are ignored and an indication is made internally that a packet error has occurred.

6.8.3 Transaction Protocol Errors

A transaction protocol error occurs when no signaling or packet errors have been detected, but an illegal or out-of-sequence packet has been detected. A transaction protocol error also results when a required packet is missing. A receiver that detects a transaction protocol error simply ignores the packet and all subsequent packets until a token packet is correctly received.

The transaction protocol errors are Incorrect Packet in Transaction Phase and Time-out Violation.

Incorrect Packet in Transaction Phase

A packet is incorrect when the wrong PID for the current transaction phase is received. For example, a handshake PID is received after an OUT PID when a DATA0/DATA1 PID should have been received. Also, a token PID should never be received by the host controller at any time.

Time-out Violation

USB has strict definitions on the maximum time allowed between packets. These time-out limits are discussed in Chapter 5 *Signaling*. A receiver waiting for the next packet of a transaction detects that the packet won't be recognized or received when the maximum time-out limit expires without receiving an SOP. If the start of the next packet of the transaction is not detected before the time-out limit, the receiver abandons the current bus transaction and returns to waiting for a token packet for the next bus transaction. Note that this next bus transaction may or may not be for the receiver, *i.e.*, a re-transmission.

If the receiver is the host controller, it will advance to initiate the next bus transaction as determined by its transaction schedule. If the receiver is a device, it simply waits for the correct reception of a next token packet to signal the beginning of the next bus transaction.

In general, the host controller can be a receiver for a data packet or a handshake packet for an IN transaction, or a handshake packet (returned by a device after the host controller sends a DATA packet) for an OUT or SETUP transaction. A device can be a receiver for a DATA packet for an OUT or SETUP transaction or a handshake packet for an IN transaction.

> The reception of a packet with a DATA0 PID instead of a DATA1 PID (or vice versa) is not a transaction protocol error. See the Transfer Errors and Data Toggle sections for more information.

6.8.4 Transfer Errors

A transfer error occurs when a transaction is retried more than three consecutive times by the host controller. Each retried transaction is due to a condition that prevents the completion of the transaction and consequently prevents the host controller from progressing to the next transaction for the transfer.

> The host controller will report an error condition to the client software after it tries a given bus transaction three consecutive times and each time receives an error. Note that other bus transactions can be attempted in between retries of a given bus transaction. It is possible that some bus transactions may not be retried for several milliseconds (frames) based on the transfer type used. See Chapter 8 *Data Transfer* for more information.

There are four errors that can lead to a transfer error: Incorrect Reception of Packet, STALL Handshake, Incorrect Transaction Type, and Data Toggle Violation.

Incorrect Reception of Packet

The signaling, packet, and transaction protocol errors previously described comprise an incorrect reception of a packet.

STALL Handshake

The transmission of a STALL handshake packet indicates that the data phase of a transaction cannot be completed due to a device problem.

Incorrect Transaction Type

A transaction is incorrect when it is the wrong form of a transaction within a transfer; *e.g.*, a three phase transaction where only two phase transactions are allowed or vice versa. See Chapter 8 for more information.

Data Toggle Violation

Data toggling to track the sequence of data packets transmitted for a specific transfer. Data toggling is discussed in detail in Section 6.6.

Data toggle retry for one transaction is not detectable until the next transaction. The transmitter must retain the old data until the next transaction to be able to retransmit the old data.

6.9 Error Possibilities

This section presents the error possibilities that can occur on USB due to the above-described errors. Each failure is described along with the response that can be taken to recover from the failure.

6.9.1 Token Packet Errors

- If a token packet decodes with a valid PID, but the EOP is not detected at the end of 24 bit periods (after bit stuffing is removed) after the SYNC field, the packet is incorrect. See later items.

- If a token packet PID field does not equal the complement of the IPID field, the packet is incorrect. See later items.

- If the CRC for a token packet doesn't compare appropriately with the CRC5 field, the packet is incorrect. See later items.

- If a bit stuff violation is detected during a packet reception, the packet is incorrect. See later items.

- If a token packet is not received correctly by a device, the device continues waiting until a token packet is successfully received. These packets may not be received correctly due to PID/IPID mismatch, CRC5 miss-compare, incorrect bit length (too short or too long), bit stuffing violation, and no EOP. An interpacket time-out (for IN, OUT, and SETUP after a PRE packet) can also cause a packet error.

- If an SOF token is not received correctly by a device with an isochronous endpoint, the device's internal SOF timer will indicate when an SOF should have occurred and the device will use that event to "simulate" the reception of an SOF. If the device is tracking frame numbers, it will also advance its frame count.

- If an IN token is not received correctly by a device, the host controller will detect a time-out violation when the device does not respond with a DATAx or handshake packet within the time-out limit. The host controller will record an occurrence of an error for that bus transaction and advance to the next bus transaction. The bus transaction that had the error recorded may be retried at a later time subject to the retry policy.

- If an OUT or SETUP token is not received correctly by a device, the host will continue and transmit the DATAx packet since it has no way to know that the device is not receiving. If the bus transaction includes a handshake phase, when the device does not respond with a handshake packet, the host controller will record an occurrence of an error for that bus transaction and advance to the next bus transaction. The bus transaction that had the error recorded may be retried at a later time subject to the retry policy. If the bus transaction does not include a handshake phase, the host controller has no way of determining that an error has occurred and simply assumes that one hasn't.

- If a PRE packet decodes with a valid PID, but the EOP is not detected at the end of 8 bit periods (after bit stuffing is removed) after the SYNC field, the packet is incorrect.

- If a PRE packet is not received correctly by a hub, the hub will not enable the downstream low speed ports, and the low speed devices will not subsequently receive a token packet. This will cause the bus transaction to time-out as described above since the low speed device will not participate in the transaction due to missing the IN, OUT or SETUP packet.

6.9.2 Data Packet Errors

- If the CRC for a DATAx packet doesn't compare appropriately with the CRC16 field, the packet is incorrect.

- If a DATAx packet is not received correctly by a receiver and there is a handshake phase for the bus transaction, the receiver will ignore the data packet and not transmit a handshake packet. The host controller may retry the bus transaction at a future time subject to the retry policy.

- If a DATAx packet is not received correctly by a receiver and there is not a handshake phase for the bus transaction, the receiver may ignore the data packet and not transmit a handshake packet. The host controller will not retry the bus transaction.

- If a DATA0 packet is received during a data phase when a DATA1 is expected (or vice versa) for a bus transaction that is employing data toggle, the receiver simply ignores the data, and, if there is a handshake phase, the receiver responds with an ACK packet during the handshake phase (*i.e.*, this is a retry from the transmitter).

6.9.3 Handshake Packet Errors

- If a handshake packet decodes with a valid PID, but the EOP is not detected at the end of 8 bit periods (after bit stuffing is removed) from after the SYNC field, the packet is incorrect.

- If there is a handshake phase for the bus transaction and a handshake packet is not received correctly by a transmitter, the transmitter can record an error for the transaction and may retry the data packet at an appropriate time subject to the retry policy. If data toggling of DATAx PIDs is being employed for the bus transaction, the PID is not toggled.

- If there is no handshake phase for the bus transaction and a handshake packet is received by the transmitter, it is ignored.

If a DATAx packet is received during a data phase and the receiver has no space for the data and there is a handshake phase in the bus transaction, the receiver responds with a NAK handshake for flow control. If the host controller is the transmitter and the NAK is received correctly, the host controller does not record an error for this bus transaction.

7. Frames

Transactions sent via the USB Bus are organized into intervals called frames. The beginning of a frame is identified by a start of frame (SOF) token packet. The beginning of the next frame marks the end of the previous frame. Transactions (*i.e.*, a sequence of token, data, and handshake packets described in detail in Chapter 6 *Packets and Transactions*) are never split across frames. Transfers that are composed of multiple transactions can span frames. Their transfer type definition and data movement requirements determine how many frames they span. Most devices don't need to be concerned with the existence of frames. Only devices that require isochronous endpoints are sensitive to the details of frames.

SOF token packets are sent at a nearly constant rate. Frames (via the SOF token packets) provide a bus global reference clock that is useful for isochronous data delivery. Isochronous endpoints can use the timing of frames to determine when they should latch data to be moved to or from the bus during the next frame time. The SOF token packet provides a common clock that all interested USB devices and endpoints can rely upon. Isochronous endpoints typically have a local clock for the purpose of producing and consuming their particular data. The SOF token packets can be used to synchronize this local clock to the bus transfer clock.

USB makes it easier for different vendors of isochronous devices to interoperate by providing a global bus clock, *i.e.*, the SOF transactions create this global bus clock. Each device can relate its local clock to the clock determined by the SOF token packets and therefore be collectively synchronized. See Chapter 9 *Isochronous Communication Model* for more detailed information about isochronous devices.

The precise timing of the rate of SOF token packets can be adjusted. This adjustment allows a host controller to correct for several sources of clock variation.

7.1 Start of Frame (SOF)

SOF token packets are broadcast to all full speed devices on the bus. Every full speed device receives the SOF token packet at the same time, within propagation time delays.

SOF tokens are transmitted only at full speed. Low speed devices will never receive an SOF token packet. Each SOF token packet also carries an eleven (11) bit field that contains the current frame number. See Chapter 6 for more detailed information about the SOF token packet.

The frame number is incremented for each frame, until the value rolls over due to the fixed length of the field; *e.g.*, a partial frame sequence is numbered: ..., 2046, 2047, 0, 1, 2, ... The frame number provides a relative time value. In general, devices don't depend on specific frame numbers and can ignore the frame number field.

7.2 Frame Timing

Each frame is 1.000 millisecond in length. The period is measured from the start of the SOF PID in one frame to the same point in the next frame. A frame is theoretically long enough to allow transmission of approximately 1500 full speed raw bytes (*i.e.*, 12,000 full speed raw bits), if all the bus time was used purely for data. Due to the protocol overhead of each transfer type and the variable overhead due to bit stuffing, the exact amount of actual data transmitted will always be less than that theoretically possible.

7.3 Requirements

SOF token packets are always transmitted on the bus at 1 ms intervals. The USB specification allows an overall full speed data rate tolerance of 2500 parts per million (ppm) in the frequency of SOF generation on the bus. This variation must take into account differences in the host, hubs, and full speed function(s). To meet this variation, the host controller's data rate must be accurate to 500 ppm. This variation allows readily available and reasonably accurate clock crystals to be used in a host controller implementation.

The host controller is required to generate SOF token packets unless the entire bus is suspended. A suspended bus has no bus activity and thus no SOF token packets.

The SOF generation rate can be adjusted and can optionally be controlled by one device driver at a time. This device driver is referred to as the master clock client.

7.3.1 Adjustments

The length of a frame is nominally 12,000 bits. The host controller allows the total length of a frame to be changed +/- 15 bits, *i.e.*, from 11,985 to 12,015 bits per frame.

The frequency of the SOF token packet generation is controlled by varying the exact length of a frame within this adjustment range of +/- 15 bits. Changes in the length of a frame must occur no faster than 1 bit adjustment every six (6) milliseconds (*i.e.*, 6 frames). This limitation in clock adjustment allows designers to build clock synchronization logic that can tolerate the allowed slew rate and still maintain an accurate local device clock.

7.4 Frame Integrity

The host controller is responsible for allocating transactions to frames to preserve frame integrity. In particular, the host controller must not allow a transaction to interfere with its ability to transmit an SOF at the required time. Hubs also play a very important role in ensuring that other devices don't transmit upstream on the bus near the end of a frame and prevent the host controller from generating the SOF token packet on time.

BABBLE on the bus occurs when a device fails to generate an end of packet (EOP) when it should. No transmitter is allowed to corrupt frame timing. The host controller and hubs have independent, but synchronized, frame timers that allow detection and preservation of frame timing.

A host controller is required to avoid transmission too close to the end of a frame such that babble would otherwise occur.

> Host controllers are assumed to never babble. Hubs are responsible to prevent devices from babbling.

Hubs are required to use their frame timers to detect a device transmitting too close to the end of a frame. When such a device is detected, the hub will isolate the device from the bus to allow the host controller to generate the SOF token packet on time. See Chapter 12 *Hub Devices* for more detailed information about hubs.

8. Data Transfers

8.1 Introduction

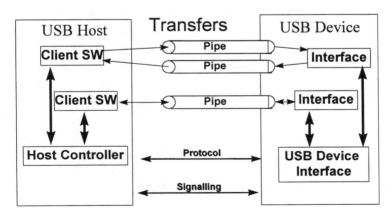

Figure 8.1: Communication via Transfers over Pipes

This chapter describes the transfer layer of USB communications between the USB host and a device. Figure 8.1 shows how pipes connect Client software on the host with interfaces on a device. The transfer layer is supported by the signaling and protocol layers below it. Previous chapters have described these lower layers. This chapter places particular emphasis on the definitions and constraints of USB transfer types. There are four different USB defined transfer types: Bulk, Interrupt, Isochronous, and Control Before each transfer type is presented in turn, some general information affecting all transfer types is described.

> In this chapter, the word "hub" will represent "hub(s)" (upstream port and N downstream hub ports with no embedded functions) and "compound package(s)" (upstream port and N downstream hub ports with embedded functions). Also, in this chapter, the word "device" will represent "hub(s)" (upstream port and N downstream hub ports with no embedded functions), compound package(s) (upstream port and N downstream hub ports with embedded functions), composite device(s) (embedded functions with no downstream hub ports), and devices (upstream device port with no downstream USB ports).

8.2 Host and Device Communications

Devices communicate with the host using their physical connection. This physical connection is made via one or more intervening connections between hubs and devices (via links) and through hubs (via hub repeaters). The physical signaling that allows communication is not symmetric. Signaling that proceeds from host to device (DOWNSTREAM signaling) is repeated by each intervening hub to all of the hub's downstream ports in the enabled hub port state. Signaling that proceeds from device to host (UPSTREAM signaling), is only repeated by the intervening hubs toward the host, *i.e.*, only the hubs on the path between the device and the host will detect any upstream signaling. This asymmetry affects the definitions of the transfer types supported by USB and places some important limitations on the functionality of devices (including hubs).

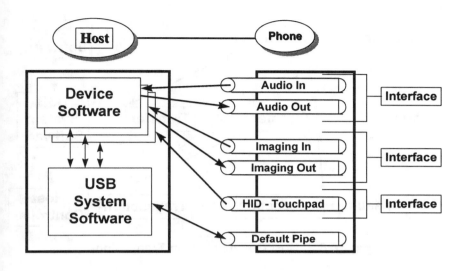

Figure 8.2: Grouping Pipes into Interfaces

The point to point logical attachment of a device to the host dictates that only the device addressed in a communication will respond to or participate in a data transfer. Further, since devices are composed of endpoints, only the addressed endpoint of the device is involved in the communication. Other endpoints of the device are not perturbed. Each device and its endpoints are independent of any other device and endpoint.

Transfers describe the communications occurring over a single pipe. Each pipe is dealt with independently of any other pipe. The information that flows between the host and a device's endpoint is completely independent of any other device or endpoint. Pipes are normally collected together into interfaces to perform some meaningful function. Such an interface is bound to a specific host software entity referred to as CLIENT SOFTWARE. Client software can be an application, a device driver, or some other software. The organization of pipes and interfaces for an example phone is shown in Figure 8.2. This example phone shows the microphone and speaker audio communication in one interface, video conferencing (local and remote camera data) as a second interface, while the third interface carries the data for the touch pad of the phone.

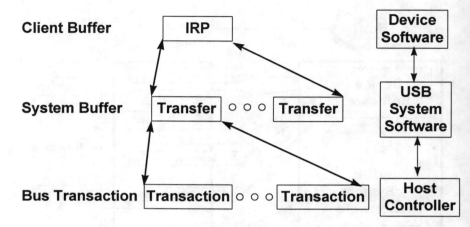

Figure 8.3: Host Communication Translations

The USB host is responsible for relating USB bus transactions to appropriate system memory buffers. Typically, the host controller and USB system software compiles several bus transactions into one or more data transfers. The data transfers move data into or out of one or more client buffers via an I/O request packet (**IRP**). The IRP is a request by client software to initiate a data transfer over USB between the host and some device.

> If the client software has data to be sent to a device, the data buffer referenced by the IRP contains the data to be transferred. If the client software wants to receive data from a device, the data buffer is empty.

Until an IRP is passed to system software, no communication can take place between a host and a device. This set of layered translations is shown in Figure 8.3.

The IRPs supplied by client software describe buffers that are meaningful to that software and device. For an audio application, this may be a buffer with enough space to hold 20 ms worth of data if the software performs its processing periodically at 20 ms intervals. USB doesn't dictate the sizes of these buffers. Specific client software indirectly determines how buffers are transformed into packets on USB by specifying the transfer type to be used for the communication and the size of a data unit (a **SAMPLE**). When an IRP is returned by USB system software to its requesting client software, the return status indicates the result of the transfer request.

USB system software uses one or more transfers to communicate the data associated with each IRP. The transfer size is determined by the transfer type requested, and implementation-specific details of the system software and USB host controller. For example, if a buffer spans physical memory pages with discontiguous addresses, a transfer may need to be split into several hardware interactions. The transfer status is similarly converted into an IRP status when the system software completely handles the IRP. If for example, a particular transfer times out due to a communication failure, the entire IRP, including all of its associated transfers, times out and the IRP return status reflects that fact.

The host controller communicates the data of a transfer by translating the transfer into one or more USB transactions. This translation is done either by the host controller hardware or by USB system software or some combination. The host controller must obey the transfer type constraints of the request. These constraints include the number of transaction phases, details of transaction error and flow control, and requirements on how to associate multiple transactions together in a transfer.

8.3 General Transfer Information

All USB transfers are composed of one or more transactions on the bus. The transactions appearing on the bus for a transfer for one pipe can be intermingled with the transactions for a transfer for another pipe. However, the packets comprising a single transaction are never intermingled with that of another transaction.

The host controller determines the order in which transactions are delivered over the bus. The host controller has substantial freedom in how transactions of different transfers can be ordered on the bus. A device can't depend on a specific order of transactions on the bus for different pipes, for example, that transactions A and B on pipe 1 will be delivered before transaction C for pipe 2. However, a device can expect that transactions for a specific pipe's transfer will be sent on the bus in first-in first-out (FIFO) order. That is, it can expect transaction A to be delivered before transaction B for pipe 1. Errors can obviously cause some transactions to be received incorrectly or not at all. But the order of transactions between the host and a device's endpoint are preserved. The host controller will not reorder the transactions comprising a transfer for a single pipe.

The token packet of each transaction is broadcast to all devices connected to the bus. Every device's serial interface engine (SIE) is responsible for decoding a token packet when it is received and determining whether this transaction involves this device. The SIE can determine this because the token packet contains the device address, endpoint number, and direction for the transaction. If the requested device address, endpoint number, and direction match those of an endpoint on this device, then it will participate in the rest of this transaction. If the transaction is not for this device, or any of its end points, the device continues decoding packets until a transaction for this device is found. Once a token packet for this device is decoded, the SIE follows the bus protocol transitions as appropriate for this transaction. The allowed transactions are determined by the transfer type of the pipe.

The bus protocol transitions described above ensure that the transmitter and receiver involved in a transaction keep their bit clocks synchronized. This is critical to ensure that the half duplex bus can provide robust data transmission even in the face of errors. USB has many features that work to deliver data transmission robustness. See Chapter 6, *Packets and Transactions* for more details.

8.3.1 Retiring Transfers

Each transfer type specifies the constraints on the maximum DATA PAYLOAD size allowed for each transaction of the transfer. These constraints are specified either as a range of possible maximum sizes or a choice from a discrete set of possible maximum sizes. The data payload of a transaction consists of the bytes in the transaction data phase, not including the SYNC, PID, inverted PID, and CRC fields. See Chapter 6 for more information.

> Even though each pipe has a maximum data payload size, the transmitter of the data should only send meaningful data. A data payload should not normally be padded to be maximum size if there is less data to transmit.

The transfer type determines the events that trigger the completion of a transfer. When a transfer completes, it is **RETIRED**, *i.e.*, the host controller and its software driver will proceed to handle the next transfer for a pipe. Each transfer type specifies what mechanisms can be used to retry a transfer if an error occurs during the transfer communication.

One retirement mechanism is called **SHORT PACKET** retirement. A short packet is a transaction whose data payload is less than its allowed maximum size. Some transfer types expect that a sequence of transactions is used to support a single communication transfer. For example, a printer data transfer to print a single document may take many transactions. The document hasn't been successfully transferred until the last transaction. Then after that transaction, another print job may follow. USB provides the short packet retirement mechanism to allow the receiver (in this case, the printer) to determine the boundaries between transfers without having to use some other indication.

For short packet retirement, each transaction of the transfer sequence is required to have a data payload of the maximum size for the pipe. When a transaction data payload is less than the maximum size, the receiver of the transaction data phase can detect that event. Such a short packet event indicates that this transfer is now complete. When the host is the receiver, it will retire the current transfer for this pipe and advance to the next transfer for this pipe. When the host is a transmitter, the IRP requesting the transfer will explicitly cause the host controller to send a short packet, if required.

A transfer can also be retired when all of the data or space of an IRP has been exhausted.

8.3.2 Transfer Characteristics

Each transfer type is defined in terms of the following characteristics:

- Data transmission direction: Unidirectional or Bidirectional. Some pipes allow bidirectional data transfers. Most pipes only allow data to move in a single direction for a given configuration of the pipe.

> The data transmission direction should not be confused with the fact that a transaction can have packets in the different transaction phases moving in both "to-host" and "from-host" directions. Data transmission direction only refers to the direction of data movement for the data phase of the transaction.

- Speed: full and/or low speed. Some transfer types constrain the speeds allowed.

- Flow Control: supported or not. Some transfer types provide mechanisms for a receiver to indicate to the transmitter whether or not there was room in the receiver's FIFO. If there was not room, then the transmitter must retry the transaction at the next appropriate time. Each transfer type also provides the definition of the next appropriate time.

- Data Delivery: Guaranteed period, Best effort, and Good effort. Each transfer type defines the type of claim a pipe has on use of the bus. Different transfer types have different qualities of bus access. A guaranteed period ensures that a pipe can rely on the host controller periodically servicing pending transfers. Transfer types with a "best effort" or "good effort" scheduling value have no ensured claim on the bus. This characteristic is described further in each transfer type.

- Data Robustness: reliable delivery or not. Each transfer type defines the mechanisms to ensure reliable delivery of data through the pipe.

- Maximum data payload size(s).

- Data payload format. Some transfer types define a required format of the payload data.

The transfer types are presented in order of simplicity: bulk, interrupt, isochronous, and control. Bulk transfers can be used for devices such as printers or scanners that want to move a large amount of data in the most efficient way possible. Interrupt transfers are used by many devices, just as hardwired interrupts would be used in other buses such as PCI or ISA. Isochronous transfers are used by devices that want to take advantage of USB's improved PC support for transfer of data such as audio or video. Control transfers are supported by every device, especially for initialization and configuration purposes, but are the most complex to describe and understand.

8.4 Bulk Transfers

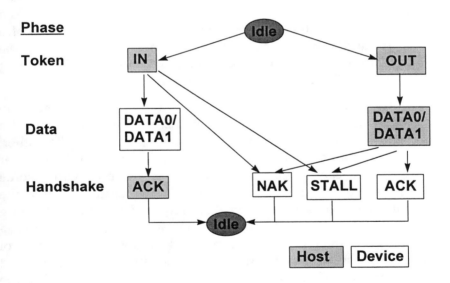

Figure 8.4: Transaction Phases and Packets for Bulk Transfers

> The drawings in the previous chapters focused only on a vertical time line. They were drawn to clearly show the packet sequencing for a transaction. In the USB bus specification and other portions of this book, a summary version of these drawings is used. Figure 8.4 is the summary version for Figures 8.5 to 8.10. The summary version indicates all possible connections between the token packet and the last packet of the transaction. In the summary version the term "IDLE" represents the link idle state between transactions. The summary version does not show the link idle state between packets in a transfer. Throughout the balance of this chapter, the summary version of the transactions will be shown followed by a series of more detailed figures of packet transmission.

Bulk transfers are best used when moving large amounts of data at irregular intervals. Bulk transfers require three phase transactions for data movement. Figure 8.4 summarizes the allowed transitions and packets from one phase to another within a bulk transaction. A bulk transaction is started with either an IN or OUT token phase. Note that if the transaction is for a low speed device, the token phase will consist of a PRE packet followed by an IN or OUT token packet. A successfully completed transaction further consists of a data and handshake phase. As discussed in Chapter 6, *Packets and Transactions*, the data phase uses alternate DATA0 and DATA1 packets to provide additional data reliability.

USB provides "good effort" at delivery of bulk data. There is no guaranteed rate provided for a bulk transfer. The transactions of a bulk transfer can occur back to back, one after the other. Transactions can also be spaced arbitrarily far apart in time. Other transfer types can be guaranteed access to the bus within some period, but bulk transfers have no such guarantee. After the guaranteed transfers have used their required bus time, pending control transfers are allowed up to 10% of the bus time (within a frame). Any remaining time can be used by both pending control and bulk transfers. If there are no guaranteed transfers present and no pending control transfers, bulk transfers can make use of all the available bus time.

It is possible to have a combination of devices configured on a USB bus that will prevent bulk transfers from being transferred on the bus, *i.e.*, bulk transfers can be "starved" from the bus. The implementation of an interface and its client software must be prepared to deal with this occurrence when it happens. For the printer example, printing can simply be delayed until enough data finally is sent to the printer. Other devices may require other approaches to preserve their desired end user behavior.

Bulk transfers can make use of reclaimed bus time. This reclaimed bus time is bus time that was budgeted to guaranteed transfers which didn't need the total time allotted to them. For example, allotted bandwidth can be unused when an endpoint has less than its maximum amount of data to transfer.

A series of transactions is used to accomplish a bulk transfer. Each transaction consists of either two phases to transmit token and handshake packets or three phases to transmit token, data, and handshake packets. The transactions are not pre-allocated USB bandwidth. Other features for the allowed bus transactions are:

- Support of the ACK handshake packet guarantees error-free delivery of the data packet.

- Retry of the transaction when the device is not ready to receive or transmit a data packet occurs when the NAK handshake packet is transmitted.

- Both the DATA0 and DATA1 data packets are used for transmission according to the data toggle protocol.

- Bulk transfers are only defined for full speed devices.

Figure 8.5 shows the transaction phases and packets required to transmit data upstream from the device to the host controller when the device was ready to transmit data. Figure 8.6 shows the transaction phases and packets required to transmit data downstream from the host controller to the device when the device was ready to receive data.

In the following figures, the term "HOST" refers to the host controller. The term "DEVICE" represents a hub, composite device, or device. The square boxes in the figures are the packets transmitted. The time line for the figures moves from left to right. The term "IDLE" in the figures represents the signal line idle link state between transmission of packets.

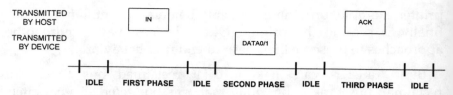

Figure 8.5: Upstream Data Packets for Transactions of a Bulk Transfer

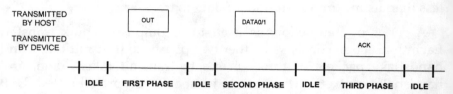

Figure 8.6: Downstream Data Packets for Transactions of a Bulk Transfer

Figure 8.7 shows the transaction phases and packets required to transmit data upstream from the device to the host controller when the device was not ready to transmit data. Figure 8.8 shows the transaction phases and packets required to transmit data downstream from the host controller to the device when the device was not ready to receive data.

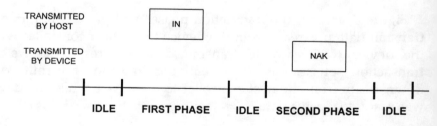

Figure 8.7: Upstream Data Packets for Transactions of a Bulk Transfer when Hub or Device not Ready for Data Transmission

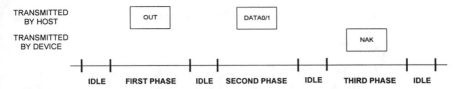

Figure 8.8: Downstream Data Packets for Transactions of a Bulk Transfer when Hub or Device not Ready for Data Reception

Figure 8.9 shows the transaction phases and packets required to transmit data upstream from the device to the host controller, and the device requires intervention by the host. Figure 8.10 shows the transaction phases and packets required to transmit data downstream from the host controller to the device when the device requires intervention by the host.

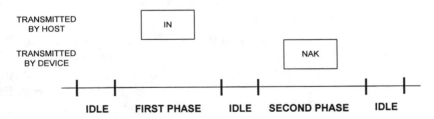

Figure 8.9: Upstream Data Packets for Transactions of a Bulk Transfer when Host Intervention is Required

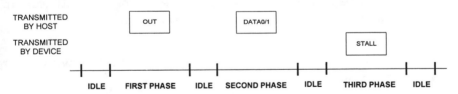

Figure 8.10: Downstream Data Packets for Transactions of a Bulk Transfer when Host Intervention is Required

In summary, the bulk transfer characteristics are:

- Data Transmission Direction: Unidirectional. A bulk pipe only supports data transfer in one direction for a given interface configuration.

- Speed: Full only. Bulk transfers are not allowed for low speed endpoints. The host USB system software responsible for configuration will not allow configuration of a low speed bulk endpoint.

- Flow Control: Supported. Bulk transfers allow NAK and STALL handshake responses during the handshake phase. NAK allows an endpoint to inform the host that there was no space or data available in the device's FIFO. A STALL handshake allows the device endpoint to inform the host that transactions will not succeed until some endpoint-specific action is taken to resolve the stall condition.

- Data Delivery: Good effort delivery

- Data Robustness: Robust delivery. The receiver responds with an ACK handshake when the CRC for the data phase checks. If an error occurred, the receiver doesn't reply with a handshake packet and the transaction will be retried at the next appropriate time.

- Maximum Data Payload Sizes: 8, 16, 32, or 64 bytes for full speed. Bulk transfers can only have the specified power of 2 maximum payload byte sizes. These sizes were selected to limit complexity in the bus transaction logic while providing reasonably efficient data transfer. As discussed above, a data payload that is less than a maximum size triggers short packet retirement.

- Data Payload Format: No USB defined data payload format. USB defines no required organization of the contents of the payload.

A bulk transfer is retired when any of the following four conditions exist:

- More than about five seconds of continuous NAKs are received by the transmitter (OS dependent).

- Three consecutive transaction timeouts (from errors) occur.

- The IRP's buffer becomes full (IN transfers) or empty (OUT transfers).

- A transaction data payload is less then the maximum packet size for the endpoint.

8.5 Interrupt Transfers

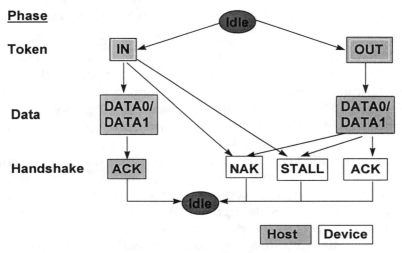

Figure 8.11: Transaction Phases and Packets for Interrupt Transfers

Figure 8.11 summarizes the allowed transitions and packets from one phase to another within an interrupt transaction. Interrupt transfers are only defined by USB Version 1.0 for carrying data from a device to the host, *i.e.*, an IN direction. USB Version 1.1 added definitions for carrying data from the host to a device, *i.e.*, an OUT direction. The interrupt transactions are the same as the bulk transaction phases.

Interrupt transfers are used to transfer small amounts of data at potentially irregular intervals. Other buses provide dedicated interrupt signals to indicate interrupt requests. Due to USB's half duplex, single logical wire bus, there are no dedicated signal wires available, and so normal bus transactions are used to make interrupt requests to the host. The interrupt transfer type has been optimized for this purpose.

Interrupt transfers provide a device with a regular opportunity to inform the host of events. Other buses typically require additional bus access before the host can determine the source of the interrupt and retrieve interrupt dependent information. USB allows an interrupt transfer to carry additional data along with the interrupt event. For example, a mouse device with a PS/2 connection typically requires three interrupts to deliver a position report (*e.g.*, x position, y position, and button state). A USB mouse can more efficiently deliver the position report in one interrupt transaction.

An interrupt endpoint specifies a period (in milliseconds) that determines how often the host controller initiates a transaction with the device endpoint. The host controller guarantees that it will initiate transactions no less than the specified rate. For example, if the specified period is 16, at least once every 16 frames the host controller will initiate an interrupt transaction on the pipe. Every 8, 10, or 13 frames is also allowed. However, every 17 (or greater) frames is not allowed. Obviously, a variety of errors can prevent the device from detecting, participating in, or completing the transaction. But the host controller manages its use of bus time to ensure that it has a regular opportunity to do a bus transaction with the device endpoint. Note that, as in the example, the host controller is free to initiate a transaction more frequently than requested. The host controller is allowed to vary the interval from period to period. The device is expected to behave appropriately when it experiences more frequent transactions.

> Typical operating systems chose a power of 2 ms less than or equal to the requested period for the interrupt period.

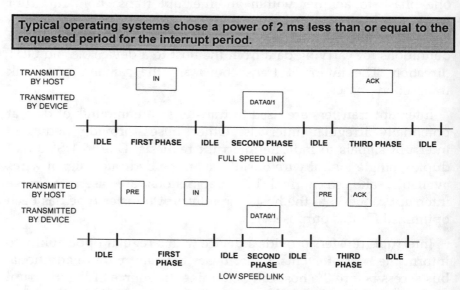

Figure 8.12: Packet Transmission for Transactions of an Interrupt IN Transfer with Interrupt Information

A device should not respond with a data phase unless it has meaningful data to supply to the host. If it has no data, it should respond with a NAK handshake packet instead of a data packet. This response allows the host to do the minimum required processing before proceeding with other transactions for other devices. When an endpoint responds with a data packet, the host controller always eventually generates an interrupt and awakens the appropriate client software. If the endpoint returns meaningless data simply to fill the data packet, significant extraneous processing is required for no purpose.

A series of transactions can be used to implement an interrupt transfer. Each transaction consists of either two phases to transmit token and handshake packets; or three phases to transmit token, data, and handshake packets. Other features for the allowed bus transactions are:

- Support of the ACK handshake packet guarantees error-free delivery of the data packet.

- Retry of the transaction when the device is not ready to transmit a data packet occurs when the NAK handshake packet is transmitted. A NAK handshake is also transmitted when the device has no interrupt pending. The device will be subsequently polled at its next interrupt period.

- Both DATA0 and DATA1 data packets are used for transmission.

- Interrupt transfers are defined for both full and low speed devices.

Figure 8.12 shows the transaction phases and packets required to transmit data upstream when the device has interrupt information. Figure 8.13 shows the transaction phases and packets required to transmit data upstream when the device does not have interrupt information. Figure 8.14 shows the transaction phases and packets required when the addressed device needs intervention by the host.

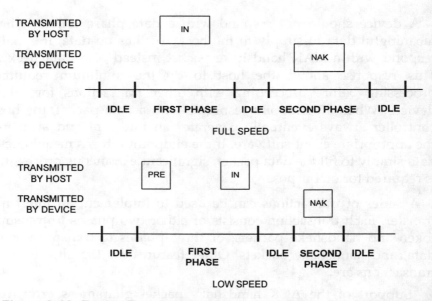

Figure 8.13: Packet Transmission for Transactions of an Interrupt IN Transfer with no Interrupt Information

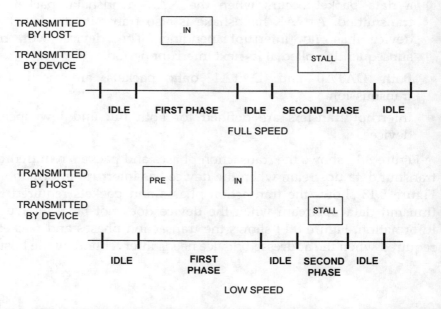

Figure 8.14: Packet Transmission for Transactions of an Interrupt IN Transfer when Host Intervention is Required

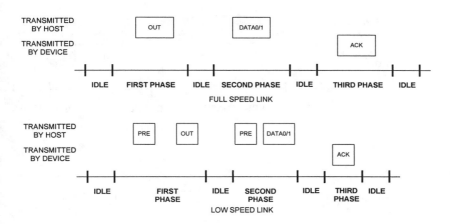

Figure 8.15: Packet Transmission for Interrupt OUT Transfer with Interrupt Information

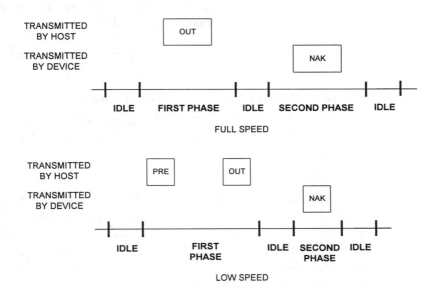

Figure 8.16: Packet Transmission for Interrupt OUT Transfer with No Interrupt Information

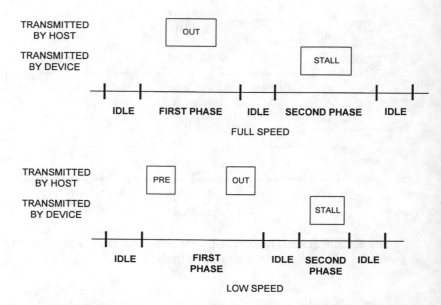

Figure 8.17: Packet Transmission for Interrupt OUT Transfer when Host Intervention is Required

Figures 8.15, 8.16, and 8.17 show corresponding transaction phases and packets for interrupt OUT transfers.

In summary, the interrupt transfer characteristics are:

- Data Transmission Direction: Unidirectional. Only IN transactions are allowed by USB Version 1.0. Version 1.1 added OUT transfers.

- Speed: Full or low.

- Flow control: Supported. Interrupt transfers allow NAK and STALL handshake responses during the handshake phase. NAK allows an endpoint to inform the host that there is no data available from the device's FIFO. A STALL handshake allows the device endpoint to inform the host that transactions will not succeed until some endpoint specific action is taken to resolve the condition.

- Data Delivery: Guaranteed period. At interface configuration time, an interrupt endpoint specifies a required maximum period for transactions. This period is specified as an integer number (N) of milliseconds (ms). The host controller initiates one bus transaction at least N ms as specified. Endpoints are in general expected to transfer data less frequently than that although that behavior is not required.

- Data Robustness: Can support robust delivery if desired. CRC checks and bus timeouts are allowed, but a device can ignore the handshake and always advance data toggle if robust data delivery is not required.

- Maximum data payload sizes: 0-64 bytes full speed, 0-8 bytes low speed. During interface configuration, an interrupt transfer can specify a maximum data payload size of any integer value from 0 to 64 bytes (full speed) or 0 to 8 bytes (low speed). Since interrupt transfers must be granted specific periodic bus time, the most accurate size prevents unnecessary over-allocation. A USB mouse could specify a 3-byte maximum size if it required one x position byte, one y position byte, and one button status byte. For such an endpoint, it might always respond with a 3-byte report. However, a mouse (or other device) could be designed that had variable length data up to some maximum. In that case, only the meaningful data would be sent, i.e., the data packet is not padded to be maximum size. Such padding wastes bus bandwidth that can be used for other transactions.

- Data Payload Format: No USB defined data payload format. USB imposes no formatting requirements on the contents of a data packet data payload for an interrupt transaction.

An interrupt transfer is retired when any of the following three conditions exist:

- Three consecutive transaction timeouts (from errors) occur.
- The IRQ's buffer becomes full.
- A transaction data payload is less then the maximum packet size for the endpoint.

Note that unlike bulk transfers, interrupt transfers are not retired due to any number of NAK handshakes. An "infinite" number of NAKs can occur and never retire an interrupt transfer. When compared to traditional interrupts, this makes sense. If there is no interrupt being generated, no interrupt should be signaled.

8.6 Isochronous Transfers

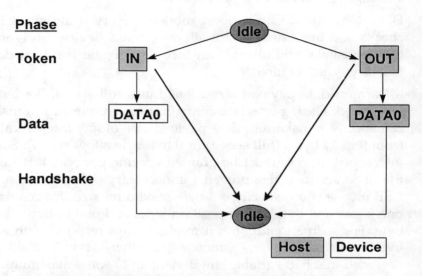

Figure 8.18: Transaction Phases and Packets for Isochronous Transfers

Figure 8.18 summarizes the allowed transitions and packets from one phase to another within an isochronous transaction. Note that there is no handshake phase for isochronous transactions.

Isochronous transfers are used to deliver better PC support for multimedia data such as audio and video. Isochronous transfers provide data delivery at regular intervals. This transfer type has been optimized for this usage and therefore has some limitations when compared to other more general transfer types. An isochronous transfer guarantees that the host controller initiates a bus transaction exactly once per 1 millisecond frame period. Obviously, a variety of errors can prevent the device from detecting, participating in, or completing the transaction. But the host controller manages its use of bus time to ensure that it has the opportunity to do a bus transaction with the device endpoint exactly once in every millisecond frame.

A series of transactions is used to implement an isochronous transfer. Each transaction consists of only two phases to transmit token and data packets. Other features for the allowed bus transactions are:

- No handshake phase is allowed. Consequently, error-free delivery cannot be guaranteed because a retry of the transmission is never allowed.

- Only the DATA0 data packet is used for transmission. DATA1 data packets are never used.

- Isochronous transfers are only defined for full speed devices. That is, no transaction for an isochronous transfer will ever include a PRE packet.

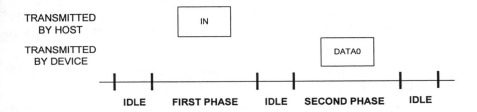

Figure 8.19: Upstream Packets for Transactions of an Isochronous Transfer

Figure 8.19 shows the transaction phases and packets required to transmit data upstream from the device to the host controller. Figure 8.20 shows the transaction phases and packets required to transmit data downstream from the host controller to the device.

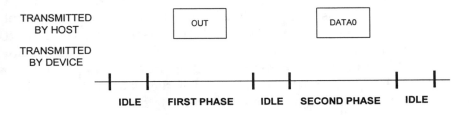

Figure 8.20: Downstream Packets for Transactions of an Isochronous Transfer

In summary, the isochronous transfer characteristics are:

- Data Transmission Direction: Unidirectional. Either IN or OUT transfers are allowed.

- Speed: Full only. Bulk transfers are not allowed for low speed endpoints. The host USB system software responsible for configuration will not allow configuration of a low speed isochronous endpoint.

- Flow Control: Not supported.

- Data Delivery: Guaranteed period. An isochronous pipe is guaranteed to have the opportunity for a single bus transaction once and only once every 1 millisecond frame. An endpoint's transaction is not guaranteed to be located at the same offset within a frame. In fact, it can occur at the end (or beginning) of one frame and the beginning (or end) of the next in extreme situations. A device must be prepared to behave correctly when such a situation occurs.

- Data Robustness: The transfer may lose data to preserve data delivery timing.

- Maximum data payload sizes: 0-1023 bytes. The data payload size is the largest of all transfer types for full speed endpoints. Isochronous transfers are the most efficient data transfer mechanism of USB in terms of bus protocol overhead.

- Data Payload Format: No USB defined data payload format

An isochronous transfer is retired when the IRP's buffer becomes full (IN transfers) or empty (OUT transfers). An Isochronous transfer is also retired when its assigned time has expired, whether or not any data was transferred. Note that unlike bulk and interrupt transfers, no handshakes are allowed and therefore no flow control is possible at the bus transaction level. There is no concept of a short packet. And finally, since there are no handshakes, timeouts are not defined as an error. Isochronous transfers have been optimized to deliver data in a timely fashion, and if the data is delayed it is assumed to be stale and no longer worth delivering.

8.7 Control Transfers

Control transfers are used to configure and initialize a device, its interfaces, and endpoints. Control transfers can also be used for ongoing, normal device operation. In general, control transfers allow flow controlled, highly reliable, bi-directional data transfer with a completion indication conveying the status of the overall data transfer. Other transfer types have fewer features in one or more areas.

Control transfers also have the most protocol overhead, yielding the least efficient data transfer. However, every device supports some minimal control transfers so that the device can be reliably recognized and configured for its intended usage.

Control transfers are different from the bulk, interrupt, and isochronous transfers in that a control transfer has additional layers of organization called stages. The other transfer types don't define stages as part of the transfer protocol.

Control transfers consist of three (3) stages: setup, data (optional), and status. The data stage can consist of several bus transactions. Stages should not be confused with transaction phases. Transactions phases are token, data, handshake. A stage consists of one or more (token, data, handshake) transaction sequences. Figure 8.21 summarizes the stages and transitions between stages of a control transfer.

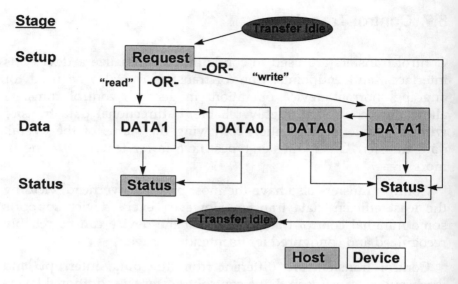

Figure 8.21: Control Transfer Stages

The setup stage consists of a single transaction. The data stage consists of zero or more transactions, and the status stage consists of a single transaction. Other features of transactions for control transfers are:

- Control transfers are defined for all types of devices, including hubs and both full and low speed devices.
- For hubs and full speed devices, the control transfer is typically used for device control, although control transfers can be used for data transmission.
- For low speed devices, the control transfer is used for both device control and data transmission.

Figure 8.22 shows the three stages in a control transfer. Each stage will be discussed individually with its associated packets.

8.7.1 Control Transfer Setup Stage

Figure 8.22 shows that a setup stage is always the first stage of a control transfer. The setup stage specifies the details of the following data stage. The setup stage describes the request that will be performed by this control transfer.

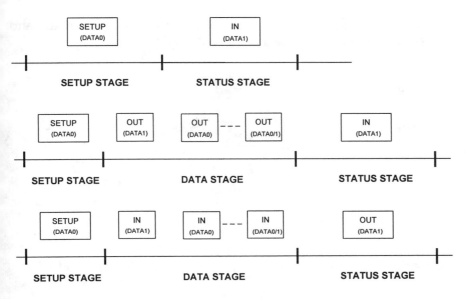

Figure 8.22: Stages of a Control Transfer

The details specified in the setup stage include whether the control transfer is a read or write operation, i.e., whether data is moved from device to host or vice versa. The setup stage always uses a DATA0 PID and is followed by zero or more data transactions with alternating DATA1/DATA0 PIDs. The first transaction following a setup stage always uses the DATA1 PID. The status stage follows the data stage and completes the control transfer. Each stage of a control transfer is described in more detail in the following paragraphs.

The setup stage of a control transfer consists of a single 3-phase transaction as shown in Figure 8.23. The token phase of the setup stage consists of an optional low speed preamble packet followed by a setup packet.

The setup packet is followed by a DATA0 packet that has a data field that is exactly 8 bytes long. The contents of the 8 byte data field specifies the parameters of the control transfer for the remaining stages of this control transfer. Chapter 11 *USB Device Framework* describes the detailed contents of the data field of a setup stage. The last phase of the setup stage is required to be an ACK handshake packet sent by the endpoint. The endpoint is not allowed to send any other handshake packets (e.g., NAK or STALL).

Phase

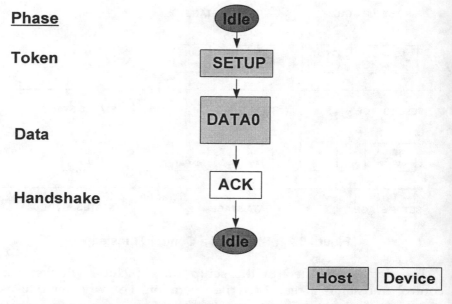

Figure 8.23: Transaction Phases and Packets for Control Transfer - Setup Stage

A setup stage must be accepted at any time by the target control endpoint. This may require aborting processing of a previous control request.

If the device is not ready to process the request when it receives the setup stage, it must still accept it with an ACK. It may, however, choose to NAK transactions of any subsequent stage until it is ready, or until five (5) seconds have passed. The setup stage of a control transfer always consists of exactly one single bus transaction, as shown in Figure 8.24.

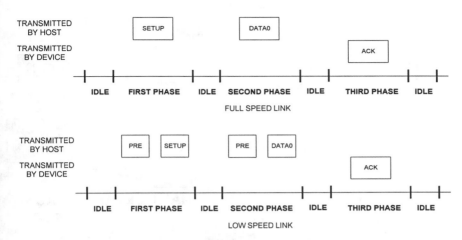

Figure 8.24: Control Transfer Setup Stage Transaction

8.7.2 Control Transfer Data Stage

The data stage of a control transfer consists of zero or more 3-phase transactions as summarized in Figure 8.25. The phases of a control transfer data stage follow the same transaction transition rules as specified for a bulk transfer type (see Figure 8.4). However, the first data transaction after the setup stage is required to be a DATA1 PID.

Part of the data contained in the setup stage indicates whether this control transfer is a read or write operation. If the data stage is a write operation, the token phase PIDs in the data stage will be OUTs. If the data stage is a read operation, the token phase PIDs in the data stage will be INs.

The setup stage also specifies the maximum allowed length of the data stage. An endpoint will never be sent more bytes than the length specified in the setup stage nor should it ever send more bytes than requested. An endpoint's behavior is undefined if the data stage is longer than specified by the setup stage.

Phase

Token

Data

Handshake

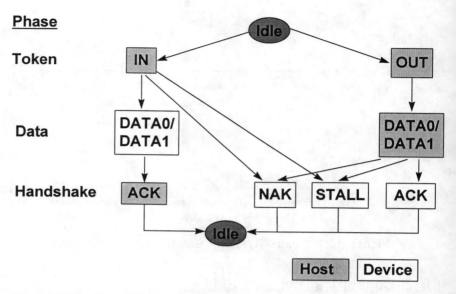

Figure 8.25: Transaction Phases and Packets for Control Transfer -
Data Stage

The control transfer's second stage is either an optional data stage
or a status stage. The data stage consists of a series of either all IN or
OUT transactions. The other features of the data stage are:

- Support of the ACK handshake packet guarantees error-free
  delivery of the data packet.

- Retry of the transaction when a device is not ready to receive or
  transmit a data packet. This occurs by the transmission of the
  NAK handshake packet.

- Subsequent to the transmission of the downstream DATA0 data
  packet in the setup stage, the transmitter of the first data packet
  of the subsequent data stage is required to transmit a DATA1
  packet.

- The data toggle protocol is followed; consequently, the next data
  packet is the DATA0 version. Both DATA0 and DATA1 data
  packets are used for transmission.

- Multiple data transactions can be transmitted within the data
  stage. The data packet direction (upstream or downstream) is

required to be the same for the entire data stage of a specific control transfer.

- When an endpoint addressed by the IN token packet has data, the device transmits a data packet. The host controller transmits an ACK handshake packet to acknowledge error-free reception.

- When the host controller transmits the OUT token packet, the host controller transmits the associated data packet independent of whether the device is ready to receive the data packet.

- When an endpoint addressed by an IN or OUT token packet does not have data ready to transmit or receive, the device transmits a NAK handshake packet.

- When an endpoint addressed by an IN or OUT token packet requires intervention by the host, the device returns a STALL handshake packet.

Figure 8.26 shows the transaction phases and packets required to transmit data upstream from a device to the host controller when the device was ready to transmit data. Figure 8.27 shows the allowed transaction phases and packets required to transmit data downstream from the host controller to the device when the device was ready to receive data.

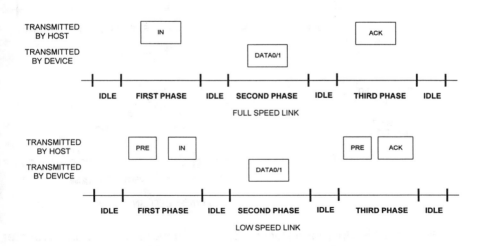

Figure 8.26: Control Transfer IN Data Transaction

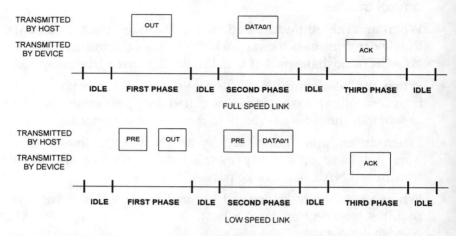

Figure 8.27: Upstream Packets for Transactions of a Control Transfer when Device is Ready for Data Transmission

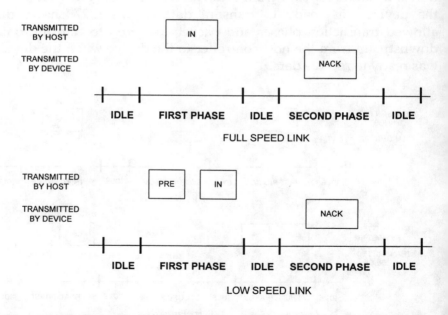

Figure 8.28: Upstream Packets for Transactions of a Control Transfer when Device not Ready for Data Transmission

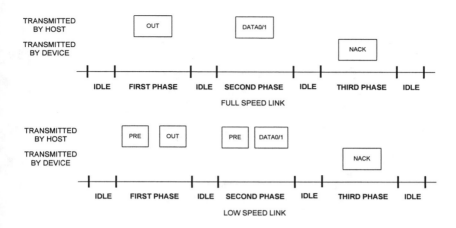

Figure 8.29: Downstream Packets for Transactions of a Control Transfer when Device not Ready for Data Transmission

Figure 8.30 shows the transaction phases and packets requried to transmit data upstream from a device to the host controller when the device requires intervention by the host. Figure 8.31 shows the transaction phases and packets required to transmit data downstream from the host controller to the device when the device requires intervention by the host.

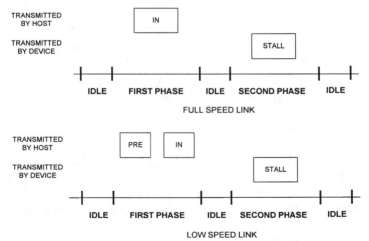

Figure 8.30: Upstream Packets for Transactions of a Control Transfer when Host Intervention is Required

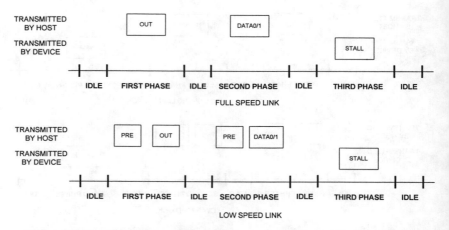

Figure 8.31: Downstream Packets for Transactions of a Control Transfer when Host Intervention is Required

8.7.3 Control Transfer Status Stage

The status stage of a control transfer consists of a single 3-phase transaction as summarized in Figure 8.32. The status stage transaction is in the opposite direction from the data stage transactions, i.e., if the data stage transactions were OUT PIDs, the status stage transaction uses an IN PID and vice versa. The status stage can be detected by the endpoint when the PID direction changes. An endpoint must be prepared to advance to status stage handling when it detects a change in PID direction. This "premature" status stage handling must be performed even if the length specified in the setup stage indicates that more data stage transactions are expected. The status stage data phase only uses a DATA1 PID with a zero length data payload.

The status stage carries information that indicates whether or not the complete control transfer has been successfully processed. The status stage has more "end to end" meaning than a USB simple handshake packet can convey. For example, if a control transfer is used to turn on a light on a keyboard, the status stage should not return success until the control transfer has been accepted and decoded by the endpoint and the light has been turned on.

Phase

Token

Data

Handshake

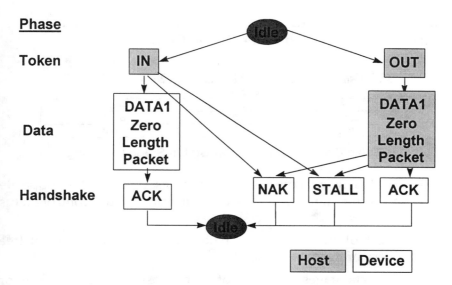

Figure 8.32: Transaction Phases and Packets for Control Transfer -
Status Stage

The status stage always conveys the status of the overall control transfer to the host. This is unlike a handshake phase of a bus transaction, since the handshake phase always returns its "status" to the transmitter of the data phase. The status of a control transfer is encoded as part of either the data phase or handshake phase of the single transaction in the status stage. The encoding is required due to the different normal data phase directions of IN and OUT transactions allowed in the data stage.

Table 8.1 shows the possible status responses defined by the USB specification and how those responses are encoded for a read or write control transfer status stage. In particular, the encoding of success is different for read versus write control operations. For a read operation, the only endpoint provided phase of the status stage is the data phase. Therefore the endpoint must return status on the data phase of the transaction, and does so with a NULL packet, *i.e.*, a DATA1 PID with zero bytes in the data field. For a write operation, the endpoint only provides the handshake phase and so must return status on that phase. It does so with an ACK handshake packet. In this way, status is always returned to the host independently of the bus transaction (normal) data transfer direction, as determined by the IN/OUT PID.

Status Response	Read Status Encoding	Write Status Encoding
Success	NULL packet	ACK
Error	STALL	STALL
Busy	NAK	NAK

Table 8.1: Control Transfer Status Stage Encodings

The status stage consists of one transaction in the opposite direction of the data stage. The other features of the control status transaction are:

- Support of the ACK handshake packet guarantees error-free delivery of the data packet.

- If the data stages consisted of all downstream data packets or there is no data stage, the data packet of the status stage is required to be upstream, *i.e.*, the host controller is required to transmit an IN token packet.

- If the data stages consisted of all upstream data packets, the data packet of the status stage is required to be downstream, *i.e.*, the host controller is required to transmit an OUT token packet.

- Only a single DATA1 data packet is transmitted. The DATA0 data packet is never transmitted for a status stage.

- When an endpoint addressed by the IN token packet has completed the control operation, the endpoint transmits a zero length data packet. The host controller transmits an ACK handshake packet to acknowledge error-free reception.

- When the host controller transmits the OUT token packet, the host controller transmits the zero length data packet whether the device is ready to receive the data packet or not.

- When an endpoint addressed by an IN or OUT token packet has not completed the control operation, the device transmits a NAK handshake packet.

- When an endpoint addressed by an IN or OUT token packet requires intervention by the host, the device transmits a STALL handshake packet.

- The protocol for non-error free delivery of the packets or missing packets is outlined in Chapter 9.

Figure 8.33 shows the transaction phases and packets required to transmit data upstream from the device to the host controller, when the device has completed the control operation. Figure 8.34 shows the transaction phases and packets required to transmit data downstream from the host controller to the device when the device has completed the control operation.

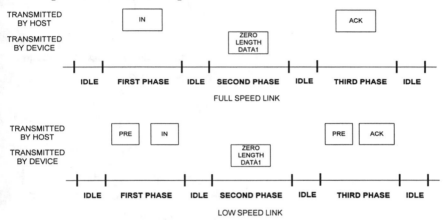

Figure 8.33: Control Transfer IN Status Transaction

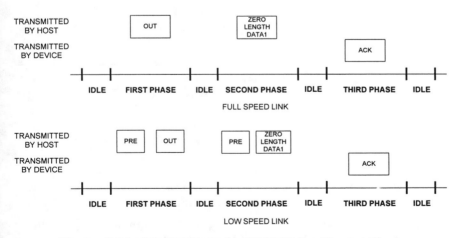

Figure 8.34: Control Transfer OUT Status Transaction

Figure 8.35 shows the transaction phases and packets required to transmit data upstream from the device to the host controller when the device has not completed the control operation. Figure 8.36 shows the transaction phases and packets required to transmit data downstream from the host controller to the device when the device has not completed the control operation.

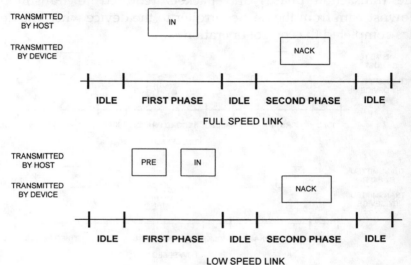

Figure 8.35: Upstream Packets for Transactions of a Control Transfer when Device not Ready for Status Transmission

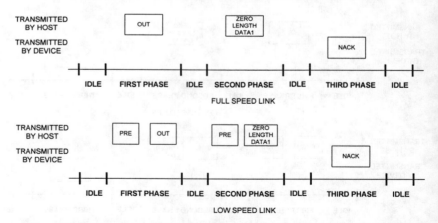

Figure 8.36: Downstream Packets for Transactions of a Control Transfer when Device not Ready for Status Transmission

Figure 8.37 shows the transaction phases and packets required to transmit data upstream from the hub or device to the host controller when the device requires intervention by the host. Figure 8.38 shows the transaction phases and packets required to transmit data downstream from the host controller to the device when the device requires intervention by the host.

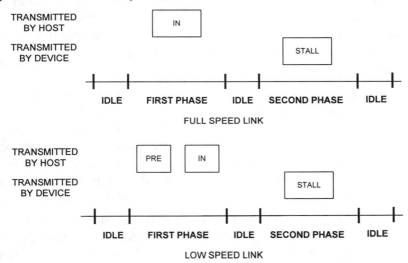

Figure 8.37: Upstream Packets for Transactions of a Control Transfer when Host Intervention is Required

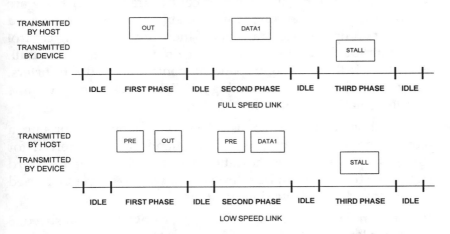

Figure 8.38: Downstream Packets for Transactions of a Control Transfer when Host Intervention is Required

In summary, the control transfer characteristics are:

- Data transmission direction: Bi-directional. Control transfers are the only transfer type that allow data to be moved in both directions with a single pipe. The pipe requires the allocation of two interface endpoints: one for each direction. The two endpoints are allocated by the device interface designer and must have the same endpoint number with opposite directions. In particular, endpoints with different numbers cannot be used for control transfers on a single pipe.

- Speed: Full or low.

- Flow control: Supported. Control transfers require three phase transactions. Handshake packets are used to defer or retry a transaction when the device doesn't have space or data available for the current transaction. The transaction retry can occur immediately after the current transaction, or it may not occur for long periods of time. A device cannot determine nor control when the retry from the host controller will be initiated.

- Data delivery: Best effort; can't specify transfer period. Control transfers can be moved over the bus whenever there is time remaining in a frame and the isochronous and interrupt transfers for the current frame have been processed. The USB specification requires that each frame keeps 10% of its time available for use by any pending control transfers. If there are no bulk transfers pending, any available bus time can be used by any pending control transfers. If there are no pending control transfers for the current frame, that time can be used for bulk transfers. If there are both pending control and bulk transfers, they will share any remaining available bus time in some implementation-specific "fair" fashion.

- Data robustness: Most robust. The transactions comprising a control transfer will be retried if no handshake is received for the data phase. The specification requires that after the third retry, the transfer must be retired and it will no longer be retried until some device driver intervention.

- Maximum data payload sizes: 8, 16, 32, 64 bytes for full speed; 8 bytes for low speed.

- Data payload format: USB Defined. See Chapter 11 for a description of the control transfer format.

A control transfer is retired when one of the following conditions exist:

- More than about 5 seconds of continuous NAKs are received by the transmitter (OS dependent).

- Three consecutive transaction timeouts (from errors) occur.

- The IRP's buffer becomes full (IN transfers) or empty (OUT transfers) during a data stage. This advances the transfer to the status stage and the transfer retires after the status stage completes.

- A transaction data payload is less then the maximum packet size for the endpoint. This advances the transfer to the status stage and the transfer retires after the status stage completes.

- The status stage completes.

8.8 Chapter Summary

Table 8.2 shows a reference summary of the characteristics of the four USB defined transfer types. Shaded transfer types are allowed for low speed devices. Unshaded transfer types are only allowed for full speed devices.

Transfer Type	Bus Access	Timing	Reliability
Bulk	As available 8,16,32,64 bytes	No Guarantee	Delivery Guaranteed
Interrupt	Guaranteed FS: <= 64 bytes LS: <= 8 bytes	Every N ms.	Delivery Guaranteed
Isochronous	Guaranteed 0 to 1023 bytes	Every 1 ms	No guarantee No flow control
Control	As available 8,16,32,64 bytes 10+% bandwidth	No guarantee	Delivery Guaranteed

Table 8.2: Summary Transfer Types Characteristics

Table 8.3 summarizes which packets are transmitted by host/controller for each transfer type.

TRANSFER TYPE	PACKETS USED IN THE TRANSACTION		
	TOKEN PACKET (Akways transmitted by host)	DATA PACKET / TRANSMITTED BY (Data0/1 used unless otherwise noted)	HANDSHAKE / TRANSMITTED BY
ISOCHRONOUS DATA UPSTREAM DATA DWNSTREAM	IN OUT	DATA0/DEVICE DATA0/HOST	N/A N/A
INTERRUPT IN ... INTERRUPT PENDING .... NO INTERRUPT PENDING	IN / HOST IN / HOST	DEVICE N/A N/A	ACK / HOST NAK / DEVICE STALL / DEVICE
INTERRUPT OUT ... INTERRUPT PENDING .... NO INTERRUPT PENDING	OUT / HOST OUT / HOST OUT / HOST	HOST HOST HOST	ACK / DEVICE NAK / DEVICE STALL / DEVICE
CONTROL TRANSFER STAGES: SETUP, DATA, STATUS **CONTROL SETUP TRANSACTION** DATA DWNSTREAM	SETUP	DATA0/HOST	ACK / DEVICE
CONTROL DATA TRANSACTION DATA UPSTREAM (opt)	IN IN IN	DEVICE N/A N/A	ACK / HOST NAK / DEVICE STALL / DEVICE
CONTROL DATA TRANSACTION DATA DWNSTREAM (opt)	OUT OUT OUT	HOST HOST HOST	ACK / DEVICE NAK / DEVICE STALL / DEVICE
CONTROL STATUS TRANSACTION DATA UPSTREAM	IN IN IN	DATA1/DEVICE N/A N/A	ACK / HOST NAK / DEVICE STALL / DEVICE
CONTROL STATUS TRANSACTION DATA DWNSTREAM	OUT OUT OUT	DATA1/HOST DATA1/HOST DATA1/HOST	ACK / DEVICE NAK / DEVICE STALL / DEVICE
BULK DATA PKT (UPSTREAM)	IN IN IN	DEVICE N/A N/A	ACK / HOST NAK / DEVICE STALL / DEVICE
BULK DATA PKT (DWNSTREAM)	OUT OUT OUT	HOST HOST HOST	ACK / DEVICE NAK / DEVICE STALL / DEVICE

Table 8.3: Packets Relative to Transfers

Note: In the above table, the term "DEVICE" represents downstream devices or hubs. The "HOST" is the host controller transmitting or receiving packets via the root hub.

9. Isochronous Communication Model

9.1 Basic Concepts

Isochronous applications produce, consume, or manipulate a data stream that is uninterrupted and has a constant volume. One of the earliest historical isochronous applications implemented by a computer is telephone switching, and the data streams first managed by these telephone switches were the audio "talk paths" used in voice communications. Today, audio applications are still common computer-based isochronous applications, as well as video imaging, data communications, and an increasing range of non-traditional applications that can take advantage of the delivery characteristics associated with isochronous data streams.

Traditionally, isochronous data streams were supported by isochronous systems, which were specifically designed for this kind of data transport. For instance they placed stringent clocking requirements on the data stream. In fact, this was the genesis of the term ISOCHRONOUS, which literally means data managed by the equal (ISO) clocks (CHRONOUS) on both ends of the data stream. For the Publicly Switched Telephone Network (PSTN) used for telecommunications in North America, this led to the single "network clock" with which all telephone equipment must be synchronized.

Personal computer systems have not, of course, usually provided that degree of native support for isochronous data. So, how do they manage audio streams and full motion video? In order to understand this, the concept of ISOCHRONOUS DATA must be separated from the concept of ISOCHRONOUS TRANSPORT. Isochronous data is a data stream in which the timing information is intrinsic. For instance, if an audio data stream has been recorded at 44.1 kHz, then, in order to faithfully reproduce that recorded experience, the playback must also occur at a continuous data rate of exactly 44.1 kHz. Isochronous transport delivers isochronous data, end-to-end, at its required data rate.

The common interconnects used in PCs today, including the ISA and PCI buses, do not provide isochronous transport. Instead, the host system or the device bundles large buffers of isochronous data together, and bursts them across the bus. For playback, the device then reconstitutes this data as an isochronous stream, playing it out over its external connection, *e.g.*, speakers or a phone line. However, this arrangement has no guaranteed time of delivery for data streams and only works as long as the occupancy of the host processor and the bus itself is low enough to ensure that the next burst always arrives before the last one is completely played out. Additionally, the large buffering required to reduce the chance that the device ever starves is both expensive and prohibitive for some applications, since it imposes additional latency in the data delivery schedule.

Isochronous streams, as experienced in the real world, have certain well-defined characteristics:

- Bounded latency for data delivery.
- Complete characterization of missing or invalid data.
- Concept of null data.

An isochronous data stream is made up of discrete items flowing across the transport. In order to fulfill the requirement of bounded latency, it must be possible to place an upper bound on the time elapsed from when the item left until it arrives. A TIGHTLY BOUND stream is one in which the actual latency varies little from the upper bound. The tighter the bound, the better the isochronous transport. Tightly bounded latency does not necessarily, however, imply low latency. A transport which is very slow, but for which the latency is a constant, meets the bounded latency criteria.

> **Isochronous transport must provide bounded latency. Additionally, some isochronous applications have low latency requirements; that is, the transport must also be fast.**

For instance, an audio stream being read from a CD ROM and played on speakers can have a very long latency, as long as that latency is bounded so that the speakers never run out of data to play. The listener does not care whether the travel time from CD ROM to speakers is 10 milliseconds or 1 second. If however, the audio stream is the voice portion of a telephone call, and originates from a microphone, reflects back to a headset, and is sent over the telephone line, the latency must be low indeed in order to spare the listener an undesirable echo.

Data integrity requirements vary widely among isochronous applications. Some applications are extremely intolerant of data that is missing or in error and will re-send large volumes of data if any portion is damaged on arrival. Other applications are quite tolerant of damaged data and may even use some simple algorithm to SMOOTH over the rough spots. Typically, isochronous applications have standard protocols associated with them to detect, and potentially correct, a damaged data stream. They do not then require a transport that guarantees data integrity. However, in order for the detection and correction algorithms to work properly, they do require the transport to provide the following information about a damaged stream:

- Type of damage.
- Exact location of the damage.
- Exact size of the damage.

Some algorithms can also take as input any of the damaged data that is available. A data stream can be damaged by incorrect, missing or late data. Given that the timing information is so tightly bound to the actual data, late data is in fact often handled as missing data. Additionally, in order to preserve the original timing of the stream, once a hole is identified in the transported stream, it must be characterized completely. This tells the application the exact size and location of the hole in the actual stream.

> An isochronous transport need not provide guaranteed data integrity. However, it must identify all damaged data, its size, and location in the stream.

Some traditional isochronous systems give each application an exact time slice for communication, thus trending the bounded latency toward a constant latency. However, many isochronous applications do not have meaningful data to communicate at every instant for which they are sampled. To take up their time slot, then, they transmit a data pattern indicating "silence". This data pattern may be standard to the application or, sometimes, to the transport. Even when not required by the transport, some isochronous applications still use some variety of NULL DATA to convey information about their data stream or their own external connectivity.

> Isochronous applications may distinguish between different types of data:
> → Data with no content errors
> → Null data (no content errors)
> → Data with content errors
> → Missing data
> → Late data

The next two sections discuss how isochronous data is transported in the traditional PC system, and how that flow is modified by USB.

9.1.1 Traditional PC Transport

The traditional PC interconnect does not provide guarantees for when data will be delivered and so transports isochronous data in bursts, with large buffers on both the host and the device. Usually, some host software manages the application and is responsible for maintaining the flow of buffers through the system.

The interactions of the full system are seen in a model where an isochronous data stream is received from an input device and then played back to an output device. Figure 9.1 depicts such a model.

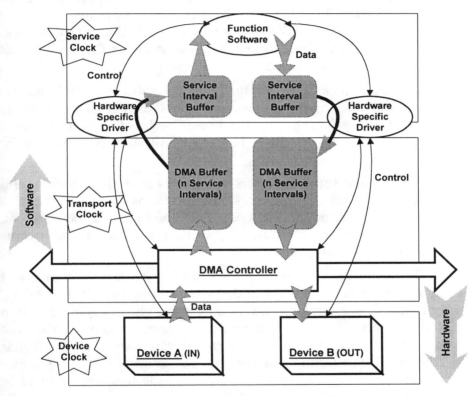

Figure 9.1: Traditional Interconnect Support

There are three clock environments in Figure 9.1:

1. Device clock used to sample the external world. The input device examines the external world in small time slices determined by its clock. It then characterizes this sampling as data and stores it in its buffer. The output device takes a buffer of these time-sliced characterizations and translates them, using *its* clock, into some meaningful interaction with the external world, for instance, the sound played by speakers.

2. Hardware clock provided by the transport itself. Data moves between the device and the host in chunks at a time. Some manager associated with the transport, *e.g.*, a DMA controller, handles this movement. The transport has a clock associated with it, but since the data movement manager does not schedule its bursts according to the transport clock, that clock is largely meaningless as far as the isochronous stream is concerned.

3. Host clock used by the function software. The function software needs a clock, which is usually manifested as events scheduled by the host. The function software uses this clock to decide when to submit additional buffers for transport.

The function software knows the rates of both the incoming and outgoing streams. It provides rate matching between the two streams as required, and as possible. If the rates are too different, the function software will simply not be able to match the streams with any degree of quality.

The device drivers handle the specific hardware characteristics of their respective devices. They do not maintain a clock themselves, but live in the clocking environments provided by the function software and the data movement manager. In general the data movement manager interrupts the device driver when it has completed transferring some specified amount of data. The device driver then either passes the new data to the function software or retrieves from the function software some new data to be transferred.

Each participant has an associated buffer, as well as a clock environment. The device maintains a buffer large enough to smooth the transferred data bursts into real world stream data.

> The size of the device buffer is a tradeoff between cost and latency on one hand, and data stream quality on the other.

If the device buffer is too small to cover the gaps inserted by the data movement manager, then an output device may run dry or an input device may overflow. Whether data is dropped, or silence inserted, a lower quality data stream results. However, large buffers incur cost, and insert additional delivery latency into the data stream. Therefore, device buffers are generally sized to cover the data stream gaps incurred by a host with "typical" occupancy.

The data movement manager also has a large buffer available to it, which is transferred in sections. When a given watermark in the buffer passes, new data is copied in or out of the buffer by the device driver. The size of the data movement manager's buffer and the number of divisions in which it is transferred are relatively independent of the data stream.

The size of the buffer used by the device driver is influenced by the time period for which the function software builds buffers and by the size of the sections in which the data movement manager moves the data. The ideal case occurs when the function software manages buffers that are the same size as the sections transferred by the data movement manager. Figure 9.2 depicts the happy situation when the input and output device driver buffer size corresponds to the function software's service interval.

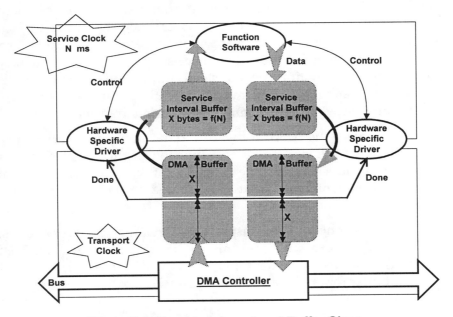

Figure 9.2: Service Interval and Buffer Sizes

The devices, data movement manager, device drivers, and function software can all have independent service intervals and buffer sizes. However, it is more likely that they will at worst be some multiple of each other. In many audio applications, for instance, the entire loop may run on a 20 ms or a 40 ms service interval, approximately. In other words, that is the amount of time represented by one of the function software's buffers. It also approximates the watermark(s) at which the data movement manager notifies the device drivers.

9.1.2 USB Transport

USB introduces some changes into the picture described above. Some, like the insertion of a software layer below the device drivers, do not affect the overall transport that much. However, exposing the transport's clock to the device via the transmittal of the Start-of-Frame (SOF) packet does change the essential nature of the transport. Figure 9.3 indicates the changes imposed by USB.

The first observation of note is that the entire software stack above the device drivers can remain unchanged in its management of isochronous streams. The device drivers themselves must adapt as they would to a new hardware interface. The device driver can also no longer directly access the device's hardware for commands, status, and event notifications. Instead, those kinds of interactions are now very similar to data transfer operations. The device drivers must sequence events and commands with data transfers.

Additionally, the USB software's data transport clock for a particular client device driver is a function of the transfer buffers submitted to it. Therefore, the function software's service interval clock environment is now *always* extended to include the device drivers' buffer management.

The bus itself no longer transports data in large, arbitrary chunks, but instead in exact slices 1 ms in length. The device, which previously needed a buffer for at least two service periods, now needs a buffer for only approximately 2 ms.

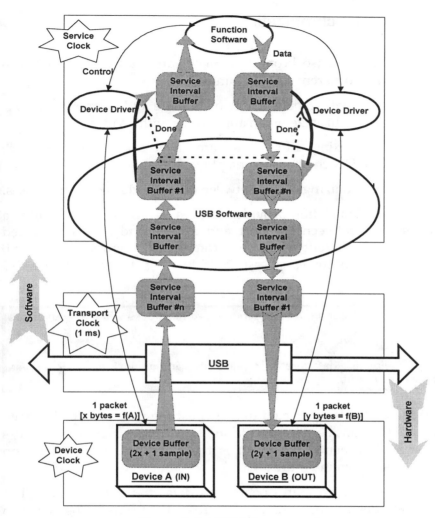

Figure 9.3: USB Interconnect

USB delivers a constant latency of 2 ms across the transport.

The total latency, between the function software and the device, is larger and more variable since it is more dependent on the function software's service interval and the operating system implementation.

9.2 USB Synchronization

When discussing isochronous data streams, SYNCHRONIZATION can refer to many different sorts of things:

1. Coordinating between two or more independent streams, *e.g.*, synchronizeing an audio track with a video image.

2. Multiplexing different streams over a common transport, *e.g.*, ISDN channels over a phone line.

3. Synchronizing clocks between different devices or processes.

USB synchronization provides a series of facilities which allow a data stream between the host and a device to be synchronized across the different clock environments it crosses. So, USB synchronization comes closest to addressing the same area as #3 above.

> USB synchronization does <u>not</u> synchronize the clocks at the different ends of a data stream.
>
> It <u>does</u> allow the data stream to match its various clock environments as closely as possible.

If Figure 9.3 is abstracted to show just the relationships between the different clock environments and how data is transported across those environments, the result is the basic USB synchronization model, as shown in Figure 9.4.

Device A provides an isochronous data stream to the host. The host provides an isochronous data stream to Device B. The host also provides a transport clock in the form of its SOF broadcast. The function software retains its overall control of the application and provides rate matching as necessary between the two streams.

At the time of device design, which other streams the device will connect to is unknown. Therefore, the USB specification only states how the device interacts with the host, even though the goal is to enable the complete connection from Device A to Device B.

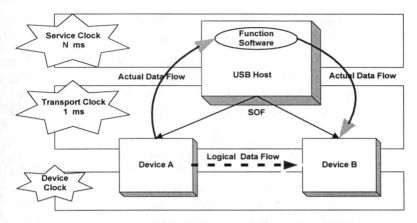

Figure 9.4: Basic Synchronization Model

9.2.1 Problem Statement

USB synchronization has been summarized as *synchronizing an isochronous data stream between a device and the host.*

However, this goal really breaks down into three independent requirements, which are addressed by the same set of solutions:

- If the data rates are compatible, the function software can match Device A's stream to Device B's stream with acceptable quality.

- If the device clock is reasonably stable with regard to the transport clock, the data stream can be managed to minimize the device buffer size while maintaining a low rate of buffer over- or under-runs.

- If data is missing or damaged, its expected size and location in the data stream must be determinable.

The host's SOF divides the USB transport into time slices of 1 ms. Slaving the device clock to the SOF, and thus creating a TIME DIVISION MULTIPLEXED (TDM) bus, would seem to handle all of the above requirements. Unfortunately, slicing a device's stream into exactly 1 ms pieces, as defined by the *USB transport*, is rarely possible.

The first difficulty arises with USB's requirement that all data be transferred in byte multiples. Not all data streams are evenly divisible by bytes into a 1 kHz clock. Padding out partial bytes adds unacceptable processing on both ends of the stream as well as the real headache of detecting such a coding scheme.

Additionally, the USB transfer architecture allows any two successive USB frames of data to be placed into different transfer buffers. Splitting samples across transfer buffers is in general a bad idea. This in turn means that, if possible, samples should not be split across frames.

Beyond the difficulty of forcing the data stream, in *sample* multiples, into a 1 kHz clock, the device clock itself may drift slightly over time with regard to the transport clock. This can be just enough to tip the balance between a complete sample and a sample minus one bit. This variability of the device clock relative to the transport clock is known as CLOCK JITTER.

In general, slaving the device clock to the transport clock (SOF) is not a reliable solution, and more complicated relationships must be allowed.

Each isochronous data stream has associated with it the maximum number of bytes it can ever accept in one USB frame (*wMaxPacketSize*). Exactly one isochronous packet transfers per USB frame for each data stream. However, that packet does not necessarily appear at the same relative position in successive frames. For instance, Figure 9.5 shows a case where the stream is scheduled at the beginning of one frame and at the end of the subsequent one.

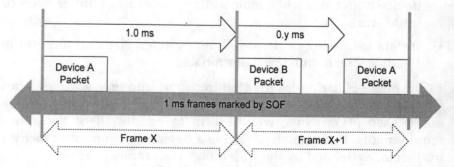

Figure 9.5: Schedule Jitter

The host is allowed to schedule the device's isochronous packet anywhere in a particular USB frame, as long as each isochronous stream has an opportunity to transfer one packet with *wMaxpacketSize* bytes in that frame. This variability causes SCHEDULE JITTER, as opposed to the clock jitter described above, in the data stream. In Figure 9.5, instead of transferring a packet each 1 ms, Device A has experienced a schedule jitter of 0.y ms in its data stream.

In order to smooth across this possible gap due to schedule jitter, the device must provide at least (2 x *wMaxPacketSize*) bytes as a buffer. Add to this buffer enough space for one additional sample, so that there is not a hard stop to processing on the frame boundary and to accommodate clock jitter, and the required buffering is now:

Required device buffer = [(2 x *wMaxPacketSize*) + 1 sample] bytes

In the initial definition of an isochronous data stream at the beginning of this chapter, there were two key concepts:

* Uninterrupted data flow.
* Constant volume.

Constant volume means that the actual amount of data transferred in a frame is as close to *wMaxPacketSize* as possible. This has the effect of minimizing *wMaxPacketSize* and thus the device buffering required.

A data stream's target volume should be to transfer either *wMaxPacketSize* bytes or [*wMaxPacketSize* - (1 sample)] bytes every frame.

In order for this volume to be achievable, given the jitter caused by clocks drifting or even just not being evenly divisible, some knowledge about the device's clock relative to the host clock must be available.

Additionally, for any given frame, both the device and the host must know the expected number of samples in order to fully characterize damaged data.

The following three statements summarize the requirements on how the three independent synchronization requirements listed above must be fulfilled:

- A variety of relationships must be allowed between the transport clock and the device clock.
- The behavior of the device clock relative to the transfer clock must be visible.
- The amount of data transferred each frame must be predictable, with allowances made for clock jitter.

USB provides ways to meet these requirements by:

1. Categorizing the possible types of device clocks relative to the transport clock.
2. Defining the knowledge required to match any compatible data stream with another data stream, keeping the flow between the host and a device as even as possible.
3. Designing facilities that make this knowledge available to devices and function software.

The following two sections are the result of this approach.

9.2.2 Characterization

Device clocks are capable of two basic behaviors relative to the transport clock:

1. They can adjust, within some tolerance, to a range of data flow clocks.
2. They operate only based on their own device clock, with no chance for adjustment.

Device clocks exhibiting the first behavior are said to be **ADAPTIVE**. Device clocks exhibiting the second behavior are referred to as **ASYNCHRONOUS**. A third category of device clocks exists which can be slaved to the SOF. These are called **SYNCHRONOUS**. Synchronous streams look like asynchronous streams, which have, through a fortuitous circumstance, a clock that exactly matches the SOF. Table 9.1 summarizes these clock synchronization types.

Referring again to Figure 9.1, the goal is to be able to match Device B's stream to Device A's data stream. So any of the sink types described above must be able to receive a compatible data stream from any of the source types. The goal is described this way (matching Device B's data stream to Device A's) because it results in the strongest requirements. In reality, of course, the device has no idea what kind of stream forms the other half of the loop. From its perspective the host is always the other end of its data stream.

Clock Type	Device	Behavior	Host Options
Asynchronous	Source	Provides data at a rate independent of the SOF.	None.
	Sink	Consumes data at a rate independent of the SOF.	Host can adjust stream to match device conditions.
Synchronous	Source	Provides data based on SOF.	None.
	Sink	Consumes data based on SOF.	None.
Adaptive	Source	Provides data at requested rate.	Host adjusts requested rate.
	Sink	Consumes data at requested rate.	Host adjusts stream as needed by source.

Table 9.1: Summary of Synchronization Types

Inserting the host in this manner allows the function software to continue to fulfill its role of managing the compatibility of the two streams. The degree of compatibility is determined by:

- The nominal data rates.
- The data formats used by each stream.

The highest degree of compatibility is achieved between two streams with the same nominal data rate and the same encoding for data format.

> Because of the different clocks involved, even streams with the same nominal data rate can experience some relative rate variations.

For instance, two audio streams may have the same nominal data rate of 44.1 kHz. At any point in time, however, the *exact* data rate of each data stream may vary, say 44.09 kHz and 44.11 kHz. The USB synchronization facilities are designed to handle this level of variation. If the nominal rates are actually different, say 44.1 kHz and 48 kHz, these streams are less compatible and the function software must intervene to drop or interpolate samples. This example is summarized in Table 9.2.

Source Data Rate	Sink Data Rate	Function Software
44.1 Khz	48 Khz	adds (interpolates) samples to sink's stream
48 Khz	44.1 Khz	drops samples from the sink's stream

Table 9.2: Example of Rate Matching

The function software must also intervene when the data formats of the two streams are different. There are two common methods by which function software performs format translations:

1. The function software maintains a "native" format for all of the data streams it manages. In other words, it first translates all incoming streams to its native format, then performs any functional manipulation required (*e.g.*, audio mixing) and then translates the native format to the format required by the output device.

2. The function software translates the input format directly to the output format.

Approach #2 has the advantage of speed, but makes it difficult to implement common functionality since there is no common hardware-independent format that can be manipulated. Approach #1 is in the exact opposite situation: slower operation but easier to implement common functionality.

> The more intervention required to translate between formats, the less compatible the streams.

USB synchronization between the host and a device ensures high quality communications between devices with compatible data streams. The primary determinant of the quality of the communications is, however, the compatibility of the streams themselves.

9.2.3 USB Isochronous Facilities

The previous section characterizes the type of device clocks and streams that can interact with the host. In order to allow quality connections across these different varieties of clocks, USB defines the following synchronization facilities:

- **FEEDBACK** information. Provides information about the data stream clocking in the *opposite* direction of the data flow.

- **FEEDFORWARD** information. Provides information about the data stream clocking in the *same* direction as the data flow.

- **CLOCK MASTERING**. Influences the host's SOF generation to allow an asynchronous device to act like a synchronous device.

The host uses these mechanisms to discover the actual state of the data stream and, where possible, adjust it or its paired stream accordingly. The "Host Options" column in Table 9.1 describes the scope of the intervention the host may undertake to adjust a particular stream. In order to intervene successfully, the host must have knowledge of the behavior of the device clocks with regard to the transport clock. This knowledge is provided as feedback or feedforward information. Table 9.3 summarizes the knowledge available about the stream and the possible interventions in the stream for each clock type and direction.

Examining Table 9.3 carefully, only one stream type can:

- Provide explicit feedback: Asynchronous Sink.

- Use explicit feedback: Adaptive Source.

Within the bounds of the nominal data rate, Adaptive Sources and Adaptive Sinks can adjust to the requirements of their current connection. Streams using all other clock types, however, require that the host intervene and match the device's needs.

Clock Type	Device	Possible Actions	Available Knowledge
Asynchronous	Source	None.	Receipt of stream provides Implicit feedforward timing knowledge to the host.
	Sink	Host adjusts stream to match device conditions.	Explicit feedback describes the exact rate at which the device consumes the stream.
Synchronous	Source	None.	Implicit feedback timing provided information provided by SOF.
	Sink	None.	Implicit feedforward timing provided information provided by SOF.
Adaptive	Source	Device adjusts stream based on host's feedback.	Host provides explicit feedback to device describing the exact production rate of the stream.
	Sink	Host adjusts stream production as needed by source. Device adjusts stream consumption.	Receipt of stream provides Implicit feedforward timing knowledge to device.

Table 9.3: Synchronization Knowledge and Interventions

Source Type	Sink Type		
	Asynchronous	Synchronous	Adaptive
Asynchronous	Sink gives feedback; Source doe not use	No adjustment possible.	Source gives implicit feed forward; Sink adapts.
Synchronous	Sink gives feedback; Source doe not use	Streams use same clock	Source gives implicit feed forward; Sink adapts.
Adaptive	Sink gives feedback; Source adjusts	Hosts mimics sink feedback; Source adjusts.	Hosts mimics sink feedback; Source adjusts.

Table 9.4: Matching Streams using Feedback/Feedforward Information

The shaded boxes in Table 9.4 indicate those pairings that can result in some number of lost or interpolated samples, even with otherwise compatible streams. Adaptive clocks provide the greatest degree of interoperability, and some amount of additional implementation complexity. Asynchronous and synchronous clocks are somewhat cheaper but have greatly reduced interoperability characteristics, with one exception: If both devices are synchronous, compatible streams "just work", essentially for free.

Unfortunately, such serendipity is rare. In one interesting case, however, it is possible to influence the odds. Some devices have access to an extremely reliable, rigid external clock that is compatible to the host's SOF; for instance the PSTN clock. So, telephone devices *could* be synchronous, if the SOF were kept in synch with the PSTN clock. The SOF (1 kHz) does not equal the PSTN clock (8 kHz), but they are divisible.

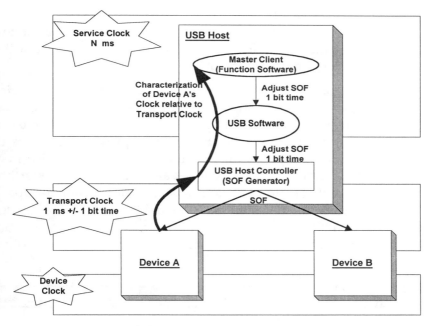

Figure 9.6: Clock Mastering

One client, the MASTER CLIENT, on the host is allowed to adjust the host's generation of the SOF slightly. Moving the SOF can disturb other devices attached to USB. Therefore the Master Client is restricted from changing the SOF faster than the bus's jitter tolerances.

> **The Master Client may adjust the SOF plus or minus 1 bit time at most once every 6 frames.**

Also, the Master Client may only shift the SOF a total of 15 bit times in either direction. There may be at most one active Master Client in a system, and that client may obtain information on how to adjust the SOF from one or more USB devices. USB does not define the format of the SOF adjustment feedback from a device to the Master Client. Some options include:

- The absolute number of bit times to be adjusted.

- The relative number of bit times to be adjusted.

- A proprietary characterization of the device's buffer states, which, over time, describe the run rate and whether or not the stream clock is correct for the device.

The format of the clock mastering feedback from the device depends largely on how much clock processing information the device manufacturer wants to implement on the device versus in the Master Client. The rate at which the device provides feedback to the Master Client is also vendor-specific. Initially, the device may need to provide more frequent feedback as the SOF could be farther from the target when the device is first attached. Later, feedback need not be so frequent, or indicate as much change. The device must either provide frequent enough feedback to handle the initial adjustment, or it must provide feedback in the form of an absolute number of bit times.

> Only one client can be the Master Client on the host.

This means that if a device is attached which needs to have access to a Master Client, and someone else already has that role, then the new device can no longer be guaranteed to be synchronous. It may now be asynchronous, with the associated drop in connection quality. So, there is a risk associated with relying on clock mastering. If it should happen that the existing Master Client is adjusting the SOF relative to the same clock that the newly attached device would have, *e.g.*, the PSTN clock, then the new device may still be able to be synchronous. However, if the two devices using clock mastering are using different clock referents, then one of the devices is forced to be asynchronous.

While USB does not define clock mastering feedback, it does define the explicit feedback which Asynchronous Sinks must provide and which Adaptive Sources use to adjust their data streams. The 1.0 version of the USB specification did not completely specify the format of feedback information and its method of delivery.

> At the time of this writing, synchronization feedback information is defined in the USB Common Class Specification, which has not yet reached a 1.0 level of maturity and is subject to change.

The feedback is defined as a characterization of the buffer on the asynchronous sink, indirectly indicating the run rate for the stream, and directly conveying the current optimum rate for the device. This exact same data is provided to the adaptive source, indicating what its target rate should be.

The feedback is a snapshot of status provided at some known, fixed rate expressed in multiples of USB frames. The more variable the device clock, the faster the rate of feedback required. Additionally, the feedback is more useful if it occurs at some rate that is evenly divisible into the service interval used by the function software. Of course, the device is not aware of the service interval for the function software. However, a number of interesting applications have relatively common service interval sizes. For instance, many audio applications use a service interval of either 20 ms or 40 ms. A useful rate for feedback from asynchronous audio sinks might be either 5 ms or 10 ms. Such a feedback rate would be timely enough that the function software could adapt the data rate in a service interval that is relatively close in time to the data which resulted in the feedback.

The 1.0 USB Specification defines the transport mechanism as an interrupt pipe from the Asynchronous Sink and the default pipe to the Adaptive Source. This is incorrect.

> Feedback is provided by an isochronous IN pipe from an Asynchronous Sink and by an isochronous OUT pipe to an Adaptive Source.

Isochronous pipes that provide synchronization feedback are known as SYNCHRONIZATION PIPES. Even though they use the USB isochronous transfer method, they do not, in fact, transfer data every frame. They only transfer feedback information during those frames indicated by their associated feedback rate. Every n frames, the host sends a packet containing the feedback to the Adaptive Source. On all frames but the nth frame, the Adaptive Source does not receive any packets on its isochronous feedback pipe. The host sends an IN token to the Asynchronous Sink every frame. However, the Asynchronous Sink only responds with feedback data on the nth frame.

The feedback is in the format of an exact, expected data rate, as shown in Figure 9.7.

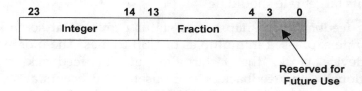

Figure 9.7: Feedback Status

The Asynchronous Sink, using the current state of its buffers, provides the feedback as its current optimum data rate. If its local device clock varies with regard to the transport clock, its optimum data rate may change over time. The Adaptive Source achieves this data rate by maintaining a sum in the same format. The fields for the *FeedbackStatus* notification are summarized in Table 9.5.

Field	Description
Integer	Indicates the number of samples currently sent in each frame.
Fraction	If an ideal data rate was maintained, a fractional amount of samples would also be sent each frame. Based on the Asynchronous Sink's buffer status, this gives the ideal size of this fractional sample.

Table 9.5: Summary of *FeedbackStatus* Fields

The *Integer* field corresponds to the number of samples sent in a frame by the Adaptive Source and received by the Asynchronous Sink, as detailed in Table 9.6.

Integer	FeedbackStatus
Offset:	bit location 14
Length:	10 bits
Legal Values:	in number of samples
Default Value:	00h
Description:	Minimum number of samples expected per frame, relative to the sink's clock. Unless the device is synchronous at a constant data rate, the sink will eventually run dry if this amount of samples per frame is never increased.
	In the case of 44.1 Khz audio being sent to a very stable Asynchronous Sink, the minimum expected number of samples per frame is 44. However, if the source does not increase the sample rate to 45 every tenth frame, the sink will run out of samples over time.

Table 9.6: Integer Field Definition

The *Fraction* portion of the *FeedbackStatus* is handled differently than the *Integer* portion. For the Asynchronous Sink it still indicates the current ideal rate. The Adaptive Source, however, uses it to accumulate fractional portions of samples to occasionally add an additional sample to a packet. See Table 9.7.

Fraction	FeedbackStatus
Offset:	bit location 4
Length:	10 bits
Legal Values:	% of a sample
Default Value:	00h
Description:	If packets were not constrained to contain full samples or bytes, this would be the current optimum fraction of a sample which would be sent to the sink every frame. This value may vary according to the variability of the device clock relative to the transport clock.
	The Adaptive Source keeps a running sum of these fractional portions and, when a full sample is indicated, it increases the number of samples in the packet by one.

Table 9.7: Fraction Field Definition

For details on how the sink provides feedback and the source uses it, see the next section. Note that the host is an integral part of this connection and makes sure that the appropriate feedback interface is always provided to the device, regardless of the paired connections.

> **Regardless of the actual sink, Adaptive Sources always receive feedback information.**
>
> **Regardless of the actual source, all Asynchronous Sinks are required to provide feedback information.**

The device must identify the type of synchronization it needs, which of its pipes are synchronization pipes, and the feedback rates for those pipes. Currently the 1.0 USB specification does not define the descriptor information required for this reporting. At the time of this writing the Common Class Specification defines endpoint-related descriptor information for these items.

9.2.4 Synchronization Processes

The preceding section describes the facilities that USB defines to allow data streams to be synchronized. But how are these facilities actually used to meet the requirements for isochronous transport? The specification requires certain behavior and descriptive information from the device in order to assure interoperability. The host, however, may interact with the device, within the bounds of the specification, in a variety of ways to implement a synchronization process. Any synchronization process used by the host must meet the USB synchronization requirements of:

- Matching input to output data streams.
- Minimizing buffer sizes.
- Fully characterizing any holes in a damaged data stream.

Two different synchronization process implementations are described: Balanced Average, and Fixed Pattern. Both implementations are supported by the 1.0 USB Specification. Although specific requests have been defined to support the Fixed Pattern model, the Balanced Average model is the more generic and reliable and is in most cases the preferred implementation.

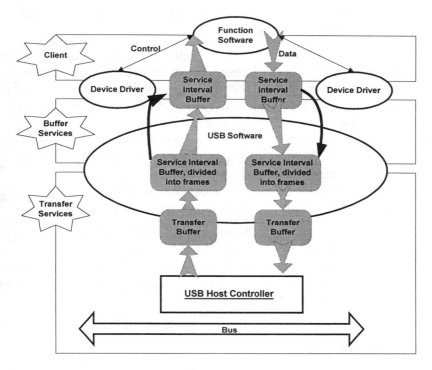

Figure 9.8: Buffer Flow Model Roles

In the USB isochronous buffer model, the function software submits a buffer for a given service interval. This buffer is then translated into separate per-frame packets. The roles which must be present in this model are captured in Figure 9.8.

The client is responsible for preparing buffers representing a single service interval for the application. Buffer services then breaks the service interval buffer into per-frame data. Transfer services is jointly implemented by the USB system software and the host controller that actually send the data to or retrieve the data from the device. Transfer services may break a buffer received by buffer services into smaller transfer buffers, depending on the requirements of the host controller. When an entire service interval buffer is complete, the buffer itself and some associated per-frame transfer status returns to buffer services. When the client receives the buffer, the data in the buffer is contiguous, with holes left for missing and damaged data.

Not all of the roles depicted in Figure 9.8 need map one-to-one with separate software processes. For instance, buffer services can be provided by the USB system software, or it can be implemented as part of the device driver. At the function software level, a service interval buffer is a contiguous data stream. At the host controller, the buffer is broken into a series of frame-sized data. Buffer services provides the translation between these two views. Whether the device driver has to worry about implementing buffer services depends on whether or not the specific operating system, or some additional helper software, implements that service layer.

Buffer services translates between a whole buffer view and a per-frame view following device-provided data stream parameters. Buffer services also implements the synchronization process for the host. Two supported examples of synchronization processes are described in the following sections.

Balanced Average

The Balanced Average synchronization process is based upon the concept of spreading the samples in a buffer as evenly as possible across all of the frames that represent the corresponding service interval. The resulting series of packet sizes varies by no more than one sample per frame. Minimizing differences in packet sizes preserves the "constant volume" requirement that minimizes device buffer sizes. Figure 9.9 shows how a service interval buffer is distributed across multiple frames using a balanced average approach.

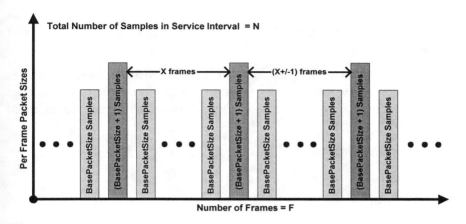

Figure 9.9: Balanced Average Spreading

The goal is to spread the N samples in the buffer as evenly as possible across the F frames that represent the service interval. The base packet size is represented by:

$$BasePacketSize = \text{integer}(\ N/F\ )$$

Equation 9.1: Base Packet Size

All packets in the stream are either *BasePacketSize* or (*BasePacketSize*+1). The number of packets with (*BasePacketSize*+1) samples in them is exactly:

$$N - (BasePacketSize*F)$$

Equation 9.2: Number of Peaks in the Service Interval

The frames with the "extra" sample in them represent peaks in the data stream. These peaks are evenly spread over the service interval. In order for buffer services to correctly spread the service interval buffer, it must be provided with the following information:

- Length in milliseconds of the service interval.
- Size in bytes of the service interval buffer.
- Sample size in bytes.

To vary the rate, the client varies the number of samples in the service interval buffer. For example, if the client is playing a data stream to an Asynchronous Sink, the client uses the synchronization feedback received from the device to determine if samples should be added or removed to the buffer for the next service interval.

If data is damaged or missing in the data stream, buffer services must identify the size of the associated hole. The three basic sources for this information follow, arranged from least accurate to most accurate:

1. *wMaxPacketSize*.

2. BasePacketSize.

3. Sample headers.

The stream's reserved bandwidth is determined by *wMaxPacketSize* and under no circumstances can a packet contain more samples than (*wMaxPacketSize*/*SampleSize*). So, in the event of damaged or missing data, this places an upper bound on the size of the hole.

Streams can use less bandwidth than they have had reserved for them. Under these circumstances (*BasePacketSize*+1) may be rather less than *wMaxPacketSize*. Since buffer services is responsible for the spreading algorithm, and thus *BasePacketSize*, it can use this more accurate characterization of the hole in the data stream.

Sample headers are instream characterizations that allow the exact size of data stream holes to be calculated. A sample header consists of one or two bytes inserted at the head of every data packet.

The sample header at the head of a packet gives the cumulative number of samples that will have been sent by the end of that packet. When this count exceeds the size of the sample header, the count rolls over and begins again. A sample header includes the number of samples in the current packet in its sum so that the host knows what should have been received, at the time that packet is received, instead of waiting for the next packet. Sample headers can be optionally inserted and stripped by buffer services.

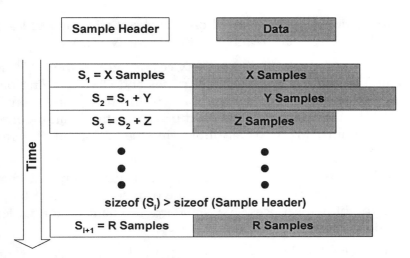

Figure 9.10: Sample Headers

So, using the Balanced Average synchronization process, buffer services provides the following:

- Matches the data streams to each other by transferring service interval buffers that are varied in size by the client.

- Minimizes device buffer size by maintaining a stream whose volume varies by at most one sample from frame to frame.

- Characterizes holes using *wMaxPacketSize*, *BasePacketSize* or sample headers depending on the accuracy required.

The Balanced Average approach therefore meets the synchronization process requirements while requiring minimal knowledge and intervention from the client or the device.

> Devices do not need knowledge of the synchronization process in order for the Balanced Average method to work.

Fixed Pattern

Spreading the data stream across multiple frames results in a pattern of packet sizes. If the device clock is very stable relative to the host clock, ideally if the device is Synchronous, a fixed, and repeating, pattern of packet sizes should develop. The Fixed Pattern synchronization process is based on this observation and relies on being able to treat data streams as if they were Synchronous.

In the Fixed Pattern, buffer services is still responsible for spreading the data across multiple frames and characterizing data stream holes. However, it accomplishes this task based on its knowledge of the data stream's fixed pattern, rather than the more generic parameters used as input in the Balanced Average approach.

In order for this approach to work, both the device and the client need to know the fixed pattern and one of them must describe the pattern for buffer services. No standard mechanism for pattern description is currently defined.

Both the client and the device also need to know on which frame the repeating pattern starts. This is accomplished using the USB defined *SynchFrame* operation. When the device receives this request, it returns the frame number at which it will start tracking the pattern. The host then schedules packets of specific sizes for specific frames in order to implement the pattern.

Buffer services knows exactly the size of data stream holes because the fixed pattern tells it what size of packet to expect in any given frame. The degree to which the stream achieves constant volume depends on the specific packet sizes in the pattern. Adjusting the data stream according to synchronization feedback is more difficult in this approach, as it requires an update to the pattern, thus varying the "fixed" pattern.

Fixed Pattern synchronization, then, works best for synchronous data streams which require no adjustment. It also requires device and host interaction to set up and track it.

> **Both device and host must have specific synchronization knowledge in order for Fixed Pattern synchronization to work.**

For this reason, *i.e.*, requiring *SynchFrame* and pattern tracking support on the device and requiring pattern administration and management on the host, Fixed Pattern synchronization is not widely implemented.

9.3 Isochronous Data Flow Management

Isochronous data streams using isochronous transport exhibit three important characteristics: constant volume, synchronized data flows, and fully characterized data streams. These characteristics impose some requirements on the device's, client's, and buffer services' management of the data flow. The device must follow timing rules for producing or consuming per-frame data. The client must manage the size and timing of the service interval buffer so that a continuous data flow results. Buffer services must provide a fully characterized data stream in order to support the data differentiation allowed for isochronous data streams.

9.3.1 Production/Consumption Model

In order to provide an end-to-end isochronous data flow, the device produces or consumes data according to the frame in which it arrived.

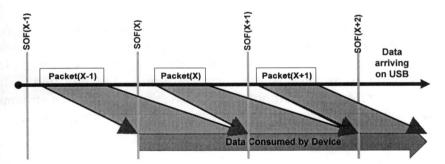

Figure 9.11: Device Consumption Rules

In frame(X) the device receives a data packet(X), which is placed into the device buffer. The device does not consume any of this data until after the device receives the SOF(X+1) demarcating frame(X) and frame(X+1). In fact, if no gaps are to be apparent externally, the device will actually still be consuming data packet(X-1) when SOF(X+1) arrives.

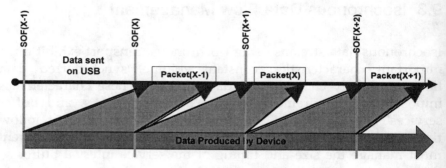

Figure 9.12: Device Production Rules

The rules for devices producing data are symmetric to those consuming it. Data collected during frame(X) is not sent during that frame. Rather, that data is sent after SOF(X+1).

> In the current frame, devices consume data received in the previous frame and send data collected in the previous frame.

9.3.2 Isochronous Buffer Model

The buffer services provided for in the USB buffer model can be designed to handle many different types of transfers using one buffer submittal and status approach. However, in order to maintain the stream's isochrony and provide the required data characterization information, clients managing isochronous streams have requirements on how they interact with the buffer services.

Submitting Buffers

The client must insure that a service interval buffer is available for filling or consumption during all frames. If the buffer is late, one or more frames in the stream will be empty, thus breaking the flow. On the other hand, any data which is submitted, but not currently being sent is considered stale and adds latency to the overall stream. Therefore, submitting too many buffers is also undesirable.

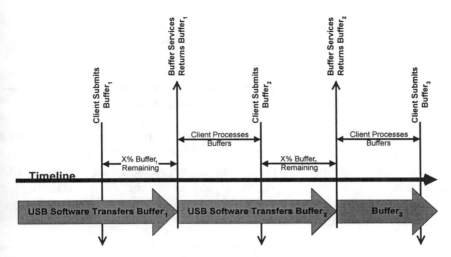

Figure 9.13: Buffer Overlapping

Ideally, only two buffers would be outstanding at any point in time. When the last X% of the first buffer is being worked on, the second buffer would arrive. The first buffer would be completed and available for use while the third buffer is X% ready. This sequence repeats continuously. This "X%" is called the DEGREE OF OVERLAP.

> The larger the degree of overlap, the more stale data, or latency, is introduced into the stream.

The smaller the degree of overlap, then, the better. However, the degree of overlap that can be tolerated is also influenced by processor and bus transport occupancy. Like device buffering, larger overlaps are required to smooth out stream gaps which could be introduced by busy systems.

```
A.          Prime the pump:
   [1]      Submit (buffer) to buffer services
   [2]      Submit (buffer) to buffer services

B.          Wait on buffer complete event from buffer services
   [1]      Receive (completed buffer) from buffer services
   [2]      Submit (next buffer) to buffer services
   [3]      Send (completed buffer) to application
   [4]      Receive (new) buffer from application
```

Figure 9.14: Buffer Submittal Algorithm

The algorithm in Figure 9.14 results in an unspecified but probably large (>50%) degree of overlap. In order to reduce the degree of overlap, however, buffer services must provide the additional functionality of notifying a client of partial buffer completion. If buffer services provides this type of functionality, the algorithm becomes as follows:

```
A.          Prime the pump:
   [1]      Submit (buffer) to buffer services
            Include the degree of completion on which to notify client

B.          Wait on buffer event from buffer services
   [1]      If (partial complete) notification
      [a]       Receive (next buffer) from application
      [b]       Submit (next buffer) to buffer services
   [2]      If (completed buffer) notification
      [a]       Receive (completed buffer) from buffer services
      [b]       Send (completed buffer) to application
```

Figure 9.15: Modified Buffer Submittal Algorithm

If buffer services does not provide a partial completion notification, the algorithm described in Figure 9.14 is the best that can be achieved. The unmodified algorithm requires two submitted buffers initially to start the data stream. This is the minimum number of buffers needed to prime the pump. Additional buffers may be required during the priming stage if the system has a long latency.

Managing Status

Isochronous data streams can support a variety of data types. All of the data in a service interval buffer must be characterized so that the function software knows exactly what the stream looks like. There are two basic approaches to providing this status:

- Packet status.
- **RUN LENGTH ENCODING** (RLE).

In both cases the data must be characterized as to whether it is:

- Non-zero length data, no errors.
- Null data (zero length data, no errors).
- Damaged data.
- Missing data. (Late data is treated as missing data.)

Packet status exposes the bus framing to the function software by providing buffer status as an array of per-packet status. In this model the buffer data is not contiguous and the function software must examine each packet for its individual status. Figure 9.16 gives an example of a packet array and its corresponding status array.

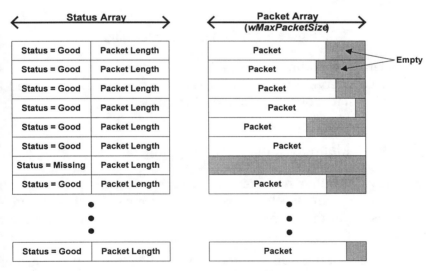

Figure 9.16: Packet Status

Run length encoding only changes status indicators when the type of status changes. Therefore, the buffer data can be contiguous, and the function software can go directly to an area of interest, *e.g.*, a hole, without processing all of the previous packets. Figure 9.17 gives the corresponding RLE array and contiguous data buffer to the results described in Figure 9.16.

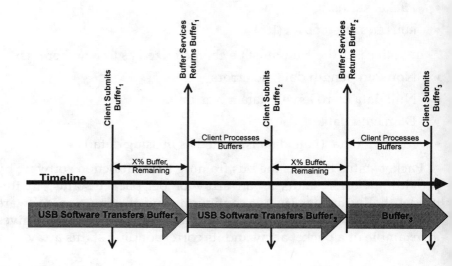

Figure 9.17: Run Length Encoding

Run length encoding is typically provided as companion status to the service interval buffer. Packet status can either be provided as companion status or as part of a packet array.

9.3.3 Pipe Management

USB provides buffer management facilities, described above, to aid in managing an isochronous data stream. It also provides mechanisms for managing the pipes along which these data streams travel.

USB does not provide a method with which to finely synchronize data moving across more than one pipe in the same direction. For example, if the application is playing out video data across one pipe and audio across another, USB assumes that the application will be using a USB-independent method of cross-synchronizing the two streams. USB does allow a client to submit multiple buffers to different pipes, specifying that all of the buffers so submitted will all begin transferring in the same frame.

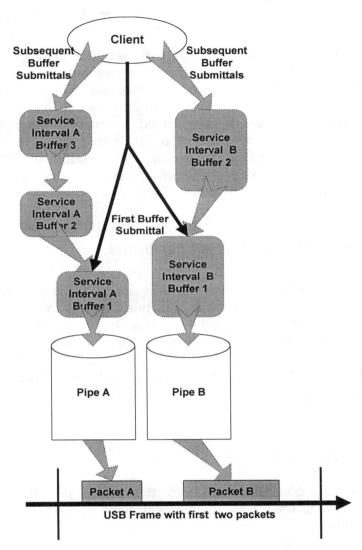

Figure 9.18: Coordinating Buffer Transfers

Once the transfers are started in the same frame, as long as all of the pipes are kept full, the individual data streams will continue to be synchronized to within 1 ms. Referring to the algorithm described in Figure 9.15, the multiple buffer submittal primes the pump. After that, the client maintains a separate event loop for each pipe.

The normal operating state of an isochronous pipe is to be continuously transferring data. However, sometimes the application wishes to change one or more of the operational parameters of a pipe. These parameters may or may not be visible to USB software. In order to change the character of a data stream cleanly, on the fly, the pipe needs to temporarily stop transferring data. The client can then restart the pipe after the changes are complete. USB allows isochronous pipes to be temporarily paused by commanding them to halt as described in Chapter 11 *Device Framework*.

9.4 Providing and Using FeedBack

Section 9.2.3 *USB Isochronous Facilities* describes the basic definition and purpose of the USB synchronization feedback information. But, how does the device produce this information? And, when it receives the feedback, how does a device modify its behavior to accommodate the feedback? The following sections describe how producing and consuming devices interact with synchronization feedback and how clients intervene in the loop to accommodate the feedback.

9.4.1 Device Point of View

All Asynchronous Sinks must provide feedback information, in the *FeedbackStatus* format, on an IN isochronous pipe. However, that is the only requirement on the feedback information. For instance, if an Asynchronous Sink is content to occasionally lose samples or deal with gaps, and thus produce lower quality output, the device may provide a value for the *FeedbackStatus* which is a constant value reflecting the nominal data rate and *not* reflecting any clock variations.

Depending on the device implementation, different algorithms may be used to give clock information feedback. The specific algorithm used depends on the expected reliability of the device clock and its compatibility with the host clock. For relatively stable data streams, a buffer monitoring method can be sufficient. For example the feedback value is started as a constant reflecting the nominal rate and then incrementing or decrementing the fractional value as low or high watermarks in the buffer are tripped.

For more granularity, the device clock itself can be accurately counted against the transport clock. One such method is described in the 1.0 USB Specification. In this method, the device, or true sample, clock is close to some power of 2 multiple of the 1 ms SOF clock (in fact the sample clock could range from 1 kHz to 1 MHz). So:

$$\text{Sample clock} = 2^P \text{ kHz; where } 1 \le P \le 9$$

Equation 9.3: Period of Sample Clock

The count of sample clock cycles is kept over a period of several frames, given by:

$$\text{Number of frames} = 2 \,^\wedge\, (10-P); \text{ where } P \text{ is as defined in Equation 9.3}$$

Equation 9.4: Number of Frames for Update

Note that the slower the sample clock, the larger the number of frames over which the sample clock cycles must be counted in order to provide accurate feedback. Faster clocks require more frequent feedback updates and tighter control of the data stream. The count of the sample clock cycles constitutes the fractional portion of *FeedbackStatus*. Equation 9.4 gives the period of the synchronization pipe. Using this method, the fractional counter is reported once every synchronization period, then cleared and the count starts anew.

The Adaptive Source receives the feedback information from an OUT isochronous pipe at its specified period. The Adaptive Source maintains a sum in the same format as *FeedbackStatus*. At its simplest, this sum has the following meaning:

Field	Operation
Integer	Send this number of samples each frame.
Fraction	Accumulates fractional amount of samples which need to be sent. When the cumulative *Fraction* rolls over, send *Integer*+1 sample for one frame and continue to accumulate in *Fraction*.

Table 9.8: *FeedbackStatus* Sum for Adaptive Source

9.4.2 Client Point of view

In actual fact, the feedback from an Asynchronous Sink is almost never passed directly, unchanged, to an Adaptive Source. Instead, a client managing an Asynchronous Sink changes the service interval buffer size according to the feedback it receives, regardless of the true source of the data. It manages the filling of its OUT buffers as required to keep up, or to drop samples in a rational manner.

A client managing an Adaptive Source always provides feedback to that source regardless of the true destination of the data. For instance, if the actual sink is Adaptive or Synchronous, the client usually provides the Adaptive Source with a constant value as feedback, indicating the nominal rate for the data stream. If, however, the client is having difficulty maintaining an even buffer flow and needs to modify the rate of the Adaptive Source, the client interferes with the nominal feedback value to adjust the source's data stream.

To speed up a data stream, the client increases the fractional amount beyond the nominal. To slow down the stream, the client decreases the fractional amount below the nominal, potentially to 00h. The client can also replace the *Integer* value if emergency, drastic action is required.

9.5 Closing the Loop, an Example

Now, how would all of this isochrony support be employed in a simple example? For example a stream of 44.1 kHz audio played to a very stable Asynchronous Sink. The client uses a service interval of 20 ms, with a 100% degree of overlap, and two priming buffers. This leads to an inherent processing latency of 40 ms (two buffers are outstanding at all times). The device provides a constant feedback of 44.1 and the client provides a constant buffer size of 882 samples. The device has been allocated a bandwidth of 384 bytes to support a top flow of 48 kHz in this configuration for stereo 32-bit audio. Using a Balanced Average spreading algorithm, nine frames of 44 samples are followed by 45 samples every tenth frame.

The client maintains a feedback sum in the same form that an Adaptive Source would. If the particular device did have a more variable clock, the feedback *Fraction* value would potentially vary and cause the client to occasionally increase or decrease the service interval buffer size.

9.6 Non-Isochronous Applications

The USB isochronous transfer type is not restricted to isochronous applications. Applications which desire guaranteed access every frame or which wish to make use of the different data types defined for isochrony, may also use isochronous transfers. Such non-isochronous applications do not, however, necessarily follow all of the requirements for isochronous data streams, *e.g.*, the production and consumption rules.

9.7 Chapter Summary

PC systems have not traditionally provided isochronous transport methods for the isochronous data they manipulate. USB takes a step towards more complete isochronous transport support by defining an interconnect which provides:

- Guaranteed delivery schedule.
- Basic data flow synchronization.
- Support for full data stream characterization.

The synchronization and isochronous transfer interfaces are also defined sufficiently to encourage interoperable devices and host software which is capable of managing aspects of a range of isochronous streams generically.

10. Host Controller Requirements

The host controller provides the connection between the host system and USB devices. Host controllers are typically a combination of hardware and software that deliver the required USB functionality. The hardware portion of a host controller provides the electrical/physical connection to the USB. The software portion controls/directs the hardware portion and provides interfaces to the USB software device drivers. Host controller designs can have different levels of functionality between their hardware and software portions.

This chapter describes the functionality that a host controller (both hardware and software portions) must provide.

10.1 Host Controller Architecture

Figure 10.1 shows a conceptual view of a USB Host controller. The software portion consists of the Host Controller Driver (HCD). This software interacts with the Host Controller hardware through the hardware/software interface. This interface is implementation specific, and the host controller driver is crafted to specifically deal with that hardware/software interface.

The hardware portion of the USB host controller consists of a root hub that provides the USB ports and data buffers (queues) where data is staged as it is moved to/from system memory.

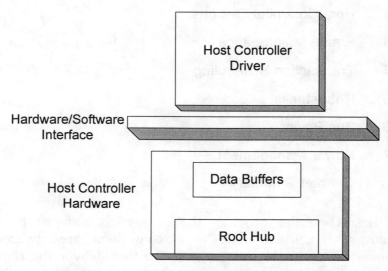

Figure 10.1: Host Controller Architecture

The root hub in a host controller is a logical abstraction of a hub. Typically, the hardware provides the base capabilities of a hub (*e.g.*, connect/disconnect detection), but the rest of the full hub capability is provided by the host controller driver. This allows the hardware implementation to be minimized but still allows the higher levels of software (USB bus driver, USB hub driver) to deal with a consistent hub interface.

The downstream ports provided by the root hub must have all the characteristics and requirements of standard hub ports. Chapter 12 *Hub Devices* describes all the requirements for hub ports.

The data buffers provide some elasticity to the data flow. USB host controllers are typically attached to the system memory via a high bandwidth parallel bus (like PCI). When moving data from system memory to USB, the host controller reads the data into the data buffers using high speed bursts and then dribbles the data out to USB. Similarly, when data is received from USB it is staged in the data buffers and then burst into system memory. A host controller makes memory accesses not just for the data that is moved on USB, but also typically for transaction descriptor and status information used to control what the host controller does or has done.

10.2 Host Controller Designs

There are two standardized implementations of the hardware portion of USB Host Controllers. These are the Universal Host Controller Interface (UHCI) and the Open Host Controller Interface (OpenHCI or OHCI). Both designs are open standards which means they can be implemented by anyone. Most operating systems provide standard drivers (the software portion) for these two designs.

The Universal Host Controller Interface was defined by Intel Corporation. The specification for UHCI can be found on Intel's web pages (http://www.intel.com). The Open Host Controller Interface was defined by Compaq, Microsoft, and National. The specification for OHCI can be found on Microsoft's web page (http://www.microsoft.com).

UHCI is defined such that the software portion of the total host controller has a large responsibility for keeping the hardware portion working on time. This allows a UHCI implementation to be relatively simple, and realized with a low gate count. OHCI is defined such that the hardware portion takes more responsibility for maintaining the data flow, so that the software portion has less work to do. OHCI implementations tend to be more complex and have a substantially higher gate count than UHCI implementations.

Both host controller designs deliver essentially the same functionality and performance for a USB interconnect.

10.3 Frame Maintenance

A USB Host Controller is responsible for all USB frame maintenance as described in Chapter 9 *Frames*. Specifically, the host controller:

- Must maintain a 32-bit frame number and provide a mechanism so that software can read the current frame number. The host controller hardware is not required to maintain more than the lower 11 bits of the frame number which are sent in the SOF packets that are sent at the beginning of every frame. Higher levels of software use the frame number value to properly schedule and synchronize isochronous transfers.

- Is the source of Start Of Frame (SOF) packets that provide frame timing. The host controller generates the SOF packets at the nominal rate of 1 every millisecond, and each packet contains the lower 11 bits of the current frame number. The SOF frequency must be within 0.05% of 1 KHz (500 PPM).

- Must provide a mechanism for software to adjust the number of bit times in a frame. This allows synchronization of the USB frame rate with external subsystems (like a PSTN). Nominally there are 12,000 full speed bit times per frame. Host controllers must allow bit time adjustments of at least 15 bits (plus or minus). It also allows the SOF frequency to be adjusted to as close to 1 KHz as possible, even though the base 12 MHz frequency may not be exact.

- Must maintain frame integrity. The host controller must not start any transactions that cannot complete before the end of the frame. This means that host controllers must do some sort of transaction length evaluation and compare it to the amount of time left in a frame before starting a transaction.

> Host controllers must properly handle the case where long memory latencies on the host side prevent the host controller from starting a transaction at its 'scheduled' time. These 'late' transactions can end up violating frame integrity if the host controller does not compare the transaction length to frame time remaining.

10.4 Transaction Scheduling

The USB host controller is responsible for scheduling queued USB transactions such that they meet the transfer characteristics for the associated transfer types.

- Isochronous transactions must occur at the frame scheduled for the transaction. If an isochronous transaction cannot or does not proceed at its required time, that transaction is skipped and status is marked accordingly. Isochronous transactions are never retried.

- Interrupt transactions must occur at a period equal to or faster than their specified period. An interrupt action that has an error (CRC, timeout, missed its scheduled time, etc.) must be retried no later than the next interrupt period. It does not have to be immediately retried and can be retried at the next normally scheduled time.

- Control transactions must be scheduled so that they are not "starved". This means that control transactions are guaranteed to eventually complete.

- Bulk transactions may be scheduled at any time as long as the previous three requirements are met.

No more than 90% of the total frame time should be allocated for periodic (isochronous or interrupt) transactions. Some of the remaining 10% must be used for control transactions (thus avoiding starvation). Any remaining frame time can be used for bulk actions.

The two host controller implementations generate schedules that meet the above requirements in different ways. Frame traffic from UHCI controllers starts with periodic transactions (isochronous transactions followed by interrupt transactions), then control transactions are done, followed by bulk transactions using any remaining frame time. Frame traffic from OHCI controllers starts with control and bulk transactions (consuming about 10% of the frame), then periodic transactions (isochronous transactions followed by interrupt transactions), and then any remaining frame time is shared by control and bulk transactions.

10.5 Robustness

Host controllers are responsible for detecting any transmission errors across the USB, and providing mechanisms so that system software (above HCD) can determine that a transmission error has occurred. There are several classes of transmission errors that host controllers must detect:

- Protocol Errors. This class of errors is detected by the host when expecting transmissions from the target device. (It is assumed the host controller never introduces protocol errors). This includes bit-stuff errors, false EOPs, and invalid PIDs.

- Time-out conditions. This transmission error arises when the host is expecting a response from a device and none occurs. This happens when the host addresses a non-existent or unresponsive endpoint. It can also happen if the host's transmission is damaged during transit such that it is not recognized by the intended target.

- Data errors. The reception of well-formed packets that have invalid CRC values are one form of data errors detected and reported by the host controller. The host controller also reports data errors when the host is unable to transmit or receive a valid packet. A typical cause for this is when delays in transferring data to or from system memory (for instance, long latencies on PCI) cause the data buffers in the host controller to overflow or underflow. Another type of data error that must be reported is when a scheduled isochronous packet is not attempted at its scheduled time.

All error detection and reporting is done from the host controller's point of view. Actual transmission errors of one type can be detected and reported as a different type of error. For instance, a packet transmitted by the host that has a data error will be detected by the target (because of an invalid CRC value) and the target will not respond with a handshake packet. This lack of handshake packet will look like a time-out to the host, and be detected and reported as a time-out error.

A non-isochronous transaction must be retired if it has three transmission errors. To meet this requirement, host controllers have to maintain an error count for each active non-isochronous transaction. If the error count reaches three for any transaction, that transaction is completed and the reported error is the last error condition that occurred. No error count is needed for isochronous transactions because they are attempted only once.

Transactions that are NAKed are not considered an error condition, since the token and data (if present) phases of the transaction were correctly received and interpreted by the target, and the target delivered an appropriate handshake. Note that this NAKed transaction is a completely well-formed transaction and this may or may not be used to reset the error count for this transaction. If NAKed transactions do not reset the error count, then a transaction that is retried for long periods of time may actually incur random data errors that eventually cause the transaction to be retired with an error.

10.6 Bus Power

As stated earlier, host controllers logically contain a hub known as the root hub. The ports on this root hub have to provide power as specified for standard hubs. The root hub for most desktop machines is normally a self-powered hub and as such can support the connection of high-power devices. On mobile computers, the root hub may be either a self-powered or bus-powered hub. Root hubs on mobile computers may even dynamically change from self-powered to bus-powered and back again based on whether or not the machine is connected to AC power. Higher levels of software (USBD) will have to be capable of supporting these dynamic changes for the system to operate properly.

When determining the USB power budget in a system, the following guidelines can be used (and are explained more in Chapter 4 *Electrical and Mechanical* and Chapter 12 *Hub Devices*):

- If the root hub is operating as a self-powered hub, each root port must be able to provide 500 ma to an attached device.

- If the root hub is operating as a bus-powered hub, each root port must be able to provide 100 ma to an attached device.

- When a port is suspended, the maximum steady state current that the port will source is 2.5 ma. This occurs when a bus-powered hub with four downstream devices attached is attached to the root port.

- Root ports have to be able to provide 500 ma even when the port is suspended. This is because a suspended device may go to its full operating power when responding to an external stimulus and generating a remote wakeup. For instance, a USB modem responding to a ring on the phone line may go to its operating power as it gathers Caller ID information and signals a remote wakeup.

As for all hubs, the root hub implemented by the host controller must provide overcurrent protection, and be able to detect and report the overcurrent condition to system software.

10.7 Power Management

The power management functions of the host controller are the same as a standard hub (see Chapter 12), at least from the perspective of the downstream ports. The root hub ports must be capable of being selectively suspended and resumed.

The root hub can also be globally suspended, which means all traffic out of all ports is stopped at the same time. Behavior of the ports on a root hub when globally suspended is equivalent to a standard hub when it has been suspended due to lack of SOFs.

Root hub ports also must handle remote wakeup signaling. The root hub ports respond identically to standard hubs ports when seeing a remote wakeup. But instead of propagating the remote wakeup to an upstream port (that root hubs don't have) the host controller must alert the system that a remote wakeup has started. System software can then do an orderly system wakeup.

Resume signaling from root ports in response to a remote wakeup must follow the timing specifications for hubs. Termination of resume signaling from the root ports may be controlled by software. If this is the case, resume signaling must last for the minimum time specified, but may last indefinitely until software terminates it.

In systems that are trying to aggressively manage power but still want to use the USB as a wakeup source, the majority of the host controller can actually lose power when the system is in a very low power state. But the root ports must still be capable of detecting and responding to a remote wakeup and the ports must continue to provide power to the downstream devices. However, the ports can continue to drive resume signaling until the whole host controller is powered and re-initialized and the system is ready to resume USB traffic.

10.8 Chapter Summary

Host controllers are the root of the USB subsystem. They provide the interface from the main system to the USB. Host controllers typically consist of a hardware portion that connects directly to the USB, and a software portion that interacts with system software. There are two standard and open host controller designs, one known as Universal Host Controller Interface and the other known as Open Host Controller Interface. The implementations are quite different but provide similar performance on the USB.

Host controllers are responsible for maintaining the integrity and frequency of USB frames, for properly scheduling USB transactions, and for detecting and reporting error conditions that happen on the USB. Host controllers provide power to USB devices and play an important role in the power management of USB devices and the ability of USB devices to wakeup a "sleeping" system.

11. USB Device Framework

11.1 Device Organization

Devices designed for plug and play dynamic attachment must be easily and consistently identifiable and configurable every time they are attached to a system. USB devices fall into this category of requirements. Additionally, USB's physical nature prevents the device's host software from having direct access to the device, interposing a host software programming interface instead. Taking plug and play interoperability to the next logical step, USB devices are also destined to be managed by adaptive host software, thus reducing software development overhead and providing minimal interoperability across systems (see Chapter 13 *USB Classes*. This combination of operational environments imposes some architectural requirements on USB devices:

- A USB device must be self identifiable, in order that the appropriate host software can be located and bound to the device.

- The USB device must describe its functional requirements in such a manner that adaptive host software can configure and minimally manage the device.

- The basic device configuration and operation must be recognizable and manageable by USB system software, not by function software.

Most recent bus architectures impose self-identification of some level on the device. Due to the interposition of a software programming interface, USB also imposes some minimal operation on the device. This chapter explains how a USB device is physically and logically organized and how that organization manifests itself to the host. It also explains how a device describes itself and how it receives and responds to host requests.

11.1.1 Physical Organization

USB places requirements on how a USB device presents itself to the host. From the host's point of view, all USB devices exhibit the same basic structure and behavior. In reality, a USB device can be implemented in a variety of ways, as long as it preserves this basic, external behavior.

It is useful, however, to examine one common physical organization. This example organization serves as a useful reference when describing the required logical device organization. Note that the description in Figure 11.1 does not extend to an illustration of how the device performs its function. Only its USB-relevant organization is depicted.

USB takes explicit notice of the power requirements of both the bus and its attached devices. Power requirements and behavior are therefore part of the configuration and behavioral requirements placed on a device by USB. The following paragraphs describe the role, including power requirements, of each physical component in USB operation.

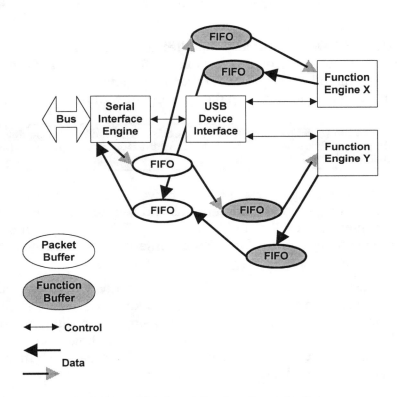

Figure 11.1: Physical Device Organization

The device attaches to USB via the SERIAL INTERFACE ENGINE (SIE), which serializes device data before sending it on the bus, and likewise deserializes the bus data before the device examines it. The SIE also handles the basic USB protocol, *e.g.*, recognizing whether a particular packet is addressed to the device and generating mechanistic portions of the protocol, such as computing the CRC, before sending the packet. The SIE must be available whenever the device is attached to the bus, even when the device has been suspended. This is so that the device can always monitor the bus at some level and know when it must wake up.

> **The SIE must be powered, and capable of monitoring the bus, at all times.**

Because of this requirement, the SIE often draws its power from the bus, which provides 100 μA of power even when the device itself is suspended.

The USB Device Interface handles the more sophisticated USB operation and protocol. It is responsible for parsing, generating, and responding to USB requests, for managing device configuration and for routing data to and from the appropriate termini on the device.

> **Because the USB Device Interface must be operational before the device is configured, it must require no more than the 100 mA of power provided initially by the bus for each device.**

The USB Device Interface may be powered completely by the bus, or through some combination of bus and self-power. While the SIE is frequently implemented as an ASIC, in a number of implementations the USB Device Interface is managed by a microcontroller.

In general, data coming from or destined for the bus is transferred via a temporary holding area known as a **PACKET BUFFER**. This is usually implemented as either a single or a dual, ping-pong buffer. Some of these buffers are capable of holding more than one packet. However, the primary purpose of the packet buffer is to hold bus-formatted data immediately before or after transmittal.

From the packet buffer, the data is sent to or received from one or more FIFO's which act as buffers for the functional capabilities of the device. For example, if the device is a printer, this would be the on-device printer buffer.

Finally, the device contains one or more **FUNCTION ENGINES**. These are the components that actually provide the useful functionality of the device; *e.g.*, printer, modem, mouse.

> **The function engine is not powered and available until the device is configured.**

When the device is configured, the function engine can be either self- or bus-powered, depending on its requirements. Aside from the power requirements, USB places no additional requirements on the function engine. Thus, it is possible to re-use an ISA or PCI function engine in a USB device.

11.1.2 Logical Organization

Externally, the USB device must act as if it is organized in a particular manner. This standard USB device organization is known as the LOGICAL ORGANIZATION of the device, and it is exhibited by all USB devices, regardless of actual implementation. The USB DEVICE ABSTRACTION:

- defines how the device describes its organization
- defines to what standard requests a device will respond and how
- defines which host software roles will own which parts of the device logical organization

To begin with, the USB device abstraction divides the USB device into a series of layers, each with its own role. The logical organization is matched to this layer structure, and thus to the assigned roles. The device abstraction also defines a series of device states and transitions, and finally, the data structures and requests which make this abstraction visible to the host.

Logical Layers

The USB device is organized into a series of logical layers. Each of these layers has its own level of communication with the host and its own associated role. Each of these roles is mirrored in the host software.

The USB BUS INTERFACE implements the USB signaling and basic protocol and corresponds to a similar component on the host.

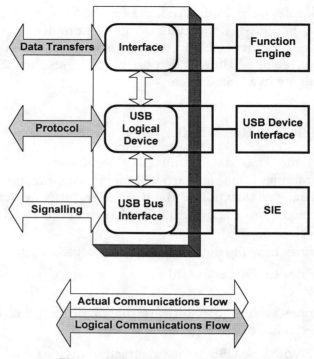

Figure 11.2: USB Logical Layers

The **USB LOGICAL DEVICE** implements the advanced USB protocol and presents the USB device abstraction to the host. It describes and maintains the USB endpoints, including managing the data routing between the bus and the appropriate source or sink. The USB Logical Device is the primary point at which the device describes itself and maintains the USB device abstraction. The majority of the requirements in this chapter apply to this layer, which is usually managed on the host by the system software and included with the operating system.

The **INTERFACE** presents USB-independent functions in terms of USB capabilities; *e.g.*, transfers and pipes. That is, it turns mouse notifications into USB interrupt transfers or audio streams into isochronous transfers. Its organization and operation may be constrained by a class specification that describes the general USB structure and behavior for this type of capability (see Chapter 13 *USB Classes*). This layer is usually owned by some type of function software on the host, whether an adaptive class driver or a device-specific driver.

Logical Structure

The logical organization of a USB device is an abstraction of the common physical organization described in Section 11.1.1 which meets the requirements of the logical layers described above.

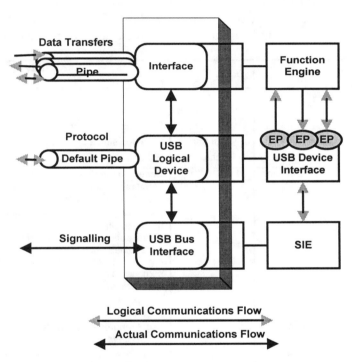

Figure 11.3: USB Logical Organization

The USB Bus Interface layer is implemented logically by the SIE. The USB Logical Device is implemented logically by the USB Device Interface. Each interface maps to a function engine.

Each endpoint is associated with a physical FIFO acting as a buffer for a function engine. Endpoints represent the smallest granularity of device addressing and are the basic device routing component. The USB Device Interface routes data to and from a function engine based on the endpoints, or FIFO's, associated with that function engine, *not* on the identification of the engine itself.

The endpoint is also the basic data transfer point for the device, and the device describes its transfer requirements on a per endpoint basis. A particular physical endpoint may be capable of supporting many different kinds of transfer requirements; *e.g.*, isochronous vs. bulk transfers or different bandwidths at different times. However, at any point in time, based on device configuration, an endpoint has just one set of transfer characteristics. Table 11.1 identifies the transfer characteristics. These will be described in more detail later.

Transfer Characteristic	Values	Variability
Transfer Type		Only 1 Transfer Type active at a time.
	Bulk	Either IN or OUT. Requires single endpoint.
	Control	Requires paired endpoints.
	Interrupt	Requires single endpoint.
	Isochronous	Either IN or OUT.
Direction	IN or OUT	Based on the FIFO capabilities.
Period		Legal range set by transfer type, see Chapter 8 *USB Data Transfers*.
		For interrupts this acts as a minimum value; transfers will occur *at least this often*, and the actual period may vary over time (as constrained above) *without* configuration changes. To change the minimum value, some level of configuration change must be accomplished.
		For isochronous transfers, this acts as an unchangeable exact value.
Packet Size		Legal range set by transfer type, see Chapter 8 *USB Data Transfers*.
		In all cases, this acts as a maximum value; that is, the size of tranfers can vary over time, *up to* the current vaule, *without* configuration changes. To change the maximum value, some level of configuration change must be accomplished.

Table 11.1: Endpoint Transfer Characteristics

The chosen transfer type determines how many endpoints are required and what the bounds will be for direction, period, and packet size. PAIRED ENDPOINTS are two endpoints with the same endpoint number, but different directions. Only the control transfer type requires paired endpoints.

Just as endpoints have associated device FIFO's, the host software managing the data transfers to that endpoint has an associated host buffer. A PIPE is the association of that host buffer with the device endpoint. Pipes, then, are the active, USB manifestation of the endpoint-host association. They use only those transfer characteristics that are currently configured for their device endpoint.

Pipes and endpoints are grouped into interfaces. Interfaces access a device capability provided by a function engine. At any point in time, the number and characteristics of the interface's pipes are fixed by the device configuration. However, changing the device configuration at some level can change both the number and characteristics of the pipes in an interface.

> The host system sees a USB device as a collection of interfaces and pipes, described by a configuration.

At any point in time, there is a configuration structure on the device that describes the device's current appearance and behavior. In fact a particular device may have several alternate configuration descriptions. The host software must choose which of these device configurations it prefers and then tell the device to assume the structure and behavior described by that configuration. This is known as configuring a device (see Section 11.2).

Only one pipe is available at the USB Device Interface layer: the Default Pipe. This pipe, typically owned by the host system software and shared by the host function software, is used to manage the USB configuration of the device. In fact, it is the only pipe available before the device is configured. After configuration, it does not appear explicitly in any interface, but is shared by all, with routing provided by a higher level request protocol.

11.1.3 Standard Device States

USB defines a series of standard device states and transitions. These primarily relate to the configuration and power states for the device. The device may have other states that are known to and managed by its own host software. However, these private states must all fit completely within the USB state management framework.

At any point in time, a USB device can be in exactly one of the following USB device states: ATTACHED, POWERED, DEFAULT, ADDRESSED, CONFIGURED, or SUSPENDED. Table 11.2 summarizes the device states. Transitions between these states occur due to events occasioned by: bus signaling, host requests, or independent device changes. Each of these states has power and configuration requirements that must be obeyed by devices in that state.

The device's capability (function engine) is only available when the device is in the Configured state. Prior to that time, only the Default Pipe is available, starting in the Default state. In fact the Default state is named for the Default Pipe and indicates a state where all of the standard requests and descriptors required by USB are available, but none of the function-specific capabilities are available.

Transitions between the standard states may be initiated by a variety of events. There are, however, a couple of universal initiators.

State	Maximum Power	Device Availability
Attached	none	Physically attached, but no power has been applied to the port on the upstream hub. Device is not aware of attachment.
Powered	500 μA	Port power has been applied. The device is now aware that it is attached. It does not see any bus traffic.
Default	100 mA	The device has observed a valid RESET signal, and will now observe bus traffic. It takes on and responds to device address 0.
Addressed	100 mA	The host has assigned a unique, non-zero, address to the device.
Configured	500 mA	The host has chosen a particular configuration for the device. All of the interfaces and pipes described by that configuration are now available. The function engine is now available and may draw up to 500 mA from the bus.
Suspended	500 μA	If the device does not observe bus activity for three or more milliseconds, it is required to enter the Suspended state. The SIE, however, must still be able to respond to wakeup signalling. When the device awakens, it returns to its pre-suspended state.

Table 11.2: Standard Device State Definitions

> Observation of a valid RESET signal in any state, except Attached, returns the device to the default state.

The reason the Attached state is exempted is that the RESET signal cannot be physically transmitted to the device without the hub powering its port. In fact the device itself is not particularly aware that it is in the Attached state.

> A bus inactivity period of 3+ milliseconds causes the device (no matter what its current state) to enter the Suspended state.

As far as the implementation requirements for availability and power consumption go, the device may treat the Attached, Powered, and Suspended states much alike. However, the transitions out of these states lead to different behaviors:

291

1. A RESET while in any of these states except Attached returns the device to the Default state. However, RESET cannot be observed while in the Attached state.

2. Only the Suspended state responds to WAKEUP signaling. When WAKEUP signaling is observed by a Suspended device, the device returns to whatever USB state it was in before it suspended.

All of the possible transitions are captured in the state diagram shown in Figure 11.4.

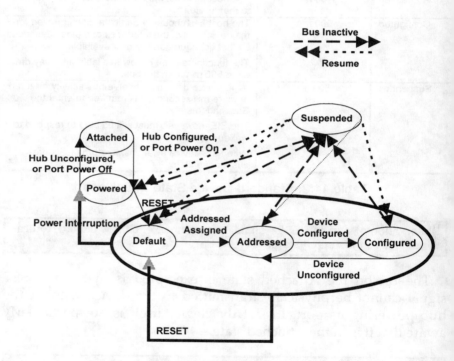

Figure 11.4: USB States and Transitions

The Attached state is unique in that the device itself cannot distinguish it. The Attached state is only entered if the user plugs the device into a hub port which is not supplying any power. Port power is not supplied under two conditions:

1. The host has turned off the port's power, probably for power conservation reasons. Since the device's SIE is no longer powered, the host has also accepted that the device will not be able to resume gracefully once the power is turned back on, but will act as if it were newly attached.

2. The hub is not configured. The hub basically acts like any other USB device, but the capability that it provides is the specialized USB hub function, rather than other, more generic functions, such as keyboard or modem. However, since a hub is also a USB device, its function engine (the actual hub) is not available and cannot draw or provide power until the hub device is configured. Therefore, until a hub is configured, all of its downstream ports are without power and cannot detect attachment changes.

If a device is attached to a configured, powered port, it can detect that it is attached to a hub. Until it sees a RESET, however, it is required to draw no more than 500 µA of power and to behave as if it were not present. Requiring the device to see a RESET before it responds to any bus traffic serves two functions:

1. It allows the host to sequence the enumeration of the bus, (see Chapter 14 *Enumeration*), so that no more than one device is responding to address 0h at any point in time.

2. It ensures that the device is in a known, coherent state before interacting with the host.

Once a RESET is received, from any state except the Attached state, the device enters the Default state. While in the Default state:

*   The device responds only to address 0h.

*   All of the USB Device Interface capabilities are available, including descriptors and requests.

*   Only the Default Pipe, which is used to access the USB Device Interface, exists. If the host attempts to use the Default Pipe for any other reason, such as accessing an interface which has not yet been configured, the result is undefined. The preferred implementation is to treat that access as an unsupported request and respond with a STALL PID.

- None of the function engines are available. Any attempt to access pipes which would normally exist only after the device is configured may result in undefined behavior. However, the recommended implementation is to simply not respond to any access on unconfigured pipes, since they do not truly exist.

- The device can draw no more than 100 mA from the bus, enough to report and manage configuration information.

The host may read all or part of the device's self description, but before it can begin to configure the device, it must first set the device address to a non-zero value.

> Once the device address is set, it is in the Addressed state.

Once the device is in the Addressed state, it may now be configured by the host, which chooses the desired configuration. Once the device is configured, it may draw up to the maximum power from the bus: 500 mA. The chosen pipes and interfaces are also available for use.

> Once the device is configured, it is in the Configured state.

At any point in time, if the bus is idle for more than 3 ms, the device enters the Suspended state. When the device is resumed, using RESUME signaling, the device returns to its previous USB state. For example, should a device in the Default or Addressed state enter the Suspended state and then be resumed, the device will return to the Default or Addressed state, respectively. In particular, the device will not be Configured and its function engine(s) will still be unavailable and its bus power draw still restricted.

Preservation of USB state is guaranteed across a RESUME, *e.g.*, the device will have the same address and configuration as before being suspended.

> Preservation of function-specific state is not guaranteed across a RESUME.

So, for example, if the device's host software has administered the function (*e.g.*, set the connection type or default communications protocol) and the device transitions through the Suspended state, the host may need to re-administer the function when the device is resumed. Whether or not this will be necessary is very specific to the device implementation and/or the requirements of its class specification (see Chapter 13 *USB Classes*).

Transitioning between states may take the device some time. If the device does not respond appropriately within the given timeframe after a transition, the host may conclude that the device is broken and either reset it or ignore it.

> **Devices must be able to respond on their Default Pipe within 10 ms of any state transition.**

However, this response can simply be a NAK. The device can then continue returning NAK's until it is ready to respond in a more reasonable fashion.

> **Devices may NAK up to five seconds on their Default Pipes before they can be considered broken.**

There are no specific requirements for the response time required for the other pipes in a configuration. However, five seconds is a reasonable bound for these pipes as well, as most hosts are disinclined to keep more than one timer when the requirements are not clear.

11.2 Device Configuration

Configuring a USB device means telling that device which interfaces and pipes are to be available, and what the characteristics of those interfaces and pipes must be. The device describes what configurations it can support, how much power each configuration requires, what its capabilities are and which interfaces and pipes will result. The host then chooses from this range of configurations and assigns a single configuration to the device. This results in a

USB configuration of the device, with USB transport and control mechanisms (*e.g.*, pipes) being made available. In order to be completely ready for use, many devices also require some functional configuration. The functional configuration is typically done by the function-specific software on the host, and may include function-specific parameters such as data format or language.

A USB device describes its requirements in terms of endpoint and interface requirements. A single configuration describes a set of these endpoint and interface requirements. The following sections describe what is included in an endpoint or an interface characterization, how configurations are chosen, and how they are changed.

11.2.1 Endpoints

An endpoint characterization consists of an endpoint number and the transfer characterizations given in Table 11.1. Endpoints never appear in a configuration by themselves, but are always part of an interface.

The Default Pipe is always implemented by the endpoint pair denoted by endpoint number 0 in both directions, and is always available, even before device configuration. After device configuration, the Default Pipe continues to be accessible, and is also logically included in all of the active interfaces. This means that the host software owning a particular interface also has access to the Default Pipe for its requests. This implies that, beyond routing data based on endpoint number, the USB Device Interface may also need to provide a subrouting capability for endpoint 0.

11.2.2 Interfaces

At minimum, an interface characterization consists of interface identification and the set of included endpoints. It may also include some capability information.

An interface is identified by two values:

1. Interface number.

2. Alternate setting number.

The interface number is the primary identifier, and serves to uniquely identify the primary function of the interface and its associated function engine. For example, the interface may relate to a set of speakers. The alternate setting number is the secondary identifier, and is used to change the characteristics of the interface. For example, different alternate settings of the above audio interface might allow different bandwidths or different audio formats without requiring different function software.

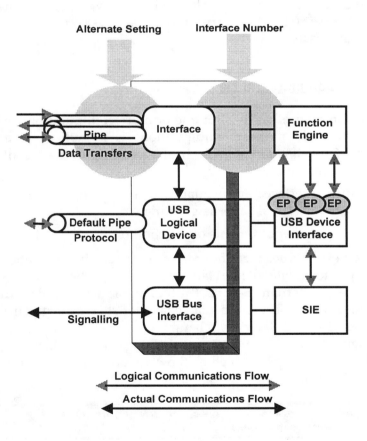

Figure 11.5: Interfaces and Alternate Settings

The interface characterization may also include capability information, *e.g.*, identifying the class to which the interface is compliant. It may also describe some specific capability information, such as the control language or data formats used. Figure 11.5 shows how the alternate setting affects the organization of an interface, *i.e.*, which pipes exist or what their characteristics are. Each interface is owned by a single host software owner. The capability information may influence which host software is chosen to own the interface, and it will impact how that host software manages the device.

The description of the interface also includes the list of endpoints and their characterizations. Although it is never included in this list, endpoint pair 0 (or the Default Pipe) is always considered to be part of the interface.

11.2.3 Configuring a Device

Each USB device has a list of one or more configurations that it can support. Each of these configurations is identified by a unique value, *bConfigurationValue*. Each of the configurations contains the following information:

- Which interfaces are available in that configuration, including all of the available alternate settings.
- The power requirements of the configuration.

The host chooses a configuration by requesting activation for the appropriate *bConfigurationValue*. When that particular configuration is chosen, Alternate Setting 0 of each of the included interfaces becomes active. The particular characteristics of a given interface can be changed later by changing the active alternate setting. Changing an alternate setting can change the number and kind of endpoints included, as well as the class and capability information for the interface.

> Alternate settings may only be changed when the pipes in the currently active alternate setting are not transferring data.

In other words, in order to change which alternate setting is active, the activity in the interface must be temporarily interrupted. This simplifies the overall operation of changing alternate settings by removing the necessity of handling changes in packet size, transfer type, etc. when existing data is already pending with a different packet size and so on.

Given the range of changes allowed between alternate settings, why would a device ever want more than one configuration?

> **Differing configurations should only be used to change the power requirements or the number of interfaces active.**

Changing alternate settings is something that can be accomplished with minimal overhead on an as-needed basis. It accommodates variances like differing audio media or the changing requirements of a phone connection. It does not affect the overall appearance of the device.

Changing configurations does in fact affect this overall appearance. For instance, the power draw for a mobile vs. a desktop configuration can be varied. Or, suppose that this particular device is a multimedia control center that supports a variety of devices such as speakers, mixers, MIDI, and so on. The number of interfaces can be varied to only provide an AUDIO OUT capability when the speakers are actually plugged in.

While changing alternate settings is comparable to "tuning" the interface, changing configurations is comparable to setting user options, or, in a more archaic time, jumpers!

Configuration Example

Let us examine a sample device that allows multiple configurations and alternate settings. This is a telecommunications device with two configurations:

- Configuration 0: a simple POTS (Plain Old Telephone Service) telephone.

- Configuration 1: either a POTS telephone with data capability or a multimedia modem, depending on availability and the requirements of the connection.

This example is somewhat contrived, in that a real telecommunications device of this sort would most likely either be rather simpler in design (exposing only a telephone + data modem interface) or significantly more complex, allowing a larger range of interfaces to be dynamically available based on connection type. However, this particular example is useful in that it exhibits sufficient complexity to be illustrative of the main concepts. Subsequent sections in this chapter will build upon this example to show other concepts.

This example conforms to, but does not fully describe, the description of the COMMUNICATION class in Chapter 13 *USB Classes*.

The description of Configuration 0, the POTS telephone, is shown in Figure 11.6. The figure shows the logical structure of the configuration description. The actual storage of this information and how the device is organized to support this configuration may be physically quite different than the illustration.

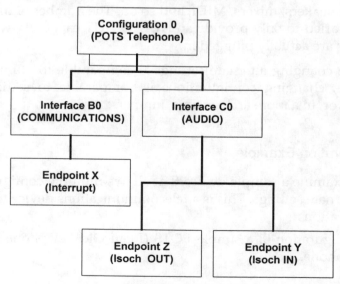

Figure 11.6: POTS Configuration

If this configuration is chosen by the host, two interfaces will be available: a call control interface (B0) and an AUDIO IN/OUT interface (C0). The call control interface will be used for receiving notifications like "ringing". The AUDIO interface provides the ability to talk/listen over a handset or speaker/microphone combination. Table 11.3 summarizes this configuration.

Interface	Alternate Setting	Endpoints	Class	Usage
B	0	EP-X	COMMUNICATION	Interrupt pipe, for call notifications
C	0	EP-Z, EP-Y	AUDIO	isochronous, normal bandwidth

Table 11.3: Configuration 0 - POTS Telephone

This configuration would be used when the user has no service provider for data connections and just wants to use the telephone aspects. Concentrating the functionality into just a POTS connection maximizes the bandwidth available for the audio connection, potentially increasing the quality.

Now suppose that the user does have data connectivity available and wants to be able to use both it and the phone functionality. Configuration 1, shown in Figure 11.7, illustrates this case.

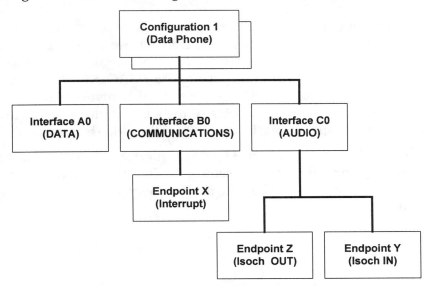

Figure 11.7: Data Phone Configuration

301

If this configuration is chosen by the host, three interfaces will be available: a DATA interface, a call control interface (B0), and an AUDIO IN/OUT interface (C0). The DATA interface has no endpoints initially, under the assumption that the bandwidth will be scheduled as needed. The audio connection must always be available, on the other hand, in order to handle normal phone calls. The initial group of alternate settings (which is always indicated by alternate setting 0) results in a device which looks much like the POTS configuration, except that the DATA interface has been defined and bound to a host driver prepared to handle it. Note that the Default Pipe is available for use by all of the interfaces, including Interface A. This configuration is summarized in Table 11.4.

Interface	Alternate Setting	Endpoints	Class	Usage
A	0	none	DATA	Available for data transfer
B	0	EP-X	COMMUNICATION	Interrupt pipe, for call notifications
C	0	EP-Z, EP-Y	AUDIO	isochronous, 2 possible bandwidths

Table 11.4: Configuration 1 - Data Phone

Now, suppose a call has been established which needs to use the DATA interface. In particular the user wishes to exchange video information. The device now needs endpoints in Interface A conforming to the IMAGING class. The IMAGING class will use isochronous transfers, and is very bandwidth intensive, so the host also changes the alternate setting of the AUDIO interface to a lower packet size to free up bus bandwidth for the video information.

Note that the data transfers on Interface B have not been disturbed while the alternate settings on Interface A and Interface C have changed. Figure 11.8 and Table 11.5 show the effects of these changes.

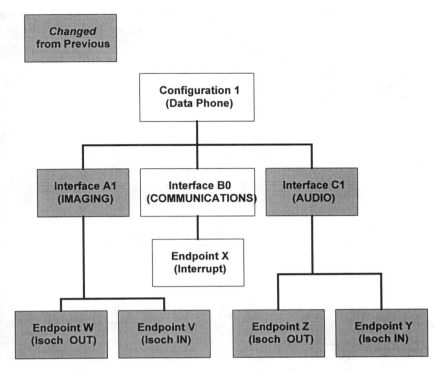

Figure 11.8: Alternate Setting for IMAGING Interface

Interface	Alternate Setting	Endpoints	Class	Usage
A	1	EP-W, EP-V	IMAGING	used to transfer video data in 2 directions; isochronous, 1 bandwidth
B	0	EP-X	COMMUNICATION	Interrupt pipe, for call notifications
C	1	EP-Z, EP-Y	AUDIO	isochronous; new, lower bandwidth

Table 11.5: Alternate Setting A1, C1: IMAGING

Now that the video exchange is completed, the user wants to download a file, so Interface A will change back to a DATA interface, using bulk transfers. This frees up some isochronous bandwidth, but increasing the AUDIO interface's bandwidth by changing the alternate setting would interrupt the conversation, so that interface's alternate setting does not change. Figure 11.9 and Table 11.6 show the changes for this case.

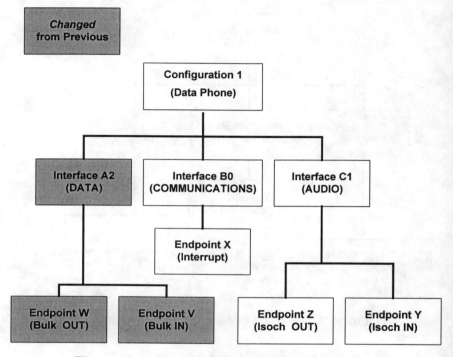

Figure 11.9: Alternate Setting for DATA Interface

The new DATA interface is now ready, although only Endpoint W will actually be transferring data. Note that the conversation on Interface C was not interrupted, but that the transfers on Interface A had to come to a complete halt in order to move to a different alternate setting.

Interface	Alternate Setting	Endpoints	Class	Usage
A	1	EP-W, EP-V	DATA	Bulk data transfers possible in 2 directions.
B	0	EP-X	COMMUNICATION	Interrupt pipe, for call notifications
C	1	EP-Z, EP-Y	AUDIO	isochronous; lower bandwidth remains

Table 11.6: Alternate Setting A2: DATA

Note that *any* of the interface characteristics can change when an alternate setting is changed. The only constraint is that no data transfers may be in progress.

11.3 Descriptors

The previous section discusses what sorts of characteristics are included in a configuration, why a configuration might be selected, and how it may be changed. This section describes the format and exact contents of the retrieved configuration information.

11.3.1 What is a Descriptor?

A descriptor is a record format used to provide information about a standard part of a logical device such as a configuration or an interface. Descriptors may be used to describe:

- Device configuration information, including interfaces and endpoints.
- User readable strings.
- Class- or vendor-specific information about control mechanisms, data formats, etc.

The 1.0 USB Specification allows for three types of descriptors:

- STANDARD: the 1.0 Universal Serial Bus Specification governs the definition of these descriptors, and all devices must support them.
- CLASS: the relevant class specification, see Chapter 13 *USB Classes*, governs the definition of these descriptors, and all interfaces compliant to that class must support them.
- VENDOR: the vendor controls the definition of these descriptors.

The standard descriptors appear in a defined hierarchy that matches the configuration structure described in Section 11.2. The complete hierarchy template is depicted in Figure 11.10.

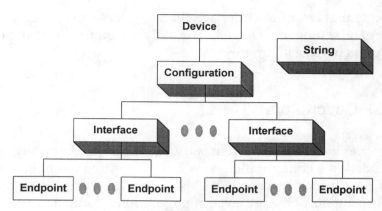

Figure 11.10: Descriptor Hierarchy

There is only one DEVICE descriptor, which characterizes the device as a whole. The device descriptor handles those items that are not impacted by a change in configuration. There is always at least one CONFIGURATION descriptor, one for each possible device configuration. Associated with the configuration descriptor are the descriptors for all of the interfaces in that configuration.

> There is one INTERFACE descriptor for each (interface number, alternate) setting combination.

Associated with each interface descriptor are the ENDPOINT descriptors for all of the endpoints that are available when that alternate setting is active. STRING descriptors are used to store user-readable strings and may be associated with any other descriptor via an index.

Standard descriptors are retrieved from the device using specific requests (see Section 11.3). The device and string descriptors are retrieved individually. However, retrieving a configuration descriptor actually results in a transfer of an ordered buffer including all of the interfaces and endpoint descriptors associated with that configuration.

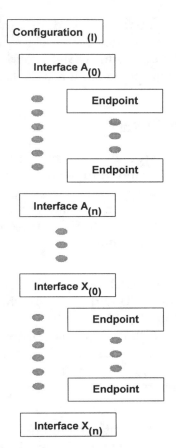

Figure 11.11: Retrieving a Configuration Descriptor

The configuration buffer that is retrieved when a configuration descriptor is requested consists first of the particular configuration descriptor, followed by a list of all interface descriptors. The interface descriptors are ordered as: interface A for alternate setting 0, then other alternate settings for interface A, interface B for alternate setting 0, then other alternate settings for interface B, and so forth. Following each interface descriptor are the descriptors for all of the endpoints available when that alternate setting is active.

Class and vendor-specific descriptors may also be retrieved using a specific request. However, they are usually returned interleaved within the configuration buffer. For example, if a given class descriptor relates to a particular endpoint in an interface compliant to that class, then an instance of that class descriptor is returned in the configuration buffer immediately following the descriptor for the particular endpoint to which it has a relationship.

11.3.2 Descriptor Storage

When the device is requested to do so, it must send descriptors over the Default Pipe, either individually or structured in a configuration buffer. The retrieval buffers have a very particular structure so that one host system-level parser can handle all USB devices. However, the descriptors and retrieval buffers were also defined to allow a range of internal device storage implementations in a cost-effective manner.

Two methods of internal storage in particular were considered during the design of the USB descriptors: the Database Method and the Buffered Method. The Database Method optimizes for efficient storage by ensuring that each descriptor is stored only once. However, this method is more processing intensive when locating and building the configuration buffer and is most likely to be used in implementations which have a microcontroller, but limited memory.

For example, the descriptor hierarchy depicted in Figure 11.12 results in the layout shown in Figure 11.13 when the Database Method is used.

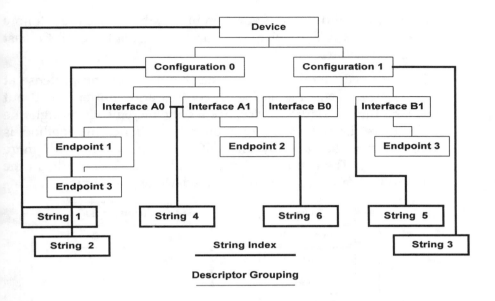

Figure 11.12: Sample Descriptor Hierarchy

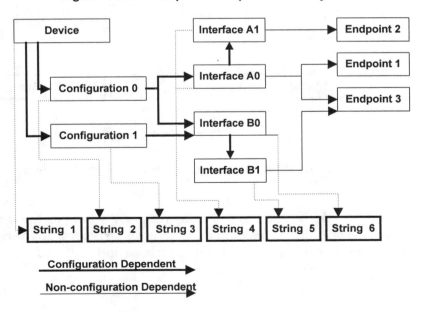

Figure 11.13: Sample Hierarchy in the Database Method

In order to build the configuration buffer, the device must follow the links from the particular configuration descriptor until the last endpoint is included.

The Buffered Method, on the other hand, makes no pretense at saving space. In this method, each configuration buffer is laid out ahead of time and the device need only increment through the buffer to retrieve the configuration information. This method is more likely to be used by an ASIC implementation with more storage space. The hierarchy depicted in Figure 11.12 results in the layout in Figure 11.14 when the Buffered Method is employed.

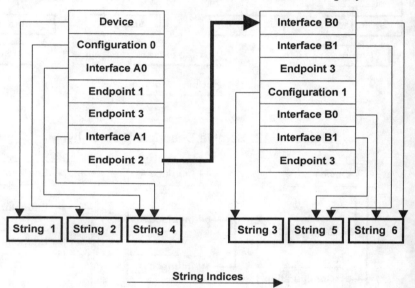

Figure 11.14: Sample Hierarchy in the Buffered Method

USB does not specify which of these methods, or any other method, should be used to store descriptors. As long as the device returns descriptors in the defined descriptor structure, any internal storage mechanism is all right. The Database and Buffered Methods are simply two sample approaches.

11.3.3 Basic Descriptor Structure

All standard descriptors use the same basic descriptor structure in order to simplify the number of different host parsers required and to reduce the chance of misidentification. For the same reasons, class and vendor-specific descriptors should use the same structure as the standard descriptors. Although this is not an explicit requirement of USB, device designers have nothing to gain and a little compatibility to lose if an incompatible class or vendor-specific structure is chosen.

All descriptors begin with the same two fields:

- *bLength*, which states the descriptor length in bytes, from beginning to end, including *bLength*.

- *bDescriptorType*, which identifies the kind of descriptor retrieved.

Besides giving the length and type of the descriptor, these fields also distinguish between descriptor versions, which may have a length change from version to version.

Some descriptor types have multiple instances; *e.g.*, multiple configuration descriptors associated with a device or multiple interfaces associated with a configuration. In these cases, the convention is always to include the number of instances in the previous descriptor type in the hierarchy. For instance, the device descriptor includes the number of configurations and the configuration descriptor includes the number of interfaces.

Table 11.7 describes the standard descriptor structure. The tables following give details about the individual fields. This is the same format used subsequently to describe the contents of each standard descriptor.

Standard Descriptor Structure

Field	Description
bLength	Size of the descriptor.
bDescriptorType	Code identifying the type of descriptor.
FIELDS	Series of fields specific to this type of descriptor.

Table 11.7: Summary of Standard Descriptor Structure

Every descriptor consists of *bLength, bDescriptorType,* plus one or more fields. This allows several descriptors to be returned in a single buffer and then parsed by host software.

bLength	Standard Descriptor Structure
Offset:	0
Length:	1 byte
Legal Values:	numbers from 3 to 255
Default Value:	none
Description:	This is the length of the entire descriptor in bytes, including this field.
	This is always the first byte of any descriptor. All descriptors are at least 3 bytes long, and standard descriptors, and most class and vendor-specific descriptors are never longer than 255 bytes.
	The one exception to this rule is the long descriptor type defined by the HID class, which allows descriptors longer than 255 bytes.
	The USB Specification makes the assumption that any changes in descriptor definitions in subsequent versions may result in a changed descriptor length. Thus, *bLength* is also used to distinguish between versions of the descriptor definition.

Table 11.8: *bLength* Description

While *bLength* is used primarily for parsing a descriptor buffer and distinguishing between descriptor versions, *bDescriptorType* identifies the usage of the descriptor and thus who might be interested in the information.

bDescriptorType	Standard Descriptor Structure
Offset:	1
Length:	1 byte
Legal Values:	constants
Default Value:	none
Description:	The supported descriptor types for the standard descriptors are defined by the USB Specification, and summarized below:

DEVICE   1
CONFIGURATION   2
STRING   3
INTERFACE   4
ENDPOINT   5

The supported descriptor types for a class descriptor are defined in the appropriate class specification, see Chapter 13 *USB Classes*.

Table 11.9: *bDescriptorType* Description

Following the *bDescriptorType* field is a series of descriptor type-dependent fields. Each field may be of any length, and are returned as a sequential stream of fields.

11.4 Standard Descriptors

This section describes in detail each of the standard descriptors and their usage. The discussion begins at the top of the hierarchy, with the device descriptor, and moves down through the list to the configuration descriptor, interface descriptor, endpoint descriptor, and, finally, the string descriptor.

The standard descriptor structure is assumed, and the *bLength* and *bDescriptorType* fields are not repeated as the first two fields in each description.

11.4.1 Device Descriptor

There is only one device descriptor per device and it is used to describe the overall device; including device identification, number of configurations, and the Default Pipe attributes. The device is

313

identified not only by vendor information, but also by class information that applies to the entire device. For more information on USB classes, see Chapter 13 *USB Classes*.

The Default Pipe does not have an endpoint descriptor to give its characteristics since it is only implicitly included in each interface. Also, the characteristics of the Default Pipe, in particular the supported data payload size, must be available as soon as possible, as the Default Pipe will be used to read the rest of the device's information and then configure the device.

Field	Description
bcdUSB	Universal Serial Bus Specification Release Number.
bDeviceClass	USB class information applying to the entire device.
bDeviceSubClass	USB subclass information applying to the entire device.
bDeviceProtocol	USB protocol information applying to the entire device.
bMaxPacketSize0	Maximum packet size for endpoint zero.
idVendor	USB-assigned vendor ID.
idProduct	Vendor-assigned product ID.
bcdDevice	Vendor-assigned device release number.
iManufacturer	String describes manufacturer.
iProduct	String describes product.
iSerialNumber	String contains device's serial number.
bNumConfigurations	Number of supported configurations

Table 11.10: Summary Table for DEVICE Descriptor

The device descriptor is identified by the DEVICE descriptor type. The current version of this descriptor is 18 bytes long.

bcdUSB	DEVICE
Offset:	2
Length:	2 bytes
Legal Values:	0x100, Version 1.0 of the USB Specification
Default Value:	0x100
Description:	This identifies the version, in binary coded decimal, of the *Universal Serial Bus Specification* to which this device was built. This version number applies to all of the descriptors and requests implemented by this device, as well as to the device abstraction and behavior.

Table 11.11: *bcdUSB* Field

USB defines several classes based on USB connectivity requirements and the capability provided by the device. If the entire device is a member of a single class, *and* the device is to be bound to its owning host software only as an entire device, this field must contain a constant indicating a valid USB class. If however, this device's interfaces (which may be of the same or different class) are to bound individually to its host software, then the "device class" is 00h.

bDeviceClass	DEVICE
Offset:	4
Length:	1 byte
Legal Values:	00h or class constants allocated by the USB implementers' Forum (USB-IF)
Default Value:	00h
Description:	Value 00h indicates a composite device, where the interfaces may be bound separately to host software.
	Value FFh indicates a vendor-specific class, where the *bDeviceSubClass* and *bDeviceProtocol* are also vendor-specific.
	Otherwise, a valid USB class code must be used and applied to the entire device.
	Class codes are not available from the USB-IF until the appropriate class specification is available at least at the 0.9 version level. Any class definition which is not yet at the 1.0 version level is subject to change, and may render its use in this field pointless.

Table 11.12: *bDeviceClass* **Field**

The following two fields, *bDeviceSubClass* and *bDeviceProtocol*, depend on the class specification indicated by *bDeviceClass* for the correct values. If *bDeviceClass* is 00h, indicating a composite device, then both *bDeviceSubClass* and *bDeviceProtocol* are 00h.

bDeviceSubClass	DEVICE
Offset:	5
Length:	1 byte
Legal Values:	constants based on *bDeviceClass* value
Default Value:	00h
Description:	This field is used to give a further classification of connection and capability requiremetns, beyond just the class label.
	The class specification indicated by *bDeviceClass* also lists the legal values for this field.
	If this is a composite device, this field must be 00h.
	Vendors may put vendor-specific values in this field only if *bDeviceClass* is FFh.

Table 11.13: *bDeviceSubClass* **Field**

The name, *bDeviceProtocol*, is somewhat of a misnomer. It really does not say anything about the protocols that this device may use.

A better name would have been *bDeviceSubSubClass*, since its real function is simply to refine the *bDeviceSubClass* definition.

bDeviceProtocol	**DEVICE**
Offset:	6
Length:	1 byte
Legal Values:	constants based on *bDeviceSubClass* value
Default Value:	00h
Description:	This field is used to give a further classification of connection and capability requiremetns, beyond just the class and subclass labels.
	The class specification indicated by *bDeviceClass* also lists the legal values for this field.
	If this is a composite device, this field must be 00h.
	Vendors may put vendor-specific values in this field only if *bDeviceClass* is FFh.

Table 11.14: *bDeviceProtocol* Field

All devices have exactly one Default Pipe that is available to all interfaces in all configurations of the device. Thus the description of the Default Pipe is placed in the device descriptor, not an endpoint descriptor like the other pipes. Most of the Default Pipe's characteristics are not explicitly described, as it has the same characteristics for all devices. It uses the control transfer type and maps the endpoint pair identified by the endpoint number 0. It is owned by the host system software and is shared across all interfaces. In fact, all of the Default Pipe's characteristics are known a priori, except for the data payload size, which could be any one of a range of values: 8, 16, 32, or 64 bytes.

The situation for the Default Pipe is complicated by the fact that the Default Pipe will in fact be accessed *before* the data payload size for the pipe is known. In fact the only way to find out the Default Pipe's data payload size is to use the Default Pipe to read the Default Pipe's data payload size.

A happy structuring of the device descriptor solves this problem. All devices must support a Default Pipe data payload size of at least 8 bytes. The eighth byte of the device descriptor just happens (!) to be the Default Pipe payload size. So, the host can use a maximum payload size of eight bytes and still be able to retrieve the Default Pipe's data payload size on the first descriptor read. The host can then set up the Default Pipe for this device to be of the correct size and continue accessing the device in the most efficient manner possible.

The host could also default to a maximum payload size of 64 bytes for the first read and only request 8 bytes. As described in Chapter 8 *Data Transfer,* if the device receives a request of a specific size, it returns only the data that was requested. This will still return at least the first eight bytes of the device descriptor and, as before, the host can now set up the Default Pipe max packet size correctly and continue accessing descriptors.

bMaxPacketSize0	DEVICE
Offset:	7
Length:	1 byte
Legal Values:	8, 16, 32 or 64
Default Value:	None
Description:	The maximum payload size for this device's Default Pipe.

Table 11.15: *bMaxPacketSize0* **Field**

The next series of fields provide vendor information about the device. This information may be used to uniquely identify the device, down to a serial number, if required.

Host systems must allow device-specific software to manage devices instead of the adaptive class driver. This vendor information is used to help identify such a device-specific driver if it exists (see Chapter 14 *Enumeration*).

idVendor	DEVICE
Offset:	8
Length:	2 bytes
Legal Values:	assigned by the USB-IF
Default Value:	00h
Description:	In order to obtain a Vendor Identifier, the device vendor must be a member in good standing of the USB-IF.

Table 11.16: *idVendor* **Field**

The following two fields, *idProduct* and *bcdDevice* are owned completely by the device vendor identified by *idVendor*. The vendor may choose to define them in any manner that makes sense for the product line.

idProduct	DEVICE
Offset:	10
Length:	2 bytes
Legal Values:	varies
Default Value:	00h
Description:	Product Identifier, determined by device vendor.

Table 11.17: *idProduct* Field

bcdDevice	DEVICE
Offset:	12
Length:	2 bytes
Legal Values:	varies
Default Value:	0x00
Description:	This is the version number for this device, given in binary coded decimal.

Table 11.18: *bcdDevice* Field

When devices are attached to a host system, the host often informs the user of that fact by displaying information about the device on the host's screen. USB uses string descriptors to allow a manufacturer to store user-readable descriptions for their device objects.

Using such strings is, of course, storage intensive. However, the manufacturer of Blake's Spiffy Device is surely happier when the host system user is informed that "Blake's Spiffy Device" has been attached, instead of the more anonymous message that a "USB Device" is now available.

iManufacturer		DEVICE
Offset:	14	
Length:	1 byte	
Legal Values:	zero:	no string description of manufacturer present
	non-zero:	must refer to a legal string descriptor
Default Value:	00h	
Description:	This allows a string description of the device's manufacturer, typically the company name. The field value is actually an index uniquely identifiying a string descriptor.	

Table 11.19: *iManufacturer* Field

iProduct		DEVICE
Offset:	15	
Length:	1 byte	
Legal Values:	zero:	no string description of product present
	non-zero:	must refer to a legal string descriptor
Default Value:	00h	
Description:	This allows a string description of the device, typically the product name. The field value is actually an index uniquely identifiying a string descriptor.	

Table 11.20: *iProduct* **Field**

USB makes provision for a manufacturer to mark the device with a serial number. However, USB does not define the format for such a serial number and instead leaves it as an arbitrary string. Some manufacturers may choose to use very extensive asset information in this field. Additionally, some host software may choose to use the serial number as a guaranteed unique identifier to distinguish between multiple instances of the same device, *e.g.*, multiple joysticks attached to the same system, but used by different players. In any case, USB devices are not required to provide serial numbers. For asset and instance management, however, manufacturers are encouraged to use serial numbers.

iSerialNumber		DEVICE
Offset:	16	
Length:	1 byte	
Legal Values:	zero:	no serial number present
	non-zero:	must refer to a legal string descriptor
Default Value:	00h	
Description:	Arbitrary string uniquely identifying this particular device instance.	

Table 11.21: *iSerialNumber* **Field**

Each USB device has one or more possible configurations, indexed from 0 to n-1. The host needs to know how many configurations to ask for when it is discovering the device information. *bNumConfigurations* gives this information and implies therefore that the device descriptor will always be completely read before the configuration descriptors are accessed.

bNumConfigurations	DEVICE
Offset:	17
Length:	1 byte
Legal Values:	1-255
Default Value:	01h
Description:	Reports the number of different configurations supported by this device. When retrieving the configuration buffers, each configuration buffer is indexed 0 to n-1, where n is the total number of configurations supported.

Table 11.22: *bNumConfigurations* Field

11.4.2 Configuration Descriptor

The configuration descriptor reports the overall device appearance and operation when the given configuration is chosen for the device. It reports the power requirements for this configuration and the number of interfaces that it includes. The configuration descriptor is never returned as an individual descriptor, but instead acts as the header record for the retrieved configuration buffer.

Field	Description
wTotalLength	Total number of bytes returned in the configuration buffer for this configuration.
bNumInterfaces	Number of interfaces in this configuration.
bConfigurationValue	Used to uniquely identify this configuration.
iConfiguration	String describing the configuration.
bmAttributes	Characteristics of this configuration.
MaxPower	Maximum power draw from the bus.

Table 11.23: Summary Table for CONFIGURATION Descriptor

The configuration descriptor is identified by the CONFIGURATION descriptor type. The current version of this descriptor is nine bytes long, as described by *bLength*. The configuration descriptor also acts as a header for the configuration buffer and, as such, also reports the *wTotalLength* of the configuration buffer so that the host software will know whether or not the entire buffer has been retrieved successfully.

wTotalLength	CONFIGURATION
Offset:	2
Length:	2 bytes
Legal Values:	varies
Default Value:	none
Description:	The total length in bytes of the configuration buffer for this configuration. This total length includes not only the length of the configuration descriptor and all the interface and endpoint descriptors, but also all of class and vendor-specific descriptors which are interleaved in the configuration buffer.

Table 11.24: *wTotalLength* Field

Within a particular configuration, there are 1 to 255 interface numbers possible. Each of those interfaces may have 1 to 255 alternate settings. Each interface is described by x interface descriptors, where x is the number of alternate settings for that interface. *bNumInterfaces* reports the number of interfaces which are in the configuration, not the number of interface descriptors in the configuration buffers.

bNumInterfaces	CONFIGURATION
Offset:	4
Length:	1 byte
Legal Values:	1 to 255
Default Value:	01h
Description:	The number of interfaces supported by this configuration. These interfaces are indexed from 0 to *bNumInterfaces*-1.

Table 11.25: *bNumInterfaces* Field

The configuration index is used to request a specific descriptor. Configuration indices range sequentially from 0 to *bNumConfigurations*-1. The usage of *bConfigurationValue* is completely different from that of the configuration index.

bConfigurationValue is used to instruct the device as to which configuration the device shall activate. It was chosen to be a distinct value from the configuration index in order to allow some implementation freedom in how the device tracks and activates configurations.

As an example, consider a device with three configurations, indexed 0 to 2. The host wants to select the configuration described by configuration descriptor index 0, which has interfaces 0 and 3.

What might be the *bConfigurationValue* for this configuration?

Option 1: use the configuration index (+ 1, to account for the requirement that *bConfigurationValue* must be non-zero); *i.e.*, 01h.

Option 2: use some bit mapping of active interfaces; *e.g.*, 00001001b, or 09h.

There are many other possibilities for defining *bConfigurationValue*, but the key concept is that separating the definition of *bConfigurationValue* from the configuration index leaves the device implementer free to choose whatever configuration value makes the most sense for the internal configuration management of that particular device.

bConfigurationValue	CONFIGURATION
Offset:	5
Length:	1 byte
Legal Values:	non-zero
Default Value:	01h
Description:	Any non-zero value which uniquely selects a valid, described configuration for this device. Devices in the Configured state have non-zero configuration values assigned to them. Devices in the Addressed and Default states have a configuration value of 00h.

Table 11.26: *bConfigurationValue* Field

As with device vendor information, the iConfiguration is an index for a displayable string that describes the particular configuration. For instance, referring to the example device described in Section 11.2.3, the string description for configuration 0 might be "POTS Telephone" whereas the description for configuration 1 might be "Data Phone".

iConfiguration		CONFIGURATION
Offset:	6	
Length:	1 byte	
Legal Values:	zero:	no string description of configuration present
	non-zero:	must refer to a legal string descriptor
Default Value:	00h	
Description:	Provides a displayable configuration name.	

Table 11.27: *iConfiguration* Field

The next two fields describe the power characteristics of the configuration. The host may choose to take power requirements and capabilities into account when selecting a configuration. For instance, a mobile system may elect not to enable configurations beyond its current budget. Or, the user may be aware the device is currently attached to a wall socket and would prefer that the device be self-powered at the time.

The default value for this field indicates a device which uses only bus power and which is capable of generating a remote wakeup event. In the USB context, a remote wakeup is not merely sourced by communications devices, but also by mice, keyboards, and even monitor controls if they are administered to do so.

bmAttributes	CONFIGURATION
Offset:	7
Length:	1 byte
Legal Values:	bitmap
Default Value:	A0h
Description:	Reports the configuration's power capabilities:

	Bit 7	Device is Bus Powered (set)
	Bit 6	Device is Self Powered (set)
	Bit 5	Device can generate a remote wakeup event (set)
	Bit 4..0	Reserved (reset to 0)

Note that all of the above are capabilities, not characteristics. The device in this configuration may be capable of running on self power; but at any given point in time it may not have self power available. Likewise, the fact that the device is capable of generating a remote wakeup event does not mean that the host has enabled that capability or that the device will in fact generate such an event.

All of these capabilities are orthogonal, and any combination of them may be set as true. If the appropriate bit is set, the capability is present.

The device may be capable of being both bus- and self-powered in this configuration. The exact source of the power at any point in time can be retrieved via the GetStatus device request. See Table 11.71.

Table 11.28: *iConfiguration* **Field**

USB sets broad bounds on device power consumption based on device state:

- 500 μA for the Powered and Suspended states.
- 100 mA for the Default and Addressed states.
- 100 mA for low power devices in the Configured state.
- 500 mA for high power devices in the Configured state.

MaxPower gives a more precise bound for the operational power the device will draw from the bus when it is in the Configured state. For instance, if a host is on a tight power budget, using 500 mA for a maximum power draw for a high power device, when the actual draw is 180 mA, might cause the host to unnecessarily refuse to configure the device. On the other hand, if the device grossly exceeds its stated *MaxPower* draw, thus causing the power budget to be drained much sooner, the device will be perceived as broken.

MaxPower describes the device's power draw from the bus, not the total power consumption for the device. Some devices use a mix of bus and self power. If the source of the self power is lost, the device may not exceed the power draw it declared for this configuration in *MaxPower*.

If such a device can continue completely on bus power, under the *MaxPower* bounds, well and good. If not, then the device must either fail operations that require the extra power, or return unrequested, to the Addressed state. In such a failure mode the host software can check the capabilities reported by *bmAttributes* and the power source status for the device (GetStatus device) and discover the problem.

MaxPower	CONFIGURATION
Offset:	8
Length:	1 byte
Legal Values:	0-250 units: resulting in 0-500 mA
Default Value:	00h
Description:	Reports the maximum power draw from the bus in this configuration, in 2 mA units. For example, a value of 150 for *MaxPower* indicates a 300 mA draw from the bus.

Table 11.29: *MaxPower* Field

11.4.3 Interface Descriptor

The interface descriptor uniquely identifies the interface, including class and capability information along with the interface number and alternate setting. Each interface descriptor describes a single alternate setting for the given interface. As such, it is associated with endpoint descriptors for all of the endpoints that will be available if that alternate setting is active.

All of the alternate settings for a particular interface are independent of each other. And, as long as none of the endpoints in the new setting for this interface are already available in another interface's active setting, switching at any time between any two alternate settings of an interface is completely legal as long as no data is currently being transferred on the interface

When the device is configured to a given *bConfigurationValue*, alternate setting 0 of each interface in that configuration is automatically activated. Past that point, changing the alternate setting for one interface has no effect on any of the other interfaces in the configuration.

> **Alternate Setting 0 of any interface should use the minimum bandwidth required for that interface, potentially 0 bandwidth.**

Designing Alternate Setting 0 to request the minimum, not the maximum, requirements is part of being a good USB device and coexisting comfortably with other USB devices. Since it uses the minimum amount of resources, it also increases the likelihood that the device will be accepted and configured by the host on any particular attachment.

Using the minimum amount of resources can mean a number of different things:

1. Choosing the minimum bandwidth required to be operational. For example, using only the minimum amount of audio bandwidth to support a phone call. This guarantees that there will be sufficient resources to accept the call. If there are more resources available at the time of call reception, which could increase the call quality, then those extra resources can be allocated at that time, instead of tying up those resources permanently.

2. Using no bandwidth until the function is required. Consider a different kind of audio interface, one used for playback. At the time of playback, the user would like to allocate as much bandwidth as possible to this task, maximizing the quality. At the same time, tying up the bus permanently, when no

playback is occurring, reduces the overall quality o experience.

3. Use the interface's Alternate Setting 0 as a placeholder unti the device or the host determines what kind of task is to be performed. This is the role of Interface A0 in the example shown in Figure 11.7.

As in #2, some of the configuration and setup of the device should be left as a matter of policy for the user. However, it is the nature of most USB host implementations that the device wil normally be initially configured without user intervention. While this approach is designed to increase the plug and play nature of the attachment process, it also places more responsibility on the device developer to choose reasonable, minimal default configurations for Alternate Setting 0.

Field	Description
bInterfaceNumber	Index uniquely identifying this interface.
bAlternateSetting	Identifies an alternate setting for this interface.
bNumEndpoints	Number of endpoints in this interface.
bInterfaceClass	USB class information applying to this interface.
bInterfaceSubClass	USB subclass information applying to this interface.
bInterfaceProtocol	USB protocol information applying to this interface.
iInterface	String describes interface.

Table 11.30: Summary Table for INTERFACE Descriptor

The interface descriptor is identified by the INTERFACE descriptor type. The current version of this descriptor is nine bytes long.

bInterfaceNumber	INTERFACE
Offset:	2
Length:	1 byte
Legal Values:	0-255; array index
Default Value:	none
Description:	Identifies the particular interface; bounded by the number of interfaces reported in the configuration descriptor as follows:

$$0 \leq bInterfaceNumber < bNumInterfaces$$

An interface descriptor is identified by an interface number and an alternate setting number.

Table 11.31: *bInterfaceNumber* Field

bAlternateSetting	INTERFACE
Offset:	3
Length:	1 byte
Legal Values:	0-255
Default Value:	00h
Description:	With, *bInterfaceNumber*, used to uniquely identify the interface descriptor and the associated endpoint list in this alternate setting.
	This field operates like *bConfigurationValue* and need not be a sequential index. Any unique value will do, however, indices are frequrently used.

Table 11.32: *bAlternateSetting* **Field**

The active setting of any interface contains zero or more endpoints. An interface without any endpoints is completely legal. In fact, such "empty" settings are commonly used as placeholders during the enumeration process so that, even though a host software owner has been located for the interface, no bandwidth is allocated until it is actually needed.

All settings of all interfaces include the Default Pipe (thus even an empty setting has a communication avenue with the host), but the number of endpoints reported in the interface descriptor never includes the endpoint 0 pair which is used for the Default Pipe.

bNumEndpoints	INTERFACE
Offset:	4
Length:	1 byte
Legal Values:	0-255
Default Value:	00h
Description:	The number of endpoints, excluding the endpoint 0 pair, which are available when this setting identified by *bInterfaceNumber* and *bAlternateSetting* is activated.

Table 11.33: *bNumEndpoints* **Field**

The following fields describe the USB class to which this interface is compliant (see Chapter 13 *USB Classes*). USB provides a single pool of class definitions for both the device class identifiers in the device descriptor and the interface class identifiers in the interface descriptor. For example, the AUDIO class can apply to a given interface on the device (*bInterfaceClass*) or to the entire device (*bDeviceClass*).

Interfaces that provide class information in the interface descriptor can be bound to the host's class driver directly.

bInterfaceClass	INTERFACE
Offset:	5
Length:	1 byte
Legal Values:	00h or class constants allocated by the (USB-IF)
Default Value:	00h
Description:	00h indicates that class information is only provided at the device level. FFh indicates that this is a vendor-specific interface.

Table 11.34: *bInterfaceClass* Field

bInterfaceSubClass	INTERFACE
Offset:	6
Length:	1 byte
Legal Values:	constants based on *bInterfaceClass* value
Default Value:	00h
Description:	This field is used to give a further classification of connection and capability requirements, beyond just the class label.
	The class specification indicated by *bInterfaceClass* also lists the legal values for this field.
	Vendors may put vendor-specific values in this field only if *bInterfaceClass* is FFh. If *bInterfaceClass* is 00h, then this field must also be 00h.

Table 11.35: *bInterfaceSubClass* Field

bInterfaceProtocol	INTERFACE
Offset:	7
Length:	1 byte
Legal Values:	constants based on *bInterfaceSubClass* value
Default Value:	00h
Description:	This field is used to give a further classification of connection and capability requirements, beyond just the subclass label.
	The class specification indicated by *bInterfaceClass* also lists the legal values for this field.
	Vendors may put vendor-specific values in this field only if *bInterfaceClass* is FFh. If *bInterfaceClass* is 00h, then this field must also be 00h.

Table 11.36: *bInterfaceProtocol* Field

Any string that labels an interface should contain more information that that which would have been provided by the class information alone. For instance, in the telephone example described earlier, a good name for the interface C0 of both the POTS and the Data Phone configuration would be "Telephone Handset" rather than a more generic "bi-directional AUDIO interface".

iInterface		INTERFACE
Offset:	8	
Length:	1 byte	
Legal Values:	zero:	no string description of interface present
	non-zero:	must refer to a legal string descriptor
Default Value:	00h	
Description:	The name of this interface.	

Table 11.37: *iInterface* **Field**

11.4.4 Endpoint Descriptor

The endpoint descriptor is the primary way of describing the transfer requirements of this configuration, including transfer type, data payload size, polling interval, and direction. When the alternate setting containing this endpoint descriptor is activated, the physical endpoint, and thus the associated pipe, will take on these characteristics.

Endpoint descriptors identify endpoints by an endpoint number and direction. This may or may not match whatever convention is used internally for routing and to identify the physical endpoint.

> There is no requirement that the endpoint number in the endpoint descriptor is actually equal to a physical endpoint number somewhere internally on the device.

It certainly may be convenient for the device if the descriptor endpoint number is the actual physical number used elsewhere on the device. However, as long as the device matches the two identifiers up correctly, the host does not know the difference. Also, bear in mind that the host reading the endpoint descriptor is actually more interested in the endpoint address, as this is what will be included in transfers across the associated pipe. The endpoint address includes direction as part of its identification.

The endpoint address, because it includes direction, can change based on transfer type. Endpoint addresses for the same physical endpoint can change between different alternate settings.

If changing the transfer type changes the direction of the transfers across the pipe, the endpoint address will change as well. This is not a problem for the host, since changing alternate settings will require it to completely tear down one pipe and set up another. Nothing, including the endpoint address, will be preserved across alternate settings of an interface.

An endpoint number and direction may not appear in more than one active alternate setting at a time. Even though the physical to logical mapping of endpoint numbers may be arbitrary, it is true that the host perceives the endpoint address as the physical identifier for the endpoint.

A given endpoint address.e.g., number and direction, may not appear in more than one active alternate setting at the same time.

The same endpoint address can, of course, be used in many different alternate settings. It is the job of the host software doing the configuration to ensure that no two active alternate settings contain the same endpoint address.

Field	Description
bEndpointAddress	Complete endpoint address.
bmAttributes	Endpoint's transfer characteristics in this configuration.
wMaxPacketSize	Data payload size for this endpoint in this configuration.
bInterval	Polling interval for this endpoint in this configuration.

Table 11.38: Summary Table for ENDPOINT Descriptor

The interface descriptor is identified by the **ENDPOINT** descriptor type. The current version of this descriptor is seven bytes long.

bEndpointAddress	ENDPOINT

Offset:	2
Length:	1 byte
Legal Values:	0-255
Default Value:	00h
Description:	Contains the endpoint address as follows:

	Bit 0..3	Endpoint number
	Bit 4..6	Reserved, reset to 0b
	Bit 7	Direction
	0	OUT endpoints
	1	IN endpoints

If the transfer type described by this descriptor is the control transfer type, the endpoint referred to is actually the endpoint pair designated by the endpoint number. In this case the direction bit is ignored and shall be reset to 0.

Table 11.39: *bEndpointAddress* **Field**

The endpoint attributes are meant to report endpoint characteristics and capabilities. Currently, the only defined attributes describe the transfer type used by the endpoint. As the specification evolves over time, this is one of the areas that may be updated to include additional endpoint information in areas like synchronization and endpoint sharing. It is critical therefore, as it is elsewhere, to maintain the existing reserved areas as reset to zero. This will allow current devices to continue to operate correctly, regardless of later specification enhancements.

bmAttributes	ENDPOINT

Offset:	3
Length:	1 byte
Legal Values:	bitmap
Default Value:	00h
Description:	Reports which transfer type is used by this endpoint as follows:

	Bit 0..1	Transfer Type
	00	Control
	01	Isochronous
	10	Bulk
	11	Interrupt
	Bit 2..7	Reserved, reset to 0b.

These are the characteristics this endpoint will take on when the *bConfigurationValue* for this configuraion buffer, and the *bAlternateSetting* for this interface descriptor are chosen by the host.

Table 11.40: *bmAttributes* **Field**

What the 1.0 USB Specification refers to as the "maximum packet size", this book refers to as the "data payload size". What both are describing is the size, in bytes, of the data the packet carries. Tokens, CRC's, etc. are considered to be overhead and are not included. For control, bulk, and interrupt endpoints, this value must be 8, 16, 32, or 64 bytes. See Chapter 8 *Data Transfer*.

For interrupt and isochronous endpoints, for which bus bandwidth is guaranteed upon configuration, the *wMaxPacketSize*, in conjunction with *bInterval*, gives the amount of bus bandwidth that must be reserved for this endpoint in this configuration.

wMaxPacketSize	ENDPOINT
Offset:	4
Length:	2 bytes
Legal Values:	0-1023
Default Value:	00h
Description:	The maximum data payload size in bytes for this endpoint when in the configuration. The actual data payload size in any particular packet associated with this endpoint may legitimately vary from 0 to *wMaxPacketSize*.

Table 11.41: *wMaxPacketSize* Field

The interval gives the guaranteed period at which the device will be polled. It applies only to guaranteed bandwidth transfer types: interrupt and isochronous.

bInterval	ENDPOINT
Offset:	6
Length:	1 byte
Legal Values:	0 to 255
Default Value:	00h
Description:	Length of polling interval in milliseconds
	For interrupt transfers, the host will poll the device at least this quickly. What the host most likely will do is to choose the power-of-2 which meets this requirement and use this as the actual polling interval. For some number of host systems, the range of values which the host will provide is actually powers-of-2 between 8 ms and 255 ms. There is no requirement, however, that the interval be a power-of-2, and a host could, in fact, choose to provide other, non-power-of-two intervals.
	By and large the device manufacturer does not need to consider what the host will provide. Instead, interrupt endpoints should state their best set of requirements, and be prepared to be polled rather more frequently.
	For isochronous transfers, the stated interval will be maintained exactly. Currently, the only legal value for *bInterval* for isochronous endpoints is 01h. Despite the fact that there is only one choice currently available, isochronous endpoints need to report an interval of 01h to ensure compatibility with future definitions.

Table 11.42: *bInterval* Field

11.4.5 String Descriptor

USB provides explicit support for user visible strings describing the device and its components. These strings are carried in special string descriptors, each of which has a sequential index that may be referred to by any of the other descriptors. These are the only optional standard descriptors. If no string descriptors are present on the device, all of the string index fields in the other descriptors must be reset to zero.

The strings are in UNICODE, to allow easy translation into different languages, based on the geographical location of the host system. For more information about the UNICODE encoding standard, refer to:

The Unicode Standard, Worldwide Character Encoding, Version 1.0, Volumes 1 and 2, The Unicode Consortium, Addison-Wesley Publishing Company, Reading MA.

The string descriptors of a particular device may support any subset of a number of languages. The desired language is designated by the LANGID, a 16 bit language ID defined by Microsoft for Windows in:

Developing International Software for Windows 95 and Windows NT, Nadine Kano, Microsoft Press, Redmond, WA.

For all languages, string index 0 lists an array of 2 byte LANGID codes to report the languages supported by this device.

> String index 0 stores the language codes. The value 00h in a string index field in a descriptor indicates that there is no string. It does **not** indicate string index 0.

USB string descriptors are not NULL terminated. The length of these strings is instead derived from the *bLength* field of the standard container.

Field	Description
bString	UNICODE encoded string.

Table 11.43: Summary Table for STRING Descriptor

11.5 Example Standard Descriptor

Recall the telephone example described in Section 11.2.3. This section expands upon that example to develop the complete set of descriptors that would be used to describe such a device. The descriptors are shown as they would be returned to the host; internal implementation may vary. In the case of the configuration buffer, the individual descriptors are shown. The layout of the configuration buffer follows after all of the descriptors are defined individually.

11.5.1 Example Device Description

This device is a communication device that has two possible configurations: POTS Telephone and Data Phone. It is a composite device that provides class information, and is bound to host software, at the interface level. The device descriptor for this device is given in Table 11.44.

The convention for the descriptor tables in this section is that real values are used wherever possible. Where no value is currently available, the convention 0xHH is used.

Field	Value	Meaning
bLength	0x12	18 bytes long
bDescriptorType	0x01	DEVICE descriptor
bcdUSB	0x0100	Release 1.0 of the *Universal Serial Bus Specification*
bDeviceClass	0x00	Composite device; see interface descriptors
bDeviceSubClass	0x00	
bDeviceProtocol	0x00	
bMaxPacketSize	0x40	Payload size for the Default Pipe is 64 bytes.
idVendor	0xHH	USB-IF Vendor ID; only available via the USB-IF
idProduct	0x01	Our first USB product
bcdDevice	0x0100	Version 1.0 of the device
iManufacturer	0x01	"Blake's Marvelous Devices" string index
iProduct	0x02	"Spiffy Communication Device" string index
iSerialNumber	0x03	"0101 0000 0000 0000"; simple serial number of arbitrary length
bNumConfigurations	0x02	2 configurations: POTS Telepone & Data Phone

Table 11.44: Sample Device Descriptor

11.5.2 Example Configuration Descriptors

This device has two possible configurations. The structure of the POTS Telephone configuration is depicted in Figure 11.15.

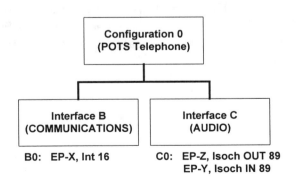

Figure 11.15: POTS Telephone Configuration

The only interfaces in the POTS Telephone configuration are B0 and C0. The second configuration of the device, the Data Phone, is more complex and is depicted in Figure 11.16.

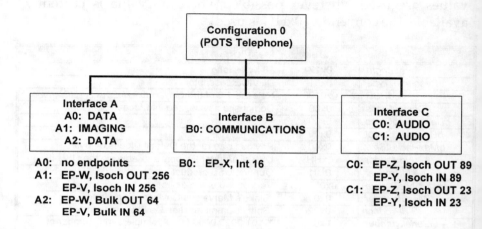

Figure 11.16: Data Phone Configuration

The two configurations for this device use the same interfaces and endpoint definitions. This reuse is not merely an artifact of the example, but is actually a good design principle, conserving device resources and ensuring that once the description is developed correctly, it will apply to all of the appropriate configurations and interfaces. Table 11.45 describes the complete set of interfaces available to this device. The Data Phone configuration uses all of the interfaces, while the POTS telephone only uses interfaces B0 and C0. The Table References column indicates where the appropriate descriptors are defined.

Interface	Class	Descriptors	Table Reference	Usage
A0	DATA	Interface A0	Table 11.48	Available for data transfer
A1	IMAGING	Interface A1	Table 11.50	Imaging Interface
		Endpoint W	Table 11.61	Isochronous
		Endpoint V	Table 11.63	Isochronous
A2	DATA	Interface A2	Table 11.48	Active data transfer
		Endpoint W	Table 11.60	Bulk
		Endpoint V	Table 11.62	Bulk
B0	COMMUNICATION	Interface B0	Table 11.49	Communications call control interface
		Endpoint X	Table 11.57	Interrupt pipe, for call notifications
C0	AUDIO	Interface C0	Table 11.50	Phone conversation
		Endpoint Z	Table 11.53	isochronous, normal bandwidth
		Endpoint Y	Table 11.55	isochronous, normal bandwidth
C1	AUDIO	Interface C1	Table 11.51	Phone conversation
		Endpoint Z	Table 11.55	isochronous, reduced bandwidth
		Endpoint Y	Table 11.57	isochronous, reduced bandwidth

Table11.45: Summary of "Spiffy Communication Device" Interfaces

The configuration descriptor for the POTS Telephone configuration follows in Table 11.46. The definition of the configuration buffer for this configuration, which includes (B0: Endpoint X) and (C0: Endpoint Z, Endpoint Y) follows at the end of this section, after all of the descriptors have been defined.

Field	Value	Meaning
bLength	0x09	9 bytes long
bDescriptorType	0x02	CONFIGURATION descriptor
wTotalLength	0x0030	48 bytes for all of the included descriptors in the configuration buffer: C0, B0, EP-X, C0, EP-Z, EP-Y.
bNumInterfaces	0x02	2 interfaces: B & C
bConfigurationValue	0x01	Chooses this configuration
iConfiguration	0x04	"POTS Telephone" string index
bmAttributes	0xE0	Bus and Self Powered (from the phone line) wakeup source
bMaxPower	0xAA	340 mA bus power

Table 11.46: POTS Telephone Configuration Descriptor

The configuration descriptor for the Data Phone configuration follows in Table 11.47. The definition of the configuration buffer for this configuration, which includes all of the descriptors in Table 11.45, follows at the end of this section, after all of the descriptors have been defined.

Field	Value	Meaning
bLength	0x09	9 bytes long
bDescriptorType	0x02	CONFIGURATION descriptor
wTotalLength	0x007E	126 bytes for all of the included descriptors in the configuration buffer: A0; (A1: EP-W, EP-V); (A2: EP-W, EP-V); (B0: EP-X); (C0: EP-Z, EP-Y); (C0: EP-Z, EP-Y).
bNumInterfaces	0x03	2 interfaces: A, B, C
bConfigurationValue	0x02	Chooses this configuration
iConfiguration	0x05	"Data Phone" string index
bmAttributes	0xE0	Bus and Self Powered (from the phone line) wakeup source
bMaxPower	0xD2	420 mA bus power

Table 11.47: Data Phone Configuration Descriptor

11.5.3 Example Interface Descriptors

The following tables show the interface descriptors for this device, indexed by *bInterfaceNumber* and *bAlternateSetting*. After all of the interface descriptors, the next set of tables gives all of the endpoint descriptors. Note that Interface B is interface number 00h, since interfaces must be zero-based indices and Interface A is not in the POTS Telephone configuration. Therefore Interface B is 00h, Interface C is 01h, and Interface A is 02h.

Field	Value	Meaning
bLength	0x09	9 bytes long
bDescriptorType	0x04	INTERFACE descriptor
bInterfaceNumber	0x02	Interface A
bAlternateSetting	0x00	Default setting for this interface
bNumEndpoints	0x00	No endpoints in this setting
bInterfaceClass	0xHH	DATA class
bInterfaceSubClass	0xHH	ASYNCHRONOUS subclass
bInterfaceProtocol	0x00	none
iInterface	0x06	"Data-Ready Interface" string index

Table 11.48: Interface Descriptor for Interface A0

Field	Value	Meaning
bLength	0x09	9 bytes long
bDescriptorType	0x04	INTERFACE descriptor
bInterfaceNumber	0x02	Interface A
bAlternateSetting	0x01	Alternate Setting 1
bNumEndpoints	0x02	2 endpoints: EP-W, EP-V in isochronous mode
bInterfaceClass	0xHH	IMAGING class
bInterfaceSubClass	0xHH	VIDEO sub class
bInterfaceProtocol	0x00	none
iInterface	0x07	"Video Interface" string index

Table 11.49: Interface Descriptor for Interface A1

Field	Value	Meaning
bLength	0x09	9 bytes long
bDescriptorType	0x04	INTERFACE descriptor
bInterfaceNumber	0x02	Interface A
bAlternateSetting	0x02	Alternate Setting 2
bNumEndpoints	0x02	2 endpoints: EP-W, EP-V in Bulk mode
bInterfaceClass	0xHH	DATA class
bInterfaceSubClass	0xHH	ASYNCHRONOUS subclass
bInterfaceProtocol	0x00	none
iInterface	0x08	"Data Interface" string index

Table 11.50: Interface Descriptor for Interface A2

Field	Value	Meaning
bLength	0x09	9 bytes long
bDescriptorType	0x04	INTERFACE descriptor
bInterfaceNumber	0x00	Interface B
bAlternateSetting	0x00	Default setting for this interface
bNumEndpoints	0x01	1 interrupt endpoint for notifications: EP-X
bInterfaceClass	0xHH	COMMUNICATION class
bInterfaceSubClass	0xHH	AT command set subclass
bInterfaceProtocol	0x00	none
iInterface	0x09	"Call Control Interface" string index

Table 11.51: Interface Descriptor For Interface B0

Field	Value	Meaning
bLength	0x09	9 bytes long
bDescriptorType	0x04	INTERFACE descriptor
bInterfaceNumber	0x01	Interface C
bAlternateSetting	0x00	Default setting for this interface
bNumEndpoints	0x02	2 isochronous endpoints at normal bandwidth: EP-Z, EP-Y
bInterfaceClass	0xHH	AUDIO class
bInterfaceSubClass	0xHH	PCM format
bInterfaceProtocol	0x00	none
iInterface	0x0A	"Telephone Handset" string index

Table 11.52: Interface Descriptor for Interface C0

Field	Value	Meaning
bLength	0x09	9 bytes long
bDescriptorType	0x04	INTERFACE descriptor
bInterfaceNumber	0x01	Interface C
bAlternateSetting	0x01	Alternate Setting 1 for this interface
bNumEndpoints	0x02	2 isochronous endpoints at reduced bandwidth: EP-Z, EP-Y
bInterfaceClass	0xHH	AUDIO class
bInterfaceSubClass	0xHH	PCM format
bInterfaceProtocol	0x00	none
iInterface	0x0A	"Telephone Handset" string index

Table 11.53: Interface Descriptor for Interface C1

Note that Interface A changes its number, class and endpoint type when it changes alternate settings. Interface C, on the other, is really only changing bandwidth allocations, and so does not change its number and class type.

11.5.4 Example Endpoint Descriptors

The following set of descriptors describes Endpoint Z and Endpoint Y in their normal bandwidth allocation. While the general rule is that the default setting for an interface should use the smallest amount of bandwidth possible, the following is a good example of when to bend that rule to assure minimal quality. These endpoints' bandwidths are based on 44.1 kHz 16 bit PCM audio, a very common format of acceptable quality. The reduced bandwidth version uses 22.05 kHz 8 bit PCM audio, a significant reduction. A third option (not included in this example) would be to increase the audio capability to a format requiring significantly more bandwidth. That option would then become Interface C2, *not* the default setting.

Note also that Endpoint Z and Endpoint Y are implemented as the Endpoint 1 pair.

Field	Value	Meaning
bLength	0x07	7 bytes long
bDescriptorType	0x05	ENDPOINT descriptor
bEndpointAddress	0x01	Endpoint Z, OUT
bmAttributes	0x01	Isochronous transfers
wMaxPacketSize	0x005A	90 byte maximum data payload size.
		This number is calculated as follows: samples are sent at the rate of 44.1 samples per millisecond. Each sample is 2 bytes; leading to a total of 88.2 bytes per millisecond.
		Since only complete samples are sent across the bus, 90 bytes must be reserved.
		Most payloads will contain 88 bytes, but approximately once every 5 ms, 90 bytes will be sent.
bInterval	0x01	1 ms polling interval

Table 11.54: Endpoint Descriptor for Endpoint Z, in Normal Mode

Field	Value	Meaning
bLength	0x07	7 bytes long
bDescriptorType	0x05	ENDPOINT descriptor
bEndpointAddress	0x81	Endpoint Y, IN
bmAttributes	0x01	Isochronous transfers
wMaxPacketSize	0x005A	90 byte maximum data payload size.
		This number is calculated as follows: samples are sent at the rate of 44.1 samples per millisecond. Each sample is 2 bytes; leading to a total of 88.2 bytes per millisecond.
		Since only complete samples are sent across the bus, 90 bytes must be reserved.
		Most payloads will contain 88 bytes, but approximately once every 5 ms, 90 bytes will be sent.
bInterval	0x01	1 ms polling interval

Table 11.55: Endpoint Descriptor for Endpoint Y, in Normal Mode

The following endpoint descriptors show the Endpoint 1 pair with reduced bandwidth.

Field	Value	Meaning
bLength	0x07	7 bytes long
bDescriptorType	0x05	ENDPOINT descriptor
bEndpointAddress	0x01	Endpoint Z, OUT
bmAttributes	0x01	Isochronous transfers
wMaxPacketSize	0x0017	23 byte maximum data payload size.
		This number is calculated as follows: samples are sent at the rate of 22.05 (1 byte) samples per millisecond.
		Since only complete bytes are sent across the bus, 23 bytes must be reserved.
		Most payloads will contain 22 bytes, but approximately once every 20 ms, 23 bytes will be sent.
bInterval	0x01	1 ms polling interval

Table 11.56: Endpoint Descriptor for Endpoint Z, in Reduced Mode

Field	Value	Meaning
bLength	0x07	7 bytes long
bDescriptorType	0x05	ENDPOINT descriptor
bEndpointAddress	0x81	Endpoint Y, IN
bmAttributes	0x01	Isochronous transfers
wMaxPacketSize	0x0017	23 byte maximum data payload size.
		This number is calculated as follows: samples are sent at the rate of 22.05 (1 byte) samples per millisecond.
		Since only complete bytes are sent across the bus, 23 bytes must be reserved.
		Most payloads will contain 22 bytes, but approximately once every 20 ms, 23 bytes will be sent.
bInterval	0x01	1 ms polling interval

Table 11.57: Endpoint Descriptor for Endpoint Y, in Reduced Mode

The following table describes the interrupt pipe in the call control interface. Note that the OUT address for the Endpoint 2 pair is not used.

Field	Value	Meaning
bLength	0x07	7 bytes long
bDescriptorType	0x05	ENDPOINT descriptor
bEndpointAddress	0x82	Endpoint X, IN
bmAttributes	0x03	Interrupt
wMaxPacketSize	0x0010	16 byte payload
bInterval	0xFF	255 ms polling interval

Table 11.58: Endpoint Descriptor for Endpoint X

The following set of tables describes the endpoints in Interface A. These endpoints vary between isochronous and bulk transfer types. Note that Endpoint W and Endpoint V are implemented as the Endpoint 3 pair.

Field	Value	Meaning
bLength	0x07	7 bytes long
bDescriptorType	0x05	ENDPOINT descriptor
bEndpointAddress	0x03	Endpoint W, OUT
bmAttributes	0x01	isochronous mode
wMaxPacketSize	0x0100	maximum of 256 bytes per payload, depending on frame rate
bInterval	0x01	1 ms polling interval

Table 11.59: Endpoint Descriptor for Endpoint W in IMAGING Mode

Field	Value	Meaning
bLength	0x07	7 bytes long
bDescriptorType	0x05	ENDPOINT descriptor
bEndpointAddress	0x83	Endpoint V, IN
bmAttributes	0x01	isochronous mode
wMaxPacketSize	0x0100	maximum of 256 bytes per payload, depending on frame rate
bInterval	0x01	1 ms polling interval

Table 11.60: Endpoint Descriptor for Endpoint V in IMAGING Mode

343

Field	Value	Meaning
bLength	0x07	7 bytes long
bDescriptorType	0x05	ENDPOINT descriptor
bEndpointAddress	0x03	Endpoint W, OUT
bmAttributes	0x02	Bulk mode
wMaxPacketSize	0x0040	64 byte payloads
bInterval	0x00	no polling interval

Table 11.61: Endpoint Descriptor for Endpoint W in DATA Mode

Field	Value	Meaning
bLength	0x07	7 bytes long
bDescriptorType	0x05	ENDPOINT descriptor
bEndpointAddress	0x83	Endpoint V, IN
bmAttributes	0x02	Bulk mode
wMaxPacketSize	0x0040	64 byte payloads
bInterval	0x00	no polling interval

Table 11.62: Endpoint Descriptor for Endpoint V in DATA Mode

11.5.5 Example Configuration Buffers

The previous section presented the descriptor definition for the "Spiffy Communication Device". Depending on the chosen storage method, each of this descriptors will appear once in the device's memory (see Figure 11.13) or already arranged into the configuration buffer format (see Figure 11.14).

The configuration buffer for Configuration 0 - POTS Telephone is shown in Figure 11.17.

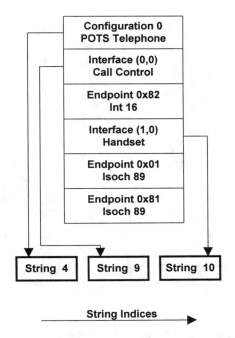

Figure 11.17: Configuration Buffer for POTS Telephone

The configuration buffer for Configuration 1 - Data Phone is shown in Figure 11.18. Note that all of the alternate settings for a particular interface are presented, in order, before the next interface is presented.

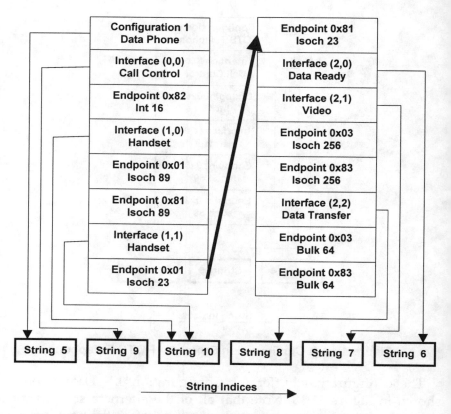

Figure 11.18: Configuration Buffer for Data Phone

This example, of course, does not fully exercise all of the possible options. Some of these are worthy of note:

- Endpoint descriptors can appear in more than one interface and/or more than one alternate setting, just as endpoint numbers can appear in more than one endpoint descriptor. If, for example, it were appropriate to define an alternate setting C2, with four isochronous endpoints, Endpoint W and Endpoint V in Imaging mode could be reused in Interface C2. However, the host would then need to take care to only allow Alternate Setting 0 of Interface A to be active when Alternate Setting 2 of Interface is active.

- Endpoint descriptors need not be grouped in pairs. It is often convenient to do so, based on the device implementation, but it

346

is not a requirement. Certainly if the particular implementation is endpoint-constrained, endpoints must be used where they are available, instead of necessarily where they are paired. For example, with a microcontroller implementation that provides a maximum of eight endpoints (four endpoint numbers, one in each direction), the example in this section uses seven of these endpoints. If an additional OUT endpoint is needed, it would be reasonable to use the OUT portion of the Endpoint 2 pair.

Note that the string descriptors referred to by the descriptors in the configuration buffer must be retrieved individually.

11.6 Class-Specific Descriptors

USB class specifications, described in Chapter 13 *USB Classes*, may define special descriptors for that particular class definition. These descriptors in general use the same basic descriptor structure as standard descriptors. They may be retrieved with a specific class command or returned as part of the configuration buffer.

When they are returned as part of the configuration buffer, this is known as INTERLEAVING, because each class descriptor is associated with a particular standard descriptor in that buffer. Class descriptors follow immediately after the standard descriptors with which they are associated, thus being interleaved within the configuration buffer. Figure 11.19 shows the Data Phone configuration buffer with the appropriate class descriptors inserted.

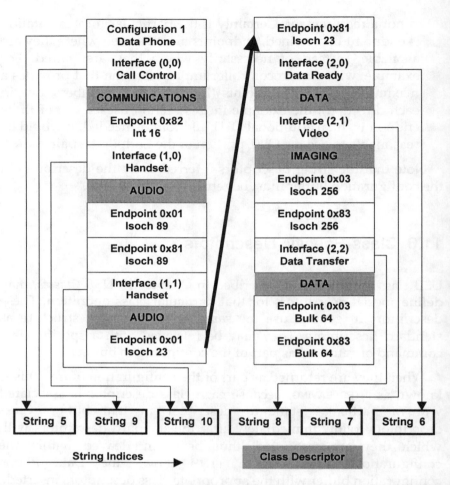

Figure 11.19: Interleaving Class Descriptors in a Configuration Buffer

The example in Figure 11.19 only shows class descriptors inserted at the interface level. This is, in fact, the most common situation, but class descriptors could also be inserted after (associated with) configuration descriptors and endpoint descriptors.

When a class descriptor is inserted after a standard descriptor, it takes on the class of the descriptor with which it is associated.

wTotalLength in the configuration descriptor, which gives the total length of the configuration buffer, must include in its tally the length of any interleaved descriptors.

11.7 Vendor-Specific Descriptors

Vendor-specific descriptors are completely under the control of the device design, although designers are *strongly* encouraged to maintain the *bLength* and *bDescriptorType* conventions to minimize the chances of misidentification.

Vendor-specific descriptors are treated much as class descriptors as far as retrieval is concerned. They may be retrieved with a vendor-specific command or returned interleaved in the configuration buffer. See Figure 11.19.

> Just as with class descriptors, vendor-specific descriptors are associated with the standard descriptors they immediately follow in the configuration buffer.

This is important because the host may choose to separate the configuration buffer into the portions applicable to specific interfaces and send these to the host software owners of those interfaces. If a vendor-specific descriptor is positioned incorrectly in the configuration buffer, it may never reach its intended software.

11.8 Requests

To repeat the introduction of the logical device organization in Section 11.1.2, the USB device abstraction:

- defines how the device describes its organization
- defines to what standard requests the device will respond and how it responds
- defines which host software roles will own which parts of the device logical organization.

Of the above aspects, all have now been described except #3. How *does* the host make requests of a device? And what are the device's response requirements?

11.8.1 What is a USB Request?

At its most basic form, a USB request is a command sent from the host to the device via the Default Pipe. This communication uses the message format described in Chapter 8, *Data Transfer*. The actual request is included in the data phase of the setup stage of a control transfer.

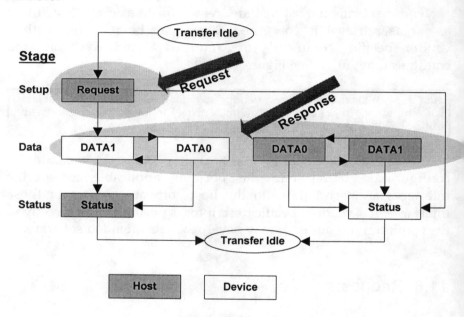

Figure 11.20: Requests using Control Transfers

Like descriptors, USB requests can be standard, class, or vendor-specific. The standard requests are defined by USB, and, in general, must be supported. The class requests are defined by the appropriate class specification, (see Chapter 13 *USB Classes*), which also states which requests are required to be supported under which circumstances. Vendor-specific requests are under the control of the device vendor. However, the same structure as that for the standard and class requests must be maintained.

There are three types of logical device information that can be separately accessible: device, interface, and endpoint. The configuration information from a device explains to the host what information is available and what logical parts there are to a device. USB requests may be addressed to any of these parts, or TARGETS.

While each request, of course, has its own specific data and usage, there are also common structural and behavioral requirements:

- All requests must follow the request structure described in Section 11.8.2.

- The actual request is always included in the setup stage of a control transfer.

- If the host needs to send information beyond that contained in the request to the device, this information is contained in the data stage following the setup stage containing the request.

- If the device's response requires information to be sent to the host, this information is contained in the data stage following the setup stage containing the request.

- The device completes the status stage successfully only after the request has been successfully executed. Devices may NAK the status stage for up to five seconds while executing the request.

- If a request is not supported by the target, or if the request is not valid based on current circumstances, the Default Pipe returns a STALL. The same action results if the request is incorrectly formulated or identifies a non-existent target. This is known as STALLING THE REQUEST.

The request structure used on the Default Pipe essentially forms a higher-level USB protocol on top of the basic USB protocol described in Chapter 8 *Data Transfer*. The rest of this section gives more detail about this higher level protocol as embodied by the request structure and the standard requests.

11.8.2 Request Structure

All requests, including class and vendor-specific requests, have the same basic structure designed to fit in the eight bytes of a setup stage. Each request must indicate the answers to the following questions:

- Is this a standard, class, or vendor-specific request?
- At what specific target is this request aimed? Device, specific interface, endpoint, etc.?
- Is there a data stage associated with this request? If so, in what direction and how many bytes?
- What is the specific request? And is there any associated data included in the setup stage?

Table 11.63 describes the overall request structure. Following this, the individual fields are described.

Field	Size	Description
bmRequestType	1 byte	Reports the request characteristics
bRequest	1 byte	The specific request.
wValue	2 bytes	Request-specific data.
wIndex	2 bytes	Identifies the particular target.
wLength	2 bytes	Length of any associated data stage.

Table 11.63: Request Structure Overview

The *bmRequestType* reports the basic characteristics for this request. The combination of *bmRequestType* and *bRequest* uniquely identifies the request.

Bits	Description	Request
7	If there is a data stage associated with this request, this indicates the direction of the stage as follows: 0: OUT 1: IN	
5..6	Reports the type of the request: STANDARD: 0 CLASS: 1 VENDOR: 2	
0..4	Reports the type of the target: DEVICE: 0 INTERFACE: 1 ENDPOINT: 2 OTHER: 3	

Table 11.64: *bmRequestType* Field

If the request is vendor-specific, the vendor has complete control over the definitions of the one byte *bRequest* codes. If it is a class request, the class specification controls the definition of the *bRequest* codes. The standard *bRequest* codes are defined by the 1.0 USB Specification, and described in Section 11.8.3.

Some requests have associated information which can fit into the request structure, *e.g.*, the *bConfigurationValue* used when establishing a device configuration. The request structure makes allowances for two bytes of such information in *wValue*.

bmRequestType specifies if the target is the entire device, an interface, an endpoint, or some other object. If the target is an interface or an endpoint, *wIndex* is used to specifically identify that target.

Requests do not necessarily have data stages associated with them. However, in some instances, the host needs to send more data than can be held in *wValue*, or the device is required to respond with some information. In these instances, the request will have a data stage. The length of that data stage is given in bytes in the *wLength* field.

11.9 Standard Requests

The currently defined set of standard USB requests is summarized in Table 11.65. For details about each request, see the section describing that request.

bmRequestType	bRequest	Code	Description
0000 0000b 0000 0001b 0000 0010b	CLEAR_FEATURE	1	Clears feature status reported by a device, interface or endpoint.
1000 0000b	GET_CONFIGURATION	8	Retrieves the *bConfigurationValue* of the current configuration.
1000 0000b	GET_DESCRIPTOR	6	Retrieves a standard descriptor.
1000 0001b	GET_INTERFACE	10	Retrieves the active *bAlternateSetting* for the specified interface.
1000 0000b 1000 0001b 1000 0010b	SET_STATUS	0	Returns feature status for a device, interface or endpoint.
0000 0000b	SET_ADDRESS	5	Assigns an address to this device.
0000 0000b	SET_CONFGIGURATION	9	Chooses the active configuration for the device.
0000 0000b	SET_DESCRIPTOR	7	Updates a device descriptor.
0000 0000b 0000 0001b 0000 0010b	SET_FEATURE	3	Activates a feature for a device, interface or endpoint.
0000 0001b	SET_INTERFACE	11	Chooses the active alternate setting for an interface.
1000 0010b	SYNCH_FRAME	12	Retrieves the frame number on which the endpoint started its frame counter.

Table 11.65: Summary of Standard Requests

Note that the *bRequest* codes in Table 11.65 are not in numeric order. This is because the codes were assigned in groups to the standard requests to make it easier to implement request handling in an ASIC implemented state machine. If we turn Table 11.65 around and look at it in code order, the grouping becomes apparent.

Code	Binary Value	bRequest
0	0000 0000b	GET_STATUS
1	0000 0001b	CLEAR_FEATURE
2		reserved
3	0000 0011b	SET_FEATURE
4		reserved
5	0000 0101b	SET_ADDRESS
6	0000 0110b	GET_DESCRIPTOR
7	0000 0111b	SET_DESCRIPTOR
8	0000 1000b	GET_CONFIGURATION
9	0000 1001b	SET_CONFIGURATION
10	0000 1010b	GET_INTERFACE
11	0000 1011b	SET_INTERFACE
12	0000 1100b	SYNCH_FRAME

Table 11.66: *bRequest* Grouped by Code Definition

Note that "gets" and "sets" are grouped, as is the collection of GET_STATUS, CLEAR_FEATURE, and SET_FEATURE. These last three requests all operate on the feature status associated with a device, interface, or endpoint. GetStatus returns the feature status. ClearFeature and SetFeature toggle the setting of the feature and/or acknowledges status changes. So, in terms of a state machine, both ClearFeature and SetFeature are "sets" in the same way SetDescriptor is (note the '1' in the least significant bit).

GetStatus, ClearFeature, and SetFeature indicate on which feature to operate through the means of a FEATURE SELECTOR. The currently defined feature selectors are presented in Table 11.67.

Feature Selector	Target	Code
DEVICE_REMOTE_WAKEUP	Device	1
ENDPOINT_STALL	Endpoint	0

Table 11.67: Feature Selector Definitions

The following sections discuss in detail the standard request definitions. The sections are in alphabetic order as in Table 11.65.

In the following request descriptions, wherever the entire device is the target of the request, *wIndex* is zero. Wherever an interface is the target of the request, *wIndex* is the interface number, or *bInterfaceNumber* of the interface descriptor, which is stored in the lower byte, while the upper byte is reset to zero. Wherever an endpoint is the target of the request, *wIndex* contains the endpoint address, or *bEndpointAddress*, of the endpoint descriptor. As with the interface number, the endpoint address is contained in the lower byte while the upper byte is reset to zero. See Figure 11.21 for a summary of this structure.

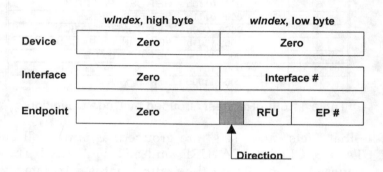

Figure 11.21: Structure of *wIndex*

In general, if byte-length data is transferred in a word-length field of the request, the data is placed in the lower byte and the upper byte is reset to zero.

Unless otherwise indicated, all of the standard requests described here must be implemented by the device.

11.9.1 ClearFeature Request

Request Code (Target) Data/Direction	Index	Value	Length	Data
CLEAR_FEATURE Device Interface Endpoint Direction: none	 Zero Interface # Endpoint #	Feature Selector	Zero	None

Table 11.68: ClearFeature Request Summary

Where SetFeature is used to enable a feature for a device, interface, or endpoint, ClearFeature disables that feature, or acknowledges and resets status. The results of a ClearFeature are retrieved via the GetStatus request. Features are identified by feature selectors, see Table 11.69. If a request uses a feature selector that is not legal or legally clearable for the given target, the device will stall the request.

The only feature that may be cleared for a device is the REMOTE_WAKEUP feature. Issuing a ClearFeature (REMOTE_WAKEUP) prevents the device from being a wakeup source. Whether or not the device would ever be capable of being a wakeup source in this configuration is reported in *bmAttributes* in the configuration descriptor. If the device cannot be a wakeup source and it receives a ClearFeature(REMOTE_WAKEUP) it will stall the request.

There are no interface features capable of being disabled at this time.

The only feature that may be cleared for an endpoint is ENDPOINT_STALL. ClearFeature(ENDPOINT_STALL) is always accepted by the device, even if the pipe is not currently halted.

ClearFeature(ENDPOINT_STALL) has the effect of resetting and restarting a pipe. In particular, it will reset all data toggles for that pipe.

Clearing an ENDPOINT_STALL which has been set by the device will restart the pipe, if the condition which prompted the device to take this action is no longer a factor. If the problem persists, the device may need to halt the pipe again and the host may have no other recourse other than to reset the entire device.

11.9.2 GetConfiguration Request

Request Code (Target) Data/Direction	Index	Value	Length	Data
GET_CONFIGURATION Device Direction: IN	Zero	Zero	One	Configuration Value

Table 13. 1: GetConfiguration Request Summary

GetConfiguration returns the current configuration value. If the returned value is zero, the device is not configured. If the returned value is non-zero, the device is Configured and the particular configuration is described by the configuration buffer containing the configuration descriptor whose *bConfigurationValue* is equal to the value returned by GetConfiguration.

11.9.3 GetDescriptor Request

Request Code (Target) Data/Direction	Index	Value	Length	Data
GET_DESCRIPTOR Device Direction: IN	Zero - or - Language ID	Descriptor Type and Descriptor Index	Descriptor Length	Descriptor

Table 11.69: GetDescriptor Request Summary

GetDescriptor returns the descriptor indicated by the combination of *wIndex* and *wValue*. *wValue* contains the descriptor type in its high byte and the descriptor index in its low byte. *wIndex* contains either a language ID for a string descriptor or a zero for all other types of descriptors. The possible values for descriptor type can be found in Section 11.9.8.

The standard GetDescriptor can retrieve three types of descriptors: DEVICE, CONFIGURATION, and STRING. Retrieving the configuration descriptor using GetDescriptor actually retrieves the entire configuration buffer, including all of the applicable interfaces and endpoints.

If the requested descriptor does not exist, the device will stall the request. If the host asks for more data than actually exists for a given descriptor, the device will simply stop sending data after that descriptor's data is exhausted. If the host asks for less data than a descriptor actually has, the device must send only the data requested by the host.

The first byte of any returned valid descriptor must be non-zero, as it is the *bLength* field.

11.9.4 GetInterface Request

Request Code (Target) Data/Direction	Index	Value	Length	Data
GET_INTERFACE Interface Direction: IN	Interface #	Zero	One	Alternate Setting

Table 11.70: GetInterface Request Summary

GetInterface returns the currently active alternate setting for a particular interface. Even if the interface has only one alternate setting (default zero), the device should implement this request. This requirement is different from that for SetInterface because, while the alternate setting may not be changeable, there is always an active alternate setting.

If the specified interface does not exist in the current configuration, the device stalls the request.

11.9.5 GetStatus Request

Request Code (Target) Data/Direction	Index	Value	Length	Data
GET_STATUS Device Interface Endpoint Direction: IN	Zero Interface # Endpoint #	Zero	Two	Device, Interface or Endpoint Status

Table 11.71: GetStatus Request Summary

GetStatus returns a two byte bit map of the status for a device, interface or endpoint in the data stage of the request. Setting or clearing the status (also a feature) is done via SetFeature or ClearFeature. Feature, in the context of a USB request, means both a feature is to be enabled or disabled and a reported status.

GetStatus is a unique request in that the device is required to always support and execute it, even if the device is currently not accepting other requests. This is so that the host can determine if there is a problem. If the host gets no response from a GetStatus, and subsequently a ClearFeature, the next most likely step will be that the host resets the device.

The status returned for a device is described in Table 11.72. Of the current device status, only Remote Wakeup may be modified by ClearFeature or SetFeature.

Bits	Name	Description
0	Self Powered	Indicates the current status of the device's own power source. If the device is currently receiving power from a source other than the bus, this bit is set.
		The host may access this status to determine the reason why the device has returned to the Addressed state (from the Configured state) or has suddenly reduced its available feature set.
		The configuration descriptor will indicate (see *bmAttributes*) whether or not the current configuration expects an auxiliary power source. This status indicates whether or not such a source is available.
1	Remote Wakeup	Indicates whether or not the device is currently enabled to generate a remote wakeup.
		The configuration descriptor reports whether or not this device configuration can act as a wakeup source. In order for the device to generate a wakeup on the bus, the host must enable the Remote Wakeup feature for the device.
		USB devices do not have a common standard way to indicate whether or not they actually have been the source of a wakeup, only that they could have been the source.
2..15	reserved	

Table 11.72: Device Status / Feature

No interface status is currently defined.

The status returned for an endpoint is described in Table 11.73. The operation of the ENDPOINT_STALL feature is potentially complex. If the device has unilaterally decided to halt the operation of an endpoint, it always sets the ENDPOINT_STALL feature for that endpoint. If the endpoint is using the control, bulk or interrupt transfer type, it will also return a STALL. Isochronous pipes simply time out if halted.

There is one complicating factor in this scenario. In one particular circumstance, a pipe can return a STALL and yet not be halted. This is the case when the Default Pipe observes an unsupported or invalid request and returns a STALL to inform the host that it will not execute the request. In this case the device will not permanently halt the Default Pipe and will not set the ENDPOINT_STALL feature for the Endpoint 0 pair.

In extremely rare cases, the device could choose to unilaterally halt the Default Pipe to indicate some critical problem with the device. If the device chooses to do this, it must also set the ENDPOINT_STALL feature for the Endpoint 0 pair. It may also choose to refuse all requests until the situation is acknowledged. The device, however, must continue to accept GetStatus and ClearFeature, so that the host can indeed acknowledge the problem. Unless the device has additional status describing the problem to share with the host, however, the host may have no other mechanism to restart the device, other than a RESET. For this reason, this ability to halt the Default Pipe should only be used with extreme caution.

0	Endpoint Stall	Indicates that the endpoint has been halted. Once this bit has been set by the device, it can only be reset through one of the following actions:
		ClearFeature (ENDPOINT_STALL)
		SetConfiguration (device)
		SetInterface (for the interface to which the endpoint belongs)
		Device RESET
		The device can not unilaterally reset this feature once it has set it. As long as this feature is set, the endpoint will exhibit the halt behavior appropriate to its transfer type: timing out on isochronous transfers, and generating a STALL for all other transfer types.
1..15	reserved	

Table 11.73: Endpoint Status / Feature

11.9.6 SetAddress Request

Request Code (Target) Data/Direction	Index	Value	Length	Data
SET_ADDRESS Device Direction: none	Zero	Feature Selector	Zero	None

Table 11.74: SetAddress Request Summary

SetAddress is used to assign an address to the device. If the address is non-zero, the device ends up in the Addressed state. If the address is zero, the device returns to the Default state.

If the device was already in the Addressed state, instead of the Default State, it logically transitions through the Default state before re-entering the Addressed state. Being re-addressed while in the Addressed state is an odd thing for a host to choose to request. It is also acceptable, therefore, for the device to stall SetAddress requests when it is already in the Addressed state. At this point, if the host really meant it, it can always reset the device.

SetAddress is the only USB request that issues a successful status before successfully executing the request. This is because if the request succeeds, the address will have changed and deciding which address to use to return the status is now difficult. Therefore, the address of the device does not change until *after* the device indicates success.

11.9.7 SetConfiguration Request

Request Code (Target) Data/Direction	Index	Value	Length	Data
SET_CONFIGURATION Device Direction: none	Zero	Configuration Value	Zero	None

Table 11.75: SetConfiguration Request Summary

SetConfiguration chooses the active configuration for the device by sending it the appropriate, non-zero, configuration value (*bConfigurationValue*) from the configuration descriptor.

If this request succeeds, the device will transition to the Configured state. If SetConfiguration sends a *bConfigurationValue* of 00h, the device enters the Addressed state. Any change in configuration value, in fact, logically transitions the device through the Addressed state to make sure that the previous device state is cleared before a new configuration is established.

If the configuration value is unknown to the device, the device will stall the request and retain its current configuration.

> **Changing a configuration resets all affected pipes. In particular, it resets all data toggles to zero.**

11.9.8 SetDescriptor Request

Request Code (Target) Data/Direction	Index	Value	Length	Data
SET_DESCRIPTOR 　　　　　Device Direction: OUT	Zero - or - Language ID	Descriptor Type and Descriptor Index	Descriptor Length	Descriptor

Table 11.76: SetDescriptor Request Summary

This request is one of the few optional standard requests. SetDescriptor is used to update the descriptors on a device. It is useful to implement easy field upgrades.

Typically, as has been seen in other plug and play bus definitions, device vendors often have problems getting the device's descriptive data correct. SetDescriptor allows the vendor to easily rectify mistakes.

The *wValue* and *wIndex* fields identify the descriptor to be updated as follows. The high byte of *wValue* contains the descriptor type and the low byte of *wValue* contains the descriptor index. The *wIndex* field is zero for all descriptor types but strings. For string descriptors, it contains the language id, see the UNICODE discussion in Section 11.4.5. Table 11.77 describes the legal combinations.

Descriptor Type	Descriptor Index	wIndex
DEVICE	Zero	Zero
CONFIGURATION	0 to bNumconfigurations-1	Zero
INTERFACE	0 to bNumInterfaces-1	zero
ENDPOINT	bEndpointAddress	zero
STRING	0 to number of strings - 1	LANGID

Table 11.77: Descriptor Identification

11.9.9 SetFeature Request

Request Code (Target) Data/Direction	Index	Value	Length	Data
SET_FEATURE Device Interface Endpoint Direction: none	Zero Interface # Endpoint #	Feature Selector	Zero	None

Table 11.78: SetFeature Request Summary

SetFeature enables device, interface, and endpoint features using a feature selector. The results of this enabling are made visible via the GetStatus request. The definitions of the feature selectors can be found in Section 11.9.5.

The only feature that may be set for devices is the REMOTE_WAKEUP feature. Setting REMOTE_WAKEUP enables the device as a wakeup source for USB. If the device is not capable of remote wakeup (see *bmAttributes* in the configuration descriptor), the device will stall the request.

There are no features that currently may be set for interfaces.

The only feature that may be set for endpoints is the ENDPOINT_STALL feature. If the host sets the ENDPOINT_STALL feature for a particular endpoint, that endpoint is now halted and its behavior is exactly the same as if the device had set the ENDPOINT_STALL feature itself. There is one exception to this rule. Devices are not required to be able to halt the Default Endpoint. If the device receives a SetFeature (ENDPOINT_STALL) for the Default Endpoint, it may do any of the following:

- Stall the request.
- Accept the request, but do not halt the Default Pipe.
- Accept the request and halt the Default Pipe.

If the device halts the Default Pipe, the same rules apply to that operation as if the device has unilaterally halted the Default Pipe. The general rule is that if the device will never unilaterally halt the Default Pipe, it should not halt the Default Pipe on the basis of a host request. If, on the other hand, it is capable of unilaterally halting the Default Pipe, it should allow the host to do so as well.

> With the exception of the Default Pipe, the device must accept a SetFeature (ENDPOINT_STALL) for any of its endpoints. Such a request halts the pipe, which results in the same behavior as if the device had unilaterally halted the pipe.

Requesting a feature that does not exist for the target causes the device to stall the request.

11.9.10 SetInterface Request

Request Code (Target) Data/Direction	Index	Value	Length	Data
SET_INTERFACE Interface Direction: none	Interface #	Alternate Setting	Zero	None

Table 11.79: SetInterface Request Summary

SetInterface selects the alternate setting for a given interface. If the device has no interfaces that have alternate settings other than the default setting of zero for each interface, the device need not implement this request. If it does not implement the request it may stall the request. It is also perfectly acceptable in this case to implement the request and simply stall whenever any alternate setting other than zero is chosen.

In general, if an alternate setting is chosen which does not exist for the interface current configuration, the device will stall the request.

Alternate settings may only be changed when the interface is not currently transferring data. It is really the host that makes the determination, from its point of view, of whether data transfer is currently in progress. The device may choose to NAK the SetInterface request until it can flush its buffers. Alternatively, the host may choose to first perform a SetFeature(ENDPOINT_STALL) for each of the affected endpoints before issuing the SetInterface request. This ensures that both the device and the host are in synch.

> Changing an alternate setting resets all affected pipes. In particular, it resets all data toggles to zero.

11.9.11 SynchFrame Request

Request Code (Target) Data/Direction	Index	Value	Length	Data
SYNCH_FRAME Endpoint Direction: none	Endpoint #	Zero	Two	Frame Number

Table 11.80: SynchFrame Request Summary

SynchFrame is optional for all USB devices in all circumstances. If the device does not support this request it will stall it.

USB broadcasts a frame number with every SOF token. This request returns the frame number in which this endpoint restarted its frame counter.

In theory it is possible to observe a pattern of packet lengths when transferring an isochronous stream. Using the frame number to report the start of the expected pattern, the host and the device can theoretically keep in synch by observing the same pattern. This is known as implicit pattern synchronization. Even where the streams can be manipulated to enforce a pattern, however, this is potentially a high overhead operation for both device and host. The same stream can be synchronized with less effort and less explicit knowledge using the methods described in Chapter 9 *Isochronous Communication Model*.

Reconfiguring the endpoint via SetConfiguration or SetInterface results in resetting the frame counter to zero, and another SynchFrame is required to start the counter again.

11.10 Other Requests

11.10.1 Class Requests

Class requests follow the structure and behavioral rules established for standard requests. However, the *bRequest* definitions are owned by the appropriate class specification, see Chapter 13 *USB Classes*.

Looking at the request structure, in particular the *bmRequestType*, one notices that, while *bmRequestType* indicates that the request is a class, not a standard request, there is no means to indicate to which class the request belongs. The class of a request is actually determined by the class of its target. In the case of an endpoint, the class is that of the active alternate setting for the interface containing the endpoint.

11.10.2 Vendor-Specific Requests

Vendor-specific requests follow the structure and behavioral rules established for standard requests. Beyond that, the definition and operation of these requests are entirely up to the vendor.

11.11 USB Common Class Specification

USB is governed by several specifications: the *Universal Serial Bus Specification*, also known as the Core Specification; the class specifications, and the *USB Common Class Specification*. The class specifications are described in Chapter 13 *USB Classes*.

The *USB Common Class Specification* does not define a "common" class in the way that the *USB Audio Class Specification* defines the audio class. Rather, this document, which is still under development, specifies items which are common to all classes and can be used by all devices, but which have not been incorporated into the Core Specification.

Currently, the following topics are addressed by the *USB Common Class Specification*:

- Appropriate structure and criteria for a class specification. This has actually been agreed to for some time by the USB Device Working Group (DWG), which owns this specification. This agreed-upon structure and content is described in Chapter 13 *USB Classes*.

- Common handling of class descriptors using expanded Descriptor Types.

- The complete definition for USB Synchronization. The synchronization definitions in Chapter 5 of the Universal Serial Bus Specification are incomplete, and thus USB synchronization is not capable of being standardized solely on the basis of those definitions. Parts of this updated definition are reflected in Chapter 9 *Isochronous Communication Model*.

- Additional power reporting and power management capabilities. These definitions take into account the total power consumption of the device, not just that from the bus. This also defines standard power states and transitions beyond those defined by the standard USB device states. These definitions are based upon Microsoft's OnNow initiative and are intended to apply to all devices.

- The ability to share endpoints. Many of today's implementations are endpoint-constrained. In addition, many device definitions use several low bandwidth pipes for operations like event notification. The intent of this definition is to allow such pipes to be shared across interfaces, just as the Default Pipe is today.

- Explicit definitions supporting dynamic interfaces. This definition does not change any of the basic configuration information provided by the device. It does, however, allow configuration to be more easily delayed until accurate information is available, based upon some external event like an incoming phone call, or the connection of additional external devices.

- Definitions which would allow implementers to group interfaces together, essentially creating meaningful sub-devices which could be managed as a unit by the host software.

While the requirements for the features included in the USB Common Class Specification are well defined, the specification is currently under development and the actual definitions meeting these requirements are subject to change.

11.12 Chapter Summary

The USB device framework permits host system software to manage common aspects of USB devices by defining the USB device abstraction, including:

- Logical device organization.
- Device layers and their corresponding roles.
- Basic device behavior.
- Descriptive mechanisms.
- Standard requests and request format.

While encouraging class definitions and allowing vendor enhancements, the USB device framework assures basic operation in a variety of systems. Standardizing those components and behaviors which all devices must implement, and which are a value-add for no device, also enables standard software and hardware, thus reducing the effort required to construct a working USB device.

12. Hub Devices

12.1 Introduction

The hub is a unique element of USB architecture. Traditional bus architectures provide connection points for devices along a fixed backplane, also known as bus segments. Different bus masters can interact with any device on a bus segment with the same maximum performance. In the USB architecture there are no backplanes, and the architecture resembles a tree structure (see Figure 12.1). The bus is composed of all the devices and the associated links.

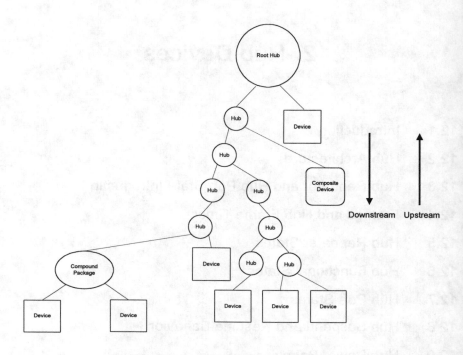

Figure 12.1: Basic USB Bus System

A traditional bus with a backplane can be divided into individual bus segments connected by bridges. Each bus segment has a limited number of connection points due to power and bus loading. In the USB architecture, the number of device connection points is expanded by the addition of unique devices called HUBS. Hubs expand the USB architecture in two ways:

- Incrementally increase connection points through additional ports, and

- Provide incremental power to the devices as the bus expands.

In the USB architecture, the bus grows by attaching additional hubs. The hubs interconnect with other hubs and devices using links. The interconnection of the ports within a hub is defined by the operation of the hub repeater. See Chapter 3, *System Architecture*, and Section 12.10 for more information.

Finally, the traditional bus architecture requires the attachment and removal of devices only after the bus is powered-off. When the bus is powered-on, the software re-establishes the configuration of the system. USB supports attachment and removal of devices when the bus is either powered-on or powered-off.

12.2 Hub Architecture

12.2.1 External Architecture

A hub is required to a have one upstream port and one to N downstream ports (see Figure 12.2) The number "N" is limited by the power that can be provided by the hub.

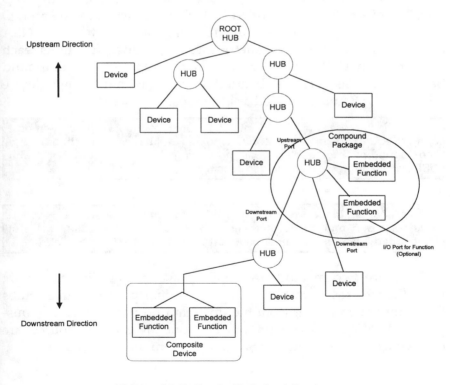

Figure 12.2: Basic Hub Architecture

The upstream port of a hub is the port that is electrically nearest to the host controller. The upstream port of a hub is connected to the downstream port of the root hub or some other upstream hub by a link. The hub's upstream port is defined by the USB specification as the root port and is numbered as Port 0.

> For the purposes of this book, the term "root port" will not be used to avoid confusion with the term "root hub". The replacement term for "root port" is "upstream port".

The downstream port of a hub is a port that is farthest away from the host controller. Downstream ports of a hub are internally connected to the upstream port of a hub. The downstream ports are numbered Port 1 to Port N.

Optionally, a hub can be packaged with one or more embedded function(s). A function may provide some function-specific I/O port. For example, an embedded LAN function will provide an I/O port as part of the embedded function for connection to the LAN. A hub that is combined with one or more embedded functions, each with its own USB device address, is referred to as a compound package. A collection of embedded functions within a single device without a USB hub is defined as a composite device.

> In this chapter, the word "hub" will also represent "hub(s)" (upstream port and N downstream hub ports with no embedded functions) and "compound package(s)" (upstream port and N downstream hub ports with USB device addressed embedded functions).

> In this chapter the word "device" will represent a stand-alone function (upstream port and no downstream hub ports) and composite device(s) (embedded functions and upstream port with no downstream hub ports).

There are two methods by which power is supplied to a hub: from the upstream port or from an external power source. Hubs that only obtain power from the upstream port are defined as bus-powered. Hubs that obtain power from an external source are defined as self-powered. See Section 12.9 for more information.

12.2.2 Internal Architecture

There are three major components to the internal hub architecture: hub repeater, hub controller, and hub ports (see Figure 12.3).

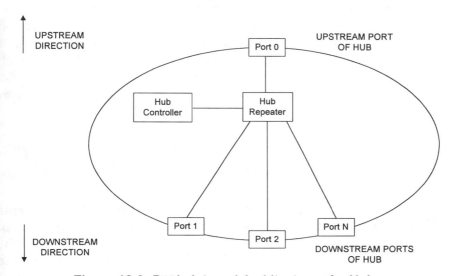

Figure 12.3: Basic Internal Architecture of a Hub

The hub repeater connects the upstream port to the downstream ports of the hub. The purpose of the hub repeater is to transmit packets between the upstream port and the downstream ports, as well as packets between the upstream port and the hub controller. The hub repeater also transmits the reset link state from the upstream port to the downstream ports and hub controller. The transmission paths are outlined in the Section 12.3.

> Since a hub presents itself as a device interface, USB could allow a composite device that has a hub interface and other interfaces; however the 1.0 USB specification requires that the hub class be reported in the device descriptor and not in a configuration descriptor. This currently precludes such a composite device.

The hub controller is responsible for configuration functions that provide control for the downstream ports of the hub. For example, the hub controller is responsible for detecting device attachment and removal on a downstream port. The hub controller is also responsible for detecting the speed of devices attached to the hub's downstream ports.

There are many states that need to be explained for a hub. Part of a hub's internal behavior is described by states and transitions. One of the complexities of a hub is that there are several interrelated entities with states. These entities are the hub repeater, the hub (as a USB device), and the hub's downstream ports. To clarify which states are being referred to, this book uses the terms *hub repeater state*, *hub functional state* (for the hub as a USB device), and *hub port state*.

12.3 Hub Repeater and Hub Port State Introduction

The hub repeater and the hub downstream ports are two elements of the hub that operate in different states for the correct operation of a USB bus system. These states are discussed in detail in the following sections. To fully understand the hub repeater and the hub downstream ports, the basic operation of the packet transmission, frame, and hub frame timer needs to be understood. Other chapters of this book provide more detailed information on these topics.

12.3.1 Packets and Packet Transmission Through a Hub

Information within the USB bus is sent in the form of packets at a specific speed (either full or low speed) (See Figure 12.4.) These are token, data, or handshake packets. The information can flow in either the upstream or downstream direction though the hubs. The upstream port of a hub is required to always support a full speed link. The downstream port of the hub is required to support the attachment of either full and low speed links. The speed of the link for a downstream hub port is established by the speed of the device connected to it. The embedded functions within a hub (compound packages and composite devices) operate at the speed of their respective links.

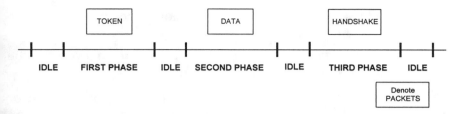

Figure 12.4: Simplified Transaction

The transfer of information in a USB system is accomplished by a series of transactions between host system memory and a hub's or device's endpoints. A transaction consists of series of packets.

The state of the hub repeater and hub ports interacts with the transmission of packets. For the purposes of the following discussion, the operation of a full speed packet (and not a low speed packet) will be outlined below. Low speed packets behave similarly.

The hub repeater is by default always ready to receive full speed packet transmissions in the downstream direction. The hub internal links connecting the hub repeater to its downstream ports are normally in the idle link state awaiting packet transmissions. Also, a hub downstream port transceiver is normally in the receive mode awaiting packet transmissions.

A token packet is only transmitted in the downstream direction. The hub will transmit a downstream full speed token packet, as follows:

- The beginning of a token packet is detected by an SOP (start of packet) from the hub upstream port transceiver.

- All of the hub downstream port transceivers that are in the enabled hub port state transition to the transmit mode, and begin re-transmitting the SOP and the following signaling received by its upstream port.

- Full speed packets are transmitted downstream only to full speed links. The hub repeater will not send full speed packets through downstream ports connected to low speed devices

- The end of a token packet is indicated by EOP (end of packet).

- The EOP is retransmitted on the hub downstream ports and the links enter the idle link state.

- The hub returns all transceivers of downstream ports in the enabled hub port state to the receive mode.

Full speed data packets can flow in either the downstream or upstream direction. Data packets in the downstream direction follow the same sequence as outlined above. Upstream packets, such as a data packet, are handled by a hub as follows:

- The beginning of a data packet is indicated by the hub transmitting an SOP. By default, the hub downstream port transceivers for ports in the enabled hub port state are in the receive mode.

- All other downstream ports are prevented from accepting an SOP.

- The hub upstream port begins re-transmitting the SOP and the following signaling received by the downstream port.

- The end of a data packet is indicated by an EOP (end of packet).

- The EOP is retransmitted on the hub upstream port and the link enters the idle link state.

- The hub returns the upstream port transceiver to the receive mode.

Full speed handshake packets can flow in either the downstream or upstream direction. Handshake packets in the downstream direction follow the same sequence as downstream packets described above. Handshake packets in the upstream direction follow the same sequence as upstream packets described above.

Full speed packets flowing downstream and upstream through the hubs are outlined in Figures 12.5 and 12.6, respectively. The downstream packets flow through the upstream port 0, through the hub repeater to the hub controller, the hub's downstream ports 1 and 2, and finally along the links to full speed devices (Figure 12.5). In this example, a downstream packet flows to all full speed devices connected to downstream ports in the enabled hub port state. The downstream packets do not flow through downstream ports 3, 4, or 5 for the following reasons:

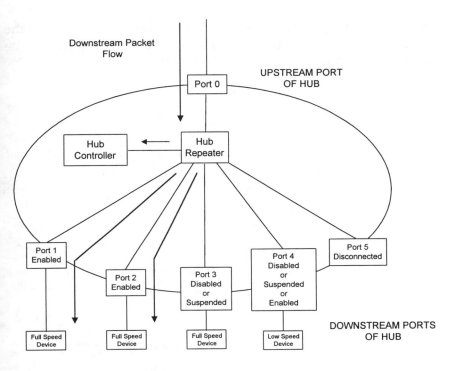

Figure 12.5: Downstream Packet Flow

- Port 3 is in the disabled or suspended hub port state

- Port 4 is connected to a low speed device. This port may be in either the suspended, disabled, or suspended hub port state. The hub repeater will not transmit any full speed packets through the low speed port. If the full speed packet is the PREAMBLE token packet, it is not transmitted through the low speed port, but prepares the hub repeater to transmit a single subsequent low speed packet through downstream low speed ports in the enabled hub port state.

- Port 5 has no devices connected to it; consequently, this port is in the disconnected hub port state.

Upstream packets flow along the link from the full speed device, through a downstream port, and finally through the hub repeater to the upstream port (Figure 12.6). In this example, the device connected to downstream port 2 was previously addressed by a

379

downstream token packet. Both downstream ports 1 and 2 are in the enabled hub port state and in the receive mode, but only one device at a time is the source of an upstream packet.

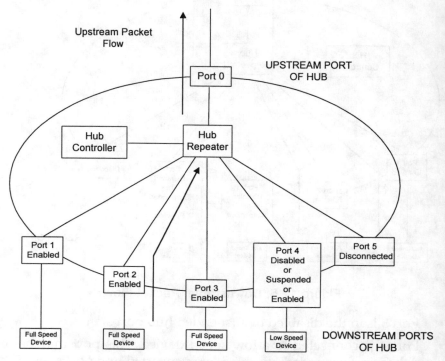

Figure 12.6: Upstream Packet Flow

12.4 Frames and Hub Frame Timer

This section reviews some basic USB frame concepts to help describe hub behavior. See other chapters for more detailed information about frames.

Information flows through the USB bus in the form of transactions within a frame. Every 1.00 milliseconds the host controller transmits a Start of Frame token packet (SOF). The frame period is from the start of the SOF packet of the present frame to the start of the SOF of the subsequent frame. The SOF packet propagates downstream only to full speed devices through downstream ports in the enabled hub port state.

> The regular transmission of the SOF packets insures that the full speed links do not enter the suspended link state. The SOF packet is not propagated through downstream ports with low speed links. The low speed links are prevented from entering the suspended link state by the associated hub transmitting a downstream EOP (end of packet) when it receives a full speed SOF on its upstream port. The transmission of the EOP is called low speed "keep alive".

12.4.1 Hub Frame Timer

Each hub contains a Hub Frame Timer (HFT) which is reset to a 1.00 millisecond value upon receipt of the SOF packet. The clock for the HFT is a 12 MHz source within each hub and is required to measure time equal to two frame periods. The HFTs enable all hubs to know when the Frame period will end prior to the receipt of another SOF packet. Thus, hubs are able to operate currently even when a packet has not completed (no EOP) or a transaction has not been correctly completed by the EOF (end of frame) as identified by the HFT.

An important consideration for proper USB bus operation is the synchronization of bit clocks between the host controller, hubs, and devices. This synchronization is achieved by the NRZI protocol applied to the packet. Both the host controller and hubs implement a 12 MHz clock, and the SOF packet transmitted from the host controller establishes the reset of the HFT of each hub. The HFT of the hubs individually count the bit periods to the subsequent SOF; consequently, the synchronization of the frame period length between the host controller and the hubs is required to be defined.

The bit periods counted by the HFT are defined as full speed bit periods independent of the number of full or low speed packets that are transmitted. The host controller is required to have a 12 MHz Frame period clock with a tolerance of +/- 500 PPM. Thus the Frame period relative to the host controller is .9995 to 1.0005 millisecond. Each hub is required to have a 12MHz HFT clock with a tolerance of +/- 500 PPM. Also, the hubs are required to have a counter accuracy of +/- 2500 PPM. Thus, the hubs' bit period range will be 83.0833 to 83.5833 microsecond Consequently, the hubs' HFT count value in a Frame period will be 11958 to 12042 bit periods (12000 nominally +/- 42).

The host controller and hubs are defined to be synchronized relative to the frame period when the following conditions are met:

- Whenever the SOF packet is received by a hub, the HFT identifies the count value. The difference between "two consecutive counts" is required to be within two counts of each other and between the minimum and maximum frame length.

- Assuming no missing SOF packet, every hub is required to be synchronized to the host controller frame period within three or fewer frames.

Once the host controller and hub are synchronized, the following protocol applies:

- The frame length count of "two consecutive counts" as detailed above is defined as the PFL (Previous Frame Length).

- Each new SOF packet establishes the previous bit period count as the PFL.

- Whenever the SOF packet is not received by a hub within the minimum and maximum HFT bit period count, the PFL is used to keep the host controller and hubs frame synchronized.

- Hubs can tolerate up to two consecutive missed or lost SOF packets and still remain synchronized through the use of PFL.

Whenever the host controller and the HFT of the hubs are not synchronized, the hub repeater cannot transmit downstream or upstream packets. The minimum frame length is used by a hub whenever the PFL has not been established or three or more sequential SOFs have not been received by the hub.

Synchronization (also called lock) is achieved when the count value of the PFL and the present count value are within two bit periods. The phase lock loop used as the clock source for the HFTs of each HUB are required to achieve synchronization within three Fame periods (assuming no missing SOF token packets). That is, the host controller and the hubs must be synchronized by the time the fourth SOP token packet is received.

Section 12.4.3 has further discussion of how the frame length and the SOF affect the operation of the USB bus.

12.4.2 Babble, LOA, and Missing Packets

The previous sections have provided an introduction to packet transmission, frames, and the Hub Frame Timer prior to the discussion of hub states. It is also important to understand Babble and LOA (Loss of Activity) prior to the discussion of hub states.

Within each Frame period, the hubs are monitoring the USB bus activity for typical operation. Typical operation includes:

- Every packet begins with an SOP (Start of Packet) and ends with an EOP (End of Packet).

- All transactions are required to begin and end within the boundaries of a Frame. The boundaries of a Frame are two consecutive SOF packets, two EOF2 events, an SOF packet followed by an EOF2 event, or an EOF2 event followed by an SOF packet. The EOF events will be described below.

- If no packet is transmitted after the transmission of the SOF packet, no SOP occurs and the transmission of an EOP will not occur.

The atypical operation of the USB bus is required to take into consideration the following:

- An SOF token packet has been transmitted and the transmission of an EOP after an SOP has not occurred prior to the transmission of the next SOF token packet. This condition of a missing EOP causes a condition called **BABBLE**.

  - If the missing EOP is associated with a downstream packet, it was the responsibility of the host controller to have transmitted it.

  - If the missing EOP is associated with an upstream packet, it was the responsibility of the downstream device that is the transmitter of the packet (not simply a hub repeater) to transmit the EOP.

- An SOP is transmitted and no bus activity has occurred prior to the next SOF. That is, the D+ and D- signal lines on the link are stuck in the idle link state (J or K state) and the EOP does not occur prior to the transmission of the next SOF token packet. This condition is called LOSS OF ACTIVITY (LOA).
  - If the SOP was transmitted by the host controller as part of a downstream packet, the responsibility for proper activity is the host controller's.
  - If the SOP was transmitted by a downstream device as part of an upstream packet, the responsibility for proper activity belongs to the downstream device that is the transmitter of the packet (not simply a repeater).
- If an SOF packet is not received by a hub after two consecutive frame periods, the value of the HFT count defaults to the minimum value of 11,968 bit periods.

By USB convention, it is always assumed that the host controller is operating correctly. As will be discussed in the following sections, the USB hubs' response to the above atypical operations associated with the host controller is different than those associated with a downstream hub or device. Consequently, the conditions of Babble and LOA only apply to the upstream packet transmission from a downstream device that is the transmitter of the packet (not simply a repeater).

> A transaction consists of a series of packets, and the entire series must be transmitted within the frame period. The aforementioned typical and atypical operations focus on the completeness of the packet and not the completeness of the transaction. Hub controllers only monitor the integrity of the packets and not the integrity of the transactions. As will be outlined below, it is the responsibility of the host controller to establish the integrity of transactions.

12.4.3 Hub Packet Handling Near EOF

This section describes EOF1, EOF2, and how hubs handle packets around frame boundaries.

The time period between two consecutive Start of Frame (SOF) packets is nominally 1.00 milliseconds. The receipt of an SOF packet by a hub resets the hub controller's Hub Framer Timer (HFT) and begins counting the full speed bit periods. The purpose of counting bit periods is to provide hub controllers advance warning that the frame period is about to end and a new SOF packet will soon be transmitted by the host controller. The hub controller only monitors the beginning and end of a packet. As the frame period is about to end, the repeater and ports of the hub are required to prepare for the impending downstream SOF packet to be transmitted. As described in the previous section, the transmission of an SOP implies that a packet with an EOP will be transmitted. When an EOP is not transmitted subsequent to an SOP, hubs are required to return to a stable state prior to the subsequent transmission of an SOF. This stable state is achieved prior to the SOF packet by the hub controller contained within each hub having advance warning that the present frame period is about to end.

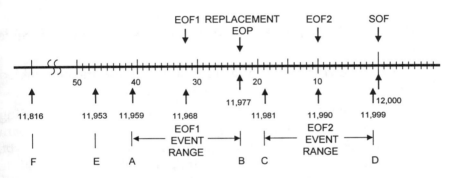

Figure 12.7: EOF1 and EOF2

To achieve this advance warning, the counting of bit periods by the hubs' controllers result in two count values: EOF1 and EOF2 (End of Frame 1 and 2) (see Figure 12.7). The following sections describe the interpretations of the two EOF count values (events).

In Figure 12.7 and subsequent sections the HFT count value is referenced to 12,000 bit periods. As previously stated in Section 12.4.1 the clock tolerance in the host controller and hubs' HFTs, and the counter accuracy, results in a HFT count value of 12,000 +/- 42 bit periods. For discussion purposes in subsequent sections the numbers 11,816, 11,953 ... 12,000 in Figure 12.7 are referenced to 12,000. The actual design values are based on 12,000 +/- 42.

12.4.4 EOF1

When a hub controller's Hub Framer Timer (HFT) count reaches the EOF1 count value, the hub is required to operate in specific ways depending on EOP details:

If an SOP was followed by an EOP before EOF1, *i.e.*, there is no EOP pending:

- The transceiver of the hub upstream ports in the enabled hub port state remain in the receive mode.

- The hub upstream port remains in the receive mode to wait for the transmission of a downstream packet; typically this will be an SOF.

If an SOP was not followed by an EOP before EOP1, *i.e.*, there is an EOP pending:

If the pending EOP was part of a downstream packet:

- The transceiver of the hub upstream port remains in the receive mode.

- The transceivers of the hub downstream ports in the enabled hub port state remain in the transmit mode.

- Between EOF1 and EOF2, the hub waits for the pending downstream EOP and the EOF2. If prior to EOF2 a downstream EOP is received by a hub upstream port, the EOP will be transmitted by the hub downstream port. Subsequent to an idle bit period, the transceivers of the hub downstream ports in the Enabled hub port state transition to the receive mode.

If a pending EOP was part of an upstream packet, the hub will transmit a replacement EOP upstream via its upstream port.

- The transceiver of the hub upstream port remains in the transmit mode and the hub will transmit the replacement EOP. The replacement EOP consists of two full speed bit times of SE0, followed by one full speed bit period of the idle link state (J state). Subsequent to the idle bit period, the hub upstream port changes to the receive mode.

  - If a hub is in the process of transmitting a replacement EOP on its upstream port when an EOP is received on its downstream port, the hub will only transmit the replacement EOP. That is, the hub will not lengthen, truncate, or duplicate the replacement EOP transmitted on its upstream port due to the receipt of an EOP on its downstream port. The EOP received on the hub downstream port may be either a replacement EOP from another downstream hub or the EOP from the downstream device that is the transmitter of the packet (not simply a repeater).

- The transceivers of a hub downstream ports in the enabled hub port state remain in the receive mode. Any upstream packet received by the downstream ports will be ignored until the completion of a downstream packet (typically the SOF) is received by the hub upstream port.

All of the hub controllers are counting bit periods from SOF. If a device does not transmit an EOP, its upstream hub will transmit a replacement EOP according to the EOF1 and EOF2 protocol. The other hubs along the path may also transmit a replacement EOP on their upstream ports or repeat an EOP received on the hub's downstream port. The clock and count skew between hubs results in a mixture of replacement EOPs and repeats of EOPs received on the hub's downstream ports.

12.4.5 EOF2

When a hub controller's Hub Framer Timer (HFT) count reaches the EOF2 count value, the hub is required to operate in specific ways depending upon the EOP details:

If an SOP was followed by an EOP before EOF2, *i.e.*, there is no EOP pending;

- The transceivers of the hub downstream ports in the enabled hub port state remain in the receive mode.
- The transceiver of the hub upstream port remain in the receive mode to await the transmission of a downstream token packet; typically this is an SOF packet.

If the pending EOP was part of a downstream packet, but is not received by EOF2, then after EOF2 the following occurs:

- The transceiver of the hub upstream port remains in the receive mode to await the transmission of a downstream packet typically this is an SOF packet.

- The transceivers of the hub downstream ports in the enabled hub port state change to the receive mode. After EOF2, the host controller will not transmit a downstream EOP. If a downstream EOP is received on a hub upstream port it is ignored.

If the pending EOP was part of a downstream packet and is received by the hub upstream port prior to EOF2, then after EOF2 the following occurs:

- The transceiver of the hub upstream port remains in the receive mode to await the transmission of a downstream packet typically this is an SOF packet.

- The transceivers of the hub's downstream ports in the enabled hub port state change to the receive mode.

If the pending EOP was part of an upstream packet but was not received by the hub downstream ports in the enabled hub port state between EOF1 and EOF2, then after EOF2 the following occurs:

- The downstream port of the hub connected to the device that was the transmitter of the upstream packet is disabled.

> The other downstream ports of other upstream hubs are not disabled because they have all received the replacement EOP.
>
> The above applies to the path of links and downstream ports between the root hub and the downstream device that is the source of the upstream packet.

If an EOP is pending that was part of an upstream packet, and is received by the hub downstream ports in the enabled hub port state between EOF1 and EOF2, then after EOF2 the following occurs:

- The transceiver of the hub upstream port changes to the receive mode.

- The transceivers of a hub downstream ports in the enabled hub port state remain in the receive mode. Any upstream packet received by the downstream ports will be ignored until the completion of a downstream packet (typically the SOF) is received by the hub upstream port.

In the above discussion the phase "...typically this is an SOF packet" reflects the fact that SOF may not be the downstream packet. According to the USB specification, the beginning of each Frame period is established by the downstream transmission of an SOF packet. If the downstream packet immediately after the EOF2 is not an SOF, the hubs will still assume the frame period has begun per the HFT count value reference to the previous SOF. For example, an SOF packet may not be detected if it was corrupted during transmission on the bus.

The hub will identify EOF1 and EOF2 relative to its internal HFT counter. As previously discussed, the clock for this counter is synchronized with the clock of the host controller frame period as defined for 12,000 bit period counts (see Figure 12.7). If the hubs' clocks were exactly synchronized with the host controller frame clock, the position of the end of frame period relative to EOF1 and EOF2 can be exactly defined.

According to the USB bus specification, the hubs are required to maintain frame period reference points even when two consecutive SOF packets have been missed by the hubs. By the third frame period, the difference between the host controller frame period and other hubs can be ± 3 bit periods. During each frame period, the root hub can adjust the actual count by one bit time to conform to other host clock requirements. Consequently, during the three frame periods associated with the missing SOFs, there is an additional difference in the bit period count value between the host controller frame period and the other hubs' HFTs.

The difference between the host controller frame period and the other hub's HFTs is calculated as follows: the first frame period results in a ± 1 bit period counter difference between host controller and other hubs, the second frame period results in a ± 2 bit periods counter difference, and the third frame period results in a ± 3 bit period count difference. Consequently, the total potential counter difference between the host controller frame period and the other hubs is ± 9 (3 +1+2+3) bit periods.

> Even though the USB specification requires that the frame period be adjusted by the USB system software no faster than one bit period every six frames, the frame counter difference is calculated allowing one bit period every frame, *e.g.*, six times faster than allowed.

As discussed previously in this section, the EOP must be received within the frame period. The EOF1 and EOF2 protocol insures that hubs provide replacement EOPs for an EOP that did not arrive from a downstream device by the correct time. For the hub to correctly transmit a replacement EOP, it uses the EOF1 event as a reference point. The EOF2 event allows the hubs to determine when the frame period is about to end. As discussed above, there is a ± 9 bit period difference between the host controller frame period and other hubs, consequently, the range of a hub's HFT count values for EOF1 and EOF2 events is defined as follows:

- All hubs are required to identify the EOF2 event prior to the host controller transmitting an SOF. Due to the potential nine bit period HFT count difference between the host controller and other hubs, the hubs identify the EOF2 event 10 bit periods before the SOF (12,000-10 = 11,990). The actual position of the EOF2 event within all the hubs relative to the host controller is within the range of 11,990 ± 9 bit periods (EOF2 range points C to D of Figure 12.7). Point C is the bit period count value by which all hubs along the path are monitoring for the completion of an EOP. Point D is the count value by which all hubs prepare for SOF.

- The transmission of an EOP requires four bit periods; consequently, a hub that records an EOF1 event is required to begin transmission of a replacement EOP four bit period prior to the EOF2 event range. Due to counter skew between hubs, a hub is required to begin transmission of a replacement EOP 23 bit periods before SOF (12,000-10-9-4 = 11,977) (see Point B Figure 12.7.) For the downstream device that began this packet, Point B is also the last chance for the device to begin transmission of the EOP.

- To enable all hubs to identify an EOF1 event prior to transmitting a replacement EOP, the clock skew of ± 9 bit periods requires the EOF1 event to be 32 bit periods prior to

SOF (12,000-23-9 = 11,968) (see Figure 12.7). The skew between the count of HFTs establishes the lowest count value for the EOF1 event at Point A of EOF1 Event Range (12,000-23-9-9 = 11,959) (See Point A of Figure 12.7.)

The above discussion outlines the protocol for upstream EOP transmission near the end of a frame period. There is a similar consideration for the downstream EOP transmission from the host controller. The host controller is required to complete all full speed packet transmissions at Point E in Figure 12.7 (11,953) and all low speed packet transmission at point F in Figure 12.7 (11,816). Point E is six bit periods prior to the lowest count of EOF1 and thus 47 bit periods prior to the SOF. Similarly, Point F is 184 full speed bit periods (rounded up from the nearest low speed bit period) prior to SOF. The protocol of packet transmission relative to Points E and F are as follows:

- If the host controller has begun the transmission of a full speed handshake packet at Point E, the handshake packet is allowed to complete. Similarly, if the host controller has begun the transmission of a low speed handshake packet at Point F, the handshake packet is allowed to complete. In both cases, the handshake packet will complete by the SOF.

- If the host controller is transmitting a packet of a transaction at Point E or F (full or low speed) and the transaction will not complete by SOF, the root hub is required to transmit a bit stuffing error plus an EOP.

A final consideration for EOF1 and EOF2 events at the end of a frame period is the receipt of an upstream packet by the host controller. The transmission of a replacement EOP has insured a correct frame period completion relative to the hubs. If any upstream packets are being received by the host controller at Point A in Figure 12.7, the host controller is required to record an error for the packet. At point A, the host controller can optionally discard an upstream data or handshake packet in progress. Thus, the host controller can optionally accept a packet that starts on or before count of point A.

The exact bit period count value of the SOF is established during HFT synchronization. When a hub is attached to the USB bus, USB bus power-on occurs, or a hub makes a transition from the suspend hub functional state; the HFT of the hub is synchronized as described in Section 12.4.1.

12.5 Hub Repeater States

As previously mentioned, each hub consists of a hub repeater, a hub controller, an upstream port, and downstream ports. The hub controller operates the hub repeater and hub downstream ports. The hub repeater states are defined when the hub is in the Awake functional state and at least one of the hub downstream ports is in the Enabled hub port state.

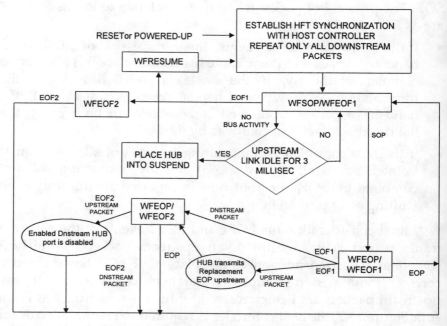

Figure 12.8: Hub Repeater States

The hub repeater is responsible for propagating signaling through the hub. The hub repeater states insure the proper protocol for packet transmission when a hub downstream port is in the Enabled hub port state. Figure 12.8 summarizes the hub repeater states. A reference point for the hub repeater to begin operation on a

USB bus is either reset or power-on. The hardware reset is defined as a downstream transmission of SE0 on the D+ and D- signal lines for a minimum of 10 milliseconds and a reception for a minimum 2.5 μseconds by receivers of upstream ports. Reset is only defined in the downstream direction. Powered-on is defined as attachment of hub upstream port to the downstream port (not in the Powered-off hub port state) of an upstream hub or when power is first applied to an assembled system.

The hub repeater states are defined relative to waiting for (WF) certain events. These events are defined for both the upstream and downstream ports as follows:

- SOP: The Start of Packet (SOP) occurs when the D+ and D- signal lines on the port transition from the idle link state to the K state. SOP can be transmitted both upstream and downstream.

- EOP: The End of Packet (EOP) occurs when the D+ and D- signal lines are driven to an SE0 (Signal Ended Zero D+ = D- = "0") for two bit times followed by driving the D+ and D- signal lines to the idle link state for one bit time. EOP can be transmitted both upstream and downstream.

- SOF: The Start of Frame (SOF) is transmitted as a packet every 1.00 milliseconds to indicate the beginning of a frame period. SOF is only transmitted by the host controller in the downstream direction.

- EOF: The End of Frame (EOF) is not transmitted on the D+ and D- signal lines and it is not a transmitted token packet. EOF is the result of the Hub Frame Timer of each hub reaching a specific time value relative to the SOF. There are two specific EOF times: EOF1 and EOF2. See Section 12.4 for more information.

- RESUME: Resume signaling occurs whenever an idle to K transition is detected after having been suspended.

Hub repeater states also define the electrical state (transmit mode or receive mode) of the transceivers of the hub downstream ports in the Enabled hub port state and the hub upstream port. Between packet transmissions, the signal lines of the link are in the idle link state. Whenever the upstream or downstream ports are waiting for a packet to begin, the transceivers are in the receive mode; these ports remain in the receive mode or change to the transmit mode according to the following protocol:

- When an SOP for a downstream packet is detected on the hub upstream port, all of the transceivers of the hub downstream ports in the enabled hub port state are changed to the transmit mode and the packet is propagated through all of the enabled downstream ports.

  - Exception to this protocol occurs when the hub downstream ports in the Enabled hub port state are connected to low speed links. If the specified downstream port is low speed and the port is in the Enabled hub port state, the hub repeater will not propagate low speed packets between it and the upstream port until a PRE packet is received by the hub upstream port. Full speed packets are never propagated through a low speed enabled port.

- When an SOP for an upstream packet is detected on one of the hub downstream ports, all of the other transceivers of the hub downstream ports are retained in the receive mode. The transceiver of the hub upstream port is changed to transmit mode and the packet is only propagated through the upstream port. Consequently, the upstream packet flow follows a unique upstream path only to the host controller. Upstream packets do not flow to other downstream ports of the hub, contrasted to the downstream packets that are broadcast to all downstream devices, with the exception of low speed packets as outlined above.

- When EOP is detected, any transceivers in transmit mode are changed back to receive mode after EOP is propagated.

There is one hub repeater state that is not identified in Tables 12.1 and 12.2. When the transceivers of the upstream port and all of the downstream ports are in the receive mode, there are no packets passing through the hub's repeater. By definition, the hub repeater is in the idle state.

Tables 12.1 and 12.2 define the electrical state of the transceivers relative to the various hub repeater states of Figure 12.8. These electrical states are defined for an enabled upstream port and the hub downstream ports in the Enabled hub port state.

HUB REPEATER STATE (1)	UPSTREAM PORT TRANSCEIVER	FULL SPEED DOWNSTREAM PORT TRANSCEIVER
WFSOP/WFEOF1	RECEIVE	RECEIVE
WFEOF2	RECEIVE	RECEIVE
WFEOP/WFEOF1	RECEIVE	TRANSMIT
WFEOP/WFEOF2	RECEIVE	TRANSMIT
WFRESUME	RECEIVE	RECEIVE

Table 12.1: Electrical State of Hub Transceivers for Downstream Packet

Note: (1) There is an exception relative to low speed packets and PRE packets as outlined in the text.

HUB REPEATER STATE	UPSTREAM PORT TRANSCEIVER	FULL SPEED DOWNSTREAM PORT TRANSCEIVER (1)
WFSOP/WFEOF1	RECEIVE	RECEIVE
WFEOF2	RECEIVE	RECEIVE
WFEOP/WFEOF1	TRANSMIT	RECEIVE
WFEOP/WFEOF2	TRANSMIT	RECEIVE

Table 12.2: Electrical State of Hub Transceivers for Upstream Packet

Note: (1) There are exceptions relative to low speed packets and PRE (special) packets outlined in the text.

There are two remaining unique hub repeater operations that must be considered:

When the hub repeater is in the WFSOP/WFEOF1 state, the typical operation is the receipt of an SOP followed by a packet that is terminated with an EOP. (See Figure 12.8.) However, this protocol may not be followed at all times; other protocol considerations are as follows:

- When a hub upstream port indicates the idle link state for more that 3.00 milliseconds, the hub transitions into the LP suspend hub functional state, and the hub repeater enters the WFRESUME state.

- The hub remains in the LP suspend hub functional state until a hub port receives bus activity according to the Resume Protocol (RP). The hub repeater remains in the WFRESUME state until receipt of the RP or a hardware reset is transmitted downstream.

> Removal of a hub from a USB system eliminates any meaning of hub repeater states for that hub. The hub repeater states for a newly attached hub don't have meaning until power is provided to the hub. Once power is provided, the hub repeater can only transmit downstream SOF packets until the HFT (hub frame timer) in the hub is synchronized with the host controller HFT as shown in Figure 12.8. As previously discussed in this chapter, when SOF packets are not received on a regular basis by a hub, the HFT synchronization is lost. Packets cannot be repeated through a hub until the synchronization is re-established.

12.6 Hub Functional States

Packets move between a host controller and devices along paths created by hubs and links. Each hub consists of a hub repeater, a hub controller, an upstream port, and downstream ports. The hub controller operates the hub repeater and hub downstream ports. The overall operational protocol of the hub is defined by functional states. Similarly, the hub repeater and the hub downstream ports operational protocol is defined by states. This section will discuss the hub functional states. The hub downstream port states and hub repeater states will be discussed in subsequent sections.

The transitions between hub functional states are outlined in Figure 12.9. Section 12.8 provides more detailed information about the definition and protocol of resume events and other related elements of Figure 12.9.

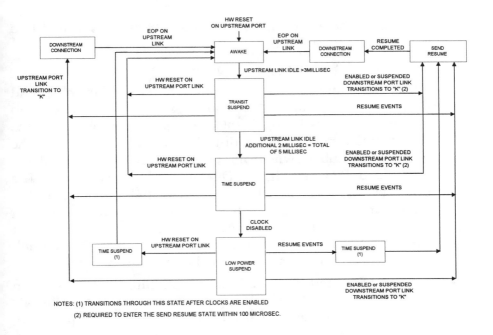

NOTES: (1) TRANSITIONS THROUGH THIS STATE AFTER CLOCKS ARE ENABLED

(2) REQUIRED TO ENTER THE SEND RESUME STATE WITHIN 100 MICROSEC.

Figure 12.9: Hub Functional States and Transitions

The transmission of packets in a USB system occurs during the awake hub functional state, the enabled hub port state, and the hub repeater states (collectively called "actively transmitting packets" states). The USB bus specification does not require all links and hubs of the bus to always be actively transmitting packets. It also defines link protocol and hub functional states that represent a non-activity level. This non-activity level is defined in terms of the suspended hub functional state and the suspended hub port state. In order to transition hubs and links between actively transmitting packets and a non-activity level, resume and suspend protocols are defined. This section will discuss the hub functional states which ensure proper USB bus operation as the hub changes between actively transmitting packets and a non-activity level.

The hub functional states are: awake, transient suspend, time suspend, low power suspend, send resume, and downstream connection. Transient suspend, time suspend, and low powered suspend hub functional states are collectively called suspend hub functional state.

The hub functional states are as follows:

- Awake: The hub is actively transmitting packets upstream and downstream through the hub upstream port and hub downstream ports in the Enabled hub port state. Additionally, the upstream port is monitoring the length of the idle on the link. Other hub downstream ports can be in the Disabled, Suspended, Powered-off, and Disconnected hub port states. The downstream ports in the suspended hub port state are monitoring for an idle to K transition on the hub downstream ports in the Disabled, Powered-off, or Disconnected hub port states. The operation of the hub is further defined by the hub repeater and hub port states defined in subsequent sections.

- Transient Suspend: The hub is not transmitting packets between the upstream and downstream ports. All control and status bits associated with the hub or the hub downstream ports are preserved. To determine if a resume will occur, the upstream port and the downstream ports in the Enabled or Suspended hub port states are monitoring for an idle to K transition. There is no monitoring for an idle to K transition on the other hub downstream ports in the Disabled, Powered-off, or Disconnected hub port states.

- Time Suspend: The hub is not transmitting packets between the upstream and downstream ports. All control and status bits associated with the hub or the hub downstream ports are preserved. To determine if a resume will occur, the upstream port and the downstream ports in the Enabled or Suspended hub port states are monitoring for an idle to K transition. There is no monitoring for an idle to K transition on the other hub downstream ports in the Disabled, Powered-off, or Disconnected hub port states. In the Time Suspend hub functional state, the internal clock is of less than or equal accuracy to the internal clock used in the Awake, Transient Suspend, and Send Resume hub functional states. The events that can be timed are:

    - Reset on the upstream port (SE0 binary pattern > 2.5 μsec.)

- Removal of a device on a downstream port in the Enabled or Suspended hub port state (SE0 binary pattern > 2.5 µsec.)

- Attachment of a device on a downstream port in the Disconnected hub port state (idle binary pattern > 2.5 µsec).

- Low Powered Suspend (LP Suspend): The hub is not transmitting packets between the upstream and downstream ports. All control and status bits associated with the hub or the hub downstream ports are preserved. To determine if a resume will occur, the upstream port and the downstream ports in the Enabled or Suspended hub port states are monitoring for an idle to K transition. In the LP Suspend hub functional state the internal hub clock has been disabled to save power. There is no monitoring for an idle to K transition on the other hub downstream ports in the Disabled, Powered-off, or Disconnected hub port states. If the Device Remote Wake bit is set in the hub's control register, attachment of a device will be monitored by downstream ports in the Disconnected hub port state.

- Send Resume: The hub transmits the resume signaling protocol upstream though the upstream port and downstream through all downstream ports in the enabled hub port state. If the Send Resume hub functional state is entered due to an idle to K transition on a downstream port in the Suspended hub port state, the resume signaling protocol will also be transmitted downstream through this port. The port will transition to the Enabled hub port state at the end of resume signaling when the hub enters the Awake hub functional state.

The hub is required to remain in this hub functional state until all of the following are achieved:

- All power and clocks are enabled and are stable.

- A minimum of one millisecond and a maximum of 15 milliseconds have elapsed.

- Downstream Connection (DS Connection): The hub transmits downstream bits received on its upstream port to all of its downstream ports in the Enabled hub port state.

399

This bus activity can also be the reflection of the resume signaling from the upstream hubs.

When the hub is in any hub functional state except Awake, and if the Device Remote Wake bit is set in the hub's control register, attachment of a device will be monitored by downstream ports in the Disconnected hub port state. The port will transition to the Disabled hub port state when the hub enters the Awake hub functional state. If the Device Remote Wake bit is set in the hub's control register, removal of a device is monitored for by downstream ports in Disabled, Enabled, or Suspended hub port states. The port will transition to the Disconnected hub port state when the hub enters the Awake hub functional state.

When the hub is in any of the hub functional states, except for Send Resume, the upstream port is required to monitor and react to the reset link state (SE0 in the signal lines for more than 2.5 microseconds).

12.7 Hub Port States

The previous section defined the overall hub functional states. This section discusses hub port states that are defined for each individual hub port.

As previously discussed, a hub has an upstream port (Port 0) and downstream ports (1 to N). During the operation of the USB bus the individual downstream ports can exist in different hub port states. The upstream port of a hub can only be in one of two possible states: Enabled and Powered-off.

The upstream port of a hub is in the Enabled state whenever it is connected to an upstream hub and the upstream hub's downstream port is in the Powered-on state. The upstream port automatically enters the Enabled state when power is supplied from the upstream link.

There are several hub port states defined for the hub downstream ports. As outlined previously, the hub repeater states define the electrical state of the transceivers of the hub downstream ports that are in the Enabled hub port state. The other hub port states of the downstream ports define the electrical state of the transceivers.

There are two stimuli that can change a hub downstream port state: software (sw) commands (also known as "requests") and hardware (hw) events.

Bus-powered hubs are required to support power switching (on/off) of each downstream port. The switching can be selected on an individual port basis, done collectively on a portion of the total ports (defined as gang), or a combination of gang and individual ports. When a hub supports a gang of ports, the power is provided for all ports in the gang when one port in the gang receives a SetPortFeature(PORT_POWER) request. Each port of the gang transitions to Powered-off hub port state independently via the Clear PortFeature(PORT_POWER) request, but power is not removed from the gang (and thus continues to be supplied downstream) until all of the ports of the associated gang transition to the Not Configured or the Powered-off hub port states. One exception is the over current hw event. This hw event is individual for each port and causes the port to transition to Powered-off hub port state and downstream power from that individual port is removed. The other ports in the gang will continue to provide power downstream.

Self-powered hubs are not required to implement power switching support for the SetPortFeature(PORT_POWER) and Clear PortFeature(PORT_POWER) requests. However, these hubs are required to support the Powered-off hub port state for the hw events of upstream port link power removal and over current on a downstream port. Even though a self-powered hub has not implemented power switching for the requests, the hub is required to support the power switching of downstream ports according to the gang and individual port protocol described above for bus-powered hubs. If self-powered hubs optionally implement power switching, their operation for both requests and hw events is the same as outlined above for downstream ports of bus-powered hubs.

The operation of a USB system does not require all links and hubs to be transmitting packets. The USB bus specification defines a protocol to suspend packet transmission individually for each downstream port. Section 12.8 goes into more detail specifically about hub suspend and resume handling. The transitions of hub downstream port hub port states are outlined in Figure 12.10. The transition from one hub port state to another occurs for specific hardware and software events.

Upstream port of hub attached or is connected to the downstream port of a hub when power is applied, or reset interpretation on D+ and D- signal lines completed ... hw

Reset encoding received by
upstream port ... hw
OR
Power to the upstream port of
the hub is removed ... hw (1)

NOT CONFIGURED

SetConfiguration (non -zero) ... sw

POWERED-OFF

ClearPortFeature (Port_
Power)...sw
OR
Non bus-power for a self-
powered hub is removed ... hw
(1)

SetPortFeature (Port_
Power)...sw
& power is applied ... hw (1)

DISCONNECTED

Device attachment
detected OR device was
connected... hw (3)

Device removed...hw (2)
OR
No device connected ... hw

DISABLED

SetPortFeature (Port_
Enable)...sw

SE0 detected on
downstream port...hw (6)

ClearPortFeature (Port_
Enable)...sw,
OR
Framing Error ... hw (1)

SetPortFeature
(Port_Reset)...sw (4)

Overcurrent detected ... hw (1)

ENABLED

SetPortFeature (Port_
Reset)...sw (4)

SetPortFeature
(Port_Reset)...sw (4)
OR
ClearPortFeature (Port_
Suspend) ...sw
OR
Selective Resume ... hw

SUSPENDED

SetPortFeature (Port_
Suspend)...sw
OR
Global Suspend (1)... hw

ClearPortFeature (Port_
Enable) ...sw (5)

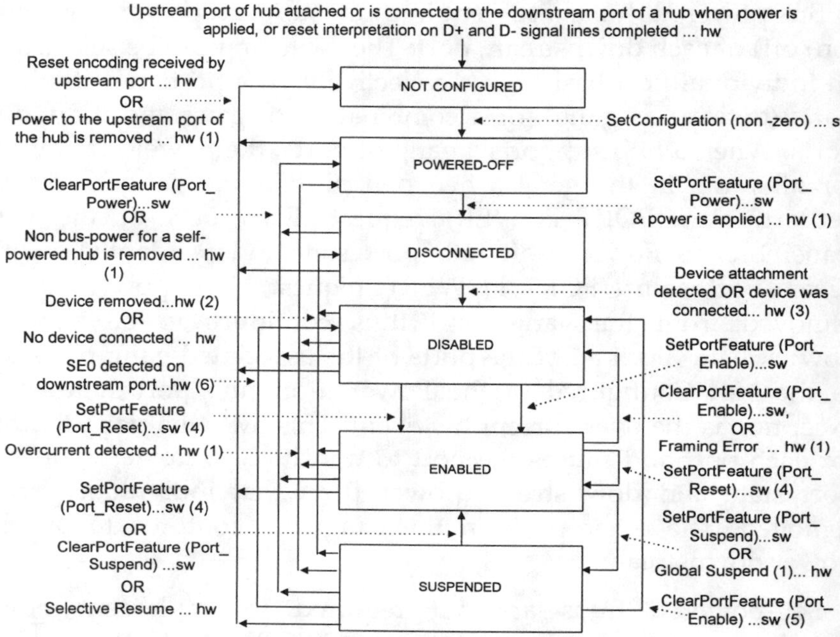

Figure 12.10: Downstream Hub Port States

Notes:
(1) See text for further information.
(2) If hub is not in the Awake hub functional state the removal of a device will transition the downstream port to the Disconnected hub port state when hub awakes. See Section 5.2.2 for more information.
(3) If hub is not in the Awake hub functional state the attachment of a device will transition the port to the Disabled hub port state when hub awakes. See Section 5.2.2 for more information.
(4) Transitioning to Enabled hub port state or remaining in the Enabled hub port state includes the downstream transmitting of SE0 encoding for a minimum of 10 milliseconds and maximum of 20 milliseconds.
(5) The transition to the Disabled hub port state is made only if the hub repeater is not in the WFFSOP (on upstream port) repeater state.
(6) The detection of SE0 encoding has no minimum timing requirement.

In Figure 12.10, the hub port states are: Powered-off, Disconnected, Disabled, Enabled, and Suspended. Hardware and software events that cause a transition from one state to another are shown. Any hardware or software event not shown for a specific state causes no transition from that state when these events occur.

402

As a hub port moves from one port state to another, the transceivers and operation of the link changes and is summarized in Table 12.3.

Hub Downstream Port State	Port Transceiver State (5)	Repeater Propagates Signaling?	Level as viewed by the hub downstream port transceiver looking downstream			Power provided down-stream
			Quiescent Level of D+	Quiescent level of D-	D+ & D- driven by	
Not Configured	Receive Hi-Z	No	"0" (2)	"0" (2)	Hub pull-down resistors	No
Powered-off	Receive Hi-Z	No	"0" (2)	"0" (2)	Hub pull-down resistors	No
Disconnected (Requirements for both D+ and D- must both be met)	Receive Hi-Z (6)	No	"0"	"0"	Hub pull-down resistors	Yes(3)
Disabled with full speed Link (Requirements for both D+ and D- must both be met)	Receive Hi-Z (6)	No	"1"	"0"	Hub pull-down and device pull-up resistors	Yes (3)
Disabled with low speed Link (Requirements for both D+ and D- must both be met)	Receive Hi-Z (6)	No	"0"	"1"	Hub pull-down and device pull-up resistors	Yes (3)
Enabled (Hub is awake)	Receive and transmit per the hub repeater state	Yes	N/A	N/A	Hub down-stream port or device up-stream port trans-ceivers	Yes (4)
Enabled (Hub is suspended)	Receive Hi-Z	No (1)	"1"	"0"	Hub pull-down and device pull-up resistors	Yes (3)

Table 12.3: Hub Downstream Port States

Hub Downstream Port State	Port Transceiver State (5)	Repeater Propagates Signaling?	Level as viewed by the hub downstream port transceiver looking downstream			Power provide down stream
			Quiescent Level of D+	Quiescent level of D-	D+ & D- driven by	
Suspended with full speed Link (Requirements for both D+ and D- must both be met. Hub is suspended or awake)	Receive Hi-Z (6)	No	"1"	"0"	Hub pull-down and device pull-up resistors	Yes (3)
Suspended with low speed Link (Requirements for both D+ and D- must both be met. Hub is suspended or awake)	Receive Hi-Z (6)	No	"0"	"1"	Hub pull-down and device pull-up resistors	Yes (3)

Table 12.3: Hub Downstream Port States (continued)

Notes:

1. When a hub is suspended and a downstream port is in the Enabled port connected, the removal of a downstream device or an upstream resume protocol is received forces the hub to the Awake state. See Section 12.9 for more information.

2. The value of "0" assumes that the speed resistor of a connected downstream device is pulled-up to the power lines of the link and not a self-powered source in the downstream device.

3. Limited to one unit load

4. Limited to one load for a bus-powered hub and five loads for a self-powered hub.

5. Receive direction for a hub's downstream port accepts packets flowing in the upstream direction. Transmit direction for a hub's downstream port sends packets flowing in the downstream direction.

6. The downstream port is sensing for a change in SE0 for attachment or removal of a downstream hub or device.

12.7.1 Software-Caused Port Transitions

The software events, *e.g.*, control transfer requests, that cause downstream port state transitions are: SetPortFeature and ClearPortFeature requests for Port_Power, Port_Enable, Port_Reset, Port_Suspend features. See later sections of this chapter for more information.

SetConfiguration(Non_Zero)

This request tells the hub controller of a USB Hub to start following the behavioral definitions of the Hub Device Class. The hub starts in the Awake hub functional state, the downstream ports start in the Powered-off hub port state (or Disconnected hub port state if power switching is not supported). The hub repeater starts operating.

SetPortFeature(Port_Power)

This request tells the hub controller to apply bus power to a specific downstream port. No power will be provided until all of the following are conditions are met:

- Power is provided by the bus. Additional power is provided by a non-bus source for self-powered hub. As shown in Figure 12.11, "Power is applied" is defined as power available to the port from a non-bus powered source for a self-powered hub or as power available from the bus via the upstream port for a bus-powered hub.
- The hub has been configured by other requests.

SetPortFeature(Port_Enable)

This request tells the hub controller to enable a specific downstream port such that packets will propagate upstream or downstream between it and the upstream port. If the specified downstream port is attached to a low speed device and once the port is in the Enabled hub port state, the hub repeater takes special action. The hub repeater will never propagate full speed signaling to ports with a low speed device attached. The hub repeater only propagates a single low speed packet between it and the upstream port after a PRE packet is received by the hub upstream port.

SetPortFeature(Port_Reset)

This request tells the hub controller to reset the specified port. The specified downstream port will drive the D+ and D- signal lines on the full speed or low speed link with the appropriate reset signal line interpretation to reset all downstream devices. The reset signal line interpretation requires the D+ and D- signal lines to be driven to an SE0 for a minimum of 10 millliseconds. The execution of this request appears as reset signaling to downstream devices. The specified downstream port is enabled after this request has completed. If the specified downstream port is low speed, the port will await a PRE packet before propagating any downstream signaling.

SetPortFeature(Port_Suspend)

This request tells the hub controller to suspend the specified downstream port. After the request, the port transitions to the Suspended hub port state. The downstream port specified by the SetPortFeature(Port_Suspend) software command cannot transition to the suspended port state in the middle of a transaction. The transaction must be completed before the specified downstream port transitions to the suspended hub port state.

ClearPortFeature(Port_Power)

This request tells the hub controller to remove bus power from a specific downstream port. This reverses the behavior described for SetPortFeature(Port_Power). If the hub supports individual port power switching, individual ports may be unpowered. Otherwise, all ports must be unpowered before power is removed.

ClearPortFeature(Port_Enable)

This request tells the hub controller to disable a specific downstream port and thus no bus packets will propagate upstream or downstream through the hub and the specific downstream port. This reverses the behavior described for SetPortFeature (Port_Enable).

ClearPortFeature(Port_Suspend)

This request tells the hub controller to resume and enable the specified downstream port. The specified downstream port will perform the Resume Protocol and transition to the Enabled hub port state. This reverses the behavior described for SetPortFeature (Port_Suspend).

12.7.2 Hardware-Caused Port Transitions

The hardware events that affect hub downstream port states are listed below:

- When a reset link state is received by the hub's upstream port, the reset link state is transmitted downstream by the hub downstream ports in the Enabled hub port state. Then all of the hub downstream ports transition to the Not Configured hub port state. In particular, downstream ports that are in the Disconnected, Disabled, or the Suspended hub port states will not transmit the reset link state downstream and will immediately transition to the Not Configured hub port state.

- If the hub does not implement power switching support by the SetPortFeature(Port_Power) and Clear PortFeature(Port_Power) requests, power is only required for the downstream port to transition from the Powered-off to the Disconnected hub port state. If the hub does implement power switching by the requests, both the SetPortFeature(Port_Power) request must have been processed and power must be present before the downstream port transitions from the Powered-off to the Disconnected hub port state.

- When a hub is in the Awake hub functional state, the attachment of a downstream hub or device or pre-existence of a connected downstream device will transition the hub's downstream port from the Disconnected to the Disabled hub port state. The attachment of a downstream device will cause an update in the Port Status and Port Change fields.

> Prior to the hub port transitioning to the Disabled hub port state, a minimum 2.5 microsecond period of non-SE0 on the D+ and D- signal lines followed by an idle state for a low or full speed devices must be observed by the downstream port. Thus, the speed of the connected link has been established prior to the Disabled hub port state. Similarly, upon entering the Disconnected hub port state, the port will transition to the Disabled hub port state if a downstream device is already connected. The protocol outlined above for the non-SE0 period and the establishment of downstream device speed still applies.

- Removal of a device results in the hub port transitioning to the Disconnected hub port state from other hub port states. If the downstream port is in the Powered-off hub port state, the removal of the device will retain the downstream port in the Powered-off hub port state. The removal of a device will cause an update in the Port Status and Port Change fields.

> Prior to the hub port transitioning to the Disconnected hub port state, the hub must transition to the Awake hub functional state if the hub is in the Suspend hub functional state. The hub must also transmit a minimum 2.5 microsecond period of SE0 on the D+ and D- signal lines to be observed by the downstream port.

- For self-powered hubs, the removal of bus power on the hub's upstream port results in all of the hub's downstream ports transitioning to or remaining in the Not Configured hub port state.

- For self-powered hubs, the removal of the external (non bus-power) power results in all of the hub's downstream ports transitioning to or remaining in the Powered-off hub port state.

- For bus-powered hubs, when bus power is lost, the hub transitions the downstream ports to the Not Configured hub port state. In the case of bus power being the only power source for the hub, the hub will rapidly stop functioning as a hub and USB device since its power source has been removed.

> If the hub is operating as bus-powered hub when configured and then bus power is lost, the hub may switch to an external (self-powered) power source and the downstream ports are not required to transition the downstream ports to the Powered-off hub port state. If the external power source is also lost prior to the restoration of the bus power, the down stream ports are defined as being in the Not Configured hub port state.

- Framing error events will occur when the EOP signaling is missing from the transmission of upstream packets and has not arrived by the EOF2 time as outlined in Figure 12.10. Framing error events result in the port transitioning to the Disabled hub port state.

- Over current on the power lines of the link will result in the hub downstream ports transitioning to the Powered-off hub port state. The over current may have caused a circuit or fuse that provides power to the link to become "open". The over current condition on any downstream port will be reported to the software by setting of appropriate bits (if supported by the hub) in the Hub Status Field and the Hub Change Field. Over current condition on a specific downstream port will be reported to the software by setting of appropriate bits (if supported by the port) in the associated Port Status Field and the Port Change Field. A port will enter the Powered-off hub port state due to over current on another port if that over current condition causes power supplied to this port to drop below electrical limits.

- A transition from idle to a K state on a link connected to a downstream port in the Suspended hub port state results in the port transitioning to the Enabled hub port state.

12.8 Hub Suspend and Resume Behavior

There are two types of USB suspend: global and selective. Both of these USB suspend states are built from the hub's ability to suspend itself and to suspend an individual port. As previously discussed, the hub functional states of transient suspend, time suspend, and low powered suspend are collectively called suspend hub functional state. A hub transitions to the suspend hub functional state when the link connected to the upstream port has an idle detected on the signal lines for three milliseconds. This idle on the upstream link will occur for one of the following reasons:

- The host controller ceases transmission of all packets
- A downstream port on an upstream hub is placed in the Powered-off, Disconnected, Suspended, or Disabled hub port states

These conditions allow the host controller to suspend operation and save power on any portion or all of the USB bus.

Global suspend occurs when the host controller ceases transmission of all packets including the SOF token packet. Each hub enters the suspend hub functional state on the USB bus after a hub recognizes a resulting Idle state on the link of more than three milliseconds. A hub that transitions to suspended hub functional state does not change the hub port state of its downstream ports, and does not change the control or status bits of the hub.

> A hub downstream ports in the Powered-off or Disabled hub port states will not monitor idle to K transitions on the downstream link. Thus, these downstream ports will not participate in a resume from a downstream device.
>
> A downstream port in the Powered-off or Disabled hub port state will not transmit any downstream packets; consequently, connected downstream devices will transition into the suspend state.

When a hub is in the Awake hub functional state, a specific downstream port will be placed into the suspended hub port state upon receipt by the hub of a downstream SetPortFeature(Port _Suspend) request. The hub's other downstream ports are not affected and stay in whatever state they were in. If the hub is subsequently placed in the suspend hub functional state, this does not effect the hub's downstream ports in the Suspended hub port state. The hubs connected to downstream ports in the suspend hub port state will see an Idle link state. After three milliseconds of Idle link state, these downstream hubs will transition to the suspend hub functional state. As this effect progresses downstream, the associated hubs also enter the suspend hub functional state (and other devices are also suspended). Thus a portion of the USB bus is suspended. This is defined as selective suspend.

Similarly, there are two types of USB resume: global and selective. Each of these USB resume states are built on the hub's ability to be resumed and to resume an individual port. Global resume really only applies when the complete USB bus has been suspended. It is more interesting and important to understand selective resume.

The selective resume is defined according to the hub's individual downstream ports that are in the Suspended hub port state.

A selective resume of a specific downstream port in the suspended hub port state can occur when the hub is in the Awake functional state and one of the following occurs:

- A hub downstream port in the suspended hub port state detects a transition from the idle to K state on its downstream link. The port will transition to the Enabled hub port state after performing resume signaling is completed.

- The receipt by the hub of a ClearPortFeature (Port _Suspend) request. The specified downstream port will transition to the enabled hub port state after resume signaling is completed.

A selective resume of a downstream port in the suspended hub port state is also possible when the hub is in the suspend hub functional state. When the port detects a transition from the idle to K state on its downstream link, a resume occurs for the hub. The transition to the Enabled hub port state occurs after the hub transitions to the Awake state. In this particular situation, the selective resume of the downstream port becomes part of a larger scope selective resume, that could ultimately be a global USB resume.

> If the Device Remote Wake bit is set in the hub's control register, the removal of a downstream device connected to a downstream port in the Suspended hub port state results in the port's transition to the Disconnected hub port state.
>
> If the hub is in the Suspended state, the transition to the Disconnected hub port state occurs after the hub transitions to the Awake hub functional state. Downstream device removal is identified by the transition from idle to SE0 signaling state on the downstream port.

A hub in the suspend hub functional state remains in this state until a resume event. The purpose of a resume is to transition the hub to the Awake hub functional state to support upstream and downstream packet transmission. The resume will occur for any of the following events:

- The upstream port of the hub detects an idle to K transition on the upstream link.

- The upstream port of the hub detects a hardware reset (SE0 for more than 2.5 microseconds) on the upstream link.
- A hub downstream port in the Enabled hub port state detects an idle to K transition on the downstream link.
- A hub downstream port in the suspended hub port state detects an idle to K transition on the downstream link. This results in setting the C_PORT_SUSPEND bit in the Port Change Field.

  Optionally, the resume may occur prior to setting the C_PORT_SUSPEND bit in the Port Change Field.

If the Device Remote Wakeup bit is set in the hub's control register, any of the following also causes a resume. In this case the previously suspended hub will also generate resume signaling on its upstream and enabled downstream ports.

- The attachment or removal of a downstream device on a downstream port for specific hub port will cause a resume. Device attachment is identified by an SE0 to idle transition on the downstream port. Detection of device attachment is defined for downstream ports in the Disconnected hub port state. Device removal is identified by an idle to SE0 transition on the downstream port. Detection of device removal is only possible for downstream ports in the Disabled, Enabled, or Suspended hub port states. Either attachment or removal sets the C_PORT_CONNECTION bit in the Port Change Field.
- The setting of the C_PORT_OVER_CURRENT, C_PORT_RESET, or C_PORT_ENABLE bits in the Port Change Field.
- The downstream port is still processing a reset to the link.
- The setting of the C_HUB_OVER_CURRENT or C_HUB_LOCAL_POWER bits in the Hub Change Field.

If an idle to K transition is detected on the upstream port of a hub, the hub transmits the resume protocol downstream through all of its ports in the enabled hub port state.

If the idle to K transition is detected on a downstream port in the Enabled hub port state, the hub transmits the resume protocol upstream through the upstream port and downstream through all of its downstream ports in the Enabled hub port state.

> If the idle to K transition is detected on a downstream port in the Suspended hub port state, the hub only transmits the resume protocol downstream through the port in the Suspended hub port state that detected the idle to K transition. The hub does not transmit the resume protocol to any other downstream ports.

12.9 Hub Power Behavior

Power is defined in terms of unit loads. Each unit load is defined as 100 milliamps of current at five volts. As discussed in Chapter 7 *Frames*, each USB device is required to initially power on with no more than one unit load drawn by its upstream port. The maximum power that a device's upstream port can draw is five unit loads. A hub is a device type, and the above power considerations also apply. Hubs come in two general classes of power capabilities: bus-powered and self-powered.

12.9.1 Hub Power Classes and Power Switching

As previously discussed, the attachment of a hub to a downstream port of an upstream hub provides additional downstream ports, and may or may not provide incremental power for additional USB devices attached downstream.

Hubs adhere to the power requirements imposed on all USB devices. After reset or system power-on, a hub is limited to drawing one or less unit load from its upstream port. During hub normal operation, its upstream port is limited to drawing five unit loads. When a hub's functional state is in the suspended state, its upstream port is limited to drawing 500 microamps plus 500 microamps for each powered downstream port of a self-powered hub. Thus a hub in the suspended hub functional state limits its upstream port to drawing a maximum of 2.5 milliamps.

There are two hub power classes: bus-powered hub and self-powered hub. Bus-powered hubs provide no more than one unit load per downstream port. Self-powered hubs provide five unit loads per downstream port.

Bus-powered Hubs

All power for the bus-powered hub itself and devices connected on the hub downstream ports is provided from the upstream port of the hub, *e.g.*, from its upstream hub downstream port.

Once a bus-powered hub is configured, its downstream ports are allowed to be powered-on under host control. When a downstream port is in the disconnected, disabled, or suspended hub port state, it provides one or less unit loads. When the downstream port is in the powered-off hub port state, it won't provide any power. When the downstream port is in the enabled hub port state, it provides one unit load.

For bus-powered hubs, the power for the hub controller, hub repeater, and the total of all power provided to its downstream ports may not exceed the five unit loads available from the upstream hub. Each individual downstream port of the hub is required to supply one unit load of power downstream independent of how much power is used by the hub controller and hub repeater. Consequently, assuming that the hub controller and hub repeater present some load, only four or fewer downstream ports can be built into a bus-powered hub.

Bus-powered hubs are required to support power switching of all downstream ports. The power switching can either be supported for all the hub downstream ports simultaneously (via a ganged control) or for each individual downstream port.

> Bus-powered hubs must be connected to the downstream port of a self-powered hub. Only a self-powered hub can provide five unit loads to each of its downstream ports. In other words, two bus-powered hubs may not be connected in series.

Self-powered hubs

In a self-powered hub, the power needed by the components of the hub is supplied by different sources. The power for the hub controller and the hub repeater is supplied from the upstream port of the hub or from a power source external to the USB bus and local to the hub. All power for other hubs and devices connected to the hub's downstream ports are supplied from a power source external to the USB bus and local to the hub. This external power source is either a physically separate power supply providing power to the hub or one that is physically built into the hub.

Once a self-powered hub is configured, its downstream ports may be powered under host control. When a downstream port is in the disconnected, disabled, or suspended hub port state, it provides one or fewer unit loads. When the downstream port is in the powered-off hub port state, it won't provide any power. When the downstream port is in the enabled hub port state, it provides five unit loads.

> For self-powered hubs, the hub repeater may draw power from the upstream port, provided the total power including the hub's controller is one unit load or less.

Each individual downstream port of the hub must provide five unit loads of power downstream. This power is provided by the external power source. Also, the external power source provides power for the hub repeater. Consequently, for a self-powered hub, the power for the hub repeater can exceed one unit load, and the number of downstream ports can exceed four. Each individual downstream port of the hub is also required to be current limited to five amps for safety reasons.

Self-powered hubs are not required to support power switching of the downstream ports. If power switching is implemented, the power switching can either be supported for all the downstream ports simultaneously (via a ganged control) or for separate individual downstream ports.

> Self-powered hubs can be connected to the downstream port of a root hub, bus-powered hub, or self-powered hub.
>
> Self-powered hubs never supply power to their upstream port.

12.9.2 Overload Protection and Power Isolation

As outlined above, there is a limit to the load a hub's downstream port must support. The hubs are also required to protect the USB bus from link attachment transient currents. The hub is required to address these issues with a current regulator.

The current regulator of a bus-powered hub must operate as follows:

- The total power requirement for all downstream ports combined may not to exceed a "trip point" of 5.0 amps. A trip point for over current can be set for less than 5.0 amps but is required to be at least five unit loads. When the total power exceeds the trip point, the current regulator removes power to all downstream ports but retains power to the hub controller and hub repeater.

- When power is removed from the downstream ports due to an over current condition, this event must be reported to the host controller via the standard port status change reporting mechanisms, described in Section 12.11.5.

- After an over current condition has occurred, the port(s) will be re-initialized by host software. This initialization is similar to the initial power-on reset initialization sequencing. This re-initialization is required because the hub removes port power when an over current condition is detected, and the host is required to intervene to re-initialize the port.

> For a bus-powered hub, the power switching must be done in such a way that minimizes excessive current transients on the hub's upstream port.

The current regulator of a self-powered hub must operate as follows:

- The total power requirement for each individual downstream port is not allowed to exceed a "trip point" of 5.0 amps. A trip point for over current can be set for less than 5.0 amps but must be at least five unit loads. When the power supplied to a downstream port exceeds the trip point, the current regulator removes the power to that port.

- When power is removed from the downstream ports due to an over current condition, this event is required to be reported to the host controller via the standard port status change reporting mechanisms, described in Section 12.11.5.

- After an over current condition has occurred, the port will be re-initialized by host software. This initialization is similar to the initial power-on reset initialization sequencing. This re-initialization is required because the hub removes port power when an over current condition is detected, and the host is required to intervene to re-initialize the port.

> The current regulator design for either bus-powered or self-powered hubs must tolerate current transients on the downstream ports during attachment and removal of downstream devices.

Another consideration of bus-powered and self-powered hubs in a USB system is the ground relative to V_{bus}. The V_{bus} on the upstream port of a self-powered hub is electrically isolated from the V_{bus} of its downstream ports. The ground on the upstream port of a low load and self-powered device is electrically connected (short-circuited) to the ground of its downstream ports. The chassis ground of a self-powered hub is required to be DC electrically isolated from the ground of the upstream and downstream ports. The chassis ground of the hub must be connected to the ground of the 120/220/240 volts AC power cable ground. The chassis ground of a bus-powered hub must be electrically connected to the ground of the upstream and downstream ports.

12.10 Hub Device Class

The USB hub device class is based on the general USB device framework model. Hub class requests and hub class descriptor data formats are designed to resemble closely the general USB device framework in order to present an already-familiar framework from which device manufacturers can base their product designs.

The hub device class consists of two areas: hub descriptors and hub requests. Each is described in detail below.

12.11 Hub Descriptors

USB hub designers must be aware of two types of descriptors: the standard hub device descriptors and the class-specific hub descriptors. The standard hub descriptors are important to the hub designer because this is what the device uses to communicate its basic capabilities to the host. Careful attention to the standard descriptors will ensure that the hub device will be correctly enumerated by the host. The class-specific descriptors are important because they describe the hub-specific capabilities to the host. This information is used by the host's hub device driver, which is the system software agent that controls and monitors USB hubs.

12.11.1 Standard hub descriptors

The hub's standard descriptors describe the device's basic capabilities to the host. This is the information the host examines to determine what type of device is attached to the USB. In the case of a hub device, the standard descriptors tell the host that the device conforms to the USB Hub Class definition, as well as specifics about the behavior of the device. The standard hub descriptors required to be supported by USB hubs are:

- Device descriptor
- Configuration descriptor
- Interface descriptor
- Endpoint descriptor

Note that String descriptors are optional in the hub class definition.

12.11.2 Device Descriptor

Field	Description
bLength:	Number of bytes in this descriptor, including this one
bDescriptorType:	DEVICE descriptor
bcdUSB:	USB Spec Revision 1.00
bDeviceClass:	Hub Class Code (assigned by USB). This field is zero if this device contains multiple configurations or multiple interfaces. If the hub device only has one configuration and that configuration only has one interface (the standard hub interface) then this field can contain the Hub Class Code (0x09).
bdeviceSubClass:	Hub SubClass Code. None defined, so this value is zero.
bdeviceProtocol:	Hub Protocol Code. None defined, so this value is zero.
bmaxPacketSize0:	Implementation dependent. This is the maximum packet size of the control endpoint. The valid values for this field are: 8, 16, 32, or 64
idVendor:	USB-assigned vendor Identification Code (see Note)
idProduct:	Vendor-specific product ID for this device
bcdDevice:	The release version of this device in "bcd" form
iManufacturer:	Index of the string descriptor that contains the manufacturer name
iProduct:	Index of the string descriptor that contains the product name
iSerialNumber:	Index of the string descriptor that contains this device's serial number.
bnumConfigurations:	Number of possible configurations. Simple hubs with only one configuration (just a standard hub configuration) will put a "1" here.

Table 12.4: Hub Device Descriptor Fields

Note that the Product ID, which is defined by the vendor, can be made somewhat indicative of the hub features. For example, a hub manufacturer that builds several models of hubs, each with a different number of ports, may wish to make the last two digits represent the number of ports. For example:

Number of Ports	Product ID
3	9303 (hex)
4	9304 (hex)

Table 12.5: Product ID Fields

This example shows a way to make the product ID somewhat representative of the product features, which makes the ID useful in helping end users or technical support professionals to quickly identify the product features and perhaps help diagnose or troubleshoot a problem in the field.

A detailed description of each of the above fields follows.

bLength	**Hub Device Descriptor**
Offset:	0
Length:	1
Legal Values:	0x12
Default Value:	0x12
Description:	Number of bytes in this descriptor, including this one

bDescriptorType	**Hub Device Descriptor**
Offset:	1
Length:	1
Legal Values:	0x01
Default Value:	0x01
Description:	DEVICE descriptor

bcdUSB	**Hub Device Descriptor**
Offset:	2
Length:	2
Legal Values:	0x100 or USB Specification Revision supported
Default Value:	0x100
Description:	USB Spec Revision 1.00 (Note: Update as necessary)

bDeviceClass	**Hub Device Descriptor**
Offset:	4
Length:	1
Legal Values:	0x09
Default Value:	0x09
Description:	Hub Class Code (assigned by USB). This field is zero if this device contains multiple configurations or multiple interfaces. If the hub device only has one configuration and that configuration only has one interface (the standard hub interface) then this field can contain the Hub Class Code (0x09).

bDeviceSubClass	**Hub Device Descriptor**
Offset:	5
Length:	1
Legal Values:	0x00
Default Value:	0x00
Description:	Hub SubClass Code. None defined, so this value is zero.

bDeviceProtocol	**Hub Device Descriptor**
Offset:	6
Length:	1
Legal Values:	0x00
Default Value:	0x00
Description:	Hub Protocol Code. None defined, so this value is zero.

bMaxPacketSize0	**Hub Device Descriptor**
Offset:	7
Length:	1
Legal Values:	0x08,0x10,0x20,0x40 [8,16,32,64]
Default Value:	0x08
Description:	Implementation dependent. This is the maximum packet size of the control endpoint.

idVendor	**Hub Device Descriptor**
Offset:	8
Length:	2
Legal Values:	Vendor ID Assigned by USB Implementer's Forum
Default Value:	Vendor ID Assigned by USB Implementer's Forum
Description:	USB-assigned vendor Identification Code

idProduct	**Hub Device Descriptor**
Offset:	10
Length:	2
Legal Values:	Vendor-specific product ID for this device
Default Value:	Vendor-specific product ID for this device
Description:	Vendor-assigned product Identification Code

bcdDevice	**Hub Device Descriptor**
Offset:	12
Length:	2
Legal Values:	The release version of this device in "bcd" form
Default Value:	The release version of this device in "bcd" form
Description:	Vendor-assigned product version code

iManufacturer	**Hub Device Descriptor**
Offset:	14
Length:	1
Legal Values:	Index of the string descriptor that contains the manufacturer name, or zero if none exists
Default Value:	Zero
Description:	Index of the string descriptor that contains the manufacturer name

iProduct	**Hub Device Descriptor**
Offset:	15
Length:	1
Legal Values:	Index of the string descriptor that contains the product name, or zero if none exists
Default Value:	Zero
Description:	Index of the string descriptor that contains the product name

iSerialNumber	**Hub Device Descriptor**
Offset:	16
Length:	1
Legal Values:	Index of the string descriptor that contains the serial number of the device, or zero if none exists
Default Value:	Zero
Description:	Index of the string descriptor that contains the serial number of the device

bNumConfigurations	**Hub Device Descriptor**
Offset:	17
Length:	1
Legal Values:	Number of possible configurations, with a minimum value of 1
Default Value:	1
Description:	Number of possible configurations. Simple hubs with only one configuration (just a standard hub configuration) will put a "1" here.

12.11.3 Configuration Descriptor

Field	Description
bLength:	Number of bytes in this descriptor, including this one
bDescriptorType:	CONFIGURATION descriptor
wTotalLength:	Total length of this descriptor, as defined in the USB Device Framework. Note that this includes the number of bytes in this configuration descriptor, all the bytes in the interface and endpoint descriptors that follow, as well as all the bytes in any class or vendor-specific descriptors that are returned for this configuration.
bNumInterfaces:	Hubs are only required to support at most one interface, so this field must be at least 1. However, a hub design may contain more than the standard hub interface in a given configuration. In such a case, this field would contain the number of interfaces in this configuration.
bConfigurationValue:	This can be any non-zero value the hub designer wishes. Whatever value is specified here is what the host will send during the SET_CONFIGURATION request, which is used to put the device into this configuration. Note that this value cannot be zero because a SET_CONFIGURATION request that specifies a configuration value of zero means the host is "unconfiguring" the device (that is, returning the device to the unconfigured state).
iConfiguration:	Index of the string descriptor that contains the description of this configuration (for example, "4 Port Self-Powered USB Hub").
bmAttributes:	Attributes of the configuration
MaxPower:	Maximum power consumption of USB device (in 2 mA increments) from the bus in this specific configuration when the device is fully operational.

Table 12.6: Hub Configuration Descriptor Fields

The configuration descriptor describes this configuration and its interfaces. In the case of a hub device, it is possible to support more than one interface, although at least one of the interfaces must present itself as a hub class interface (see the Interface Descriptor section below).

A detailed description of each of the above fields follows.

bLength	Hub Configuration Descriptor
Offset:	0
Length:	1
Legal Values:	0x09
Default Value:	0x09
Description:	Number of bytes in this descriptor, including this one

bDescriptorType	Hub Configuration Descriptor
Offset:	1
Length:	1
Legal Values:	0x02
Default Value:	0x02
Description:	CONFIGURATION descriptor

wTotalLength	Hub Configuration Descriptor
Offset:	2
Length:	2
Legal Values:	Non-zero value that is the sum of all the bytes in the configuration descriptor and all its associated descriptors
Default Value:	N/A
Description:	Total length of descriptor data for this configuration. This length includes the number of bytes in this configuration descriptor, all the bytes in the interface and endpoint descriptors that follow, as well as all the bytes in any class or vendor-specific descriptors that are returned for this configuration. This field is usually examined by the host during enumeration so the system software can determine how many bytes to request to retrieve all the descriptor data for this configuration, since the number of bytes is dependent on the number of interfaces, endpoints, etc.

bNumInterfaces	Hub Configuration Descriptor
Offset:	4
Length:	1
Legal Values:	1 or greater
Default Value:	0x01
Description:	Hubs are only required to support at most one interface, so this field must be at least 1. However, a hub design may contain more than the standard hub interface in a given configuration. In such a case, this field would contain the number of interfaces in this configuration.

bConfigurationValue	Hub Configuration Descriptor
Offset:	5
Length:	1
Legal Values:	Any non-zero value
Default Value:	0x01
Description:	Value to use in SET_CONFIGURATION request to set device to this configuration.

iConfiguration	Hub Configuration Descriptor
Offset:	6
Length:	1
Legal Values:	Index of the string descriptor that contains the product name, or zero if none exists.
Default Value:	0x01
Description:	Value to use in SET_CONFIGURATION request to set device to this configuration.

bmAttributes	Hub Configuration Descriptor
Offset:	7
Length:	1
Legal Values:	D7: 0 = not bus-powered 1 = bus-powered D6: 0 = not self-powered 1 = self- powered D5: 0 = **not** a Remote Wakeup Source 1 = Remote Wakeup Source D4-0: Reserved (must be zero)
Default Value:	Configuration dependent
Description:	Defines the attributes of this configuration

MaxPower	Hub Configuration Descriptor
Offset:	8
Length:	1
Legal Values:	0 – 0xFA [0 – 250 decimal]
Default Value:	Dependent on device power design
Description:	The maximum amount of power (expressed in 2 mA increments) that the hub draws from USB. If a self-powered hub doesn't draw any power from USB, this value would be zero. Conversely, if a bus-powered hub draws power from the bus for its downstream ports, this value may be as high as 250 (0xFA) to indicate the hub requires the full 500 mA from USB.

12.11.4 Interface Descriptor

Field	Description
bLength:	Number of bytes in this descriptor, including this one
bDescriptorType:	INTERFACE descriptor
bInterfaceNumber:	This is a zero based index into the array of interfaces supported in this configuration. This is similar to an array index in C.
bAlternateSetting:	Value identifying an alternate setting for this interface.
bNumEndpoints:	Number of endpoints in this interface. This count doesn't include the default endpoint (endpoint zero). A value of zero indicates that this interface only uses the default endpoint.
bInterfaceClass:	Hub Class code (0x09)
bInterfaceSubClass:	Hub SubClass code. Since none are defined, this must be zero.
bInterfaceProtocol:	Hub Interface Protocol code. Since none are defined, this must be zero.
iInterface	Index of string descriptor identifying this interface.

Table 12.7: Hub Interface Descriptor Fields

The interface descriptor is crucial in the hub descriptor layout because it identifies the device as a hub class device. Note that this class code can be specified in the interface descriptor as well as in the device descriptor. However, if the device supports *more than one interface* in a given configuration, the class code should only be specified in the interface descriptor. In that case, the *bClassCode* field in the device descriptor should be set to zero. The host will enumerate the device on an interface-by-interface basis (recognizing that the device has specified that each interface presents its own class code).

A detailed description of each of the above fields follows.

bLength	**Hub Interface Descriptor**
Offset:	0
Length:	1
Legal Values:	0x09
Default Value:	0x09
Description:	Number of bytes in this descriptor, including this one

bDescriptorType	**Hub Interface Descriptor**
Offset:	1
Length:	1
Legal Values:	0x04
Default Value:	0x04
Description:	INTERFACE descriptor

bInterfaceNumber	**Hub Interface Descriptor**
Offset:	2
Length:	1
Legal Values:	0-bNumInterfaces (from configuration descriptor)
Default Value:	0x00
Description:	Identifies the interface index of this interface. If there is only one interface on this device, this field would be zero. If a hub is part of a composite device that supports more than one interface, then this value would indicate the interface number of this interface.

bAlternateSetting	**Hub Interface Descriptor**
Offset:	3
Length:	1
Legal Values:	0 – 255
Default Value:	0x00
Description:	Hubs are not required to support any alternate interfaces, but if the device designer wishes to do so, this field would indicate the alternate setting index.

bNumEndpoints	**Hub Interface Descriptor**
Offset:	4
Length:	1
Legal Values:	1-255
Default Value:	0x01
Description:	Number of endpoints in this interface. In most cases, this value is 1. In cases where the hub designer wishes to offer additional endpoints for extensions to the hub's basic functionality, this value would be greater than one.

bInterfaceClass	**Hub Interface Descriptor**
Offset:	5
Length:	1
Legal Values:	0x09
Default Value:	0x09
Description:	Hub class code

binterfaceSubClass	Hub Interface Descriptor
Offset:	6
Length:	1
Legal Values:	0x00
Default Value:	0x00
Description:	Interface subclass code.

binterfaceProtocol	Hub Interface Descriptor
Offset:	7
Length:	1
Legal Values:	0x00
Default Value:	0x00
Description:	Interface protocol.

12.11.5 Endpoint Descriptor

Field	Description
bLength:	Number of bytes in this descriptor, including this one
bDescriptorType:	ENDPOINT descriptor
bEndPointAddress:	Address and direction of this endpoint
bmAttributes:	Attributes of this endpoint (transfer type)
wMaxPacketSizse:	Maximum number of bytes that will be sent in a single packet by this device.
bInterval:	Interval that the endpoint should be polled by the host.

Table 12.8: Hub Endpoint Descriptor Fields

The endpoint descriptor specifies the hub endpoint's characteristics. For hub devices, the only endpoint in the hub interface is the INTERRUPT endpoint that is used to report hub change notifications to the host. If the hub device designer adds other endpoints to the interface, the standard hub device driver probably won't use those endpoints. The safest approach is to keep the hub interface simple and report only one endpoint with the appropriate characteristics.

A detailed description of each of the above fields follows.

bLength	Hub Endpoint Descriptor
Offset:	0
Length:	1
Legal Values:	0x07
Default Value:	0x07
Description:	Number of bytes in this descriptor, including this one

bDescriptorType	Hub Endpoint Descriptor
Offset:	1
Length:	1
Legal Values:	0x05
Default Value:	0x05
Description:	ENDPOINT descriptor

bEndpointAddress	Hub Endpoint Descriptor
Offset:	2
Length:	1
Legal Values:	Bits 3-0: the endpoint number (usually one)
	Bits 6-4: reserved, must be zero
	Bit 7: Must be 1 = Input Endpoint (for this hub class)
Default Value:	0x81 (endpoint 1, direction = IN)
Description:	Endpoint's address and direction. This can be thought of as a sub-addressing of the device's overall bus address.

bmAttributes	Hub Endpoint Descriptor
Offset:	3
Length:	1
Legal Values:	0x03
Default Value:	0x03
Description:	The endpoint's transfer type is INTERRUPT.

wMaxPacketSize	Hub Endpoint Descriptor
Offset:	4
Length:	2
Legal Values:	0, 0x40 (depeneding on number of ports on the hub)
Default Value:	Depends on the number of hub downstream ports
Description:	The maxpacket size for the interrupt (status change) endpoint. Since the status change endpoint must report its data in 8-bit increments, this value must round up to an 8-bit multiple. For example, if a hub has 9 downstream ports, the natural data payload in the hub would be 9 bits, which would be rounded up to 16-bits (to the next byte).

bInterval	Hub Endpoint Descriptor
Offset:	6
Length:	1
Legal Values:	0xFF
Default Value:	0xFF
Description:	The hub status change endpoint should not be polled any more frequently than once every 256 msec. Note that the host may actually poll the endpoint more frequently.

12.12 Hub Requests

As with the descriptors, hubs support two general categories of requests: standard requests that are common to all devices, and hub class-specific requests that are specific to the hub device class.

Standard device requests must be supported in hubs as for all other USB devices. Requests that are not supported should be STALLED by the USB hub. Example of such requests in a hub device are:

- SET_CONFIGURATION to an unknown or unsupported configuration value
- SET_INTERFACE to a non-zero alternate interface value
- All optional device requests (example: SET_DESCRIPTOR).

For the GET_INTERFACE request, the hub should return a zero indicating the alternate setting is always zero.

Hubs also support a set of class-specific requests. The requests are modeled after the standard requests in order to reuse as much of the device framework as possible. This approach maximizes the designer's familiarity with the hub requests. The actual request codes are, indeed, identical to the request codes used in standard requests. The key difference is that the request *type* (*i.e.*, the *bmRequestType* field in the setup packet) indicates that the request is a *class* request. This differentiates the hub class request from the standard device request.

Table 12.9 shows a summary of the class-specific requests that hubs support and Table 12.10 shows a summary of the hub class request codes. More detailed explanations of each of the requests follow.

Request	bmRequestType	bRequest	wValue	wIndex	wLength	Data
ClearHubFeature	00100000B	CLEAR_FEATURE	Feature Selector	Zero	Zero	None
ClearPortFeature	00100011B	CLEAR_FEATURE	Feature Selector	Port	Zero	None
GetBusState	10100011B	GET_STATE	Zero	Port	One	Per Port Bus State
GetHubDescriptor	10100000B	GET_DESCRIPTOR	Descriptor Type and Descriptor Index	Zero or Language ID	Descriptor Length	Descriptor
GetHubStatus	10100000B	GET_STATUS	Zero	Zero	Four	Hub Status and Change Indicators
GetPortStatus	10100011B	GET_STATUS	Zero	Port	Four	Port Status and Change Indicators
SetHubDescriptor	00100000B	SET_DESCRIPTOR	Descriptor Type and Descriptor Index	Zero or Language ID	Descriptor Length	Descriptor
SetHubFeature	00100000B	SET_FEATURE	Feature Selector	Zero	Zero	None
SetPortFeature	00100011B	SET_FEATURE	Feature Selector	Port	Zero	None

Table 12.9: Summary of Hub Class-Specific Requests

Feature Selector	Recipient	Value	Request
C_HUB_LOCAL_POWER	hub	0	ClearHubFeature
C_HUB_OVER_CURRENT	hub	1	ClearHubFeature
PORT_CONNECTION	port	0	None
PORT_ENABLE	port	1	SetPortFeature ClearPortFeature
PORT_SUSPEND	port	2	SetPortFeature ClearPortFeature
PORT_OVER_CURRENT	port	3	None
PORT_RESET	port	4	SetPortFeature
PORT_POWER	port	8	SetPortFeature ClearPortFeature
PORT_LOW_SPEED	port	9	None
C_PORT_CONNECTION	port	16	ClearPortFeature
C_PORT_ENABLE	port	17	ClearPortFeature
C_PORT_SUSPEND	port	18	ClearPortFeature
C_PORT_OVER_CURRENT	port	19	ClearPortFeature
C_PORT_RESET	port	20	ClearPortFeature

Table 12.10: Summary of Hub Class Feature Selector Codes

bRequest	Value	Comments
GET_ STATUS	0	Hub or Port status retrieved through this request.

CLEAR_ FEATURE	1	The hub accepts feature selectors to clear following change bits:
		ClearHubFeature: c_hub_local_power
		                         c_hub_over_current
		
		Ports accept feature selectors to disable the following features:
		ClearPortFeature: PORT_ENABLE (disable port)
		                         PORT_SUSPEND (resume port)
		                         PORT_POWER (remove power)
		
		Ports accept feature selectors to clear the following change bits:
		ClearPortFeature: C_PORT_CONNECTION
		                         C_PORT_ENABLE
		                         C_PORT_SUSPEND
		                         C_PORT_RESET
		                         C_PORT_OVER_CURRENT

GET_STATE	2	This is an optional request.

SET_ FEATURE	3	The hub does not accept any Set_Feature requests. Class-specific Set_Feature requests sent to the hub (i.e., the recipient bits in bmRequestType specify the "device") should be STALLED by the hub.
		
		Ports accept feature selectors to enable the following features:
		SetPortFeature: PORT_ENABLE (enable port)
		                    PORT_SUSPEND (suspend port)
		                    PORT_POWER (apply power)
		                    PORT_RESET (reset port)
		
		Ports never accept feature selectors to enable change bits. Change bits are set by hardware events such as device attach, end of reset signaling, etc. Thus, it is illegal for the host to send a SET_FEATURE request with any of the "change" feature selectors (e.g., c_port_enable, etc.) in the wValue field of the setup packet. If the hub device receives such a request, it should respond with a STALL handshake.

Reserved for future use	*4-5*	
GET_DESCRIPTOR	6	The host retrieves the hub class descriptor using this request. The hub class descriptor is variable in length, so the setup packet's wLength field will vary depending on the number of ports. See the description of the GET_DESCRIPTOR request below.
SET_DESCRIPTOR	7	This is an optional request.

Table 12.11: Summary of Hub Class Request Codes

Since hubs support both standard and class-specific device requests, the hub designer should be aware of the possible device requests and ensure that the hub behaves appropriately. This section describes the standard and class specific flavors of each applicable request. The corresponding hub behavior is outlined in each case.

12.12.1 GET STATUS

Request Code (Target) Data/Direction	Index	Value	Length	Data
GET_STATUS Hub Port Direction: Device to Host	Zero Port #	Zero	4 4	Hub Status Port Status

Table 12.12: STATUS Request Summary

The GET_STATUS request can be directed at one of four entities on the hub device:

1. The device

2. The endpoint(s)

3. The hub

4. The port(s) on the hub

Note that standard device requests are used to get status from the device and the endpoint(s), while class-specific requests are used to get status from the hub and the ports.

Standard request:

- Get Device Status:

This is the standard device request to get the device status. The details of the request are defined in Chapter 11 *USB Device Framework*. The hub device should return the appropriate information about the device status.

- Get Endpoint Status:

This is the standard device request to get the endpoint status. The details of the request are defined in Chapter 11. The hub device should return the appropriate information about the endpoints supported.

Note: this request may be directed at either the default endpoint (endpoint zero), or the hub's status change endpoint. If the request is directed at the status change endpoint and the hub has not yet been configured (a SET_CONFIGURATION request has not been received and successfully completed by the hub device), the hub should respond with a STALL. This indicates an error condition on the GET_STATUS request. The rationale for this behavior is that the hub, not having been configured, does not yet present any endpoints other than the standard default endpoint.

Class request:

The class-specific GET_STATUS requests use the standard GET_STATUS semantics, but the request is designated as a class-specific request. When used as a class-specific request, the GET_STATUS request can be used to retrieve status from the *Hub* (GetHubStatus) or from the hub's *Ports* (GetPortStatus).

The "recipient" bits in the bmRequestType field differentiate the GetHubStatus request from the GetPortStatus request.

* GetHubStatus:

The GetHubStatus request is a class-specific GET_STATUS request. The host uses this request to check hub status, usually after some change has occurred in the hub.

Retrieving the *Hub* status is done via the GetHubStatus request:

Field	Value	Meaning
bmRequestType	10100000	Device To Host (1) Class Request (01) Recipient is Device (00000)
bRequest	0	GET_STATUS
wValue	0	None
wIndex	0	None
wLength	4	Four bytes requested

Table 12.13: GetHubStatus Setup Packet

The hub returns four bytes of hub status data in the data stage of the control transfer. The status data is defined as follows:

STATUS FIELDS (1st 16-bits of data returned)	
BIT	**DESCRIPTION**
0	**Local Power Status:** This is the state of the local power supply. This field only applies to self-powered hubs whose USB Interface Engine (SIE) is bus-powered or hubs that support either self-powered or bus-powered configurations. This field is returned as a result of a change to the hub's power source. This field reports whether local power is good. This field allows system software to determine the reason for the removal of power to devices attached to this hub or to react to changes to the local power supply state. If the hub does not support this feature, then this field is RESERVED and follows the definition of the RESERVED bits below. This field reports the power status for the SIE and the remainder of the hub. 0 = Local power supply good. 1 = Local power supply lost (inactive).
1	**Over-Current Indicator:** This field only applies to hubs that report over-current conditions on a global hub basis (as reported in the Hub Descriptor). If the hub does not report over-current on a global hub basis, then this field is RESERVED and follows the definition of the RESERVED bits below. This field indicates that the sum of all the ports' current has exceeded the specified maximum and power to all the ports has been shut off. For more details on Over-Current protection, see Section 7.2.1.3.1 (Over-Current Protection) in the "Self-Powered Hubs" section of the USB Specification. This field indicates an over-current condition due to the sum of all ports' current consumption. 0 = All power operations normal. 1 = An over-current condition exists on a hub-wide basis.
2-15	**Reserved** These bits return zero when read.

434

	CHANGE FIELDS
	(2nd 16-bits of data returned)

BIT	DESCRIPTION
0	**Local Power Status Change:** (c_hub_local_power) This corresponds to Local Power Status, Bit 0 above. This field only applies to locally-powered (i.e., self-powered) hubs whose USB Interface Engine (SIE) is bus-powered, or hubs that support either self-powered or bus-powered configurations. This field is returned as a result of a change to the hub's power source. If the hub does not support this feature, then this field is RESERVED and follows the definition of the RESERVED bits below. This field reports whether a change has occurred to the local power status. 　　　　0 = No change has occurred on Local Power Status 　　　　1 = Local Power Status has changed
1	**Over-Current Indicator Change:** (c_hub_over_current) This corresponds to Over-Current Indicator, Bit 1 above. This field only applies to hubs that report over-current conditions on a global hub basis (as reported in the Hub Descriptor). If the hub does not report over-current on a global hub basis, then this field is RESERVED and follows the definition of the RESERVED bits below. This field reports whether a change has occurred to the Over-Current Indicator. This field is only set if an Over-Current condition has occurred (i.e., acknowledgment of this change by system software will not cause another change to be reported). 　　　　0 = No change has occurred on the Over-Current Indicator 　　　　1 = Over-Current Indicator has changed (i.e., Over-Current condition has occurred).
2-15	**Reserved** These bits return zero" when read.

Table 12.14: Hub Status and Change Fields (returned in GET_STATUS request)

- GetPortStatus:

The GetPortStatus request is a class-specific GET_STATUS request. This request is used by the host to check port status, usually after some change has occurred such as a device attachment event.

Retrieving the *Port* status is done via the GetPortStatus request as shown in Table 12.15:

Field	Value	Meaning
bmRequestType	10100011	Device To Host (1) Class Request (01) Recipient is Other (00011)
brequest	0	GET_STATUS
wValue	0	None
wIndex	0	Port Number for which status is being requested
wLength	4	Four bytes requested

Table 12.15: Get Port Status Setup Packet

If the hub receives a wIndex that specifies a non-existent port, the hub must STALL the request.

The hub returns four bytes of port status data in the data stage of the control transfer. The status data returned in that data stage is shown in Table 12.16:

STATUS FIELDS	
(1st 16-bits of data returned)	
BIT	**DESCRIPTION**
0	**Current Connect Status:** (port_connection) This field reflects whether or not a device is currently connected to this port. This value reflects the current state of the port, and may not correspond directly to the event that caused the Insertion Status Change (Bit 0 in below) to be set. 0 = no device is present on this port 1 = a device is present on this port **NOTE:** This field is always "1" for ports that have non-removable devices attached.
1	**Port Enabled/Disabled:** (port_enable) Ports can be enabled by host software only. Ports can be disabled by either a fault condition (disconnect event or other fault condition, including an over-current indication) or by host software. 0 = Port is disabled 1 = Port is enabled
2	**Suspend:** (port_suspend) This field indicates whether or not the device on this port is suspended. Setting this field causes the device to suspend by not propagating bus traffic downstream. Resetting this field causes the device to resume. Bus traffic cannot be resumed in the middle of a bus transaction. If the device itself is signaling a resume, this field will be cleared by the hub. 0 = Not suspended 1 = Suspended
3	**Over-Current Indicator:** (port_over_current) This field only applies to hubs that report over-current conditions on a per-port basis (as reported in the Hub Descriptor). If the hub does not report over-current on a per-port hub basis, then this field is RESERVED and follows the definition of the RESERVED bits below. This field indicates that the device attached to this port has drawn current that exceeds the specified maximum and this port's power has been shut off. Port power shutdown is also reflected in the Port Power field above. For more details, see Section 7.2.1.3.1 (Over-Current Protection) in the "Self-Powered Hubs" section of the USB Specification. This field indicates an over-current condition due to the device attached to this port. 0 = All power operations normal for this port. 1 = An over-current condition exists on this port. Power has been shut off to this port.
4	**Reset:** (port_reset) This field is set when the host wishes to reset the attached device. It remains set until the reset signaling is turned off by the hub and the reset status change field is set. 0 = Reset signaling not asserted 1 = Reset signaling asserted
5-7	**Reserved** These bits return a "0" when read.

Table 12.16: Port Status and Change fields (returned in GET_STATUS request)

STATUS FIELDS	
(1st 16-bits of data returned)	
BIT	**DESCRIPTION**
8	**Port Power:** (port_power) This field reflects a port's power state. Since hubs can implement different methods of port power switching, the meaning of this field varies depending on the type of power switching used. The device descriptor reports the type of power switching implemented by the hub. Hubs do not provide any power to their ports until they are in the configured state. 0 = This port is powered OFF 1 = This port is powered ON NOTE: Hubs that do not support power switching always return a "1" in this field.
9	**Low Speed Device Attached:** (port_low_speed) This is only relevant if a device is attached. 0 = Full Speed device attached to this port 1 = Low speed device attached to this port
10-15	**Reserved** These bits return zero when read.

Table 12.16: Port Status and Change fields (returned in GET_STATUS request) (continued)

	CHANGE FIELDS
	(2nd 16-bits of data returned)
BIT	**DESCRIPTION**
0	**Connect Status Change:** (c_port_connection) Indicates a change has occurred in the port's Current Connect Status. The hub device sets this field for any changes to the port device connect status, even if system software has not cleared a connect status change. **(See Note)** 0 = No change has occurred on Current Connect Status 1 = Current Connect Status has changed **For ports that have non-removable devices attached, this field is set only after a RESET condition to indicate to system software that a device is present on this port.**
1	**Port Enable/Disable Change:** (c_port_enable) This field is only activated when a change in the port's enable/disable status was detected due to hardware changes. This field is not set if system software caused a port enable/disable change. 0 = No change has occurred on Port Enabled/Disabled status 1 = Port Enabled/Disabled status has changed
2	**Suspend Change:** (c_port_suspend) This field indicates a change in the host-visible power state of the attached device. It indicates the device has transitioned out of the suspend state. Going into the suspend state will not set this field. The Suspend Change field is only set when the entire resume process has completed. That is, the hub has ceased signaling resume on this port and three milliseconds have passed to allow the device to resynch to SOF. 0 = No change 1 = Resume Complete
3	**Over-Current Indicator Change:** (c_port_over_current) This field only applies to hubs that report over-current conditions on a per-port basis (as reported in the Hub Descriptor). If the hub does not report over-current on a per-port hub basis, then this field is RESERVED and follows the definition of the RESERVED bits below. This field reports whether a change has occurred to the port Over-Current Indicator. 0 = No change has occurred on Over-Current Indicator 1 = Over-Current Indicator has changed
4	**Reset Change:** (c_port_reset) This field is set when reset processing on this port is complete. As a reset of completing reset processing, the enabled status of the port is also set and the suspend change field reset. 0 = No change 1 = Reset Complete
5-15	**Reserved** These bits return zero when read.

Table 12.16: Port Status and Change fields (returned in GET_STATUS request) (continued)

Note: If, for example, the insertion status changes twice before system software has cleared the changed condition, hub hardware will be "setting" an already-set bit (*i.e.*, the bit will remain set). However, the hub will transfer the change bit only once when the host controller requests a data transfer to the Status Change endpoint. System software will be responsible for determining state change history in such a case.

12.12.2 GET STATE

Request Code (Target) Data/Direction	Index	Value	Length	Data
GET_STATE Other Direction: Device to Host	Port #	Zero	One	Per-port bus data

The GET_STATE request is an optional hub class-specific request. This request is typically used to facilitate system debug. This diagnostic feature provides a glimpse of the USB bus state as sampled at the last EOF2 sample point at a particular port number (which is specified in the request).

Hubs that implement this diagnostic feature store the bus state at each EOF2 state, in preparation for a potential host poll in the following USB frame.

The data returned is bit-mapped in the following manner. The value of the D- signal is returned in the field in bit 0. The value of the D+ signal is returned in the field in bit 1. Bits 2-7 are reserved for future use and are reset to zero.

Hubs that do not support this request respond with a STALL handshake in either the data stage or the status stage of the control transfer.

12.12.3 CLEAR FEATURE

Request Code (Target) Data/Direction	Index	Value	Length	Data
CLEAR_FEATURE Hub Feature Port Direction: Host to Device	Zero Port #	Feature Selector Feature Selector	Zero Zero	None None

The CLEAR_FEATURE request is used by the host to perform standard and class-specific feature manipulation. Therefore, the hub can expect to receive both the standard and the class-specific versions of the CLEAR_FEATURE request. The CLEAR_FEATURE request is generally used to disable features in the USB device.

Standard Request:

The standard CLEAR_FEATURE request can be directed at one of two entities:

1. The device
2. The endpoint

The features that can be selected are:

• Clear Endpoint Stall Feature

This is the standard device request to clear the endpoint STALL. The hub can receive this request to either of its two endpoints, if the endpoint has stalled.

See Chapter 11 for a complete description of the Clear Endpoint Stall Feature request.

Note: If this request is directed at a non-default endpoint (*i.e.*, not at endpoint zero) while the hub is UNCONFIGURED, the hub must STALL the request. Only endpoint zero can be specified for this request when the hub is UNCONFIGURED.

• Clear Device Remote Wakeup Feature

This standard device request is used to clear (*i.e.*, disable) the hub's ability to be a remote wake-up device. By sending this request, the host masks the hub's ability to remotely wake-up a suspended segment of USB. This means that the hub is no longer able to signal a remote wake-up sequence based on a port or hub status change.

All hubs are capable of being remote wake-up sources on USB. Therefore, hubs report their ability to be remote wake-up sources as ENABLED by default.

For more information on the standard CLEAR_FEATURE requests, please refer to Chapter 11.

Class Request:

- ClearHubFeature

This class-specific device request is used to clear hub change bits that were set by the hub device in response to hardware events. The host specifies which change bit to clear by the value of the feature selector, which is specified in the wValue field of the setup stage.

Feature Selector	wValue	Meaning
C_HUB_LOCAL_POWER	0	Clears the local power change bit
C_HUB_OVER_CURRENT	1	Clears the over current change bit

Table 12.17: Hub Feature Selector Values

Note that no other feature selector values are valid for the hub. That is, no hub "features" can be disabled using this class-specific CLEAR_FEATURE request.

- ClearPortFeature

This class-specific device request is used to *disable* port features and to clear port change bits that were set by port hardware events. The host specifies which feature is being disabled or which change bit is being cleared by the feature selector specified in the wValue field of the setup stage.

> Note: Only one feature selector is specified per request. This means that only ONE feature can be disabled and only ONE change bit can be cleared at a time. There is no provision for disabling multiple port features or clearing multiple change bits in one request in the hub class definition.

The following feature selectors are valid for class-specific CLEAR_FEATURE requests directed at a port. These values appear in the setup stage's wValue field.

442

Feature Selector	wValue	Meaning
PORT_ENABLE	1	Disables the port. No bus traffic is propagated upstream or downstream on the port.
PORT_SUSPEND	2	Resumes the port. Bus traffic resumes on this port, in accordance with port resume functionality.
PORT_POWER	8	Removes power from the port.
C_PORT_CONNECTION	16 (0x10)	Clears the C_PORT_CONNECTION change bit
C_PORT_ENABLE	17 (0x11)	Clears the C_PORT_ENABLE change bit
C_PORT_SUSPEND	18 (0x12)	Clears the C_PORT_SUSPEND change bit
C_PORT_OVER_CURRENT	19 (0x13)	Clears the C_PORT_OVER_CURRENT change bit
C_PORT_RESET	20 (0x14)	Clears the C_PORT_RESET change bit

Table 12.18: Clear Port Feature Selector Values

12.12.4 SET FEATURE

Request Code (Target) Data/Direction	Index	Value	Length	Data
SET_FEATURE				
Hub Feature	Zero	Feature Selector	Zero	None
Port	Port #	Feature Selector	Zero	None
Direction: Host to Device				

The SET_FEATURE request is used by the host to perform standard and class-specific feature manipulation. Therefore, the hub can expect to receive both the standard and the class-specific versions of the SET_FEATURE request. The SET_FEATURE request is generally used to **enable** features in the USB device.

Standard Request:

The standard SET_FEATURE request can be directed at one of two entities of the hub:

1. The device

2. The endpoint

The features that can be selected are:

• Set Endpoint Stall Feature

This is the standard device request to force an endpoint to exhibit STALL behavior. The hub can receive this request to either of its two endpoints (the standard default endpoint, or the status change endpoint). Upon successful completion of this request, the hub must return a STALL handshake on transactions directed to the endpoint that was stalled by the request.

See Chapter 11 for a complete description of the Set Endpoint Stall Feature request.

> **Note: If this request is directed at a non-default endpoint (i.e., not at endpoint zero) while the hub is UNCONFIGURED, the hub must STALL the request. Only endpoint zero can be specified for this request when the hub is UNCONFIGURED.**

- Set Device Remote Wake-Up Feature

This standard device request is used to set (i.e., enable) the hub's ability to be a remote wake-up device. By sending this request, the host allows the hub to remotely wake-up a suspended segment of USB. This means that the hub will be able to signal a remote wake-up sequence.

All hubs are capable of being remote wake-up sources on USB. Therefore, hubs report their ability to be remote wake-up devices as ENABLED by default.

For more information on the standard SET_FEATURE requests, please refer to Chapter 11.

Class Request:

- SetHubFeature

> **The hub does not accept any Set_Feature requests. Class-specific Set_Feature requests sent to the hub (i.e., the recipient bits in bmRequestType specify the "device") should be STALLED by the hub.**

- SetPortFeature

This class-specific device request is used to enable port features. The host specifies which feature to enable by the value of the feature selector, which is specified in the wValue field of the control transfer. The port number is specified in the wIndex field.

Only one feature selector is specified per request. This means that only ONE feature can be enabled at a time. There is no provision for enabling multiple port features in one request in the hub class definition. The only exception to this rule is the PORT_RESET feature selector. This request performs a RESET and then ENABLES the port. However, this is due to electrical requirements imposed by the USB bus architecture and not to the hub class design.

The following feature selectors are valid for class-specific SET_FEATURE requests directed at a port. These values appear in the control transfer wValue field.

Feature Selector	wValue	Meaning
PORT_ENABLE	1	Enables the port. Bus traffic is propagated upstream or downstream on the port.
PORT_SUSPEND	2	Suspends the port. Bus traffic is suspended on this port. Device(s) attached to this port go into suspend since they subsequently do not see bus traffic on this port.
PORT_RESET	4	Causes the hub to send reset signaling down this port, and then to enable the port. Note that the hub maintains USB bus reset timing, as outlined in Chapter 4. The hub is responsible for automatically enabling the port after the reset.
PORT_POWER	8	Applies power to the port.

Table 12.19: Set Port Feature Selector Values

The hub will set only the Reset Change bit (C_PORT _RESET) in response to a successful PORT_RESET. The hub will not set the Port Enable Change bit (C_PORT_ENABLE) since this port enable/disable change was caused by the host sending the PORT_RESET request and not by a hardware event on the port.

The Port Enable change bit is set only when the port is disabled due to a hardware event (*e.g.*, port was disabled due to a device babble condition).

12.12.5 GET DESCRIPTOR

Request Code (Target) Data/Direction	Index	Value	Length	Data
GET_DESCRIPTOR Device Direction: Device to Host	Zero or Language ID	Descriptor Type and Descriptor Index	Descriptor Length Requested	Descriptor Data

The GET_DESCRIPTOR request is used by the host to get the standard and class-specific descriptors. Hubs differentiate standard GET_DESCRIPTOR requests from class-specific GET_DESCRIPTOR requests via the bmRequestType field in the control transfer. The GET_DESCRIPTOR request can be used to retrieve the standard descriptors and the hub class descriptor.

Standard Request:

The standard GET_DESCRIPTOR request is used to retrieve the standard USB device descriptors, such as the device descriptor, configuration descriptor, etc. This is outlined in more detail in Chapter 11. Hubs respond to the standard GET_DESCRIPTOR requests as specified in the USB device framework.

Class Request:

The class-specific GET_DESCRIPTOR request is used to retrieve the hub descriptor. The host identifies the request as being class specific by setting the appropriate bits in the bmRequestType field of the control transfer. The remaining fields in the GET_DESCRIPTOR control transfer are very similar to the standard GET_DESCRIPTOR request. For the class-specific request, the request is defined as follows:

Field	Value	Meaning
bmRequestType	10100000	Device To Host (1) Class Request (01) Recipient is Device
brequest	6	GET_DESCRIPTOR
wValue	0x2900	High byte: Descriptor type (0x29) Low byte: Descriptor index (0)
wIndex	0 or Language ID	Zero indicates default language, or a non-zero 16-bit Language ID is supplied
wLength	Varies	Number of bytes of descriptor data requested. The host may request less or more than the actual size of the hub descriptor, and devices should be prepared for such cases.

12.12.6 SET DESCRIPTOR

Request Code (Target) Data/Direction	Index	Value	Length	Data
SET_DESCRIPTOR Device Direction: Host to Device	Zero or Language ID	Descriptor Type and Descriptor Index	Descriptor Length Requested	Descriptor Data

The SET_DESCRIPTOR request is used by the host to update standard and class-specific descriptors. However, this request is optional and is not required for USB hub class compliance.

Standard Request:

The standard SET_DESCRIPTOR request is used to update the standard USB device descriptors, such as the device descriptor, configuration descriptor, etc. This is outlined in more detail in Chapter 11. Hubs respond to the standard SET_DESCRIPTOR requests as specified in the USB device framework.

Class Request:

The class-specific SET_DESCRIPTOR request is used to update the hub descriptor. Hubs should STALL this request if the device does not support it. The host identifies the request as being class specific by setting the appropriate bits in the bmRequestType field of the control transfer. The remaining fields in the SET_DESCRIPTOR control transfer are very similar to the standard GET_DESCRIPTOR request. For the class-specific request, the request is defined as follows:

Field	Value	Meaning
bmRequestType	00100000	Hot To Device (0)
		Class Request (01)
		Recipient is Device
brequest	7	SET_DESCRIPTOR
wValue	0x2900	High byte: Descriptor type (0x29)
		Low byte: Descriptor index (0)
wIndex	0 or Language ID	Zero indicates default language, or a non-zero 16-bit Language ID is supplied
wLength	Varies	Number of bytes of descriptor data that follows. The host may update only a portion of the hub descriptor, which would result in a length that is less than the full Hub Descriptor Length.

13. Universal Serial Bus Classes

13.1 What is a USB Class?

USB classifies devices and interfaces by grouping their capabilities according to the connection requirements of USB and their application. A given class, then, describes a set of capabilities and how it can appear to the host. A class definition governs how an interface is defined, how it interacts with the host, and how it interacts with other interfaces on the same device.

Why use classes, except as a handy shorthand identification? Because a class describes the baseline specification for a given set of capabilities. As such, an interface using that class can be bound to and managed by adaptive host software known as a CLASS DRIVER, in any system, without requiring a specific driver to be loaded. This means that devices can in fact be developed without any additional software development being required. Or that a device which conforms to the class definition, but which uses a specific driver to enhance its operation, can still retain its basic function when used in a system without that specific driver. Or that a device implementer building a very complex, advanced device, can use class drivers for those interfaces which only require a basic class functionality and restrict software development to just the value-added areas.

Each class is defined by a USB CLASS SPECIFICATION. With the sole exception of the HUB class, class specifications are separate documents from the USB Specification. Each class specification is developed by a group of interested companies and then ratified by the **USB IMPLEMENTERS' FORUM** (USB-IF) through the agency of the **USB DEVICE WORKING GROUP** (DWG).

> When the DWG approves a USB class specification, it assigns a class code to the new class and posts the class specification on the USB-IF web page (http://www.usb.org).

While the USB-IF controls when and what class code is assigned to the new class, all of the other definitions for the class, including sub-class and protocol codes, are controlled solely by the working group defining the class. All of these definitions must be documented in the class specification before it is approved and released. See Section 13.1.2.

The HUB class specification was so pivotal to the overall USB definition that it was released as a chapter in the original USB Specification. As such, the documentation of its definition does not conform to the same template as the other class specifications. The Hub chapter in the USB Specification does, however, have all of the required content of a class specification.

> The HUB class is a USB class like any other and governed by the same rules, plus additional requirements due to the role it plays in USB connectivity.

Although summarized briefly in this chapter, the HUB class is described in detail in Chapter 12 *Hub Device Class*.

The following sections describe what must be defined in a class specification and how those definitions are applied to USB. In addition to describing the basic appearance of the USB interfaces conforming to the class, using the class definition also provides some guidance to the host on how to bind those interfaces to their corresponding host software. That process is further discussed in Chapter 14 *Enumeration*.

Finally, this chapter summarizes the USB classes currently defined by or in progress in the DWG. Only class specifications that are at a release level of 0.9 or above are publicly available. The definition of any class whose specification has not yet reached 1.0 may change before the 1.0 version is released. Implementers should therefore approach with caution any pre-release definition.

13.1.1 Device *vs.* Interface

Although frequently referred to improperly as "Device Classes", USB classes in fact most closely apply to interfaces and not necessarily to the entire device.

USB categorizes devices in many different ways:

- COMPOUND PACKAGES. This is actually a packaging option in which a hub is physically included with one or more other USB devices. Each of the non-hub devices connects to a FIXED PORT on the hub. The hub may additionally expose some ports externally so that more devices can be attached.

- SIMPLE DEVICES. All of the interfaces on a simple device are of the same class *and* the class code in the DEVICE descriptor is non-zero (see Chapter 11 *USB Device Framework*) and identifies the class of the interfaces. The class codes in the INTERFACE descriptors are ignored. The intent of a simple device is that it is bound as a single object to its owning host software.

- COMPOSITE DEVICES. The original intent of a composite device was that it contained interfaces that were of different classes. However, this has evolved to meaning simply a device whose interfaces can be bound individually to owning host software. A composite device is indicated by a class code of 00h in the DEVICE descriptor, see Chapter *13 USB Device Framework*.

Class specifications generally define how an interface of that class appears and interacts with the host. Few classes define how an entire device must interact.

Even when used in a simple device, the class really describes how the individual interfaces on that device are defined.

Defining class usages, and thus software bindings, at an interface rather than a device level, is more than an accident of history.

Having complete class definitions at an interface level means tha class drivers can bind directly to that interface and its data, withou having to go through the complication of additional intervening software layers. As well as having performance implications, thi: can simplify host organization by reducing the number of standar(software interfaces that must be developed.

Using classes at an interface level also allows device developer: to mix and match interfaces to create interesting devices. Thos(parts of the device that only require the base capabilities of ar existing class, *e.g.*, a keypad, can use standard components and standard class driver. The device implementer is free to concentrat(on those areas that provide additional value and differentiate tha particular device.

Interesting devices can also be created out of a number o standard class interfaces. For instance, a phone can include AUDIC interfaces for talking and listening and a HID interface for keypac input.

13.1.2 Class Definitions

A USB class specification describes the common characteristics and requirements of interfaces adhering to the class. It must have content that answers the following questions:

- What kinds of interfaces or devices are described by this class and how are they categorized?

- How do the interfaces, endpoints, and other standard USB objects used by this class behave in isolation and/or with other interfaces?

- What descriptions are required, both within the bounds of the standard USB descriptions and of the class-specific capabilities?

This all boils down to a class specification which must describe how this class relates to the standard objects, descriptors and requests described in Chapter 11 *USB Device Framework* and how it describes its class-specific capabilities and semantics.

The USB-IF owns the assignment of a class code to a USB class, as described by a class specification. The class specification, however, owns any further categorization by subclass and protocol codes, relative to the particular class.

The class specification must specifically describe the appearance of an interface implemented to the class definition. What are the endpoint requirements? Number of endpoints? Transfer characteristics? Any restrictions on legal bandwidths? Class-specific formats of data transfers? Do the pipes attached to these endpoints have any standard uses or roles with regard to the owning application? Does this interface interact in any standard way with other interfaces of the same or different class? How does this interface interact, if at all, with other interfaces on the same device?

Just as the STANDARD descriptors provide the information required for the host to adapt to the device's USB connection requirements, the CLASS descriptors allow the host software to adapt to its functional requirements. CLASS descriptors describe class-specific capabilities, connection requirements, data formats, and command languages.

> As a general rule, a class should re-use existing standards for its functional capabilities, instead of inventing new ones.

For instance, the AUDIO class provides descriptors identifying which of the existing audio formats are used for its streams, rather than describing a new USB-specific audio format.

As described in Chapter 11 *USB Device Framework*, the device may handle its class-specific descriptors in a variety of ways: interleaved vs. singly, dynamic vs. static. A class specification may choose to restrict how the device manages its class descriptors.

Classes generally use the Default Pipe to issue class-specific requests to the interface. A class may define new USB class-specific requests, or it may wrap an existing command language in a USB shell and use that. If the applications for this class require that requests down the Default Pipe be coupled to data transfers, the specification must account for this, since there is no standard mechanism defined in USB for coordinating data transfers and Default Pipe requests.

Many classes additionally use an Interrupt pipe to send class specific notifications to the host. In this case a class-specific notification format may also be defined.

13.1.3 Choices: Class *vs.* Vendor-specific

A class definition provides its primary value by enabling adaptive host software to work with a wide range of implementations of class capabilities. In particular, a class driver provides application access to many different class-compliant interfaces, regardless of implementation. All class-compliant interfaces must be capable of being managed by the appropriate class driver. For the device vendor this means that these interfaces must:

- Support the minimum class functionality by implementing al *required* portions of the class specification.

- Implement any extensions in a compatible manner. Some class definitions make specific allowance for compatible extensions. At a minimum, any implementation extensions should no interfere with device operation when a class driver is managing that device.

Class drivers are adaptive device drivers that support a particular class definition and that may be provided by the operating system vendor, by a device vendor, or by a third party software vendor. Regardless of source, a class driver must be able to manage any class-compliant interface. For the class driver provider that means that the class driver must:

- Support the minimum class functionality by implementing all *required* portions of the class specification.

- Adapt its operation to any of the options defined in the class specification.

- Ignore any extensions not described by the class specification. Implementing support for non-class-defined extensions is not helpful and may actually cause interoperability problems since each device vendor may have implemented these extensions in a widely divergent manner.

But, if the interface and its host software interaction is already defined by a class, where can an implementer provide product differentiation other than cost?

Remember that a class definition describes only the baseline capabilities for that class. If the implementer provides only those baseline capabilities, then, yes, differentiating the product in ways other than cost is going to be a challenge. In some cases, the raw performance of different implementations may vary widely while providing the same basic functions. Or, where options exist within the class, the range of baseline capabilities supported in a particular implementation may vary.

When constructing a USB device, a vendor has two types of options for balancing class-defined capabilities and vendor value-adds:

1. Provide a better or more flexible implementation of class functionality, including enhancements in cost, performance, range of options supported, etc. This option requires no additional host support beyond the minimally provided class driver.

2. Add supplemental, vendor-specific features to the basic interface definition. This option requires additional host support beyond the minimally provided class driver. That additional host support can take a variety of forms:

    -   Application-level enhancements in the capability stack above the provided class driver.

    -   An enhanced class driver, that must support all other interfaces conforming to the class definition.

    -   A device-specific driver.

Replacing the existing class driver is potentially a large commitment on the part of the device vendor, since a class driver must support *all* class definitions, not just those that particular vendor has implemented. Additionally, as the class definition changes over time, it will be difficult for the device vendor to keep up with the definitions required. If replacing a class driver makes other devices break, the device vendor who has chosen that strategy will take the blame, along with the support calls.

> Potential interoperability problems and the consequent support burden are excellent reasons to never replace an existing class driver.

All systems allow device-specific drivers to be bound to particular interfaces and/or devices. Using a device-specific driver has the advantage of granting the implementer significantly increased freedom, and, of course, a higher development and support cost. Identifying a device or interface as belonging to a specific class does not prevent the implementer from also providing a device-specific driver.

> All interfaces that belong to a specific class must minimally conform to that class definition, even if a device-specific driver also manages the device.

This allows the device to maintain compatibility with other host software and to operate at a minimum level even if the more capable device-specific software is not present.

13.2 Communication

The *USB Communication Class Specification* provides definitions for devices that present remote connections to the host system, such as telephones, modems, LAN adapters, and bridges to other environments and buses. In order to provide these connections in a coherent USB-compatible manner, the *USB Communication Class Specification* defines a COMMUNICATION FRAMEWORK to present and manage remote connections. It also defines two USB classes:

- COMMUNICATION class; which governs the operation of the communication framework.

- DATA class; which allows the host to receive undifferentiated data from a remote interface.

The communication framework is designed to present a series of interfaces to the host. Each of these remote interfaces act as if they were local, *e.g.*, the talk and listen paths required for a telephone may be implemented as paired AUDIO interfaces. The source or destination of such an AUDIO interface is remote, but the host system can manage it as if it were a local, native AUDIO interface such as a speaker or a mike.

13.2.1 Definitions

Most class specifications define one USB class, with a single set of USB connectivity requirements and a coherent set of functional requirements that can be met by a single class driver. The *USB Communication Class Specification* actually defines two such USB classes: the DATA class and the COMMUNICATION class. While the DATA class definition fulfills a role similar to other USB classes, the COMMUNICATION class is used to identify the control and notification interface associated with the communication framework.

Data Class

The DATA class can be used in any device, not just communication devices. It denotes a data stream, in either direction, which displays no native interface type. In other words this stream is not known a priori to be another USB class such as AUDIO, HID, or IMAGING. The data moving over a DATA interface is thus referred to as UNDIFFERENTIATED DATA, and the interface itself must be managed by host software which discovers the actual data format through some means other than class identification.

DATA interfaces come in two basic forms:

- Asynchronous, which uses the bulk transfer method.
- Synchronous, which uses the isochronous transfer method.

The different forms of the DATA interface are used to indicate USB connectivity REQUIREMENTS, not functional requirements. In communication devices, data interfaces are used primarily for the following purposes, to handle:

- Data transfers that are not relevant to any defined USB class, *e.g.*, file transfers.
- Data streams that are pulled directly from the remote connection, without any interpretation by the device.

Communication devices may split the data stream from the remote connection into native USB classes or forward it on, unmodified, to the host software.

If the communication device interprets the data stream, the device uses the communication framework to organize the resulting streams into recognizable USB interfaces, as seen in Figure 13.1.

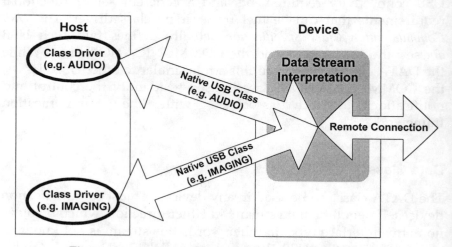

Figure 13.1: Device Interpretation of Data Streams

On the other hand, if the host software is responsible for splitting or merging the data, then the USB device will present the remote stream as an undifferentiated data interface, as seen in Figure 13.2.

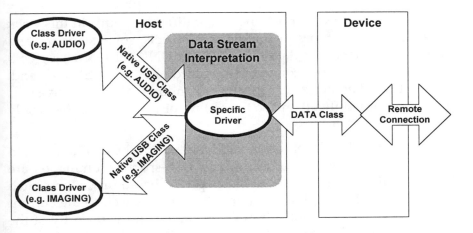

Figure 13.2: Host Interpretation of Data Stream

Communication Class

The communication framework describes how a series of interfaces are organized and managed in a manner that supports a remote connection. The communication framework consists of:

- A **BASIC CALL CONTROL INTERFACE** used for communication requests and notifications.

- Models which describe the level at which the control of the remote interface occurs.

The class of the basic call control interface is always the COMMUNICATION class. The basic call control interface is used for managing the remote connection and the communication aspects of the device. It consists of an interrupt pipe for connection status notifications (*e.g.*, incoming call, call dropped) and the Default Pipe for communication requests.

Remote connections are traditionally managed by a capability stack in which the undifferentiated data from the remote connection enters and exits at the line level at the bottom of the stack and application-oriented commands and data are exchanged at the top of the stack. In any given combination of host and device implementations, some portion of this stack is implemented on the device and some on the host.

Inserting the device/host division at different points in this stack exposes different types of command protocols, some standard and some proprietary. By defining a COMMUNICATION class, USB requires that these command protocols be identifiable and, preferably, standardized. However, handling arbitrary divisions would be very difficult and so the communication class defines only three division points:

1. A very low level device model in which the communication device acts as a codec. A few USB-specific commands are defined to handle specific telephony-based procedures such as dialing. Such a definition corresponds well to the current understanding of soft modems, in which the majority of the communication features are implemented on the host, in software.

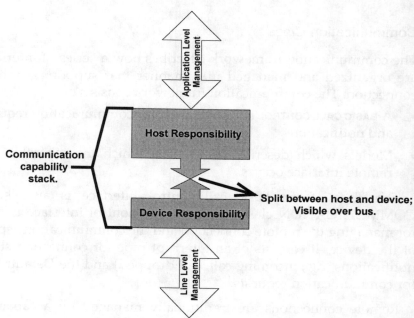

Figure 13.3: Dividing the Communication Stack Between the Host and Device

2. An intermediate device model in which the communication device can accommodate a relatively sophisticated data stream.

In this case the device can perform tasks such as compression and security, but does not perform any interpretation of the data stream itself. The commands used by such a device model are also USB-specific, augmented by proprietary commands. Such a definition corresponds well to the cost-reduced "data pump" modems, which do more work in hardware but which still have most functional activity implemented in host software.

3. A reasonably high-level device model in which the communication device looks more like the traditional modem or telephone. This definition requires a standardized command set and assumes relatively sophisticated device hardware (such as a microprocessor) and some level of stream interpretation on the device. The COMMUNICATION class supports only two standard command sets: V25ter (the "AT" command set) and Q931 (an ISDN protocol). These standard protocols are embedded in a USB-specific communication wrapper before transportation over USB.

Besides the basic call control interface, the communication device also presents interfaces which deliver the actual data carried over the remote interface. These other interfaces can be any USB class, including the DATA class. Whether the DATA class is used or some other more meaningful class is primarily determined by sophistication of the communication device.

Communication devices by their nature are very dynamic. An interface that is appropriate during one connection may not be useful in the next. Sophisticated communication devices may implement completely dynamic interfaces, as described by the *USB Common Class Specification*. Such interfaces are only valid during the connection period, and are unavailable at other times.

13.2.2 Design Targets

The *USB Communication Class Specification* allows support of any device that is presenting remote connections to the host; including:

*   Telephony devices.
*   LAN devices.

- Remote or wireless communications and control devices.

- Remote input devices.

- Home control devices.

- Bridges for host-to-host communications and device sharing.

Although the specification does not specifically disallow any of the other types of communication devices, it has really only been validated for telephony devices. A telephony device is "any device which could attach to a phone line" and includes telephones and modems using mechanisms such as POTS, DSVD, and ISDN.

Telephony devices also present a very wide range of design targets from the simplest codec to the most sophisticated multimedia modem; from telephone handsets to multi-line ISDN telephones. The definers of the *USB Communication Class Specification* divided these telephony design targets into the following categories:

- Undifferentiated DATA Devices. Such devices provide only DATA stream access and require a specialized driver for interpretation.

- Remote Interface Devices. The device provides the pertinent class interfaces, which the host class drivers access directly.

- Fancy Schmancy Devices. These are very intelligent devices which not only provide the appropriate USB class interfaces, but which complete most, if not all, of the stream manipulation. They also exploit all of the abilities of the dynamic interface definition in the *USB Common Class Specification* and are capable of associating their interfaces into sub-devices as required.

The *USB Communication Class Specification* has been primarily validated and optimized for the Remote Interface Device. Communication devices presenting only undifferentiated data are completely valid to build, but require little standardization. Fancy Schmancy Devices are also very interesting devices to build, but require extensive standardization, beyond what would be likely for a v1.0 specification.

13.2.3 Examples

A simple communication device example might consist of a telephone with data capability. Such a device has a basic call control (COMMUNICATION) interface, a pair of DATA interfaces, and a pair of AUDIO interfaces for the telephone talk and listen paths.

Interface	Class	Transfer Type	Bandwidth
Basic call control	COMMUNICATION	Interrupt	256 ms
Data capability	DATA	Bulk	Defaults to 0.
Speaker, microphone	AUDIO	Isochronous	Defaults to 0. Varies with available bandwidth and connection quality.

Table 13.1: Data Phone Example Interfaces

The basic call control interface is always present, with bandwidth allocated. The data capability is only allocated bandwidth on an as needed basis. The AUDIO interfaces may either default to zero bandwidth, and refuse calls if no bandwidth is available, or may allocate the minimum bandwidth required for a phone connection and augment that bandwidth for increased quality if it is available. Such a device might also provide a HID interface for direct keypad access.

A more complex device uses approximately the same interfaces but allows more variability in the class types and availability of the interfaces. For instance, a comparable Fancy Schmancy Device might allow an IMAGING interface as an alternative to the DATA interface. Which class of interface the device used would be determined during the connection process.

13.3 Hub

The HUB class is a USB class like any other and conforms to the USB class structure. However, hubs also have very specific roles in maintaining USB connectivity. As such the HUB class is the only

USB class defined by the *USB Specification* and is described in detail elsewhere in this book, see Chapter 12 *Hub Devices*.

13.4 Other Classes

A variety of other USB classes are under definition. These include Audio, Human Interface Device (HID)(*e.g.*, mouse, keyboard, joystick), Mass Storage, Monitor (*e.g.*, for controlling position, size, alignment, etc.), Physical Interface Device (*e.g.*, force feedback), Power (*e.g.*, UPS), Printers, and Imaging (*e.g.*, video and still).

Details on these classes can be found on the USB web site (http://www.usb.org).

13.5 Chapter Summary

USB classes characterize the USB connection requirements for an interface and its basic application capabilities. Thus, they provide both a basic operational structure and enumeration hints for locating and binding the correct host software to manage the device.

Each interface of a USB device may be of a different class, thus allowing the device implementer to mix and match software resources, reusing definitions where it makes sense and inventing new ones as needed. Host systems, in general, provide a minimal set of class drivers. Thus, when a device implementer uses class definitions on his device, he not only can decrease the cost of software development and support but also increase the interoperability of the device.

14. Enumeration

14.1 Introduction

This chapter describes how USB devices are handled as they are added to, or removed from, the system. USB can be a very dynamic environment, where one or more devices may be attached or removed from the system at any time. When a user adds or removes a hub device that has downstream devices connected to it, the system must properly adapt to the new environment.

Enumeration is generically the process of detecting, initializing, and configuring devices. Because USB is a hot-plug/unplug environment, enumeration also covers the proper handling of device insertion and removal. Both hardware and software are involved in the process of enumeration. On the hardware side, USB hubs play a very important role in enumeration, because they are the devices that initially detect the connection or disconnection of a USB device (or devices). On the software side, the hub device driver interacts with the hub to take the basic steps that enable hub ports, and assign a unique device address to new devices. Individual device driver software (for the added device) is typically the agent that actually configures the USB device.

This chapter covers enumeration from three different perspectives. First enumeration from a device's viewpoint is explored. Second, the interactions with a hub during enumeration

are described. And third, a description of how information from a
USB device should be used to locate an appropriate device driver is
explained.

14.2 Enumeration Sequence

This section describes the sequence needed to enumerate a device as
seen by a device. Hub interactions associated with enumeration are
covered in the next section.

The first transactions are typically generated by operating system
(OS) software. Transactions after that may be generated either by
the OS, or by the loaded device driver. Steps in the enumeration
sequence are detailed below.

- The device is plugged into an available hub port. For bus-
  powered devices, this is when the device first gets power and
  can start its power-up sequence. If the device is self-powered,
  the device may not be able to tell that it went from disconnected
  to connected.

- Some time later a RESET is driven on the bus. This RESET will
  last at least 10 milliseconds but could last longer (50
  milliseconds or more).

- At the end of RESET, the device starts receiving SOFs (or low
  speed keep-alives). The device should be completely reset at this
  point and its device address should be reset to 0 (the default
  address).

- Some time later, a GetDescriptor (Device) request is sent to the
  default device (*i.e.*, the device with an address of 0). The main
  purpose of this first transaction is to determine the
  MaxPacketSize for the newly connected device's default pipe.
  (Recall that MaxPacketSize for control endpoints can be either 8,
  16, 32, or 64 bytes.) The byte at offset 0x07 in a Device Descriptor
  contains the MaxPacketSize for the device's default pipe, so the
  GetDescriptor(Device) has to read at least the first eight bytes to
  determine the default pipe Max Packet Size.

Ideally, the GetDescriptor(Device) request has a length of eight bytes. For well-behaved devices, this will result in a data stage consisting of eight bytes, followed by a status stage to complete the transfer. However, if the device is ill-behaved and doesn't pay attention to the Length field in the Setup transaction, the device could send more than eight bytes (if its MaxPacketSize is larger than eight). This can result in a babble condition back at the host controller and the control transfer won't have a status stage.

To avoid babble, host software may decide to make the size of this first GetDescriptor(Device) request 18 bytes (the size of a Device Descriptor) or larger. This guarantees that there is enough buffer space in the host to hold the complete Device Descriptor. If the device's default pipe MaxPacketSize is 32 or 64, the full Device Descriptor will be returned and the control transfer will terminate normally (from both the device and host perspective). If the default pipe MaxPacketSize is 8 or 16, the full Device Descriptor won't be returned during the data stage. This will look like a short packet to the host, and the host will immediately start the status stage of the control transfer. From the device's perspective, this status stage looks like an early termination of a control transfer (since the complete Device Descriptor was not sent). Well-behaved devices handle early termination of control transfers without a problem. Ill-behaved devices may miss the status stage from the host, because they are still waiting for the next IN transaction to finish sending the Device Descriptor. This will result in an incomplete control transfer.

In both of the above ill-behaved cases, the device may be in an undetermined state, but should still respond to the next SETUP packet to continue operation. But to be safe and guarantee the state of the device, host software may drive another RESET. Since enough data was returned in both cases (at least the first eight bytes) to get the default pipe's MaxPacketSize, future control transfers can operate without fear of babble or early termination.

- A SetAddress request is sent next to assign the device a unique address. This control transfer has no data stage because the new address for the device is contained in the SETUP transaction. The status stage transaction (an IN) is addressed to the default address (0). The device should not take on the new address until successful completion of the status stage.

Recoveries from transient errors in the SetAddress control transfer are as follows:

- If the SETUP or DATA packets of the setup stage are corrupted, the device will ignore them, resulting in a timeout. The host will retry the transaction.

- If the host does not receive the ACK packet in the SETUP transaction, a timeout will occur and the host will retry.

- If the IN packet of the status stage is corrupted, the device will not see it, and the transaction will timeout. The host will retry.

- If the zero-length DATA packet sent by the device in the status stage is corrupted, the host will not see it, the transaction will timeout. The host will retry.

- If the ACK packet of the status stage is corrupted, the device will not see it and will consider the SetAddress control transfer incomplete. The host, however, will believe that the device has taken on the new address. The following step in the enumeration sequence is sent to the new address and will timeout (since the device is still at the default address). Host software must be able to detect and correct this case. Backing up to any previous enumeration sequence step can make the correction.

- The device is sent another GetDescriptor(Device) request. This time the host software knows the default pipe's MaxPacketSize and the Length field in the SETUP transaction is sufficient to send the whole Device Descriptor. This will involve multiple IN transactions during the data stage if the device has a MaxPacketSize less than 32 bytes.

Operations through this point are typically generated by OS software. After successfully reading the device descriptor, the OS has enough information to look for a specific device driver for the newly connected device. See Section 14.5 *Device Driver Loading* for

.nformation on what descriptor information is used to locate a device driver.

The following two steps complete the process of configuring the device. The OS performs these steps if no device driver was found and loaded; otherwise the device driver performs them. Note that if a device driver is loaded, it may issue a GetDescriptor(Device) request before performing these steps so that it has the complete descriptor information.

• The device is sent a GetDescriptor(Configuration) request. If the device has multiple configurations, then several GetDescriptor (Configuration)s may be sent to read each of the configuration descriptors.

When doing the initial read of a configuration descriptor, the total length of the descriptor is unknown. If the initial request did not have enough buffer space to hold the whole descriptor, another request is made with a sufficient buffer size.

• The device is sent a SetConfiguration request. This request tells the device which configuration to assume. The value sent should be the bConfigurationValue field from (one of) the device's configuration descriptor(s).

14.3 Hub Interactions

This section describes the interactions with a USB hub necessary to establish connectivity with a newly added USB device. This description assumes that the new device is plugged into a port of a hub that is fully configured and ready to accept new devices. The primary requirements for a hub to be in this state are that the hub is configured, and the appropriate hub requests have been sent to the hub so that power is enabled to the downstream ports.

• When a device is plugged into a hub port, the hub detects the insertion because the USB signal lines go from a single-ended 0 (SE0) to either a differential 1 (when a full speed device is inserted) or a differential 0 (when a low speed device is inserted). This change is reported upstream through the hub's

Status Change pipe (interrupt endpoint) the next time the hub is polled.

- The host software receives the Status Change notification from the hub. The information delivered precisely identifies which of the hub's ports had the change in status.

- Host software issues a Get Port Status request to the hub, requesting status information for the port where the change occurred.

- The hub responds with four bytes of data containing port status information (first two bytes) and port change information (last two bytes). Port Status indicates that a device is connected (bit 0) and port power is ON (bit 8). Bit 9 in Port Status will indicate whether a full speed (bit 9 = 0) or low speed (bit 9 = 1) device is connected. Port Change indicates that there has been a change in connect status (bit 0).

- Host software sends a request to the hub telling it to clear the Connect Status Change bit for the port. Clearing this bit keeps the hub from reporting another Status Change Indicator on the hub's Status Change pipe the next time it is polled. The request sent to the hub is a Clear Port Feature request with the feature selector set to C_PORT_CONNECTION.

- Host software sends a request to the hub telling it to drive a RESET to the newly attached device. This RESET is required to put the device into a consistent state and guarantee that the device is at the default address (0). The command sent to the hub is a Set Port Feature request with the feature selector set to PORT_RESET.

- When the hub is finished driving RESET (a minimum of 10 milliseconds), it sets the RESET_CHANGE bit in its Port Change register. The hub also enables the port for downstream (and upstream) traffic and indicates this by setting the PORT_ENABLE bit in the Port Status register.

- The asserted RESET_CHANGE bit in the Port Change register causes the hub to send a Status Change Indicator on the hub's Status Change pipe the next time the pipe is polled.

• Host software receives the Status Change Indicator from the hub. The information only indicates that there has been some change on the port. Host software cannot assume that the RESET is complete.

• Host software issues a Get Port Status request to the hub, requesting status information for the port where the change occurred.

• The hub responds by returning the values in its Port Status and Port Change registers. Port Status indicates that a device is connected (bit 0 = 1), the port is enabled (bit 1 = 1) and port power is ON (bit 8 = 1). Bit 9 in Port Status will indicate whether a full speed (bit 9 = 0) or low speed (bit 9 = 1) device is connected. Port Change has RESET_CHANGE asserted (bit 4 = 1) indicating that the reset process is complete.

• Host software sends a request to the hub telling it to clear the Reset Change bit for the port. Clearing this bit keeps the hub from reporting another Status Change Indicator on the hub's Status Change pipe the next time it is polled. The request sent to the hub is a Clear Port Feature request with the feature selector set to C_PORT_RESET.

At this point, the hub and its port have been fully enabled for USB traffic to the newly-connected device. The enumeration process for the new device (as described in the previous section) now occurs.

14.4 Device Removal

Users can remove USB devices at any time. There is no interlock mechanism that prevents a device from being removed until the software is ready. Because of this, OS software and vendor-supplied device drivers need to handle the case where a device suddenly disappears. The exact method for doing this is OS-specific, but some basic features are required.

1. There has to be a way to notify device drivers that the device they were using has been removed from the system.

2. There has to be a way for any pending or in-progress transfers to be aborted and cleaned up.

Device removal from a device viewpoint is pretty straightforward. Self-powered devices will stop seeing SOFs and will suspend. Unless they provide special hardware (like detecting a voltage on the USB power line) they really can't tell that they have been disconnected[1]. Bus-powered devices lose power when they are disconnected.

When a device is removed from a port, the hub detects the change and reports the change to host software. The sequence is described in the following steps:

- When a device is first unplugged, the hub detects that the USB signal lines float to a single-ended zero. This causes the hub to reset its Connected and Enabled bits in the Port Status register, and to set the Connect Change bit in the Port Change register.

- The asserted Connect Change bit in the Port Change register causes the hub to send a Status Change Indicator on the hub's Status Change pipe the next time the pipe is polled.

- Host software sends a request to the hub telling it to clear the Connect Change bit for the port. Clearing this bit keeps the hub from reporting another Status Change Indicator on the hub's Status Change pipe the next time it is polled. The request sent to the hub is a Clear Port Feature request with the feature selector set to C_PORT_CONNECTION.

Now the hub's port is ready for the next device connection. Host software can notify the device driver that the device has been removed, and begin the process of cleaning up outstanding transfers.

---

[1] This is one reason why the port driven RESET on device connection is so important. Without the reset, self-powered devices may retain the device address they were assigned on a previous insertion.

14.5 Device Driver Loading

The dynamic nature of USB requires that OS's be able to load (and perhaps unload) device drivers as USB devices are added to, or removed from, the system. This section provides guidelines about how USB device information (information from the standard descriptors on a device) should be used to identify an appropriate device driver for the device.

The strategy for finding a device driver is to look for one that is targeted for the device using very specific criteria, and then if no driver is found, gradually lessen the specificity of the criteria and continue the search. For a USB device, there are two stages that this driver search can take. The first stage is to look for a driver that is designed for the whole device. The search for this driver is done before the device is configured. If a driver is found, this driver is responsible for configuring the USB device.

Many devices are composite devices having more than one interface and each interface may require its own driver. Composite devices won't have a driver designed for the whole device, so the Stage 1 driver search will be unable to locate a driver. At this point, the device has to be configured so that the interfaces are established and the Stage 2 search for a driver for each interface can begin.

14.5.1 Stage 1 Driver Search

Criteria for the Stage 1 driver search are shown in the table below. The criteria come from fields in the Device Descriptor. Entries in the table are in priority order. If a driver is not found based on criteria from one entry, the search is continued with the less selective criteria found in the immediately following entry. If no driver is located, then the device has to be configured so that the Stage 2 driver search can begin.

Criteria	Description
Vendor ID, Product ID, Device Revision	This provides the most selective choice of device driver. Vendors can provide a driver that is targeted at the specific revision of their device.
Vendor ID, Product ID	This allows a driver to be loaded for any revision of the device, even if a device revision is shipped after the driver is in the field.
If Class=FFh then Vendor ID, SubClass, Protocol	This allows a device vendor to build a set of devices with different product IDs, but with largely the same functionality and use a single driver to support them.

Table 14.1: Stage 1 Driver Search Criteria

14.5.2 Transition from Stage 1 to Stage 2

The transition from Stage 1 to Stage 2 involves selecting a configuration and configuring the device. For devices with a single configuration descriptor, it is a simple matter of telling the device to take on that configuration (using a Set Configuration request). For devices with multiple configuration descriptors, a choice has to be made as to which configuration the device should have.

There are several possible strategies for choosing which configuration to assign to the device. These range from very simple (like choosing to use the first one) to very sophisticated (like providing some interaction script to allow the user to help in the decision).

Most devices will probably not have multiple configurations. Those that do will most likely have a driver that loads during the Stage 1 driver search and the driver will use some device specific criteria for determining which configuration to use.

14.5.3 Stage 2 Driver Search

The Stage 2 driver search is based on information from interface descriptors in combination with device descriptor information. At this point the device has been configured so that specific interfaces are enabled. There should be a separate driver search for each interface.

Criteria for the Stage 2 driver search are shown in the table below. Entries in the table are in priority order. If a driver is not found based on criteria from one entry the search is continued with the less selective criteria found in the immediately following entry. If no driver is located, then that particular interface of the device will be unused.

Criteria	Description
Vendor ID, Product ID, Device Revision, Interface Number	This provides the most selective choice of device driver. Vendors can provide a driver that is targeted at the specific interface of a specific revision of their device.
Vendor ID, Product ID, Interface Number	This allows a driver to be loaded for a specific interface of a device, regardless of the device revision.
Interface Class, Interface SubClass, Interface Protocol	This allows a generic driver to be loaded for the interface. Devices from different vendors can utilize the same driver using this (or subsequent criteria). This is typically how drivers for Device Classes are chosen.
Interface Class, Interface SubClass	Similar to the previous case, but not relying on the Interface Protocol.
Interface Class	The least selective Class based criteria.
If Class=FFh then Vendor ID, SubClass, Protocol	This allows a device vendor to build a set of devices with different product IDs, but with largely the same functionality and use a single driver to support them.

Table 14.2: Stage 2 Driver Search Criteria

15. Software Programming

15.1   Overview

15.2   Host Controller Interface

15.3   Driver Interface

15.1 Overview

Software support for USB in modern operating systems is divided into separate drivers, each responsible for a different degree of hardware and bus abstraction. Each of these drivers is responsible for its domain, and provides interfaces for the other drivers to use. The driver architecture is typically a layered one, similar to the popular models used in the Win32 and UNIX operating environments.

The USB specification makes no mention of the specifics of a particular USB software implementation, keeping that level of detail up to the operating system vendors, each of whom may implement USB support differently. In this way, each operating system could implement software interfaces whose details need not match that of any other operating system, but who's basic functionality and feature set satisfy the requirements of the USB bus architecture.

The USB software architecture can be roughly divided into three basic software domains—the host controller driver layer, the hardware abstraction layer, and the data transfer layer (see Figure 15.1). Each domain has its own device driver interface. This chapter will describe those interfaces in detail, using the Microsoft Windows USB programming model.

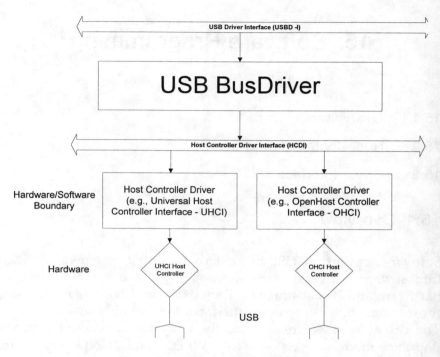

Figure 15.1: USB Driver Stack

15.2 Host Controller Driver Interface

At the bottom of the USB driver stack, the host controller driver is responsible for abstracting the hardware details of the host controller (*e.g.*, I/O addresses, memory ranges, data structures, interrupt mechanisms, and event masking).

The host controller driver is responsible for controlling the USB host hardware, and as such is a critical element in the USB system software architecture. Typically, host controller drivers are supplied as part of the operating system, as is the case with the Microsoft Windows family of operating systems. However, in some cases it may be necessary to write a host controller driver to replace that supplied by the operating system. This is done by replacing the host controller driver with one that conforms to the HCDI published by the operating system.

478

Note that the HCDI is not a widely-used interface, since it is part of the USB hardware abstraction layer, and since there are only two USB host controller standards (UHCI and OHCI). For this reason, this chapter will not focus on the HCDI, but rather will focus on the hardware-independent USB Driver (USBD) interface that most driver writers will need to understand in detail.

15.3 USB Driver Interface

The USB Driver Interface (USBDI) is the primary interface that USB device drivers use for communicating with their respective USB devices. USBDI provides the functionality necessary for performing USB configuration, USB control transfers, and USB data transfers using bulk, interrupt, and isochronous data transfer types.

The most common USBDI is that employed by Microsoft Windows, and is the interface described in this chapter. There are other USBDI-like interfaces defined for other special-purpose systems, although their basic mechanisms are very similar to the USBDI defined by Microsoft. Grasping the concepts in the Microsoft Windows USBDI can help clarify the approaches used by other USBD interfaces.

In the Microsoft Windows environment, the USBDI is an internal interface between the USB client device drivers and the USB Driver. The interface is similar in concept to the SCSI driver interface in Windows NT, and consists of a basic Request Block approach. The USBD functions are made available to other drivers via the I/O Request Packet (IRP) mechanism native to the Win32 Driver Model (WDM).

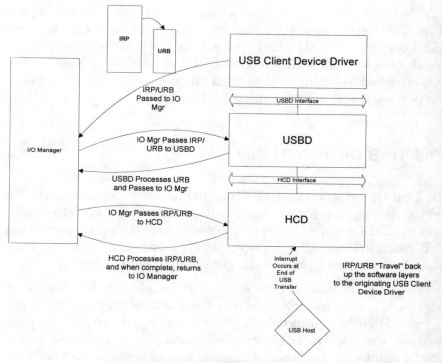

Figure 15.2: IRP and URB Flow Diagram

Figure 15.2 shows the basic flow of the IRP and its associated USBDI structures as they are processed by the USB software layers. The USB software stack provides a set of USB data structures that are used to submit work requests to the USB software stack. The data structures use a "request block" paradigm, and are defined by the USBDI.

USBDI defines a USB Request Block (URB) data structure. Client device drivers use the URB to submit USB data transfer requests to the USB software drivers. Clients must submit a URB in order to transfer data *to* a USB device *or* to retrieve data *from* a USB device. In order to use the existing IRP models, the URB is simply added to an IRP as a parameter in the IRP and the IRP is used as the work order shell in which the USB transfer requests reside.

Client device drivers create and format their desired USB transfers using the URB definitions, and then submit the URB within an IRP to the USB software layers. How IRPs are created or managed is specific to the client device driver design. In some cases, the client USB device driver receives the IRP from a higher layer driver. An example of this would be a USB HID mini driver that translates standard operating system HID semantics to USB semantics. In this case, the HID class driver would supply the USB-to-HID client driver with the IRP with which to submit its URB requests. The client driver would still be responsible for filling in and tracking the URB, but the IRP would be created by a higher layer driver in this case. In other cases, the USB client driver is the highest layer driver, and thus it creates its own IRPs and URBs to perform USB transfers. An example of this case would be a monolithic driver that exports its own interface to User-Mode applications via DeviceIoControl or Read/Write interfaces.

USBDI allows drivers to perform the basic functions necessary to use the USB device as defined by the USB specification. This involves configuration, data transfer, and error detection and handling. To allow client device drivers to use USB devices, USBD permits client drivers to attach to USB device objects that are created when a new USB device is detected (see Chapter 14 on USB Enumeration for more details on how USB enumeration sequences are handled by the Windows Plug and Play subsystem).

Figure 15.3 shows how the Microsoft Windows USB Driver Interface transfers two types of data: control data and raw data. The control data corresponds to transfers to a device's default endpoint, or any other control endpoints that a device may implement (other than the default control endpoint). The raw data corresponds to bulk, interrupt, and isochronous endpoints implemented by the device. The raw data interface is only usable after the device has been configured, while the control data interface may operate on the default endpoint before the device has been configured.

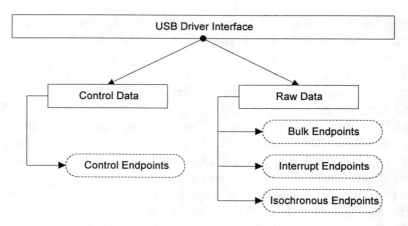

Figure 15.3: USB Driver Interfaces

15.3.1 Structure of a USB Request Block (URB)

In order to perform transfers on USB, every USB client device driver must use the USB Driver Interface (USBDI). A core structure of the USBDI is the USB Request Block (URB). Every call to USBD must use a specific type of URB. A pointer to the URB is attached to the IRP that is then submitted via the IoCallDriver WDM service, as described above. The URB structure is defined by the USBD header file USBDI.H, and there are supporting macros to facilitate using the URB in header files such as USBDLIB.H and USB100.H.

USB Request Blocks are similar to SCSI Request Blocks in the Windows NT Device Driver model. Each of the USBD requests is intended to provide a service that client device drivers can use to perform data transfers to their respective USB devices. There is a different URB defined for each of the USBD functions that are submitted to the USB stack by client device drivers. USBD distinguishes the URBs by the function code supplied in each of the URBs. Client device drivers use the URB to submit both USB control and data transfers. That is, URBs can define USB control traffic such as GET_DESCRIPTOR, as well as pure data traffic such as bulk or isochronous data transfers.

A URB is composed of two main sections: the *header* and the *body* that consists of zero or more fields (see Figure 15.4). The URB header definition is identical in all URBs. To achieve this commonality, a URB is defined as a Union C structure that contains both the header URB as well as all the other function-specific URBs. To make sure each URB has a header in it, each of the individual URBs for all the USBD functions contain a URB header as the first parameter.

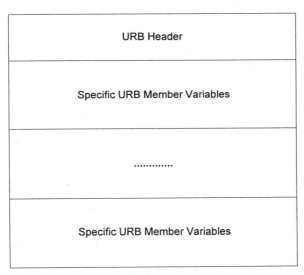

Figure 15.4: URB Structure

For example, the URB to perform a Get_Interface request and a bulk data transfer request are defined as follows. Note the common header section that defines the function-independent parameters.

```
struct _URB_CONTROL_GET_CONFIGURATION_REQUEST {
      struct _URB_HEADER;
      PVOID Reserved;
      ULONG Reserved0;
      ULONG TransferBufferLength;
      PVOID TransferBuffer;
      PMDL TransferBufferMDL;     // *optional*
      struct _URB *UrbLink;       // *optional* link to next urb
                                  // request
                                  // if this is a chain of commands
      struct _URB_HCD_AREA hca;   // fields for HCD use
      UCHAR Reserved1[8];
};
```

15.3.2 Configuration Interface

Device drivers configure USB devices by using the USBDI configuration interface. This interface is not explicitly defined in the USBDI, so this description simply focuses on the subset of USBD calls that are used by drivers during configuration.

The USBD functions that are used during normal device configuration are as follows:

```
URB_FUNCTION_GET_DESCRIPTOR_FROM_DEVICE
URB_FUNCTION_SELECT_CONFIGURATION
URB_FUNCTION_SELECT_INTERFACE
```

Other USBD functions can also be used during configuration. Those functions are discussed below. We will focus on the above three functions in this section.

URB_FUNCTION_GET_DESCRIPTOR_FROM_DEVICE

During configuration, the device driver typically queries the device for which it has been loaded to determine the device's exact capabilities. Also, the device's descriptor data must be provided to the USB Driver in subsequent configuration calls, so retrieving the data from the device is usually a necessary step during the configuration process.

USB devices can contain several types of descriptors that outline the device's characteristics. The descriptors that are typically retrieved during configuration are

- Device descriptor
- Configuration descriptor

The *device descriptor* contains general information about the device, such as its vendor ID and product ID. The contents of the device descriptor are described in more detail in Chapter 11 *USB Device Framework*. To retrieve the device descriptor, the driver takes the following steps:

1. Allocate memory where the device descriptor data should be placed. This must be non-paged memory, and is allocated using the ExAllocatePool WDM service.

```
Buffer = ExAllocatePool(NonPagedPool, sizeof (USB_DEVICE_DESCRIPTOR));
```

. Allocate memory for the URB. This must also be non-paged memory, allocated using the ExAllocatePool WDM service.

```
Urb = ExAllocatePool( NonPagedPool,
                sizeof (struct _URB_CONTROL_DESCRIPTOR_REQUEST));
```

. Next, build the URB for the GET_DESCRIPTOR request, using a macro supplied by USBD.

```
sbBuildGetDescriptorRequest(urb,
                sizeof (struct _URB_CONTROL_DESCRIPTOR_REQUEST),
                USB_DEVICE_DESCRIPTOR_TYPE,
                0,
                0,
                deviceDescriptor,
                NULL,
                size,
                NULL);
```

. Submit the URB to the USB driver stack by using the IoCallDriver WDM service and supplying the *StackDeviceObject* that was obtained during the enumeration process.

. Wait for the completion of the bus transfer by either using a kernel synchronization object, or using an I/O Completion routine. In this example, we will use a kernel synchronization object since this is not a performance sensitive operation, and one that is likely to complete in a relatively short period of time.

. Examine the URB and NT status codes to determine the result of the request. If the URB was successful, then the descriptor data will be in the buffer supplied to the USB driver stack.

The *configuration descriptor* contains information about a specific configuration supported by the device, such as the number of interfaces, the endpoints, and their characteristics, etc. The contents of the configuration, interface, and endpoint descriptors are described in more detail in Chapter 11. To retrieve the configuration descriptor, the driver takes the following steps.

1. Allocate memory where the configuration descriptor data should be placed. This must be non-paged memory, and is allocated using the ExAllocatePool WDM service.

> The amount of data that a device returns in response to a request for its configuration data depends on the details of the configuration. However, the device reports the total length of all the descriptors in a particular configuration in the *wTotalLength* field of the configuration descriptor. Therefore, only enough memory is allocated for the configuration descriptor in this step.

```
pBuffer = ExAllocatePool(NonPagedPool, sizeof
(USB_CONFIGURATION_DESCRIPTOR));
```

2. Allocate memory for the URB. This must also be non-paged memory, allocated using the ExAllocatePool WDM service.

```
pUrb = ExAllocatePool( NonPagedPool,
          sizeof (struct _URB_CONTROL_DESCRIPTOR_REQUEST));
```

3. Next, build the URB for the GET_DESCRIPTOR request, using a macro supplied by USBD.

4. Submit the URB to the USB driver stack by using the IoCallDriver WDM service and supplying the *StackDeviceObject* that was obtained during the enumeration process.

5. Wait for the completion of the bus transfer by either using a kernel synchronization object, or using an I/O Completion routine. In this example, we will use a kernel synchronization object since this is not a performance sensitive operation, and one that is likely to complete in a relatively short period of time.

6. Examine the URB and NT status codes to determine the result of the request. If the URB was successful, then the descriptor data will be in the buffer supplied to the USB driver stack.

7. Determine the length of all the descriptors in this configuration by examining the configuration descriptor's *wTotalLength* field.

```
wTotalLength = pcdConfigurationDescriptor->wTotalLength;
```

8. Free the memory created for the configuration descriptor in step 1, and allocate enough memory for the entire set of descriptors that describe this configuration.

```
ExFreePool (pBuffer);

pBuffer = ExAllocatePool(NonPagedPool, wTotalLength);
```

9. Repeat steps 3 through 6 to retrieve the configuration descriptor.

10. Free the resources allocated in this procedure

```
ExFreePool (pBuffer); /*after configuration data has been used
                       or copied*/

ExFreePool (pUrb);
```

Now that we have successfully retrieved the device's onfiguration information, we can proceed to configure the device. n this example we assume that the device driver decides which onfiguration to use for this device. It's also possible for a device lriver to leave a device in the unconfigured state, and only onfigure the device in response to an external event such as a User Mode application opening the device driver, or through driver-pecific IoControl notifications. The configuration process is xplained below.

URB_FUNCTION_SELECT_CONFIGURATION

Device drivers use the URB_FUNCTION_SELECT_CONFIGURA-TION function to initially configure the device. A specific onfiguration descriptor and alternate interface setting is specified or each interface. This function configures the device by sending he device both the SET_CONFIGURATION and the SET_INTER-ACE requests.

To use this USBD function, device drivers can either build the JRB on their own, or use a helper function supplied by the

USBDLIB function library. We will describe how to build the URB
in the driver using some helper macros. To use the helper function
consult the USBDLIB documentation in the Win32 Driver Mode
(WDM) Device Driver Kit.

To configure the USB device, the following steps should be taken
in the USB device driver:

1. Call a USBD helper function to parse the configuration
   descriptor and select a particular interface. The
   InterfaceNumber below is obtained from the interface
   descriptor's *bInterfaceNumber* field.

```
pInterfaceDescriptor =
USBD_ParseConfigurationDescriptor(ConfigurationDescriptor,
                        InterfaceNumber,
                        AlternateSetting)
```

2. Determine the number of interfaces and pipes (endpoints) in
   this configuration.

```
numberOfInterfaces = ConfigurationDescriptor->bNumInterfaces;
numberOfPipes      = interfaceDescriptor->bNumEndpoints;
```

3. Determine the size of the URB based on the number of
   interfaces and the number of pipes (endpoints) in the
   interface. Allocate memory for the URB to select the desired
   configuration. This must be non-paged memory, allocated
   using the ExAllocatePool WDM service.

```
nBytes =
GET_SELECT_CONFIGURATION_REQUEST_SIZE(numberOfInterfaces,
numberOfPipes);
urb = ExAllocatePool(NonPagedPool, nBytes);
```

4. The URB contains an interface "object" (a data structure
   that describes the interface. This interface object is used
   during configuration, and is used to describe the interface in
   the driver. The driver fills in certain fields of the interface
   structure before submitting the URB.

```
interfaceObject =
  (PUSBD_INTERFACE_INFORMATION) (&(urb-
>UrbSelectConfiguration.Interface));
```

```
// set up the input parameters in our interface request
structure.
interfaceObject->Length =
  GET_USBD_INTERFACE_SIZE(interfaceDescriptor->bNumEndpoints);

interfaceObject->InterfaceNumber      = interfaceDescriptor-
>bInterfaceNumber;
interfaceObject->AlternateSetting     = interfaceDescriptor-
>bAlternateSetting;
interfaceObject->NumberOfPipes        = interfaceDescriptor-
>bNumEndpoints;
```

5. USBD requires that a maximum transfer size be specified for each endpoint. The maximum transfer size indicates the largest buffer that will be submitted for transfer to or from the endpoint. The following code fragment shows how the maximum transfer size is set.

```
for (j=0; j<interfaceDescriptor->bNumEndpoints; j++) {
  interfaceObject->Pipes[j].MaximumTransferSize =
  USBD_DEFAULT_MAXIMUM_TRANSFER_SIZE;
} /* for */
```

6. A USBD helper macro is used to construct the Select Configuration URB, as follows.

```
UsbBuildSelectConfigurationRequest(urb, nBytes,
ConfigurationDescriptor);
```

7. The URB is now ready for submission to USBD. The URB is "attached" to an IRP by putting the pointer to the URB in the Parameters.Others.Argument1 field of the IRP.

8. If the USB software driver stack successfully processes the URB, the client device driver can then store information about the configuration in the device extension area. Typically, the device driver would store the configuration handle, and the information in the interface object(s) in the device extension area. The information in the interface object includes the Pipe Handles, which are required for data transfer on the USB endpoints. The following code fragment shows an example of how this could be accomplished, but in general this step is up to the device driver designer.

```
deviceExtension->ConfigHandle = urb-
>UrbSelectConfiguration.ConfigurationHandle;
deviceExtension->Interface = ExAllocatePool(NonPagedPool,
interfaceObject->Length);

// save a copy of the interfaceObject information returned
RtlCopyMemory(deviceExtension->Interface, interfaceObject,
interfaceObject->Length);
```

URB_FUNCTION_SELECT_INTERFACE

Device drivers use URB_FUNCTION_SELECT_INTERFACE to select an alternate setting for a given interface. The device must have previously been configured using the URB_FUNCTION_SELECT_CONFIGURATION function (see above).

Device drivers typically use this function in response to a request from their clients. For example, if an audio device driver is opened with certain parameters that imply a specific USB data transfer rate, the device driver can select the appropriate alternate setting by using this request.

15.3.3 Control Transfer Interface

To perform control transfers on USB, device drivers use the USBD control transfer interface. This interface simplifies USB control transfers so the device drivers can use an abstraction to perform such transfers.

GET_ and SET_ DESCRIPTOR

This function is used to get and set descriptors from the device. The URB function discriminates between the two types of requests. To get or set a descriptor, device drivers use the URB structure "struct _URB_CONTROL_DESCRIPTOR_REQUEST" to perform the transfer. Device drivers supply a buffer that either supplies or receives the descriptor data.

Note that the 8-byte setup packet is formatted and sent to the device by the USB stack as an implicit result of this URB.

The GET_ and SET_DESCRIPTOR functions use the following RB structure. The fields are filled in as described below.

```
struct _URB_CONTROL_DESCRIPTOR_REQUEST {
      struct _URB_HEADER;                  // function code
                                           //indicates get or set.

      PVOID Reserved;
      ULONG Reserved0;
      ULONG TransferBufferLength;
      PVOID TransferBuffer;
      PMDL TransferBufferMDL;              // *optional*
      struct _URB *UrbLink;               // *optional* link to
                                           //next urb request
                                           // if this is a chain
                                           //of commands
      struct _URB_HCD_AREA hca;           // fields for HCD use
      USHORT Reserved1;
      UCHAR Index;
      UCHAR DescriptorType;
      USHORT LanguageId;
      USHORT Reserved2;
};
```

GET_STATUS

This function is used to get status from the device, as defined in the USB device framework's request mechanisms. To get status from the device, the device driver must fill in the corresponding URB structure "struct_URB_CONTROL_GET_STATUS_REQUEST". Note that the "Index" field in the structure indicates the recipient of this request on the USB device.

The GET_STATUS function uses the following URB structure. The fields are filled in as described below to retrieve the status of the USB device, interface, or endpoint.

```
struct _URB_CONTROL_GET_STATUS_REQUEST {
      struct _URB_HEADER;
      PVOID Reserved;
      ULONG Reserved0;
      ULONG TransferBufferLength;
      PVOID TransferBuffer;
      PMDL TransferBufferMDL;              // *optional*
      struct _URB *UrbLink;               // *optional* link to next urb
                                           //    request
                                           // if this is a chain of
                                           // commands
      struct _URB_HCD_AREA hca;           // fields for HCD use
      UCHAR Reserved1[4];
```

```
    USHORT Index;                    // zero, interface or endpoint
    USHORT Reserved2;
};
```

The following fields must be specified by the caller before submitting this URB to the USB stack:

TransferBuffer –buffer where status data will be placed (must be allocated from NonPagedPool)

TransferBufferLength – length of above buffer

TransferBufferMDL – if caller uses a Memory Descriptor List to describe the supplied buffer, this field is a pointer to that MDL. If no MDL is used, this field should be NULL.

UrbLink – pointer to next urb if this is a chain of URBs. This is an optional field.

hca – host controller structure embedded in request. This is an unused field by the caller.

Index – Specifies the device (zero), the interface number, or the endpoint address for this GET_STATUS request

GET_CONFIGURATION

This function is used to get the current configuration from the device, as defined in the USB device framework's request mechanisms. To get the configuration from the device, the device driver must fill in the corresponding URB structure "struct _URB_CONTROL_GET_CONFIGURATION_REQUEST."

The GET_CONFIGURATION function uses the following URB structure. The fields are filled in as described below to retrieve the current configuration of the USB device.

```
struct _URB_CONTROL_GET_CONFIGURATION_REQUEST {
    struct _URB_HEADER;
    PVOID Reserved;
    ULONG Reserved0;
    ULONG TransferBufferLength;
    PVOID TransferBuffer;
    PMDL TransferBufferMDL;          // *optional*
    struct _URB *UrbLink;            // *optional* link to
                                     // next urb request
```

```
                                    // if this is a chain
                                    // of commands
        struct _URB_HCD_AREA hca;   // fields for HCD use
        UCHAR Reserved1[8];
    };
```

The following fields must be specified by the caller before submitting this URB to the USB stack:

TransferBuffer –buffer where status data will be placed (must be allocated from NonPagedPool)

TransferBufferLength – length of above buffer

TransferBufferMDL – if caller uses a Memory Descriptor List to describe the supplied buffer, this field is a pointer to that MDL. If no MDL is used, this field should be NULL.

UrbLink – pointer to next urb if this is a chain of URBs. This is an optional field.

hca – host controller structure embedded in request. This is an unused field by the caller.

SET_ and CLEAR_ FEATURE

This function is used to set and clear features on the USB device, as defined in the USB device framework's request mechanisms. Device drivers use this function to set or clear standard and vendor or class specific device features. To set or clear features, the device driver must fill in the corresponding URB structure "struct _URB_CON-TROL_FEATURE_REQUEST". This URB is used for both SET_FEATURE and CLEAR_FEATURE requests.

Before the URB is sent to the USB Driver, the fields must be filled in as described below to set or clear a feature on the USB device.

```
        struct _URB_CONTROL_FEATURE_REQUEST {
            struct _URB_HEADER;
            UCHAR Reserved[20];
            struct _URB *UrbLink;      // *optional* link to
                                       // next urb request
                                       // if this is a chain
                                       // of commands
            struct _URB_HCD_AREA hca;  // fields for HCD use
            USHORT Reserved0;
            USHORT FeatureSelector;
            USHORT Index;              // zero, interface or
```

```
                                               // endpoint
            USHORT Reserved1;
      };
```

The following fields must be specified by the caller before submitting this URB to the USB stack:

FeatureSelector –This corresponds to the particular feature selector as defined in the Set_Feature request setup packet. This field will be placed in the appropriate field in the setup packet when the transfer is executed on USB.

Index – This corresponds to the wIndex field, as defined in the Set_Feature and Clear_Feature request setup packets. This field should be zero if no interface or endpoint is being addressed. If an interface or endpoint is being referenced in the request, this field indicates the interface or endpoint to which the request pertains.

UrbLink – pointer to next urb if this is a chain of URBs. This is an optional field.

hca – host controller structure embedded in request. This is an unused field by the caller.

Vendor and Class Requests

This function is used to send vendor- and class-specific requests to a device. Since these requests are not defined in the core USB specification, the client driver specifies the fields of the URB. The client driver must be aware of the device's capabilities before submitting vendor- and class-specific requests to the device. Devices that do not understand a particular vendor- or class-specific request will often return a STALL handshake, and the client driver will be informed of this in status fields in the URB and the IRP.

The following are the fields of the URB to perform vendor- and class-specific requests.

```
      struct _URB_CONTROL_VENDOR_OR_CLASS_REQUEST {
            struct _URB_HEADER;
            PVOID Reserved;
            ULONG TransferFlags;
            ULONG TransferBufferLength;
```

```
    PVOID TransferBuffer;
    PMDL TransferBufferMDL;              // *optional*
    struct _URB *UrbLink;               // *optional* link to
                                        // next urb request
                                        // if this is a chain
                                        // of commands
    struct _URB_HCD_AREA hca;           // fields for HCD use
    UCHAR RequestTypeReservedBits;
    UCHAR Request;
    USHORT Value;
    USHORT Index;
    USHORT Reserved1;
};
```

The following fields must be specified by the caller before submitting this URB to the USB stack:

TransferFlags – specifies direction of this request (see "TransferFlags" constants in USBDI.H)

TransferBufferLength – length of TransferBuffer in bytes

TransferBufferMDL – if caller uses a Memory Descriptor List to describe the supplied buffer, this field is a pointer to that MDL. If no MDL is used, this field should be NULL.

UrbLink – pointer to next urb if this is a chain of URBs. This is an optional field.

hca – host controller structure embedded in request. This is an unused field by the caller.

15.3.4 Bulk and Interrupt Data Transfer Interface

Since USB device drivers transfer data on bulk and interrupt endpoints in similar fashions, the USBD interface is identical for interrupt and bulk pipes. The interface is a buffer-oriented one, whereby the client driver supplies a data buffer for the USB driver to source or sink data from or to, depending on the direction of the transfer. To perform a data transfer to a bulk or interrupt endpoint, the client driver allocates a virtually contiguous buffer (usually from the NonPagedPool using ExAllocatePool) and references the buffer in the URB.

The data buffer can be described to the USB driver stack either through a pointer returned from the ExAllocatePool service, or by using a Memory Descriptor List (MDL). In the former case, the US Driver stack will accommodate any potential physical pag crossings that a buffer contains. The client device driver is no required to ensure that the buffers do not cross physical pag boundaries.

Once the data buffer has been allocated and described in th URB, the remaining parameters are specified as follows:

```
struct _URB_BULK_OR_INTERRUPT_TRANSFER {
    struct _URB_HEADER ;
    USBD_PIPE_HANDLE PipeHandle;
    ULONG TransferFlags;              // note: the direction
                                      // bit will be set by USBI
    ULONG TransferBufferLength;
    PVOID TransferBuffer;
    PMDL TransferBufferMDL;           // *optional*
    struct _URB *UrbLink;             // *optional* link to next
                                      // urb request
                                      // if this is a chain of
                                      // commands
    struct _URB_HCD_AREA hca;         // fields for HCD use
};
```

The following fields must be specified by the caller befor submitting this URB to the USB stack:

PipeHandle – This is the pipe handle returned to the client drive for each pipe opened through a SELECT_CONFIGURATION or SELECT_INTERFACE request.

TransferFlags – Any transfer-specific flags are set here. Usually the only flag that is set by the client is the USBD_SHORT_TRANSFER_OK flag. The direction of the transfer is *implied* from the endpoint's characteristics, so the client driver need not set the direction bit.

TransferBufferLength – length of TransferBuffer in bytes

TransferBufferMDL – if caller uses a Memory Descriptor List to describe the supplied buffer, this field is a pointer to that MDL. If no MDL is used, this field should be NULL.

UrbLink – pointer to next urb if this is a chain of URBs. This is an optional field.

hca – host controller structure embedded in request. This is an unused field by the caller.

Note that the device driver writer usually is not required to exercise control over the data toggle characteristics of a data transfer. The USB driver stack handles the data transfer details. However, if your device must have its data toggle reset to DATA0, you can do this via either a RESET_PIPE URB, or by un-configuring and then re-configuring the device. In both cases, the data toggle will be reset to DATA0 and transfers can be submitted to the interrupt or bulk endpoint.

Note also that the TransferFlags field indicates whether a short transfer from the bulk or interrupt endpoint should be considered an error. If the USBD_SHORT_TRANSFER_OK flag is *not* set and a bulk or interrupt endpoint sends less than its MaxPacketSize, this will be considered and reported as an error to the client device driver. Otherwise, if the USBD_SHORT_TRANSFER_OK flag *is* set, short transfers will simply terminate the transfer but not indicate an error.

15.3.5 Isochronous Data Transfer Interface

The isochronous data transfer interface differs substantially from the bulk and interrupt data transfer interface. This is mainly due to the differences in the Microsoft Windows data transfer model between isochronous endpoints and bulk/interrupt endpoints. For example, bulk and interrupt data transfers are not specified on a per-frame basis. Isochronous data transfers, by contrast, must specify per-frame data buffer parameters.

Isochronous data transfers are usually designed to start on a particular frame, and to continue data transfers at a regular rate. Usually, each frame consists of a data packet that can contain up to the *wMaxPacketSize* number of bytes. However, the isochronous data transfer model allows for shorter transfers in any given frame.

Just as with bulk data transfers, the device driver must specify a data buffer for isochronous transfers. However, since the USB Driver does not determine exactly how to split up the given data buffer into individual packets in each frame, the device driver writer must also determine how much data should be sent in each packet. This is called per packet transfer information. This information must be supplied when the isochronous transfer is submitted to the USB Driver. By providing the per packet transfer information, the USB device driver writer is specifying how to spread the data buffer over the number of frames specified.

To specify an isochronous data transfer using the USBD Interface, several new items must be considered (as compared to bulk and interrupt data transfers):

- Data buffer sizes for each USB frame (each 1 msec interval)
- Starting frame number for the data transfer (*i.e.,* the first frame in which to commence data transfers)
- Flags specific to isochronous data transfers only

The USBD Interface defines an isochronous URB to contain a fixed amount of information in the first portion of the URB and a variable sized array of isochronous descriptors in the latter portion. Isochronous descriptors are defined below.

The array of isochronous descriptors is variable in size because each isochronous URB could represent a different buffer size and a different number of USB frames' worth of data. A field in the fixed portion of the isochronous URB specifies how many packets are described in the array of isochronous packet descriptors.

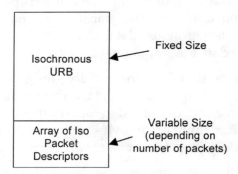

The isochronous URB is defined by the USBD Interface (in the file "usbdi.h") as follows:

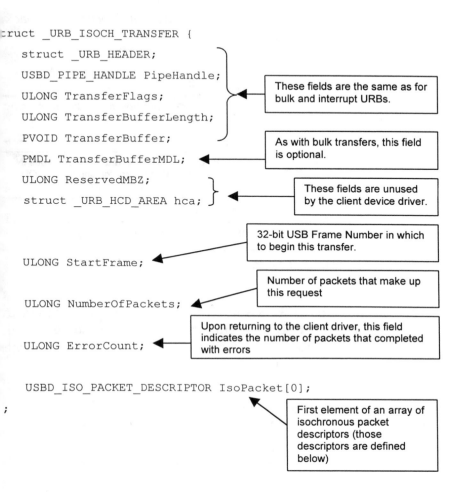

```
:ruct _URB_ISOCH_TRANSFER {

    struct _URB_HEADER;

    USBD_PIPE_HANDLE PipeHandle;

    ULONG TransferFlags;

    ULONG TransferBufferLength;

    PVOID TransferBuffer;

    PMDL TransferBufferMDL;

    ULONG ReservedMBZ;

    struct _URB_HCD_AREA hca;



    ULONG StartFrame;



    ULONG NumberOfPackets;



    ULONG ErrorCount;


    USBD_ISO_PACKET_DESCRIPTOR IsoPacket[0];

;
```

These fields are the same as for bulk and interrupt URBs.

As with bulk transfers, this field is optional.

These fields are unused by the client device driver.

32-bit USB Frame Number in which to begin this transfer.

Number of packets that make up this request

Upon returning to the client driver, this field indicates the number of packets that completed with errors

First element of an array of isochronous packet descriptors (those descriptors are defined below)

The isochronous packets are described in an isochronous packet descriptor, which is defined in usbdi.h as follows:

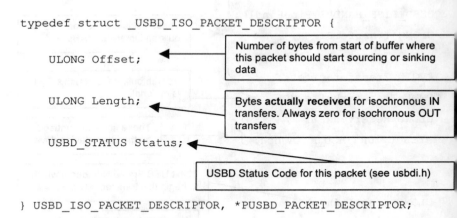

```
typedef struct _USBD_ISO_PACKET_DESCRIPTOR {

    ULONG Offset;          ◄── Number of bytes from start of buffer where
                               this packet should start sourcing or sinking
                               data

    ULONG Length;          ◄── Bytes actually received for isochronous IN
                               transfers. Always zero for isochronous OUT
                               transfers

    USBD_STATUS Status;    ◄── USBD Status Code for this packet (see usbdi.h)

} USBD_ISO_PACKET_DESCRIPTOR, *PUSBD_PACKET_DESCRIPTOR;
```

The isochronous URB is somewhat more complicated than the bulk and interrupt URB definition. Here are some of the considerations device driver writers should bear in mind when specifying an isochronous URB.

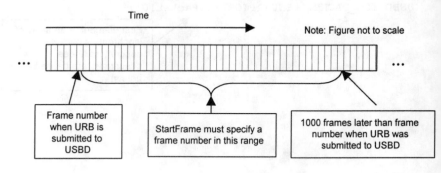

- Providing a starting frame number (StartFrame) is optional. However, if a starting frame number must be specified, that frame number must be within 1000 frames of the currently executing USB frame number. This limitation is due to the fact that the USB driver must specify the exact frame in which the

Host Controller driver should start the transfer. Since this essentially translates to scheduling a transfer "in the future," there must be some limitation on how far in the future the transfer can be scheduled. For example, specifying a starting frame number that is, say, 65000 frames in the future would require that the USB Host Controller driver maintain a very large and complex schedule of transfers. Therefore, to bound the scheduling parameters of the Host Controller driver to a reasonable size and complexity, the client device driver writer can only specify a starting frame number that is 1000 frames in the future.

To provide a starting frame number, the client device driver must first determine the current frame number. There is a USBD service that provides that information. The URB function is URB_FUNCTION_GET_CURRENT_FRAME_NUMBER. To use this function, the following URB must be used:

```
struct _URB_GET_CURRENT_FRAME_NUMBER {

    struct _URB_HEADER;

    ULONG FrameNumber;

};
```

> USBD returns the current frame number here.

Once the current frame number has been obtained, the client device driver can specify a starting frame number for the isochronous transfer. Keep in mind that there is a small latency built into the USB software stack that client device drivers must account for. This means that client drivers should provide a realistic offset from the current frame number when specifying the starting frame number.

Using empirical methods, a typical value that can (usually) safely be specified for starting frame numbers is:

Starting Frame Number = Current Frame Number + 5

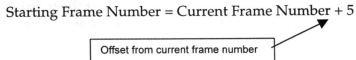

> Offset from current frame number

In this case, the starting frame number is five frames later than the current frame number. This translates to approximately 5 msec of latency in the starting transfer. Note that it may be possible to use an even smaller offset, and lab studies have shown that the USB driver stack may also accept offsets of two or three frames.

However, when specifying such aggressive low latency isochronous starting frame offsets, device drivers must account for the error case. That is, if the USBD interface returns an error when the URB is submitted, device drivers must be able to handle the error case that could be a result of specifying an overly aggressive starting frame number (*i.e.*, too small of an offset from the current frame number). In this error case, the device driver would have to re-check the current frame number and attempt a larger offset when specifying the starting frame number.

Despite the provision for explicitly indicating the starting frame number, keep in mind that device drivers are not *required* to specify the starting frame number. USBD provides a flag that device drivers can set when submitting the starting URB (the flag is USBD_START_ISO_TRANSFER_ASAP, and is specified in the `TransferFlags` member variable of the URB structure Setting this flag tells USBD to start the transfer as soon as it can.

Empirically gathered data shows that this latency is usually on the order of five USB frames. Hence, device driver designers may choose to let the USB driver stack decide in which frame number to start the transfer. This approach would also have the side benefit of removing the need for checking the current frame number. Using this flag means that the USB driver stack manages the frame numbers inherently.

- Another key area to consider when writing an isochronous client device driver is the size of the data buffer. The size implications differ depending on the direction of the transfer. In the isochronous OUT (host to device) case, the data buffer must exactly match the isochronous packet descriptors.

  For example, suppose a USB audio client device driver wishes to transfer digitized sound sampled at 44.1 kHz to the USB audio output device (*e.g.*, speakers). In order to maintain fidelity, the audio device driver must ensure that exactly 44,100 samples are delivered to the speaker every second. If each audio sample were one byte[2], then the device driver (and the USB device) could be designed to transfer 441 bytes every 10 msec. In this fashion, the exact numbers of time-sensitive bytes are delivered over USB as are delivered over an analog audio out implementation.

To solve this problem on USB using this example, the audio device driver could be designed as follows:

• Deliver 9 packets of 44 bytes each

• Deliver 1 packet of 45 bytes

• Total: 10 packets delivered for a total of 441 bytes in a 10 msec period (44.1 kSamples/sec)

In order to deliver the data in this fashion, the client device driver must provide the per-packet information in the URB. Specifically, this information is provided to USBD in the isochronous packet descriptors. By providing a size and offset in each of the descriptors the client driver allows USBD to break apart the data buffer into individual USB data packets. Since this is an isochronous data transfer, each packet would be sent in a separate frame. Since isochronous endpoints are guaranteed USB bus access in every frame, this means that a packet will be sent in each frame until the number of packet descriptors has been exhausted. At that point, the USB drivers will consider that transfer complete and return the URB to the calling (client) device driver.

In the above example, the client device driver would provide ten isochronous packet descriptors to describe each of the ten packets. Each packet descriptor must provide the offset into the data buffer as well as the number of bytes to be sent. The following figure illustrates the concept of providing per-packet information in the isochronous packet descriptors that are submitted as part of the URB to USBD.

---

[2] This is not the typical case for stereo audio, but is used for illustrative purposes only in order to keep the example simple.

45 Bytes	Packet 9		Offset: 396 Sz: 45	Packet 9
44 Bytes	Packet 8		Offset 352 Sz: 44	Packet 8
44 Bytes	Packet 7		Offset 3082 Sz: 44	Packet 7
44 Bytes	Packet 6		Offset 264 Sz: 44	Packet 6
44 Bytes	Packet 5		Offset 220 Sz: 44	Packet 5
44 Bytes	Packet 4		Offset 176 Sz: 44	Packet 4
44 Bytes	Packet 3		Offset 132 Sz: 44	Packet 3
44 Bytes	Packet 2		Offset 88 Sz: 44	Packet 2
44 Bytes	Packet 1		Offset 44 Sz: 44	Packet 1
44 Bytes	Packet 0		Offset 0 Sz: 44	Packet 0

Data Buffer   **Isochronous Packet
                                Descriptors**

The URB for the above transfer would contain a linear data
buffer (or a non-linear buffer if a Memory Descriptor List is
specified) that contains the data to be transferred. The URB
would also contain an array of isochronous packet descriptors
that specify how the USB stack should break apart the linear
buffer into individual isochronous transfers. In the above
example, the first packet descriptor specifies that the data for the
packet should be fetched from offset 0 and for a length of 44
bytes. The second packet descriptor specifies that the packet
data should be fetched from offset 44 (the byte that follows the
last byte in the first packet) and for a length of 44 bytes from
that offset. The same applies to the other packets in this
isochronous data transfer.

Note that the last packet specifies a slightly different length than
the other 9 packets. This last packet specifies a 45 byte length,
which allows the client device driver to achieve the precise 44.1
kHz data transfer rate for this audio data transfer over USB.

- After the isochronous transfer has been started, the device
  driver must ensure that there is a continuous flow of URBs to
  the USB stack in order to maintain the data stream. To
  accomplish this, the client driver must:

- Initially submit multiple URBs (when starting the isochronous stream). This ensures that the USB drivers will always have at least one URB in process, which ensures that the data stream will not be interrupted. Exactly how many URBs to submit depends on the data transfer design in the client device driver and the USB device. At a minimum, two URBs should be submitted initially.

- Continue to re-submit URBs to the USB driver stack such that there is no "drying up" of the data transfers due to a lack of active URBs in the driver stack. This means the client device driver must (in the IoCompletionRoutine, or elsewhere on a separate thread) continue to submit URBs that maintain the data transfer flow through the USB driver stack and over the bus itself.

- Respond to errors quickly and either drop data errors or fill in the data so as to keep the isochronous stream intact for the higher level layers in the data transfer stack. The fill data can be a pre-determined pattern or an extrapolation based on the surrounding correct data.

- Error codes for isochronous packets are returned in the isochronous packet descriptors. The client device driver should examine the error status in the isochronous packet descriptors in order to determine if there has been a packet error. Note that if there are individual packet errors, this may not be reflected in the URB's overall status (which is in the URB_HEADER structure). That is, an individual packet error does not necessarily mean that the overall status for that entire URB will also reflect an error.

- When submitting URBs after the initial "start-up" URB, the START_ISO_TRANSFER_ASAP flag *must* be set if the URB is attempting to keep the isochronous data stream going. That is, subsequent URBs after the first URB should not calculate a frame number. Setting the START_ISO_TRANSFER_ASAP flag in the `TransferFlags` field ensures that the USB driver stack will queue the requested transfer after the last actively queued transfer is completed.

15.3.6 For more information

For more information on the USB device driver programming model for Windows 95 and Windows 98, please consult the following:

- **Microsoft Windows 95 OSR 2.1 USB Device Driver Kit**
  - This kit requires the Windows NT 4.0 Device Driver Kit to already be installed.
  - This kit supplies the supplemental header files and libraries to support the OSR2.1 USB driver stack. These files must be added to (and in some cases replace) the Windows NT DDK components.
  - This kit contains all the header files necessary to compile a USBD client device driver.
  - This kit can be obtained from the Microsoft Developer Network Level II, starting January 1997.
- **Microsoft Windows 98 Device Driver Kit**
  - This kit contains sample drivers that have sample isochronous routines for performing the above functions.
  - This kit also contains all the header files necessary to compile a USBD client device driver.
  - Contact Microsoft for more information on obtaining this DDK. It is expected that after the official shipment date of Windows 98, the Windows 98 DDK will appear on the MSDN package.

16. Administration and Compliance

6.1   USB Administration

6.2   Compliance Program

6.3   USB Logo

6.4   Chapter Summary

This chapter describes the organizational bodies that control and administer the USB specification and related documents. It also covers the Compliance Program that is used to help ensure and measure compliance to the USB specification and the USB logo.

16.1 USB Administration

There are several different organizational bodies that control and administer the USB specification and related documents. The first is the USB Core Team, which consists of the original companies that wrote the specification and holds the copyright for the USB specification. The second is the USB Implementers Forum (USB-IF) which is a consortium of companies that are implementing USB products. The third is the Device Working Group (DWG) whose charter is to develop USB class documents. The following sections provide more detail on each of these.

16.1.1 Core team

The USB Core Team consists of Compaq, Digital, IBM PC Co., Intel, Microsoft, NEC, and Northern Telecom. These companies hold the copyright on the USB Specification and are responsible for any updates or revisions to the specification. The core companies have also formed the USB Implementers Forum.

507

16.1.2 USB Implementers Forum (USB-IF)

The USB Implementers Forum is an ongoing program facilitatir product development based on the USB Specification. Th Implementers Forum encourages design activity among PC OEM Peripheral Vendors, Independent Software Vendors, Operatin System Vendors, Independent Technology Vendors, Telephon Equipment Vendors, and Value Added Resellers. The Implemente Forum sponsors activities such as Developers Conferences an Compliance Workshops. The IF is also the organization tha maintains the list of Vendor IDs that are used in USB products.

Membership in the USB-IF costs $2500 per year, and upon joinin the first time the joining company is assigned a Vendor ID. Othe benefits of membership include:

- Free technical support
- Whitepapers, design guides, application notes, etc.
- Participation in Developers Conferences
- Participation in Compliance Workshops
- Invitation to participate in marketing events
- Company listing in USB key contacts list
- Participation in USB committed products list
- Ability to purchase Hardware Development Kits
- Participation in industry discussion groups

More information about the USB-IF can be found on the Worl Wide Web at http://www.usb.org.

16.1.3 B.1.3 Device Working Group (DWG)

The USB Device Working Group (DWG) was formed to manage an oversee the development and revision of USB Class Specifications As part of their technical responsibilities, the DWG also collects an resolves technical issues pertaining to the USB Core Specificatior These approved Core Specification change recommendations ar sed as input when the Core Companies release new versions of the ore Specification.

The DWG is divided into individual Class Working Groups CWGs). CWGs are formed to take responsibilty for particular class pecifications and/or particular focused issue areas as they arise. ny DWG member can propose a new class document or issue area, nd the DWG will decide if the proposal is pertinent and if an xisting or new CWG should handle it. A sampling of current Class Working Groups include:

Human Interface Devices (HID)

Printers

Audio

Imaging

Communication

Any person who is employed by a member company of the USB-F may participate in the DWG. The DWG meets about every six weeks. More information on the DWG can be found on the web at ttp://www.usb.org/developers.

6.2 Compliance Program

The USB 1.0 specification defines the operation of USB devices at he level of interfaces and mechanisms. To complement the pecification and enable measurement of compliance in product pace, the USB-IF has instituted a Compliance Program that rovides reasonable measures of compliance and acceptability. The oal of the compliance program is to make the end-user experience with USB be as pleasant and problem-free as possible. Products that ass this level of acceptability are added to the Integrator's List. 'roducts are placed on the Integrator's List after having met the ollowing three requirements:

Completed the appropriate Compliance Checklists. The checklists are self-disclosure statements of specific areas of product compliance.

- Passed Compliance Testing. Compliance testing is done
  Compliance Workshops and provides limited configuratic
  testing of interfaces and behavior. Areas such as complian
  with USB Device Framework (Chapter 11), and appropria
  power consumption (Suspend, Unconfigured, and Configure
  are measured.

- Demonstrated Operation. Product operation is demonstrated
  a Compliance Workshop where the product is run with a typic
  application for a period of time. Other USB devices (*e.g.*, hub
  are included during the test to exercise interoperability acros
  devices.

16.2.1 Integrator's List

The Integrator's List is a list of USB products that have met the thre
criteria (Checklists, Compliance Testing, and Demonstrate
Operation) of the USB-IF Compliance Program. This list
proprietary to USB-IF members and is used as a tool to help mak
selections for product integration and bundling. The list cannot t
used in any public marketing. Products on the list are n
guaranteed or warranted in any way.

16.2.2 Compliance Checklists

Compliance checklists are a simple set of yes/no questions th
measure product compliance in areas that are difficult to tes
Checklists are useful during the design phase of a product as
"memory jogger" to make sure products are designed to b
compliant. Upon completing a product, checklists are sel
disclosure statements of specific areas of product compliance. Whe
a company completes a checklist, it is indicating that their produc
was designed for compliance and in their estimation met th
compliance criteria in the checklist.

The USB-IF collects and examines completed checklists fc
correctness. Once a product has a completed and "passed" checklis
the product is added to the Integrator's List if the other two parts c

USB compliance (Compliance Testing and Demonstrated Operation) have also been successfully completed.

The table below shows some sample questions from the Peripheral Checklist and provides an example of how checklist questions are phrased.

Does the USB peripheral drive no power upstream over the power cable pair?	yes____ no ____
Does the USB peripheral enumerate with DC bus voltages over the range of 4.150V to 5.25V?	yes____ no ____
Does the peripheral have its ground connected to the ground line of the USB cable?	yes____ no ____
Does the USB peripheral have its connector shell tied to the PC board ground plane?	yes____ no ____
Does the peripheral have one and only one root port?	yes____ no ____

There are six different checklists that are targeted at different kinds of USB products. In some cases more than one checklist may apply to a single product. For instance, a compound package would have both the Hub and Peripheral checklist apply to it. Some USB devices are integrated from building blocks that already have completed checklists. For example, a USB peripheral with an attached cable could complete the Peripheral Checklist and reference the already completed and submitted Cable/Connector checklist for the cable and connector that the product is using. Most end-user USB products will have to complete, or reference, the Peripheral Checklists, the Peripheral Silicon Checklist, and the Connect/Cable Checklist. The list of checklists is provided below:

- Peripheral Checklist, used by vendors building end-user USB peripherals. This checklist covers areas like power consumption, voltage margins, and suspend/resume for both self-powered and bus-powered devices. It focuses on areas outside of the USB silicon.

- Host Checklist, used by vendors building end-user systems with USB ports (*i.e.*, motherboards and add-in cards). This checklist covers the electrical and mechanical requirements of a USB host.

It does not cover construction or operation of the USB host controller.

- Peripheral Silicon Checklist, used by vendors providing USB building-block silicon (controllers, interfaces, etc.). This checklist covers the details of the USB protocol for both normal and error conditions. Operation of both full speed and low speed devices is covered. This checklist should be reviewed by anyone doing silicon design.

- Hub Checklist, used by vendors building standalone hubs or compound packages including a hub. This checklist covers areas like power capabilities of the hub, termination resistors, and EMI and safety considerations. It focuses on areas that are affected when hub silicon is integrated into a product.

- Hub Silicon Checklist, used by vendors providing USB building-block silicon for Hubs. This checklist covers the details of the operation of hubs, including its protocol requirements, repeater requirements, suspend/resume requirements, and the required behavior at the end of frames. This checklist should be reviewed by anyone doing hub silicon design.

- Connector/Cable Checklist, used by all cable and connector vendors, and any peripheral with attached USB cables and connectors. This checklist covers the electrical and mechanical requirements of USB cables and connectors.

16.2.3 Compliance Testing

Compliance testing focuses on specific areas of the USB Specification where compliance is easily measured. This includes compliance with the Device Framework (Chapter 11) where proper inclusion and formatting of descriptors is checked, along with proper operation of the standard command set. The USB-IF has test programs that check compliance with device framework requirements, and for hub devices. These programs are available from the USB-IF web pages (http://www.usb.org).

Compliance with the power requirements of USB is also measured, specifically measuring suspend current (<500µa), unconfigured current (<100ma) and configured current (<500ma).

All compliance testing is done at Compliance Workshops.

16.2.4 Demonstrated Operation

Demonstrated operation is the third component of the USB-IF compliance program. Demonstrated operation means using the device in its normal mode for its intended usage. Device drivers (either provided in the OS, or provided by the vendor) are required to demonstrate operation. Testing includes operation with other devices (including through tiers of hubs) and validating that the other devices are not adversely effected by the device under test. Testing also validates the ability of the device and driver to gracefully handle hot-insertions and hot-extractions. All demonstrated operation is done at Compliance Workshops.

16.2.5 Compliance Workshops

Compliance Workshops are USB-IF sponsored events where USB-IF members can come and complete the compliance testing and demonstrated operation portions of the USB-IF Compliance Program. USB Compliance Workshops are held regularly to promote USB product development, validate product compliance with the USB specification, and ensure that USB devices operate together.

Compliance workshops usually begin with a training session where the latest information about USB is presented. This training can range from proposed specification changes to common problem areas that have been discovered at previous workshops or in the implementation/debug process.

After the training, private test sessions are scheduled between system vendors and peripheral vendors. During these test sessions, the vendors validate that their products work well together. Results of these test sessions are collected as part of the Demonstrated Operation portion of USB compliance. The USB-IF provides special test teams (acting as both system vendor and peripheral vendor) who validate the Compliance Testing portion of the Compliance Program.

The workshop also includes a "Grand Melee" that is typically held in the evening. At this event, the USB-IF sets up a typical system and invites all peripheral vendors to attend and plug in their devices. This goal of this social event is to see how many peripherals can be plugged in while the system and devices remain operational. At publication time, the record number is forty-six devices.

Compliance Workshops are held at hotels (usually ones with suites) in various locations and typically run for two or three days. The USB-IF arranges room blocks at special rates and meeting rooms for the training and melee. Participants pay for the hotel rooms, and the USB-IF provides lunch.

Latest information about scheduled Compliance Workshops can be found on the USB-IF developers web pages (http://www.usb.org/developers).

16.3 USB Logo

The USB Implementers Forum (see Figure 16.1) has developed a logo to be associated with the USB. The logo was developed to be easily recognizable by end users and can be used by vendors in promoting products based on USB. The USB-IF requests that the logo be used only for compliant devices, but there are no real restrictions on its use. The logo can be used in any type of promotional material, including sales collateral, print ads, TV commercials, promotional videos, web sites, software applications, etc. The logo is provided by the USB-IF in several electronic formats, allowing usage in varying medium (print, online, display, etc.). There are usage guidelines for how the logo should be displayed including minimum size and spacing from other information. Several versions of the logo are available for use with light and dark backgrounds, and where color is available. The complete logo package and usage guidelines are available on the USB-IF web pages (http://www.usb.org).

Figure 16.1: USB Logo

16.4 Chapter Summary

The organizational bodies that control and administer the USB Specification and related documents are the Core Team, the USB Implementers Forum (USB-IF), and the Device Working Group. The Core Team holds the copyright for the USB Specification and controls revisions of that document. The USB-IF is a consortium of companies geared at making USB successful and enabling USB product development. The Device Working Group (DWG) is chartered with managing Device Class specifications. The DWG also collects and resolves technical issues with the USB Specification.

The USB-IF runs a Compliance Program whose goal is to make the end-user experience with USB be as pleasant and problem free as possible. The program uses three components (compliance checklists, specific compliance tests, and demonstrated operation) to determine compliance, and successfully passing products are rolled up into an Integrator's List. The USB-IF sponsors Compliance Workshops where USB product vendors can complete compliance testing and demonstrate that their products operate together.

Index

Notes

Notes